GOING AND SON:

A NOVEL.

By "MONK."

NEW YORK:
(PUBLISHED FOR THE AUTHOR BY)
THE AMERICAN NEWS COMPANY,
117, 119, & 121 NASSAU STREET.
1869.

PREFACE.

I HAVE taken the plot and the characters of this narrative from the midst of New York life, where they presented themselves to me in a manner undoubtedly more striking and interesting than my talents permit of portraying. My object, however, is rather to tell a story, than to present a fine moral picture with all the proper light and shade—contrasts between high and low life. Should any of my characters be recognized by my fellow-citizens, or by the originals themselves, I can only claim that I have attempted to remember their noble and good qualities as well as their vices, and if I have committed injustice, I have erred on the side of good will toward them, and confidence in the better and purer side of human nature in general.

GOING AND SON.

A NOVEL.

BOOK I.—FANTASY.

CHAPTER I.

THE MANIAC'S STORY.

> " Whose horrid image doth unfix my hair,
> And make my seated heart knock at my ribs,
> Against the use of nature? Present fears
> Are less than horrible imaginings."
> MACBETH.

NEAR the center of the Black Forest in Germany, in a wild and remote spot, stands the old, half-crumbled castle of Unkstein, which for many generations had been the home of my ancestors; and my father, the count of Unkstein, after having lost his fortune, found himself obliged to choose this, the remnant of his former estates, for a home, where his scant income would maintain him, though sparingly indeed. My mother died while I was yet in the cradle. I was an only child, and without a relative in the world, when my father also died, about the time I arrived at the age of manhood.

I was a sad enough boy. The influence of my surroundings did not fail to tinge my growing mind with their own characteristics. The gigantic black trees, from which the forest derives its dark name, the terrors of the wilderness, the awful loneliness of nature, the old castle, my melancholy father, the old housekeeper dressed in black and looking like a ghost,—with such companions what could be more natural than that I should grow up a morose, ill-tempered man, unfit for that bright world which lay somewhere beyond my black trees, and even without desire to go forth and seek society.

Superstition and religion meant the same to me. My few servants and poor retainers were under the reign of a rogue of a priest who gleaned my domain and swayed the scepter of his accursed craft without opposition. My days were spent in praying and eating, and I was fast sinking into a state of imbecility, when an event occurred which woke up my latent mental powers and stirred them to activity, bringing me an amount of knowledge which has been mistaken for madness, and which has brought me to this prison, where I linger, without hope of release, without one ray of joy. and yet in the perfect possession of my senses, as this manuscript must show the world.

If she would only not come here! Can I never convince the doctor that he and the rest of them are wrong on this one point? Should I not know, I, who have held her a thousand times in these arms; should I not know if her face is a *wolf's* instead of a woman's, as it was when I first saw her? But I cannot make them believe it, and they send her to me again and again until I have raved myself sick, until the terror of her white teeth has nearly eaten my life away; until I tried to kill her; and now she only dares to come and grin at me through these bars. Oh, at such times I feel my brain whirl and a living, roaring fire just underneath my skull.

It was in the Black Forest, three years ago, that I had the first warning of my life's curse. I had been hunting, and was returning home with an old gamekeeper and my dogs. The sun was setting as we gained the crest of a mountain, whence we could see my castle towering above the trees on an opposite hill. Twilight and hazy mists were fast obscuring familiar objects as we descended into the valley. The path was narrow, through the black trees, somber and silent like huge monsters at rest, while a shadowy crowd of shapeless things seemed to dodge around their sturdy trunks and flit across our way.

Hark! a rustling of the leaves; a low growl, a loud bark, and my dogs are off like a flash into the depths of the forest.

" What is it, Hans ?"

" A wolf, sir; let's after him," he cried, and hardly could I keep him in sight, so dexterously did he glide through bush, and branch, and briar, following the baying of the dogs.

An exclamation of pity from Hans brought me to where he had just stumbled over the body of my favorite hound. We hurried on, even my slow blood was roused with the desire for revenge of my pet.

"On, on," cried Hans, brave always, but rarely impetuous;" we *must* have him to pay for this!" Ah, it cost him his life, and me more than a thousand lives!

We pushed on, recklessly, madly,—losing all sense of fear or danger. We reached an opening in the woods; a flat meadow lay before me, inclosed on every side by a wall of black trees, and with a strange shudder I saw that, though I had known the woods from my boyhood, I had never before come to this clearing.

"I hope we have him!" cried Hans, and spoke the last words that ever passed his lips. A wild shriek—a shriek that rings in my ears now—a shriek so terrible that the woods re-echoed it as did my heart—and I saw Hans on the ground, his throat in the huge mouth of a monstrous black wolf.

At a distance of about ten feet I fired, without causing the brute to change his murderous position. I made another step, and discharged the other barrel, with the muzzle almost touching his shaggy coat;—he did not seem aware of my presence. It was then that an awful, superhuman fear, came over me; then I became certain that the tales of spirits in the Black Forest were true, and that I now stood face to face with a creature of hell. Spell-bound, I watched that horrid monster with straining eyes, every faculty obscured by terror except that of sight. Vainly endeavoring to rouse myself and flee away, I saw the white teeth leave the throat of my poor Hans, and with a sickening, craunching noise, bury themselves in his breast, and tear out his heart. In unconscious fulfillment of my destiny, I drew a small pistol, loaded with silver balls by the priest, who assured me that no evil spirit was proof against them, and fired full at the demon. With a human groan the wolf bounded into the air and fell—a sudden gust of wind filled the clearing with a dense black fog—it shaped itself—it approached me, and I heard a voice like that of the storm which now howled around me, shrieking,—

"Thou hast killed my son! but I will avenge him."

I fled—fled through the woods which all around seemed strange to me; fled through the storm, and the rain, and the lightning and thunder, which had all awakened as at the call of a master spirit; I thought I heard the wild huntsman riding on the shaggy clouds as they flew before the gale, following close, and spirits innumerable, in hideous shapes, barking and yelling behind me in pursuit. Next morning I was found, by the aid of my faithful hounds, insensible, bruised, and battered by my wild race through the forest, and with scarce a shred of clothing. Yet the bodies of Hans, the black wolf, and the dog, could not be found; nor could any one recognize, from my description, the clearing in the woods that had been the scene of that night's terrors.

*   *   *   *   *   *

My illness was the more distressing, that the specters of this awful tragedy nightly visited my brain, and there held high carnival, feasting on my life-blood until my strong constitution prevailed, and health, the most potent charmer of wicked fancies, drove them out, and made me for awhile a different man. For the first and only time in my life, did I feel a desire to see the world; so the next summer found me at Baden-Baden, with such money as I could raise from a Jew by mortgage upon my castle. From the world of the Black Forest, with its

specters and horrors (which *do* exist in spite of all the teachings of all philosophers),—out from the world of my own gloom and melancholy—out of my routine and acquaintance. I emerged into the center of high life and gayety, frivolous *bon-ton* and all that induces men and women to live for the hour alone.

The scenery around Baden-Baden helped to infuse a new spirit into my distracted mind, and but little did the gay throng, with whom I mingled, imagine that the pale man who walked in their midst had deep experience with spirits so dread and terrible that their simple appearance in the sparkling ball-room, as they had appeared to me in the forest wilderness, would pale every cheek, and turn all the hilarity of the place into dismay and horror.

But the pale and silent man changed. For the genius of that gay watering-place, the irresistible force of example and association held their sway over him, and the more entirely, that his previous life had been one of utter seclusion, was he now carried away by the world of music and laughter, of dancing and gaming, of voluptuousness and high life in all its customs. And thus I plunged headlong into the world of dissipation, and with my noble name and better gold, I soon found myself a lion at Baden, courted by the men and not disliked by the women.

And I gambled. The green-table—the croupier with his marble face—the diabolical chink of gold—the distant music calling to pleasures and charms which gold alone can procure—the sparkling wine and glaring eyes; all the appendages of this shrine of gold drew me on, and *I played*.

I played—played with success—played on, on, on—lost. Lost heavily, lost again, lost all I had in the world but a few hundreds. Won again; played on like a maniac. I concentrated my whole being upon the game and won more. I was chained to the table by as irresistible a power as that which nailed me to the ground while I saw my huntsman torn into shreds by the wolf-fiend; now, as then, I was under the control of Satan, but how different the circumstances! Instead of wind, and horror, and demons, a paradise of light, and music, and beauty, and *gold* flowing instead of the blood of my poor Hans!

And *gold* I am winning, that *gold* which holds you all, men and women of Baden, in deepest bondage, and though I am mad, yes, raving mad, there is a system in my madness, and I shall win more, until I am acknowledged *king* of Baden's gaming-tables.

Yes, you are right; I will stop—I will be cool—yes, cold and hard as fashionable charity itself. I will stop. I rise from the table and bear my winnings home. Was it not Satan whose money I won and whose counsel I followed in carrying away my ill-gotten treasure? Truly the money won in a gambling hell is but a curse, and will be a curse as long as God in Heaven reigns high above the Arch-fiend!

*   *   *   *   *   *

I now was as rich as though my father had transmitted to me, unimpaired all the estates and revenues of the domain of Unkstein.

A summer night at Baden! An inexpressible charm in every object—the moon at the full, and gilding the streets, lanes, and avenues—a happy, busy hum of music and laughter softened by distance, and mingled with the soft tones of the nightingale, as I walk with my love among the perfume-laden trees. Oh, how different the white cloud-drapery which only heightens the beauty of the coquettish moon, to the rent garments of the storm-god which whirl in grand confusion in the wild sky of the Black Forest. And instead of the weird specters on the dark path, I see the soft moonbeams break through the cultured foliage and dance on the graveled walk like voluptuous elfs; and instead of the angry voice of the whirlwind my ear is drowsy with the delicious sounds near and far, and blissful with the soft voice of love at my side.

Love? Yes: and though I knew years ago that it was bought with the gold of the gaming-table; yet when it first broke upon my lonely heart it gave me a foretaste of heaven, that I now thank God for, from the midst of the night which has closed so hopelessly around me.

If they would only keep her away from me, now! They compel me to see her glaring eyes—the white teeth—the horrible snarl of the ferocious beast—the expression of hungry wolfishness which lusts after my heart as it did for that of my faithful Hans, in the wilderness!

And then again, it seems so ludicrous to me! Strange, that a man in adversity does not lose his sense of the ridiculous! A woman, a lovely female with a wolf's face! Ha! ha! ha! I laugh in the keeper's face sometimes, when he brings this woman-brute, and I laugh to myself for hours together when they have left me again.

She was an Italian. Her parents, her birth, her station were never known to me; she came in the suite of the king of Holland. Her name was Angelica.

I married her and took her to my castle of Unkstein, spending a large portion of my gains in the wedding festivities. Never can I forget my wedding night. The storm-king was abroad in his might, and all the spirits of the Black Forest were set loose in the air. The wild huntsman, with his mad train, sped around and about the old tower, and the atmosphere was heavy with vague terrors. Even when I fell asleep, I dreamed of the black wolf in the spectral clearing; but, oh agony—this time he was gnawing at my own heart.

*   *   *   *   *

From this period my misery commenced. The money won at the gaming-table was all I possessed in the world, except my weird homestead, and no sooner had my wife discovered the true state of my affairs than she concentrated all her vicious energies upon the task of obtaining possession of it. By scheming and device, by false pretenses and hypocrisy, she succeeded. By degrees, in small sums at first, her importunacy increasing as did the extent of her desires, she finally placed the whole of my fortune beyond my control, and when I proved myself a beggar, her protesta-

tions of love ceased and she showed her real face.

Her real face! Yes; by horrible degrees slowly and stealthily, she changed her face. As we sat by the fire, lost in gloomy thought, she would suddenly turn her eyes upon me and then it was I saw a new, strange look in them—a fierce, hungry look. This was the first. She rarely laughed and I prayed that she might *never* laugh! Her teeth, always white, enlarged, her mouth doubled in size, and when she now showed that fierce and glittering array, accompanied by that horrible flashing of her eyes, I became frenzied with fear and disgust, for as a wild beast snarls and shows its horrid fangs, so it snarled and showed them when *my wife* laughed.

Call me mad, all the world? Read this manuscript, man or woman, and dare to tell me I was mad when I wrote it.

I have eyes—eyes that lie not, and I saw the hair grow upon her face. I saw the nose recede day by day as her countenance sharpened and her jaws grew longer. The very servants, though they would not acknowledge the fact to me, must have noticed this change, for they studiously avoided her and me; and yet the horror to which I was chained by day and which threatened me by night, did not drive me mad or kill me!

One faithful valet I had who finally acknowledged to me that his lady, my wife, resembled a wolf more than a woman. This indorsement of what I knew to be the truth was a great comfort to me. I embraced the good fellow with tears in my eyes. I even laughed—laughed long and heartily, until I saw that he looked at me fixedly and with a sort of apprehension. So I explained to him that my joy was because no one could now call me a fool or a lunatic, since he could corroborate my opinion.

He had relieved me of the worst of my miseries, the mistrust of my own sanity; for I must acknowledge that when I was not believed, at times my brain would burn and whirl, while I queried again and again whether my senses were lying to me or not; but whenever I met her by chance, I saw the lupine visage, plain and appalling as ever.

We now occupied separate parts of the castle, and seldom encountered each other—never by my desire; but my health and strength began to leave me, until I could no longer blind myself to the fact that this wild beast, whom I had taken to my heart, was devouring my vitals, inch by inch, even as I had seen the black wolf eat the faithful heart of my poor Hans. And as I have now recurred to that fatal subject, I will finish it, and with it close my terrible story.

In hope of a reaction from my low spirits, I took with me my valet, and sauntered out for a hunt, caring more for the fresh air and exercise than for the probable sport.

My dogs found plenty of game, and, roused by the excitement, I followed the chase with an unwonted energy through the mazy forest, and losing all my gloomy fancies, recked not that night was approaching.

The massing of heavy clouds enveloped the

sun before he set, and the gathering darkness, from its melancholy associations, brought back at once a sickening revulsion of feeling. The excitement of the chase having passed away, my sorrows returned, and settled like a huge black cloud upon my breast, heavy as lead.

We emerged from the woods, and found ourselves upon the crest of a hill; under our feet lay a valley, buried in thick woods, and over yonder, on the next hill, I saw the castle of Unkstein.

My heart knew the spot, and stood still, while an icy chill drove the blood back upon it. Yes, I knew the spot well; I turned to my companion—he shrank from me with an expression of fear on his face.

"What day of the month is it," I asked him and though I knew the answer, when he replied,

"The thirteenth day of May, dear master," the answer made me tremble like an aspen, for, two years ago on this very day Hans had met his death.

As if these words had aroused the fury of the elements, the storm-king awoke with a roar and a shriek; the rocks and mountains caught the sound and hurled it through the forest, while the distant thunder answered the summons with a fierce growl. Up rose the pile of clouds in mad fantastic shapes, and sped across the sky, to cover it in an instant with a waving angry chaos, like a tempestuous sea.

"Home!" I cried, in an agony of fearful apprehension. "Home! for God's sake, if you love your life!"

We ran at full speed, pursued by the storm with blinding flashes of lightning, and pelted by rain. Again I heard the wild huntsman careering madly onward * * * *
"Lord have mercy upon us, we have lost the path!"

Night had closed around us as if sent down from heaven or sent up from hell in an instant: *but there*—was I mad, or was I dreaming a horrible dream? There, a clearing in the woods, I knew it well; there a black heap on the ground, a groan, a growl. *Hans writhing in mortal agony under the teeth and claws of the black wolf!* I stood spell-bound for a moment, it seemed ages. Fear, mortal fear possessed me, and increasing, still mounting higher, it well-nigh snapped the thread of life. The phantom stayed, it was there before my eyes, it was *real;* but thank God, I found strength to break the spell of the fiend and flee away, to rush through the woods as I had done two years before.

My brain did not do it, for I had no brain then; my heart did not do it, for it was like a lump of ice in my bosom; by the power of instinct alone I found my way to the castle, to my own room, I burst open the door, and there stood, not my wife, *but the wolf, dressed as a woman.* I receded, appalled; she advanced. I saw the hungry eyes; I heard a snarling growl, such as was still in my ears; she threw herself upon me; a faint struggle; her teeth were in my heart and I knew no more.

This is my story—after a long night of blissful oblivion, I awoke in this cell, the cell of a mad-house. I do not wish to leave it, for it protects me. If I went abroad she would follow me and get my heart, though now when she comes, and she *will* come, she snarls words of treacherous kindness to me.

If they would only leave me in peace! Oh, if she would only die! But the insatiable spirit of the Black Forest would send another instrument of his vengeance, and it is better that I should end my miserable existence here.

And if the reader of this, should hear that the noble Count of Unkstein died a maniac, raving, laughing, and cursing, let him reflect on my dreadful condition, and consider what his own conduct would be were he subjected to similar horrors. *I am not mad.* This is what I ask the world to concede, and in unswerving faith I point to this manuscript as a witness.

CHAPTER II

GOING.

> "I have a mind presages me such thrift,
> That I should questionless be fortunate."
> MERCHANT OF VENICE.

THE wind was on the beam, and blowing fresh, and the "Glad Tidings" was plunging along through the billows of the Atlantic. On her deck were two young men, sitting in chairs propped and braced to defy the law of gravitation, so often embarrassing to the ship-passenger.

Judging from their plain attire, neither seemed to belong to the wealthier class of society; but the refined and intelligent face of the younger (he might have barely reached his majority) at a glance told you that he was a gentleman. The other contrasted strongly with his companion; but especially in the expression of his face. He was short and slim, while his countenance, though intelligent and of an effeminate regularity bore the stamp of craftiness, and perhaps deceit. He might have been his companion's senior by some ten years.

They discussed the future which lay before them in the new world—for the "Glad Tidings" was bound for New York, and another day of fair weather would bring them within sight of the promised land.

"Stilletto," said Ernest Montant, for that was the name of the younger; "it is my firm conviction that I will succeed in America."

"Quite a natural sentiment at your age," said Stilletto, dryly; and you have a great advantage in speaking English as well as you do."

"Why, as to that, although I am a German, as you know very well, and born and brought up in Hamburgh, my mother was an English lady, and my father, one of those intellectual Germans whose only fault is their ill-fortune, after having lost all his money, is now living in England on my mother's estates. But I asked my parents for a hundred pounds and a few letters to parties in New York, and here I am."

"You are certain of a situation upon your arrival?"

"Yes: the arrangements were made before I left London, and there seems no doubt about the high standing and respectability of the firm of Going & Son, Bankers and Commission merchants, New York."

"American business-houses are not founded upon rocks."

"I must take my chances; I am young, and have no apprehension for my own future."

"I have told you that this is not my first visit to America," continued Stilletto, "and to the little information I have given you, I will add a good deal after our arrival. As for me, I like New York. The women are beautiful."

Montant's face colored slightly as he answered half audibly,—

"I am glad of it. More than most men, I think, I am inclined to admire and appreciate female beauty. I love a beautiful woman, for to me she is the master-piece of God's creation."

"You speak too hotly for one of your age," said Stilletto, sneeringly. "Let us return to the consideration of your future, which seems altogether in your own hands. For your own good, I tell you that New York is a very queer place. All the old teachings of conservatism, the 'systems' of the old world, fall to the ground there. We find variety and pleasure in being rich to-day and poor to-morrow; we make a fortune in a day and spend it in a week, and our business principles do not savor of great nicety, or of what the old world calls 'strict honesty.' *Smartness* is our watchword, and our foremost men have a better reputation than their consciences will warrant."

"I have heard this before," answered the German, "but I don't, can't, and won't believe it."

That is the answer of youth and inexperience! In New York we only laugh at your old-fogy routine. And why not? D'Israeli somewhere says of the English that they think too much of system and too little of men. You will find that the American idea of business is—a great struggle among *individuals*, and that struggle is pushed to the utmost limits of the common law, without reference to any rules of hackneyed propriety or overstrained conscientiousness. This is the world into which you are stepping, so you may as well make up your mind to it."

"My mind *is* made up"—answered the other, gravely. "I intend to stand above all your irregularities, nor will I work for any man, though he be the wealthiest in that great city, who is not strictly conscientious in all his dealings."

Stilletto paused for a moment; but finally said, quietly,—

"You are twenty-one."

"True, but I lay this down as my law and mean to stick to it. I know that I am young; but I have left my home, with all its luxuries, because my pride would not let me be a pensioner. I have proved that I am old enough to choose my own road through the world, and I have the example of my father's failure before me. He was honest at heart,

but too generous and confiding. As a consequence he reaps a sad harvest in his old age. I mean to do differently."

He arose and walked away. Stilletto, deeming it best to drop the subject, went below to amuse himself by tormenting a little monkey, which he kept to vent his spite upon, when his fellow-men objected too strenuously to his efforts in that line on themselves.

* * * * *

"How different are the faces I meet, to those in Europe," thought Ernest Montant to himself, as he made the best of his way to the office of Messrs. Going & Son, in Exchange Place, New York City, to pay his respects to that firm, for the first time. "There seems to be much more life, wit, and intelligence in the faces of these men. Each seems to be thinking and acting for himself, regardless of others," he added, as a bank-messenger darted from an office door and nearly knocked him down, without ever stopping to apologize. "I don't see any human *machines*, and I should not wonder if Stilletto was right in saying that here is a constant strife for *individual* superiority."

So meditating, he reached a fine building, over whose door was suspended a black and gold sign, GOING & SON. A highly ornate carriage drove up as he read the name and he saw two gentlemen descend, whom he correctly surmised to be his future employers, Mr. Charles W. Going and his son Walter. The former was a remarkably handsome gentleman, about sixty years old, with a noble head, a hale, stout figure, and venerable white hair. His son, taller, and perhaps thirty years his junior, resembled his father in manly attractiveness, but his gait, as he walked into the office, told of a reckless boldness, which might become offensive.

"They must be a monstrously wealthy house," thought he. "But few London merchants would be seen driving to their places of business in such a dashing equipage."

He entered the office; but not with beating heart, for Ernest Montant knew nothing of trepidation, although his quiet, self-reliance was entirely free from the taint of arrogance.

He entered—the floor was inlaid with a mosaic of tiles, the doors and furniture were of black walnut, the counters topped with very fine French plate glass. Elegantly dressed clerks were moving around, trying to look busy, and a scornful expression on each seemed to proclaim that they considered themselves part of the great house of Going & Son.

"Is Mr. Going in, sir?"

"Engaged, sir,—can't you tell me what you want?"

Our hero did not relish the tone in which the reply was made, so he said, rather peremptorily,—

"Take this note in to him." The boy in man's clothes made an impudent bow and turned to deliver the note. At this moment, Mr. Walter Going stepped out of the private office, and noticing Montant, said carelessly—

"Why don't you sit down?" but our hero thought to himself, "Either pay no attention to me at all, or else be courteous."

Mr. Walter Going disappeared with the note

and soon there came a summons for the new-comer to the private office. As he entered, its appointments impressed him with the idea of a dandified nobleman's study, modified by feminine tastes into a lady's boudoir, were it not for a large, double desk, which occupied the center of the room, where sat Mr. Going and his son.

Mr. Going's face assumed a pleasant look as he arose slowly, drawing himself up to his full height, and held out his hand with graceful, dignified cordiality.

"My dear Mr. Montant," he said. "I welcome you here and to my house, with the assurance that I am most pleased to see you."

There was no pomposity in the tone or manner, though, perhaps, too much dignity; but when Mr. Montant took the proffered hand, and looked its owner full in the face, he found him so highly bred, yet so kind and gentle, that his own heart beat warmly and gratefully in response.

"Walter," said Mr. Going, "this is Mr. Ernest Montant, the son of a gentleman I once knew very well, in Hamburg. He is here as a clerk in our house."

"Halloo!" said Walter, looking up from the newspaper, which he had been reading carefully, and, rising with a sigh at the effort, he shook our hero roughly by the hand, adding, in a reckless, but not unkind manner, "How are you, sir? Well"—taking a good look at him from top to toe—"you'd better go and see my tailor. Of course, we don't care how a man is dressed; but for your own sake I must tell you that your appearance, at the present moment, is a little verdant."

A glance from his father caused him to turn away with a shrug of the shoulder, and resume his newspaper and cigar, whose flavor had somewhat astonished our hero when he entered the room, for in English offices such luxuries are generally considered irreverent.

"Mr. Montant," said Mr. Going, senior, upon resuming his seat, and motioning the new clerk to a chair, "I remember your father as an honorable gentleman, and a remarkably clever business man."

"His success in life seems hardly to warrant the latter compliment, Mr. Going," he replied, with a sigh.

"I know of his misfortunes;" replied the merchant, "but these may happen to any man." (This was spoken so earnestly, that our hero noticed it with some wonder.) "Success in life is accidental, and knowing what are your father's talents and principles, I can not blame *him* for what, as I said before, may happen to any one."

Montant felt that he would like to argue the point; but, young as he was, he had already learned that it is sometimes best to hold one's tongue, so he merely bowed an assent.

"I have a situation for you," continued Mr. Going, "but I can not promise to make it a permanent one until we have tried what you can do. You shall be the Assistant Cashier and Book-keeper. As you speak English perfectly you have every chance of success, and since you are recommended so highly, I will give you a thousand dollars a year."

"I am very much obliged to you, sir," said our hero, honestly; "it is more than I had any right to expect."

Mr. Going nodded graciously, and added: "We have a little German correspondence, if you feel competent, I will make this a part of your duty."

"Very well, sir," he replied; but thought what a strange system there must be in the house where one young man was intrusted with being assistant cashier, book-keeper, and corresponding clerk.

The door opened without an announcing knock, which seemed very strange to our hero, and when a gentleman entered (without taking off his hat), the new clerk naturally arose to leave the room; but Mr. Going told him to keep his seat, which seemed stranger yet. "What a country!" he thought.

The new-comer was very young, and either employed an excellent barber, or had no need to be shaved. He was dressed like a coxcomb prepared for a promenade, and wore diamond studs. He looked like a Jew, he spoke like a Jew, and, in fact, he *was* a Jew. Mr. Walter Going immediately asked him:—

"How is Pumpernickle Mining, Solomon?"

"I'll sell at four'n'af, buy at three-eighths, give you a good option at three-quarters, or sell, you buyer three at five-eighths, sell you a put for a thousand, for two thousand shares at a half, buy you a call at the same price for five hundred, market going down, corner in it, think they'll *dandrew* the stock, just bought three thousand at an eighth cash."

Montant looked at him in astonishment, for all this had been said in one breath, and with a rapidity which seemed perfectly marvelous.

"Well," said Walter, leaning back and lighting a fresh cigar, "how is Melodram Quicksilver?"

"Just sold two thousand shares at an eighth, market strong, bulls buying up all they can lay their hands on. I'll sell at three-sixteenths, buy at a quarter, sixty days' margin, ten per cent, no puts in the market, calls plenty at a quarter a share; think I'll sell another thousand at a quarter cash."

"He always ends with 'Cash,'" thought our hero, biting his lips to keep from laughing outright. "It seems to be the 'Amen.' I wonder if all the stock-brokers in New York resemble this one, in having an enlargement of his windpipe and the St. Vitus' dance in his jaws."

"Come here," said Walter to Mr. Solomon, and they retired into a corner of the room. As Montant now rose to leave, he heard the Jew say, with a suppressed vehemence, which made his voice sound like a distant crackling:

"Bet you two to one Erie ain't going up; ten to one, gold will be lower; even, that Blackhead & Co. are busted higher than a kite, and Whitefoot made piles of greenbacks. So you see I'm right, you're wrong always. So don't believe it? Stake your money, here's mine Cash!"

Mr. Going accompanied our hero to the door.

"I fancy that you would prefer to commence work to-morrow," he said. "We count upon seeing you to-night, at dinner—Number —— Fifth Avenue, at six, punctually."

As Ernest thanked him, he continued, "Another point,—Walter shall look into your personal comforts. Have you found a respectable boarding-house and reasonable prices? A stranger, you know——"

"Through the introduction of a fellow-passenger I am comfortably quartered in Brooklyn, at five dollars a week."

"I am glad to see you begin by living within your means. Few young men stick to that principle in this city, Mr. Montant, and now let me ask, are you provided with ready money? If not, I will allow you to draw a month's salary in advance."

"I have yet a hundred pounds, so I do not need it; but, believe me, sir, I appreciate your kind offer. I do not intend to draw my salary for the first year."

"You will find it a hard task."

"I have done harder things than that, sir. Again I thank you for your kindness. It is greater than I dreamed of. Good morning, sir."

"To-night, at six—Remember!"

When our hero reached his boarding-house he partook of his luncheon and philosophized over the events of the day.

"It is all very strange, this house of Going & Son," he soliloquized. "They volunteer more salary than I could expect—they drive to their office in a dashing carriage—and that heavy compromise between a swell and a lout, Walter Going. By St. George, an English papa would send him off shooting, racing, betting, any thing to keep him out of his counting-house! And this sandy-haired lion domineers over the coxcomb clerks, and is a full, active partner withal! But Mr. Going—I would like to put him in the center of the London merchant-princes and say to them, 'Gentlemen, here is a specimen I caught in America; but I will match him against any of you!' But only personally—yes, only personally! His *business* principles—(and here the young sage shook his head)—well, they are not *mine*; and as long as they are not mine of course I can not admire them. And how singular that a man in his position should say, 'A merchant's success is *accidental!*' Indeed I do not think so. But, come what may, I mean to rise in that house, and anyway I shall never forget my reception by an American gentleman in New York!"

Punctually at six o'clock he arrived at the superb mansion of Mr. Going in Fifth Avenue. He had crawled into his full dress suit, made by a London artist, and looked graceful, refined, and even captivating, when he met the members of Mr. Going's family. He returned to his boarding-house about midnight; but was in dreamland long before he could get to sleep

"Her face—her figure—her speech—*every thing*," he cried, as he paced the room.

"She is the most beautiful girl under the sun—she *must* be the most beautiful girl under the sun! I am not in love—that would be impossible, so soon; but, as the Maniac says, 'I soon shall be, if I go there often. What a pretty name; 'Jessie Going.' She will be *gone* soon, doubtless, for half New York must be running after her."

He was quite excited by the impression made upon him by Mr. Going's only daughter, whose name, perhaps not so pretty as our friend then imagined it was, as we have just heard, neither Angelica, nor Evangeline, nor yet Madeleine, but simply Jessie, which, being considered too long by her father and brother, called for abbreviation into Jess. And as our hero called that name to memory, there seemed a heavenly melody in the monosyllable, which must have originated in his own brains.

"Such splendid black hair—what a contrast to her yellow brother! Such eyes—and the classic face! I can draw it from memory—and the graceful yet stately figure—such a neck! and—and—I'll go to bed," he cried, angry with himself; but, before he commenced that action, lost himself in dismal reflections. "She is rich and at the top of the ladder, and I am poor and at the very bottom, what can she be to me," &c., &c. But suddenly recalling Stilletto's assertion, that business in America was a strife amongst individuals, he consoled himself with the thought so common to youth—"Perhaps I have just as good a chance as any one."

CHAPTER III.

MR. STILLETTO'S ABODE.

" If thou wert honorable,
Thou would'st have told this tale for virtue, not
For such an end thou seek'st, as base as strange."
CYMBELINE.

ERNEST MONTANT made his appearance at the office at eight o'clock next morning, but found that at this hour the porter was wont to begin sweeping the rooms, with his mind perfectly easy as to the arrival of the gentlemanly clerks.

Somewhat astonished at this discovery, although it seemed in perfect keeping with the general style of matters in the house of Going & Son, our hero determined not to make that mistake again. So he passed the time as well as he could out of doors until the sweeping was finished, when he learned from a little chat with the porter, that Mr. Going was the finest gentleman in America, Mr. Walter a born prince, and Miss Jessie, an angel, body and soul.

"How coarsely these uneducated people pronounce names," thought our hero, in whose ears that word Jessie, was ringing and re-echoing in accents of heavenly music as performed by his enthusiasm, with a chorus of angels.

The clerks, as he soon discovered, were in the habit of " coming down " at half-past nine to ten, the cashier at half-past ten exactly, and the partners in their carriage at eleven o'clock. The hour of leaving was not less peculiar, but more on a par between the " castes " of the office, for the partners would leave at four o'clock; and five minutes later, *all* the clerks would follow, which made things very pleasant for the porter and janitor, with their various friends, who would hold *conversaziones* in the offices during the balance of the afternoon.

At first, the porter resented the impertinence of the new clerk, in "coming down" altogether too early," whereupon the insulted one narrowly escaped being knocked down, and only got a lecture.

"My good friend, if I were Mr. Going, I should tell *you* that this is *not early enough;* but quite late enough for you to find another situation. Besides, I intend to stand no impertinences from you, and if you differ from me, we will argue the point in the private office as soon as the firm arrive."

To which the porter made no reply; but informed his wife that Mr. Mountain was an *aristocrat,* and no mistake. But his silence at the moment calmed the rising choler of our hero, and by a little generalship, he won the porter's confidence (although he remained an *aristocrat* in the honest man's eyes all his life), and the friendly conversation brought about the first-quoted outbursts of eloquence on the subject of the Messrs. Going and Miss Jessie.

During the day our hero had but little to do, as usual on first appearances; but he saw a good deal. He saw that Mr. Solomon was sent for twice, and that his lightning-like eloquence exceeded yesterday's, that bank-messengers were received and dispatched — that Mr. Going's face was troubled—that the old cashier frowned and figured away violently all day—that Walter swore great oaths at somebody and at the bank—that said bank had refused a discount, although Mr. Going was one of the directors—in short, that the firm was pressed for money and did not make up its balance at the bank—all of which seemed more and more strange in so large a house, for he did not read in the newspapers that money was "tight" in the market.

But he also had reason, even that day, to believe that the firm was largely and handsomely connected—that Mr. Going stood very high—that his private property was comparatively immense, though somewhat encumbered, and to come to the conclusion that it was good-hearted confidence in his employees, and want of management on their part, which so put matters out of shape. His final resolve was —I shall stand by the old gentleman until I can be of service to him, and as long thereafter as God pleases."

So he went home to his modest dinner at his quiet boarding-house, and then, in accordance with a promise given on board ship, he went out to hunt up Stilletto's present place of abode.

Somewhere in the suburbs he found a neat house, in a quiet street, over whose door was the sign "August Müller, Attorney and Counsellor at Law." As this corresponded with the address given him by his friend, he rang the bell.

A bright boy, with blue eyes, flaxen hair, and German physiognomy, opened the door, and, upon inquiry, said that his papa and Mr.

Stilletto had just finished supper, and would be found in the parlor.

He entered the designated room; but it was so filled with smoke, that at first he could not distinguish the inmates. By advancing toward the center of the room, and straining his eyes, he discovered first a nose, which was red, then some disheveled hair, and a long goatee, —also red, then a long attenuated face, which was pale, then a pair of mischievously blinking eyes, which were of no color at all, and finally, when he had wiped away the tears that the acrid fumes had brought, he found a long, bony body of a man, which, together with the clothing thereon, gave a general impression of dirt.

All these articles joined together constituted a human shape, which was sitting up at a table playing cards, supported by a glass of lager-bier and a pipe, and confronted by Mr. Stilletto, with his sallow and treacherous-regular face, with his piercing impudent eyes, and his small body curled up like a snake.

At the sight of our hero, the mysterious philosophy of the cards was left to itself, and the introduction by Stilletto of "his esteemed friend and fellow-passenger, Mr. Montant, son of Mr. and Lady Montant, of London," to the red nose and appendages of his "old and intimate friend, August Muller, late of the Court of Wurtemburg, and now lawyer by profession and philosopher by inspiration."

"Mr. Montant," said the philosopher, in a voice like a cracked kettle-drum, "Mr. Montant, you are welcome! when August Muller says, *welcome,* he means not the hackneyed term of hypocritical worldliness, he means not a hollow sound, an empty, shallow epithet, he means welcome to his heart and to his home, now and hereafter. I can not *yet* call you friend (holding the guest's hand in his own, which was rather moist and slightly clammy), for a *friend* of August Müller has to earn his spurs—but you are a friend of *my friend,* and therefore, I repeat to you now and forever— welcome!"

Mr. Muller was, to all appearances, intoxicated.

"So you are living here, Stilletto," said our hero, in want of a remark that would not show his disgust, but a slight stress of voice on the last word of the sentence betrayed him.

"Yes, sir, I am living here, and very comfortably. You must excuse my friend" (with his usual blunt impudence), "for he has drunk too much beer."

"I like it," said Muller, coming from the sublime to the ridiculous; "it makes me sleep well."

"Do drunken men dream?" asked Stilletto, maliciously.

"I am not drunk," remonstrated the philosopher. "I shall repose to-night by the side of my beloved wife—an angel who condescends to perambulate the rough path of life with —"

"A drunkard, who beats her occasionally," interposed Stilletto, dryly.

"That, Mr. Stilletto," replied Mr. Muller, gravely, "is not so much a mistake of *yours,* as the result of the vile tongues of this world, who delight in calumniating a man who despises it."

"And the world returns the compliment, hey?"

"The world is hard, very hard on the poor," said Mr. Muller. "The world has driven me from posts of honor to the dens of misery; from the service and confidence of a king to the vocation of a Tombs lawyer, whose humiliating profession consists in snatching criminals from the grip of the law. But my family must have bread, sir, and I—"

"Must have whisky and beer," interposed Stilletto, disagreeably. (It was evident that the monkey would rest in peace *that* night.) Then he added, seriously,—

"My friend Muller is an excellent man at heart, and you can trust him. I am very glad that you came in, as I want to speak to you on a matter of business, which will give you a big chance to make money—more money in six months than you can save from your salary in six years, in the meek and lowly capacity of an honorable, half-paid, kicked-und-cuffed clerk."

"Stay," said Mr. Muller, "stay but a moment, and allow me to introduce my family to the friend of my friend, for greater title than that I would not give to the Emperor of all the Russias, were he now present."

"Which he is not," interposed the genial Mr. Stilletto.

Mr. Muller went to the door, and bawled at somebody to come in, "and quick at that."

"Now you will see some fun," said Stilletto.

In came a woman, a neat, docile creature, who might once have been possessed of character and beauty. The former had turned to total apathy; the latter still remained visible in her face and figure, for physical beauty often is ineradicable.

With her were three boys, in one of whom our hero recognized the lad who had opened the door for him. But the bright, childlike cheeriness which had struck him at first was now gone—chilled into submissive fear in the presence of his father.

After Mrs. Muller had been introduced as the philosopher's "loving and adored better-half," she retired to a far corner of the room, and sat down near a table.

"Now, boys!" cried Muller; "Attention!" The boys stood like leaden soldiers.

"Forward, march!"

They marched as if their lives depended on their accuracy.

"By the right flank!" — "By the left flank!" — "Right face!" — "Left face!" —"About face!" &c., all was done as if by puppets moved with wires. No animation, no childlike pleasure, no soul in the presence of the great philosopher.

"Halt!"

There they stood, immovable—a piteous sight.

"Karl, who is the god of the Jews?"

"Moses," was the half-unconscious answer.

"Friederich, who is the god of the Turks?"

"Mohammed," was the parrot-like reply.

"Now look out, gentlemen! George! who is the god of the Christians?"

"Blockhead," replied the youngest, with a listlessness, as though he intuitively felt the monstrosity of the answer.

"Ha! ha! ha!" laughed Muller, and Stilletto joined in; but our hero looked toward the mother, who sat at the end of the room—not mechanically, as at first, but with bowed head, and weeping bitterly.

In a few moments, however, she arose, and stepped boldly up to her children, kissing every one in quick succession, and hurried them to the door; but Muller interfered, in a vindictive tone,—

"Mariana, I am not done."

She tried to turn around in defiance, but her spirit was broken; she could not confront him; yet her motherly instinct to save her children prevailed, and in spite of him she pushed them out of the room, and followed them without a word.

"My wife, like all good women, is religious, you know. But this—this that you have heard, Mr. Montant, is *my* teaching, and the teaching of our present enlightened German philosophers."

"Mr. Muller," said Ernest, unable to control his contempt, "you are my countryman, and I shall not accuse you of a desire to belittle and disgrace German philosophy; but if you were a stranger and a foreigner, and told me what has just past was German, in any sense of the word, I would give you the lie, as plumply and as broadly as you could wish." Mr. Muller was not prepared to do battle with his equals; so he took some more beer.

"Come, now, let us have a sociable talk about the business project I mentioned, which originated in the philosophic brain of Mr. Muller, and which is to be given to the world by the practical ingenuity of Antonio Stilletto, now pauper; but millionaire '*in spe*,' which being latin, is to be translated for friend Muller's benefit. It means, in the future, August."

"My education, sir," commenced the injured philosopher.

"Go on with our business," interrupted Stilletto, impatiently.

"Well, sir, in the western part of this State there is a county called Hocus County. One of its townships, called Pocus Township, contains the Hobgoblin farm. This farm is owned by August Muller, and August Muller proposes to sell the said Hobgoblin farm to the Hobgoblin Mining and Manufacturing Company, for the sum of fifty thousand dollars, in cash, and three hundred thousand dollars in shares of the capital stock of said company, taken, of course, at their par value. Antonio Stilletto will, on his part, sell and convey certain patents he holds, to said company; patents which will enable them to utilize the mined material, for the sum of twenty-five thousand dollars, in cash, and two hundred thousand dollars, in stock."

"Is the company to know what you paid for these lands, Mr. Muller?" asked our hero.

"August Muller's affairs are open to the world," was the pompous answer. "He knows not what it is to *conceal*, unless it becomes his solemn duty towards his friends, and humanity in general, to do so. On this point, then, I feel obliged to answer you by a courteous negative."

While Montant moralized over this strange speech, and its unexpected *finale*, Mr. Muller descanted on the great benefits to be derived by wandering underneath the surface of the Hobgoblin farm, and of the immense obligation to himself and Stilletto, humanity in general would stagger under, all of which, as Ernest Montant did, we shall pass over, as being of no possible interest.

"The capital stock of the company is to be two millions of dollars," concluded Mr. Muller. "You will see that of this, one quarter must be transferred to Mr. Stilletto and myself. This would leave a million and a half to the subscribers. Of course *some* money must be raised at once—at least two hundred thousand dollars; for I must have my fifty thousand, cash, and my friend twenty-five thousand, and then one hundred thousand must be spent on the farm, in mining, and building the factory. The remaining twenty-five thousand will do for minor expenses, such as fitting up a splendid office, advertising, and feeing editors, &c.

"And how do you expect to pay a respectable dividend on such an enormous sum as two millions of dollars?" asked our hero in astonishment.

"I confess that I miss my accustomed confidence in my plans, on that little point," answered the philosopher, with a slightly troubled look. "It is true, that though our profits will be immense, I can not see that we can possibly pay more than seven per cent."

"Why," cried Montant quickly, "if they would be satisfied with calling the capital stock a million, the dividend would be fourteen per cent., and the shares would be worth double as much."

"My dear friend Stilletto and I will be in the ring, and we shall want all that stock to operate with. It is absolutely necessary to make a large show; we shall lend the company money, if necessary, to declare one or two *large* dividends, and quietly work off our stock during the excitement."

"I see it all now," said our hero, with ill-concealed sarcasm. "It is a beautiful idea. I suppose poor tradespeople, tailors and shoemakers, will buy that stock and pay their hard-earned money into your hands. Of course it will be a *safe investment* for them," he added, bitterly.

"I have told you before," interposed Stilletto, dryly, "that moralizing is not a word in the American vocabulary."

"And I have told you that you are mistaken in your one-sided view of the American character," cried Montant, angrily, but he controlled himself, and, as he had no objection to hear more of the scheme, he submitted to a long and minute disclosure of one of the most intricate and deeply laid plans for defrauding the public, imaginable.

The result was that he left the house, having promptly refused to mix himself up with

Hobgoblin or to bring it to the notice of his employers, whose capital and influential name were coveted by this worthy pair. From his immediate acceptance by one of the wealthiest firms in New York, Stilletto believed our hero possessed a great hold over the firm of Going & Son, and tried hard to coax him to exert his influence in favor of Hobgoblin.

As he walked home that night from August Muller's house, he thought to himself, wonderingly, "How can these men be so absurd as to expect *me*, a young fellow just entering an office, to have such an influence with the principals as to be able to induce them to enter on such a vast enterprise upon *my* recommendation."

But he did not know Stilletto's ideas on that subject, or that men remote from such society as that in which Mr. Going moved, are only too apt to overrate all those who seem to them on an equality with the coveted aristocrats, or he would not have been surprised at Messrs. Muller and Stilletto for grasping eagerly at the slightest chance of opening negotiations with Going & Son, and entirely overestimating his influence with that firm, from their ignorance of all above their own low cunning.

A few days after our hero's interview with Messrs. Stilletto and Muller, Mr. Stilletto, who seemed to have forgotten the rather sharp remarks of Ernest Montant, prevailed upon the latter to accompany him to the house of a friend, in fact, a relation.

Not yet acquainted with the different localities of the city, our hero was not aware that Antonio led him toward the lowest, vilest neighborhood, until the character of the streets, and the people they encountered, reminded him of similar sights in London, and he recognized that class of dens which resemble each other the world over—sailors' dance-houses.

It was a scene not without a sort of fascination for those who like to study the different phases of human society without stopping at what offends delicate taste. The streets were alive with a queer company of men and women, many of them inebriated, some singing, others talking very loud. Glaring lights streamed from the windows of the tottering houses, from the unobstructed hallways, from the old-fashioned half-doors. Sounds of shrill music and coarse laughter filled the air, which seemed to roll sluggishly in this conglomeration of dens of vice and crime, while mocking hilarity marked the wretches that only came forth in the night like wicked owls.

Many a shadow flitted by, once filled with sound flesh and quick blood, but long ago shrunk into a grim ghost of its former self; in many a face, haggard despair and awful depravity struggled for mastery. In that queer and shocking crowd there glittered many uniforms in dignified contrast, for the police had perfect control of this ward, as Stilletto informed our friend.

"I am glad of it," said Montant, somewhat relieved.

"Do you know why?" asked the Italian.

"I dare say, New York is becoming civilized."

"That is not the reason. The police are inefficient and corrupt enough, but in this Fourth Ward they are absolutely forced to be masters or they would be annihilated in a week."

"I am not surprised at that," said Montant, "and yet I like to observe these people at times. I dare say, there are many among them who deal out much charity to their wretched neighbors. And a certain joviality is not to be mistaken. True, that the misery and terrible vulgarity staring out at every corner are horrible, but there is a quaintness in the whole lively scene that stands in interesting contrast to the gilded high-life of fashionable quarters."

"You see, people are more *Parisian* here! They live more in the streets than up-town folks."

"I prefer even these crooked and tumble-down streets to the interior of those houses, each looking like a tottering temple of iniquity, rotten with the excess of depravity. But since you have brought me here, where are you going to take me? Although a visit to such quarters can not be misinterpreted as a tour of dissipation, yet I confess that another place might be deemed more fit for a young clerk—"

"Here!" interrupted Stilletto, as they now stood at the door of a crooked dwelling, all lighted up within, and strains of confused music bewildering the visitors, whom it was calculated to entice.

"I won't go in here! What place is it?"

"The Countess," answered Stilletto. "It is the most noted among the Italian boarding-houses in the city."

"And does your *relative* live here?"

"No," answered the other, after a moment's consideration.

"Then, where lives your friend?"

"We shan't go to see her—or him to-night. Come in."

Montant, with the imprudence of youth, entered. It was a queer place. A spacious room filled with wild dancers; the women all old and homely, dressed in very short frocks, and atrociously painted, and without youthful appearance in spite of gay ribbons and luring, indecent behavior; the men mostly belonging to the nautical persuasion and all inebriated; the room hung around with queer ornaments, consisting in endless strips of yellow and red papers pinned up to the ceiling in the form of hanging baskets and large stars.

On one side there was a platform, perched upon which an old *maestro* was fiddling away, his gray hair nearly gone with dissipation, his toothless mouth grinning demonlike, his cadaverous face in ugly grimaces, and his lean body distorted like a Pickwickian goblin on a tombstone. Near him a lad was playing the tamborine, holding it in a dozen places at once—over his head, under his feet, on his back, and everywhere except in a natural position.

But the most interesting personage was the countess. She looked tall, behind the bar over which she sold vile liquors to the reeling guests.

When Montant had been told by his companion that she was the titled mistress of the house, he remarked,—

"What a strange face! Although she is an old and withered hag, I am certain she must have been beautiful. But what a mouth she has!"

"What is the matter with her mouth?" asked Stilletto, quickly.

"When she laughs her coarse laugh, she looks like a—"

"Like a what?"

"Like some snarling animal. Like a *wolf!*"

Stilletto started. Grasping his companion's arm, he cried, fiercely:

"Have you—do you know—"

"Let me go!" replied our hero, shaking him off, "What has possessed you? She does look like a wolf, and this place has satiated my desire to see low life. Let us go."

At this moment one of the dancers pushed violently and intentionally against Montant, who was neither difficult to irritate nor slow in action, so he knocked his assailant, a dirty-looking but broad-shouldered fellow, into the middle of the room. In an instant an ugly crowd threatened our hero. The countess jumped into the midst of it, and Montant noticed that she was a small woman, for she habitually stood upon a bench behind the counter. A little man, very round and short-haired, also interfered, and, although he wore no weapon or emblem of authority, the assailants recoiled from him.

"You're a gintleman," said the little man quickly, to Montant, "Come out o' this. This ain't no place for *you!*"

And, before he knew it, he found himself in the street with the little man by his side.

"Now you're out of it—*cut!*" said the latter.

"You are a police officer?"

"Yes, and can tell a gintleman. You're a stranger here?"

"Yes, and would like to know the nearest way to a hack-stand."

"Come along, then; I'll show you."

"My friend has remained in there," said Montant, whose quick eyes the fact had not escaped, that Stilletto had slipped away behind the counter as soon as symptoms of a disturbance occurred.

"Let him go," said the little man, and as they walked on briskly, he asked,—

"What the devil makes you come to sich places?"

"My friend—"

"Yes—I forgot your friend!"

After a short walk, during which neither spoke, they reached a place where they found a carriage.

Montant comprehended the policeman's motives quite easily. He had indeed recognized in him a gentleman, and had taken him out of that "no-torious den of stubborn thiefs and mankillers," as he called it, with a view to earn a good fee. After our hero had volunteered the latter, he asked,—

"What is your name, sir?"

"Mr. Stump, sir—of the Metropolitan head-quarters in Mulberry Street."

"Well, good night, Mr. Stump!"

"Good night sir and thankee."

As our hero rode home, he came to the conclusion that Stilletto had taken him to the "Countess," for the purpose of drawing him into a row, and probably with the hope that his late traveling companion, who had given his views too plainly during the interview at Mr. Muller's, would receive a good thrashing.

"What a fool I was to be led away in this manner," soliloquized Montant. "I think, however, that this experience will suffice to make me wiser."

CHAPTER IV.

THE PRIORY.

There's nothing ill can dwell in such a temple;
If the ill spirit have so fair a house,
Good things will strive to dwell with it."
TEMPEST.

MISS JESSIE GOING might have commenced it, or the old gentleman might have brought it about, or Walter Going might have been the cause; but the fact is, that after a few months our hero found himself not only a personal friend, but an always welcome guest at the grand house in Fifth Avenue.

Miss Jessie decided that she liked him because he was so different from other gentlemen she had met. Mr. Going, for reasons of his own, had, at first, treated him with more consideration than the other clerks, and soon became convinced that, in business or away from the office, he was in every way their superior; and even Walter, after finding out that the new clerk would not allow him to patronize or tyrannize, treated him first as his equal, then as a first-rate fellow, and finally selected him as his especial friend and companion.

It would have been unnatural had so young a man as Ernest Montant not been gratified and proud at his personal success with people who, in point of education, name, wealth, and position, were among the tip-top aristocracy of New York; but he tried hard so to shape his conduct toward his fellow-clerks, as to allow them to forget as much as possible that he was an object for envy. But he did not entirely succeed, for he was never admitted into that sort of masonry which always exists among the clerks in one office.

Mr. Going, with the fine instincts of a true gentleman, observed and appreciated his efforts to overcome the prejudices of his colleagues. Walter Going laughingly advised him to let them go to the devil, and promised to clear them all out, if he found cause for serious complaint, while Miss Jessie declared that he was the only gentleman from the office that she ever could endure.

So it will not surprise us very much to see, in this phaeton, just driving away from the door of the house in Fifth Avenue, Ernest Montant, seated by Walter Going, who was driving four-in-hand, while Mr. Going occupied the back seat with another gentleman. This other gentleman was very fat, and his face was very red, and his head very bald underneath his pompous, broad-brimmed hat. His features were good—even attractive to some; but the close observer noticed something disagreeable in his expression. Was it selfishness? Was it sensuality? Was it brutality? Was it conceit? But his acts and words, as recorded in this veracious narrative, will tell us plainly the character of Mr. Christian Fatman, the great banker and financial man of Broad Street. He was well dressed, even foppish in his appearance, and had a fat laugh that sounded fatly good-natured.

Away they went on that fine, bracing spring morning. It was one of the few holidays permitted in New York, and the party were going to visit a large estate fifteen or twenty miles from the city, which Mr. Going contemplated purchasing. The four splendid bays, well handled, danced through the city, through the park, out on the wide smooth road in the welcome sunlight, where Walter cracked his whip, and away they flew, while everybody looked out as they passed, some admiring, some envying, some even scowling; but the boys on the road-side cheered them vociferously.

"It is a palatial residence, the 'Priory,'—a palatial residence, Mr. Going," said Mr. Fatman. "I would like to buy it myself, if I could afford it."

"I am not so sure that I can afford it," said Mr. Going, gravely. "And then the expense of keeping up such an establishment."

"You may get it for two hundred thousand," replied Mr. Fatman." "And, besides, they will leave one hundred and fifty on mortgage."

Our hero pricked up his ears at the word "mortgage," and ruminated gravely. "When I buy a palatial residence, I shall pay cash for it. Mortgages are the first underminers of a house, and betoken a poor foundation."

"The property is sure to rise in value," said Mr. Fatman, "and I expect to see the day when that two hundred acres will be worth double what you will have to pay for them. If I understand the matter, old John Jacob Van Strom would never sell it, if his son were not a sort of cross between an idiot and a maniac."

"He has been in the lunatic asylum once already, has he not?" asked Walter Going.

"Yes; and should be there now. It is a great pity that the elder son, George, died of drink. He was a fine fellow, and I knew him well. What in the world made him, rich as he was, and married to a beautiful woman, go to the dogs, I cannot imagine."

"She is very handsome, eh?" asked Walter.

"Superb! A figure like Venus; in fact, the most voluptuous woman I ever saw—excuse the expression, Mr. Going. Look to your heart, Walter; and you too, Mr. Montant."

Walter whipped up his horses, and made no reply; except an incredulous smile, which our hero seemed to understand, for he half-smiled himself.

"The old fellow, you know, is a queer fish," said Mr. Fatman. "His son's craziness is not altogether an original accomplishment, and old Van Strom, for some reason or other,—'pon my word I don't believe he knows himself,—hates this young widow, this Josephine

Van Strom. He barely permits her to live at the 'Priory,' although she is as poor as Job's turkey, having only a few hundreds a year from the estate of her father, General McLane. I wonder what she will do when the place is sold, for the old man intends to take John to Europe, immediately, I understand?"

"Old Mrs. Van Strom is dead, and young John unmarried?" asked Mr. Going.

"John Jacob is a widower," answered Mr. Fatman. Mr. Going heaved a sigh, for a few years ago he had buried his own wife.

"I am quite interested in all this, Mr. Fatman," said the old gentleman, "for, though I have met Mr. Van Strom, I never heard his family history. I wonder if I could not make some arrangements for the comfort of the young widow, in case I buy the estate."

"Always chivalrous, father," laughed Walter.

"Yes, as an old man should be. You, young gentlemen, as a rule, are chivalrous only to the young and fascinating; I endeavor to protect and assist all the sex, young or old, handsome or homely." He said this quietly, without ostentation, and many of his friends knew that it was true.

Time passes rapidly when one is in motion, and the square, fast gait of the horses shortened the tedium of the long drive. Walter Going and our hero kept up a conversation in a confidential undertone, probably on a confidential subject, for they had become intimate friends since Ernest had showed that he loved cricket and played it well. "No man who is fond of violent exercise can be an entire fool," reasoned Mr. Walter, and upon coming more in contact with his friend, he found that he was the most taciturn man he ever had met, with reference to his own or other people's affairs, so he gradually unfolded to him a secret, a great secret—that which had made our hero smile when Mr. Fatman cautioned Walter to look to his heart when in Josephine Van Strom's presence. This secret we must leave unraveled for the present, for here we are at the "Priory." "Turn to the right, Walter, over that bridge, for Van Strom's estate consists of that island, and this bridge spanning that small arm of Long Island Sound, connects it to the main-land, and Westchester County."

"Splendid trees!" said Mr. Going.

"Noble, royal trees!" added Mr. Fatman.

"So far the thing is glorious!" cried Walter, as they dashed along a winding road through the park.

"List to the rooks," quoted Mr. Fatman, laughing, as they startled some old crows overhead.

"Swell place this," said Walter.

"A palatial residence," corroborated Mr. Fatman, leaning back in style and comfort, as they emerged from the woods, and a long curve around a beautifully sloping lawn brought them to the door of the house, massive and noble in its appearance.

"Good architecture, good walls, no humbug about this," said Mr. Fatman, gathering up his fatness to alight.

"Woodbine and honeysuckle to the very roof. This is indeed a place after my own heart!" said old Mr. Going, with real enthusiasm.

"A palatial residence, indeed," said Mr. Fatman.

They were met at the door by a small old man, with thin legs and a bald head, who bade them welcome in a whining voice. This was John Jacob Van Strom. Behind him, in the doorway, loomed up a shadow—a creature of the imagination, a lank creature, an awkward creature, whose arms were too long, whose forehead was too low, whose eyes were too small, and whose nose and jaws were too protuberant. This was John Jacob Van Strom, Junior.

Leaving the horses to the care of the groom, the party went into the house, where they were expected. Mr. Going, Mr. Fatman, and Mr. Van Strom walked together, and John Jacob, Junior, followed his father like a cur, with a vapid grin, leaving Walter and our hero to make observations to each other.

"The very doors have a port-wine look about them; see how the old varnish has become crusty. This is the place for a gentleman to live in. What dinners could be given in this dining hall! Do you see these oak panels?— these old carved side-boards?— this grand old table?—And can't you imagine my father sitting at the head of it, a large company around it, and the dinner arranged by me? By George! we must buy the place! And then the view from this bow-window! Look at the Sound, and the boats, and think of fishing, and yachting, and smoking a fine cigar in this back piazza after dinner, hey, my boy!"

They walked back into the great hall, which reached up to the very roof of the house.

"Look at these confounded old family portraits," said Walter. "I dare say they are the old Van Stroms; but if the old fellows were as ugly as they now look, all covered with dust and cob-webs, I do not wonder at the physical attractions of their last edition, J. J., Jr."

"I see you can become quite enthusiastic, Walter."

"About a place like this, certainly. Like a fine old English gentleman, all of the olden time," he hummed gayly in response.

They visited the bedrooms up stairs and the billiard-room, and the picture gallery (without any pictures.) Walter decided that it would make a capital ball-room, and so they finally came down stairs to the reception room, where a lady awaited them. She had superb golden hair, framing a face of exquisite complexion, and a softness of manner, an unspeakable delicacy, and yet warmth, in all that she said and did, which especially charmed the young men.

"This, gentlemen," said old Mr. Van Strom, in his cracked voice, "is my daughter-in-law, Mrs. G. Van Strom, with whom I am not on very good terms."

She colored deeply; but her features remained unmoved, and with downcast eyes she made a courtesy.

"Madame," said old Mr. Going, coming heartily over toward her, "I am half ashamed to force so many gentlemen upon your solitude at once; but I hope you will excuse us, and believe that we are doubly honored by your father-in-law's kind introduction."

Mr. Van Strom did not notice this well-merited rebuke.

"This gentleman, who is so kind to you, Josephine," he continued, brusquely, "is Mr. Going, who will probably buy the place, and this, is my friend Mr. Fatman."

Mr. Fatman spoke out hastily: "Madame, I am quite sure that were I your father-in-law, my taste is sufficiently cultivated to appreciate you, and remain on the best terms with you."

Mr. Fatman meant well enough; but his coarse nature prevented him from seeing that he only brought up the unpleasantness again, and in far worse taste. Josephine, after having bowed to the gentlemen, said softly, but in a pained voice,—

"It seems strange to me to receive you, gentlemen, in this house; but being the only lady here, I must do the honors, and welcome you all, as though it were mine, for to-day."

"Come along to the stables," cried Mr. Van Strom.

So they left the poor widow in the drawing-room and inspected the stables and paddocks in which some ancestorial Van Strom had once kept his racers, perhaps with a crazy idea of introducing the "Derby" into America before America was sufficiently civilized for that amusement, as Walter Going remarked to his companion.

At all events, the stables were now empty and dilapidated, and the paddocks resembled the ruins of some field fortification, interesting, perhaps, to the antiquarian, but not in the least to a horseman.

"I shall repair the inclosures, take out the stones and rocks, rebuild the stables, and make a place of it that will challenge all England!" cried Walter, who this day seemed to have exchanged his usual dull and blasé manner for the merry fire of a school-boy.

"Do you keep no horses, Van Strom?" asked Mr. Fatman.

"Yes, sir," was the reply, as he led the way to a tumble-down barn, standing separate from the stables. "I keep a pair of carriage horses, and my son has a light mare."

"The best mare in the country," said John J., Junior, smiling timidly.

"Let us see them," suggested Walter; and after groping amongst hay and dirt, and the rotten remnants of stalls, they discovered two black animals, and one yellow one.

"These black ones are the carriage horses," said the lord of the "Priory," "they were bought—"

"By your grandfather, sir?" queried Walter, dryly, as he examined hem.

"By my father, sir," answered the other, a little severely. "They are only about twenty years old."

Walter nodded his unqualified belief in the statement, and proceeded to look at the apparition in the third stall.

"I'll lead her out, sir," said John J., Junior, mildly; and by a good deal of "Whoa, pet!" and "Come, girl," and great exertion, he finally produced the creature to full view.

"That's a noble mare," said Walter, biting his lips.

"I thought you were a horseman!" cried John, with delight. "You look like a horseman, give us your hand, sir. Indeed, you are a judge of a horse. Now, this mare, gentlemen, I love. She is the dearest, faithfullest creature in the world, and unless she stands still, I tell you she can go!"

"You don't say! That's wonderful," cried Walter, much amused.

"What I mean by standing still is this, that sometimes she takes a notion to stop short on the road, and when she does, I don't attempt to make her go."

"I would not if I were you," said Walter, sagely; and so the mare was dismissed, and the party turned toward the house once more.

"These lawns remind me of "merry England," said Mr. Going, "and the trees are the finest I have seen on any gentleman's place this side of the Atlantic."

Mr. Van Strom looked pleased, as though he thought the price of his estate was growing larger in his guest's mind, and led the way to the gardens, graperies, and hot-houses. Mr. Going enjoyed the examination exceedingly, and busied his imagination with planning the improvements he would make after he had bought the "Priory."

"How did the name originate?" he asked.

"The 'Priory?' Oh, there is a long story connected with that," said old Van Strom.

"Tell us the story," suggested Mr. Fatman, but the lowering brow and melancholy expression of Mr. Van Strom's face forbade further questioning, as he said,—

"I would rather not. It is an old family legend, and discusses subjects which, at my age, I should shrink from approaching, lest I arouse the dead too soon to receive me among them. Let it pass, and I will show you the last vestige of the actual 'Priory.'"

By this time they had walked entirely around the house, and reached an old but still mighty elm, upon one of whose branches hung a large bell. It was a very curious bell, of a yellow composition, and not unartistically decorated with bas-reliefs, representing deformed human figures, such as monks, with dwarfed legs and wooden coats, and women, with outlandish noses and horrible mouths.

"Its proper place is in the turret on the roof," explained Van Strom, "but I had it taken down and put here for convenience sake, as I use it to call the men from the field at dinner-time."

"And they say—"

"Never mind it, John," said his father. "It can not interest the gentlemen."

But Mr. Fatman was not to be balked thus; so, with an engaging smile, he encouraged the young man to continue.

"They say, that whenever any of the family are going to be very sick or die, or something dreadful is going to happen, that bell rings on the night before, and, if it happens only the next night instead of the next morning, it rings again while things are going on."

"This is indeed the story, gentlemen," said old Van Strom, "but, of course, we can not expect you to believe it."

"Why, everybody must believe it, father," said John, fearful lest his wonder should lack credence, "for it rang the night before mother died, and the night before George died, and the night before Joe's little girl died, and the night—"

"Never mind, John," said the old man, dismally, "this is not a pleasing subject anyway, and the bell can only ring twice more and then it may burst."

"These are cheerful specimens of humanity," said Walter Going, in the ear of Ernest. "I think they have a couple of ghostly bells ringing in each of their monstrous ears."

"May I inquire," he said aloud, "who it is that rings this instrument on such occasions."

"God only knows," replied the old man, looking upward."

"If my father buys the place, I shall make a vigorous attempt to share that knowledge, and if I find a human brute at the rope, I'll lower the bell, just over his head, and ring him deaf and dumb," said Walter, decidedly.

From the discussion of this mystery they were called to lunch, which was served in the dining-room and presided over by Mrs. Van Strom. As the three elder men had now arrived at the question of price and terms of payment, they, with young John, occupied one end of the table, so that Walter Going and our hero found their places on either side of the fair widow.

"We shall have the pleasure of your company till evening, gentlemen, I hope," she said, in her rich, deep voice, that had withal a sort of metallic tone, indicative of a very warm heart. Our hero, too, watched her closely, and admired her considerably.

"Yes, madam," replied Walter, "we will take the liberty of resting till four o'clock, and, as it is only half-past twelve now, you will have to put up with us for some hours yet."

"It is quite a change, and a real pleasure for me, to see any one nowadays," she said, with a sad smile. "This place, which, with hospitality and good company, could be made all that is delightful, is dreary and lonely enough for the solitary woman incarcerated here."

Although the words glided from her lips in a half whisper, old Van Strom had, in all likelihood, overheard them, for, when luncheon was barely finished, he said with an angry scowl:

"Josephine, my dear, coffee and cigars are not generally graced with ladies' society, as you should know by this time."

She arose and moved to the door, but all the guests arose with her. In their respectful manner she recognized that they felt for her, and as old Mr. Going shook her by the hand, with that kindness and delicacy which every woman appreciates, and thus manifested his sympathy; she felt the tears starting to her eyes and was forced to leave the room abruptly.

Mr. Fatman could not restrain himself·

"Van Strom," he said, angrily, "I have known you many years, and I take the liberty of telling you plainly, that your treatment of your daughter-in-law is a disgrace to your good name."

"No, no, no, my friend," answered the half-witted old man, "You don't understand the case — I have remembered her handsomely in my will," and he winked at the young men, and smiled cunningly.

"I bet he lies," whispered Walter to his companion, "and we may as well inform the reader that his opinion proved correct. John Jacob Van Strom, among other freaks of eccentricity, had taken such a dislike to his fair relative, that he indeed denied her all assistance during his life and after his death, beyond the bare permission to remain under his roof. Even this was so much accompanied with coarse insult, such as we have witnessed, that she only staid there for a few weeks at a time, preferring to live as she might, on her almost beggarly means, than to submit and endure, where submission and endurance became revolting.

No definite result, with regard to the purchase of the property, could quickly be reached with so whimsical a character as old Van Strom. One moment he would be ready to close the bargain, but the next would suddenly change it to the conclusion that, after all, he would keep the estate, were it only out of respect to the seedy-looking, ancestorial assemblage in the hall.

After coffee, cigars, and *petits verres*, they inspected the wine cellars, closets, and plate, finding many treasures laid up by the great-grandfathers of the present owner, probably unknown, and certainly unappreciated by him.

Finally, they resolved to spend the remaining hours before their departure in the open air, so they sallied forth in a body into the park. As the conversation still ran upon matters of business uninteresting to our hero, he sauntered apart to enjoy an uninterrupted soliloquy. The sky being very blue and the air very balmy, his heart warmed to a sunny object— and he thought of Jessie Going.

"Am I in love with her or not?" he asked himself, thoughtfully, "I hope not," he continued, sagely, and after considering all the *pros* and *cons* with care and close scrutiny of his heart, he finally came to the conclusion, that, although he might be 'smitten,' yet there was nothing like a settled passion—a love, which, if disappointed, would interfere with his peace of mind.

"It is certainly quite natural that I should be fascinated by a beautiful and accomplished woman in a station above me, who has shown, by many kindnesses and little marks of attention, if not decided preference, at least hearty, goodwill toward me. On the other hand, I am convinced, after cool deliberation, that I am *not* in *love*, which shows that I am not so very easily won, and that I possess quite a modicum of independence. The conquest of a weak heart can not give a woman much satisfaction, I should fancy."

Losing himself in thought, he also lost his way in the park, and was wandering whither his rambling would lead him, when a few steps brought him out of the trees, and showed him a fine view of the Sound. Within a stone's throw stood a summer-house, fantastically built upon a rock, and, approaching it, he found himself in the presence of Josephine Van Strom.

CHAPTER V.

JOSEPHINE VAN STROM.

"I am too fond; and therefore thou may'st think
my 'haviour light,
But trust me, gentleman, I'll prove more true
Than those that have more cunning to be strange."
                        ROMEO AND JULIET.

SHE was reclining in a rustic arm-chair, apparently unconscious of her surroundings, and lost in thought. Though her gaze was directed toward the extended view of the Sound, there appeared no enthusiasm in her dreamily lustrous eyes for the beautiful scene. Our hero did not wish to disturb her, but could not forego the pleasure of watching her, unobserved himself. At this moment of supreme repose, her purely classic face presented to his enthusiastic mind, a living image of the Queen of Heaven, as painted by Raphael; with womanly holiness; but also the passions and sufferings of her sex written in it, all framed in the golden glory of her hair. The beautiful *contour* of her figure was half hidden, half indicated by her loose summer dress, her round and snowy arm peeping out of the white folds, and her hand, itself a gem of soft perfection, rested upon a little table beside her, where she had laid her straw hat and some wild flowers.

Ernest Montant was not bashful nor yet systematically bold, and gazing, he finally made up his mind to speak to her.

"Mrs. Van Strom," he said, when he found that she had not heard his approach, "I hope you will pardon me for this interruption."

She started at his unexpected voice, and with a woman's instinct turned full upon him to judge his motive. The inspection was satisfactory, for she smiled, a smile which blended the little stray wrinkles of care and sorrow about her full and charming mouth into the loveliness of youth and beauty to which her years entitled her, though the littleness of man had imbittered her short life.

And indeed she was not the only woman who would have graciously smiled upon him as he stood in the vigor of young manhood, with his clear red and white complexion, his eyes sparkling, perhaps with admiration for *her*, his attitude graceful, and his voice deep and melodious. Long afterward, Josephine acknowledged that the strength of will he unconsciously displayed, in trifles as in more eventful moments, formed his greatest charm for a woman, and on his forehead seemed written:—Indomitable moral courage, unfaltering, inflexible integrity of character; and through every change of his dark blue eyes there shone an earnestness, which proved none the less powerful because often softened and diverted by the sprightliness of his youth.

"No interruption, sir," she said, gathering her light shawl around her shoulders, "for I was doing nothing in the fullest sense of the word. Will you take a seat?"

So he took a seat, and, when invited by her, he produced his cigar-case and lighted a fragrant Havana.

"My husband was a great smoker," she said, with a sigh, "so I am accustomed to it."

"I have heard of your misfortunes and with deep regret Madam," replied our hero.

"They have been great, sir, and you will find in me a very lonely woman, and much to be pitied, for I am only twenty-one."

There was a charming *naïveté* in her manner of speaking.

"Do you not go into society, Mrs. Van Strom?" he asked.

"My father-in-law," she replied, coloring slightly, "does not see fit to permit me any pleasures, with the exception of tolerating me here for a few months in the year. Now that the place is to be sold, even that comfort will be denied me."

She said all this very simply and uncomplainingly, and then, changing her tone, added,—

"I do not know what makes me speak of myself to a stranger, as if I could expect him to find it interesting."

"Perhaps he is finding it more so than some of your nearest friends," said he, smiling.

"I know to what you allude; but I am so resigned to what I have to undergo, at the hands of my father-in-law, that my feelings have become blunted." Something in her tone contradicted this assertion, and as she rapidly turned her gaze to the endless watery waste of the Sound, there ensued a pause.

"Do you know, sir, that I have not yet become acquainted with your name?" she said after awhile.

"My name is Ernest Montant," he answered promptly. "I am a clerk with the house of Going & Son. My father is in England, and is a former friend of our senior partner."

"In England? But I should have taken you to be a German."

"I am German," was the answer; "German by birth, half German by blood, and entirely German by persuasion, if I may so call it."

"I like Germans," was her reply. "They are more intelligent than other people, and have more heart, *I* think."

"If I were not a German I would venture to say you are right."

"I can not bear people who seem to have no heart," said Josephine, warmly.

"Because you have a very warm one yourself," cried our hero, boldly, for her simplicity and artlessness seemed so genuine that her words went to his heart, and he felt impelled to speak without restraint.

"Do you think so?" she asked, coquettishly, and looking him full in the face with her great blue eyes. He could scarcely meet her gaze unflinchingly, so he answered,—

"I can only tell you, Mrs. Van Strom, that, in my humble opinion, you would command the devotion of many, so that I think you should not be altogether dissatisfied with the lot accorded you. Call this flattery, if you choose. I never flatter, and seldom speak as plainly, I assure you, as I have just spoken to you."

"I believe you are sincere, Mr. Montant, and it would be absurd and untruthful in a woman like me to deny being truly gratified by your praise."

It would be hard to tell how it came about, but rarely do two people approach intimacy as rapidly as did our hero and the lovely widow. They arose to take a walk.

"There is another little island, quite stony and deserted, connected with this one by a sort of dilapidated dam or mole—if you are not too fatigued I will show it to you." So said Mrs. Van Strom, and our hero followed her most willingly. The wind was fresh, and blew the folds of Josephine's light summer-dress tightly around her. Her companion possessed a high and manly purity which we shall always find in him, but he could not help wondering, as the spring breezes revealed to him more of the widow's palpable charms, that George Van Strom should have been such a fool as to kill himself by drinking.

They stood upon the rocks which reached boldly out into the sound, and watched the waves breaking at their feet with useless perseverance. He spread her shawl out upon the sunny stones, and sat at her feet. As he looked at the water, and the sky, and at her face, and into her eyes, the genial sun shone into his heart; and she—had she not, at their very first meeting, felt that sympathy toward him, that confidence, that budding affection, which knows no cause or reason, but is one of the mysterious works of Nature?

"Near this place," she said, "I first heard the vows of my husband. I was then but seventeen, and I believe I was so inexperienced and impressible that any man whom I did not positively *dislike* could have prevailed upon me to accept him. The moon was shining brightly and the night was divine. He was a handsome, good-hearted fellow, and I was a foolish child. I accepted him—we were married that same summer, and before my child was born I was a widow. My happiness had been buried long before the grave received the remains of his weakness and folly. This is my history."

"And it is a history," said he, gravely, "which, though its outlines be before the world, can not be understood by a soul on earth but yourself. A loving heart forced to witness the gradual living decay of the being it most cherished. Oh, Mrs. Van Strom! I can not mention but I can guess at the *details* of your sufferings, and if, to-day, you were to be married to a friend of mine, I would take him aside and say to him, 'From the moment you claim her as your wife, you should consider yourself the means selected by Providence to reward her for her trials. Her sufferings in times past must be present with you

always; they must stand between you and your faults, between you and all temper and discord; and they should inspire you with the sacred duty of living for her happiness to the latest breath of your existence!'"

He did not know why he thus spoke to her. She did not know why it was, that, although he raked up the buried past, his words did not wound her, but solaced and comforted her beyond measure. She looked at him—in her eyes there stood sacred tears.

"Speak on," she said, softly. "I could listen to you forever."

Beware, Ernest Montant! You and this woman are on dangerous ground; and if you had more experience with the sex, you would read danger in the throbbing of your own heart, danger in the expression of that Madonna-like face, danger to you and your prospects with Jessie.

But he talked away, in manly and yet sympathetic accents, until the bright tears streamed, unchecked, down her cheek. He arose, took her hand and begged her pardon.

"Pardon? For what, my friend," she said, composing herself. "This conversation has been like a sunbeam in my dreary life, and yet I never knew you before to-day. It is very singular—" she ended, shaking her head dreamily; and he echoed the sentiment, and the drowsy trees heard it and rustled it to each other, and the zephyrs breathed it over the silver ripples of the water—all nature heard it and knew it before. "Singular," and yet not new.

"Well," he said, in an altered manner. "Well, I suppose that this gentleman, to whom I was going to give all this wholesome advice, with such astounding impudence, will soon make his appearance."

Josephine shook her head with a smile. "No," she said, "I have not been in love since I was a widow. I don't know how it is, but my heart has become unimpressible."

He stole a sly but searching look at her face as she said the last words, and said, laughing,—

"I believe, if the right man should come along, your stoicism would melt away like snow in the sun."

"Quite possible," she answered, coquettishly, "but the right man has *not* come, as yet."

What a fool Ernest Montant is making of himself. Those words "*not come as yet*" have vexed him as though he had thought *he* might be the right man.

"Mrs. Van Strom," he said, "I must appear very impertinent. Tell me, is it really a fact that you have not been in love since your widowhood, or are you politely telling me that the affairs of your heart are no business of mine, and that you have no intention of making a confidant of an entire stranger?"

"What I have told you is true," she answered. "I have been free from even a passing fancy for any one, and for that matter—"

"Well, for that matter?"

"I do not know why I should thus confide in you. Do you believe that some natures are wrought in shapes of sympathy with each other so that when they meet there is a sort of instinctive freemasonry established at once —a confidence which is from God?"

"Indeed I do," he replied earnestly. "Have you read Goethe's Wahlverwandtschaften?"

"Yes, that is, a translation of it, for my acquaintance with German is limited. I think the English title, 'Elective Affinities,' does not quite express the meaning; but the novel is superb, and I have pondered over it often. Well, then," she continued, "I think that our meeting has proved the truth of Goethe's belief, that the mysterious affinity between human natures will have its way in spite of conventionality and the natural distrust of new acquaintances."

"And upon that theory, which I joyfully, thankfully accept," said he, "you base the desire of telling me—what?"

"I was going to tell you that I have only loved once, in my whole life, and that was a school-girl's whim, which fortunately resulted in—nothing."

"And your husband?" he asked, almost appalled by the manner in which this lovely, guileless woman was opening her secret heart.

"I never loved him," said Josephine, so softly that the manner in which it was uttered, almost hid the awful significance of the speech: "I never loved him."

He remained silent.

"Do you see those waves, swelling and surging, and beating against this rock? They have probably bathed it, embraced it, and rested by its side for centuries; but there is no love in their contiguity, their natures are different, there is no *affinity* between them, and though the rock may sink into the sea, or the sea rise up and cover the rock from view, they will be enemies forever. Though the rock may conceal a handful of water in a crevice, though the water may wash away particles of the stone, the stone will return to stone again, and the water to water, at the first opportunity. They never may unite. Such has been my married life."

"And yet," continued the widow, dreamily, "I think I know what love is, though it has not fallen to my lot, *as yet*. I am sure that I could be so enwrapped in love that my individual existence would be entirely lost sight of. It may be that my guardian angel has kept me from this danger, knowing that it might destroy me."

With these words she arose; something, it might have been that guardian angel, told her that she was going too far. He followed her, respectful and self-possessed.

By a mutual impulse they took a silent farewell of the spot where Josephine's husband had first plead his cause so successfully, and where she had this day formed a new friendship, and, perhaps,—but who can tell?

Mrs. Josephine Van Strom has been placed before the reader, in a very peculiar position, and one which might lead to a hasty decision that she was a very weak and silly woman, yet her unrestrained, impulsive, and, may be, unwise speaking, arose from no weakness, no silliness, no levity, or lack of modesty. She had tasted too deeply of the fountain of disappointment to be easily lead to unveil her heart, but when the outside covering of reserve was once cast aside from her, the warmth of her nature gushed over all bounds of worldly-wise caution. Yet so correct is the intuition of such passionate hearts, that it preserved her from misplacing confidence, and the extraordinary intimacy sprung up between them, as just narrated, astonished her thoroughly, as she thought it over. Still, her heart had dictated it; her heart, in spite of reason, approved it, and her heart, that sole authority in a woman's breast, was full of the image of Ernest Montant, with his earnest face and musical voice.

They walked together over the meadows toward the house, with its massive pillars and stately air, arm-in-arm, and conversing on the topics of the day. They lingered, and their footsteps dragged as they approached the door where they must part.

"When can I see you again?" he asked, eagerly.

"When you wish. It will give me great pleasure to see you soon."

"And should this house be sold, Mrs. Van Strom?"

"Then I shall move into a quiet cottage, somewhere in New England. I like the country and the people there, and have many friends among them. You know my father, Gen. McLane, although a Southerner, married a Boston lady, and lived in Boston after going on the retired list. Besides, I think I can make a *cheap* arrangement, and yet live respectably, near that city; and I assure you that money is a great consideration with me."

Ernest Montant's thoughts instantly went out toward this lady's needs. "So young, so beautiful, and so poor," he thought, "how I wish I could do something for her."

"How can I make an excuse to come here?" he said, dolefully. "Mr. Van Strom would certainly never invite me."

"And I *can not*; so here it can not be, unless some business matters between Mr. Going and my father-in-law should require a messenger," she said, slily.

"Oh! the ingenuity of woman," cried our hero, laughing. "I can easily arrange that, even though the business were only of sufficient importance to save my dignity as embassador. I know Walter Going so intimately, that I am sure of a satisfactory result there. But suppose you should be away when I come," he suggested.

"Well, perhaps you had better send me word,—a card or note."

"And suppose you could not stay at home on the day that I appoint, or should be indisposed. You know that I could not come here *on business* very often. Will you answer my note?"

"Well—as it seems necessary—yes."

He took her hand and kissed it. She left it in his listlessly for a moment, and looked at him tenderly, with her glorious eyes. It was a dangerous moment. She broke the spell by giving him a slight tap on his cheek.

"After all," she said, "you are only a boy."

And yet Josephine Van Strom was not a coquette. Never in her previous experience had she permitted a flirtation like this, and certainly this sudden attack seems rather severe. So, at least, thought our hero, as he turned the matter over in his mind afterward; and he even reproached himself severely for having carried matters so far. So chivalric and high-minded was he, that he never thought of attributing part of the blame to her; but accused himself of having perhaps convinced her that he had fallen desperately in love with her, which, as he assured himself, was a mistaken impression.

He had been many times enraptured with Jessie Going; we have seen him fascinated by Josephine Van Strom; but he *loved* neither the one nor the other.

Mr. Van Strom, with his guests, were now coming over the lawn, still in earnest conversation, and the first words we overhear are from the old gentleman.

" Well, Mr. Going, in a week from to-day I will give you a definite answer whether I will sell the Priory, or not. Mark you, two hundred and twenty-five thousand dollars is the price, two-thirds to remain on bond and mortgage, five thousand cash on the day of sale, when we sign the papers, and the balance after the title is searched out, and the deed is delivered into your hands.

" Exactly so," replied Mr. Going; " and now we must ask for our carriage, to return, for it is five o'clock."

So the horses came up with a great deal of unnecessary stamping, and rearing, and neighing, and snorting, and after the usual amount of hand-shaking had been done, and Mr. Going had almost affectionately bidden Josephine good-bye, and after that lady's soft little fingers had given our hero's hand a little soft squeeze, which he did not forget immediately, there came a crack of the whip, a general farewell, and away they went, all too soon out of the widow's sight, who stood watching them to the last. And when the rattle of the wheels had died away, she felt that the load she had carried so long, though lifted off for one bright afternoon, had fallen back upon her heart, heavier than ever.

She sank into one of the chairs on the front piazza, and wondered why the gentle breezes, coming freshly from the hills of Westchester County, did not waft to her listening ear even an echo of those noisy wheels, which had seemed to fairly *fly* away from her—perhaps forever.

Before her lay the flower-beds surrounding the house, and yonder was the lawn falling away in gradual slopes. As she looked attentively at the little flowers and grasses, it seemed to her dreamy imagination, that they were crowding and jostling each other in dwarfish disturbance, trying to get a last look at the fast dying sun in the West. At the foot of the lawn, the grand group of dark and silent trees, tinged by the sun, wore golden-crowns and the hills and rocks were lighted up by his last rays with an infinity of colors. What a study for the painter. The hovering shadows rolling over the green hillsides, the granite rocks shining now in silver, now

fading away to blue, now to violet; the gray-blue clouds towering in massive shapes, while the little white ones clustered around like effigies of cherubim upon a background of endless blue, shaded by the last rays of the sun to gold, as though the fields of heaven lay there, according to the teachings of our childhood.

Josephine Van Strom watched the scenery till her eyes moistened and the little tears stole out to catch the sunbeams like the flowers at her feet. Her heart throbbed and her face glowed as if a meteor had arisen on the horizon of her soul, while the sun was sinking yonder. Was it so? Had the morning dawned upon her which brings to woman new light, new life?

She laid her hands on her throbbing breast: had the stranger only stimulated a fleeting fancy, or had she already, in one of those moments upon which hangs a lifetime, set her heart upon his image, clutching it firmly to have and to hold till death should part them? As yet there is but a zephyr astir in her heart, as in the air around her rippling the water but gently and only rustling softly the leaves of the trees; but, it may soon increase to a gale and arouse the horrors of the tempest. It may grudge the moon to the patient earth this very night, it may hang this beautiful world now spread before her admiring gaze, in cheerless mourning, and sleep may be banished from your couch before you think it possible—poor Josephine.

Already the breeze becomes stronger, and now that the sun has fairly set, it brings with it a warning chill. A change comes over the scene; but, what is that streak of pale gold glinting through the trees? It spreads its luster and expands like magic over the lawn, it trembles from leaf to leaf, from flower to flower, and coats the dark trees with silver, it lies on the roads, runs along the fences, lightens the whole country in an instant, it flashes up the water and glitters greeting from the distant hills—it is the new moon.

" Welcome, oh star of love!" said Josephine, from the depth of her passionate soul. "Light up his pathway wherever he goes; shine into his heart and bring him tidings of what you have read in mine own, for—God help me—*I love him!*"

*　　*　　*　　*　　*

And, meanwhile, the four bays were scampering along the road and stamping through Central Park, and rattling over the pavements to the house where Jessie Going awaited the company to a late dinner. Ernest Montant did not speak a word during the whole ride, but sat biting his lips and comparing Jessie Going and Mrs. Josephine Van Strom, repeating to himself again and again, that, since he did not love both (of that he was quite certain), and was unable to decide upon a preference, he therefore loved neither of them, which conclusion invariably proved very provokingly unsatisfactory.

CHAPTER VI.

HOW JOHN JACOB VAN STROM, JR., GOT MAR-
RIED.

> "If thou wilt needs marry, marry a fool."
>   HAMLET.

JOHN JACOB VAN STROM, Junior, was, as we
have seen, the happy proprietor of a yellow
mare. Her poetical name was "Bella." She
was not quite sound in body; but, in the
language of her owner, "she knew as much as
any human being," which might have been
correct had John considered his own mental
caliber as the standard.

Like most of her gender she was born with
a strong will, and had never quietly submitted
to the humiliation of having her mouth pulled
to the right or left by the degrading machinery
called reins and bit. She only tolerated a
bridle upon the condition that it should be
strictly considered as a head ornament, and
she alone decided upon the road to be traveled
upon, the speed adopted, and upon the proper
moment and place to turn her yellow nose
homeward for dinner. John's greatest amusement was to harness this strong-minded
female, sit lazily in his rickety wagon, and
leave it to her superior judgment to decide
upon a pleasant excursion for the day. Entertaining himself then by conversing with the
mare, he was dragged along as resistlessly as
a child in a baby-wagon, and great was his
delight whenever his motor made an unexpected turn and varied the more familiar
drives, by attempting short cuts through the
woods or other unfrequented places. It must
not, however, be omitted that when "Bella"
came jogging back through the park, John
made a pretense of handling the reins in fine
style, and when she considerately stopped for
him to alight, he always cried "whoa" very
imperiously, just as other folks with more
sense are apt to do, when wishing to hide
their incapacity before a criticizing world.

On a fine afternoon, not many days after
the events chronicled in the last chapter, John
and Bella were peacefully traveling along the
high road, when suddenly the mare shook her
head, gave a saucy little kick at the traces,
and stood still.

"Hallo!" said John to himself, "there is a
reason for this; she never stops unless something is in the wind. I shall wait and see."

It so happened that close by the road there
stood a rustic tailor's shop; but John took no
notice of his surroundings, being too busily
engaged watching the mare with intense expectation of a *dénouement*. There he sat, the
reins thrown over Bella's back, curved like a
cat on a grindstone, his thin, smooth chin, and
protruding jaws resting on his bony hands,
his sharp elbows braced upon his angular
knees, his attenuated legs drawn up under
him, and his low, narrow forehead wrinkled
in wonder, for he was thoroughly convinced
that something remarkable was certain to
happen soon; when the door of the shop
opened and out stepped the tailor's daughter,
tolerably good-looking, robust, sprightly, neat,
and clever

"Good morning, ma'am," said John, touching his hat.

"Good morning, Mr. Van Strom."

"Eh! you know my name? What is
yours?"

"They call me Bella."

"The devil," cried he, "and don't you
know, my pretty girl, that I call my mare,
this mare, Bella, too."

"You surprise me, sir," she said, amused.

"And as your name is Bella, and the mare's
name is Bella, too, you must take a ride with
me. Don't object, jump in just as you are,
right off. I tell you, a Van Strom don't wait
for any one."

"I'll ask father," she commenced.

"Ask fiddlesticks!" he interrupted, angrily.
"Come this instant. The mare might start
if you don't hurry," he added, under his
breath, with a troubled glance at that animal,
who certainly seemed to have awakened from
her recent nap.

Bella had but little desire to avoid the frolic
offered her, and when he answered her suggestion of the propriety of dressing up by an
impatient "Now or never," she jumped up
alongside him with an alacrity that threatened
to dislocate the springs, and the old mare,
seeing her namesake finally bagged, started
with a jerk that threw the still unseated fair
one upon the willing support of John's extended arm.

The laborers in the field stopped their work
to see the strange couple. Stragglers and
country folk whom they met, laughed and
passed impertinent jokes in a half-audible
tone as they passed; but "he laughs best
who laughs last," and, before half an hour
Bella, the tailor's daughter, had the best of
the joke, for the sole heir of the wealthiest
man in the county had made her a declaration of love.

Without waiting for an answer he took her
to his "throbbing heart," thus saving her a
world of remonstrance, gradual yielding,
blushing, and all other fine effects of propriety used by maids in such cases—all of
which could so advantageously be dispensed
with, according to John's example.

"Bella, you don't speak, you don't answer,"
he cried, agitated by his rapidly changing
whims. "But let us leave the answer to your
noble namesake! Look there, my darling, see
yonder is the cross-road! My mare was never
guided by a strip of leather since I had her.
Now, if she turns to the right, we will be
married at once, within the hour. If she
turns to the left, we are parted forever!"

Bella agreed to this arrangement by which
the whim of an animal was to decide her destiny; but, as they neared the spot, she determined upon trying a plan of her own to secure
the fortunes of the day. It was very deceit-
ful, doubtless very wicked; but did not the
prize at stake warrant the action, and was she
not a woman? Blinding John with caresses,
she softly put out her hand toward the reins
and grasping one, gave one little but decided
pull to the right; but ah! there she missed
it. The mare, totally unaccustomed to such
liberties, stood still with amazement; then in-

dignation filled her soul, and, with a snake of her head and a defiant whisk of her tail, with true feminine contrariness, she wheeled to the —*left*, and jogged on leisurely in that direction.

"Ha, Bella, woman!" cried John, in great excitement, "would you try to deceive me? Its foul—didn't I see you pull that left line? Its awfully mean, I say. Oh, ye women, ye women!"

Delighted at his mistake, Bella proposed to try another experiment. But it proved not so easy to suit John's whim. He suggested that the next trial should be the first fowl that crossed the road. If it should prove a rooster —but she stopped him right there, and something else had to be thought of.

While he sat musing, almost in despair, her quick eye saw a team approaching in the distance. "I have it," she cried, instantly. "If the first team we meet is a double one, two horses, you know, I will consent to—never mind what, if only one horse, farewell happiness!"

Agreed. The team approaches, nearer, nearer — two horses, of course, as Bella thought, but when she prepared for a final embrace, she was startled by the look of utter misery which overspread his countenance.

"Bella," he sighed, "it's all over. It is of no use tempting the fates any more, so let us be resigned!"

"Oh, wretched tailor's daughter! Oh, disconsolate Bella!"

"What can be the matter now?" she gasped.

"Oh, darling of my heart," he cried, mournfully, "that team, that team."

"Well, those two horses—"

"There were not two horses. Oh, my dear, my sweet, my—there was but one horse! The other was a *mule!*"

For a moment the temptation to laugh outright at the intensely comical expression of his face nearly overcame her, then her good sense prompted her to end the farce at once, but she acted differently. Like a good general, who keeps his presence of mind on a battle-field half lost, and knows how to turn the scale to victory at an opportune moment, she was equal to the emergency and sent her tears, as light troops, in advance, to gain time.

"Oh! you bad man," she sobbed, "*you*, to talk of love. Oh, you deceiving, two-faced, deep-plotting, scandalous wretch—Oh, you heartless, mean, low, false, unprincipled—oh! oh! oh!" (Strong symptoms of hysterics.) "Thus to treat me (gasps and sobs), thus to—trifle with me—such merciless tor-rr-ture from one I loved *so* well!" Here came a perfect cataract of tears.

"Don't cry, Bella," he blubbered, in imploring tones. "It is not my fault. Have I created that cursed mule? Can I help it that his father was an ass?"

"He was not," she cried, vehemently, "the thing's father was a *horse!*"

"But his mother was an ass!" he suggested, mildly.

"I tell you, John, the animal is a horse. I know his father is a horse! Ask old Ben Smith, who owns him; he lives next door to us, and I k-n-o-w it is a horse, a sweet, little,

black horse, with a star in its forehead, right here!" and she pointed at her own forehead, to prove this an accurate description of the sweet, black, little horse.

"I admit that, darling, I admit that, but that does not prove him a horse. For his mother must have been—must, you know—"

"If your mother," she interrupted, hopefully, "if your mother was Miss Jones, and your father Mr. Van Strom, what are you? Answer me that!"

"My name is Van Strom," he conceded, puzzled.

"Then that beast is a *horse*," she cried, triumphantly ("and you are the ass," she added, good-humoredly, to herself).

So, proving her superior knowledge to his utter discomfiture, she took advantage of his amazement and addressed herself to his affections, for he really seemed to love her, and finally he gave up the point.

The mare proved to be an inconsidered, though not inconsiderable, ally, and just then helped matters amazingly by coming to a standstill just in front of a little country meeting-house on the road-side.

"When *she* decides, it is all right," said John, with a sigh of relief; and they alighted without hesitation on finding the door open, to be married on the spot. They found the minister inside, engaged in patching up a broken window with an old newspaper, so before long they were standing before him, in front of the great pulpit.

While the parson was going through the ceremony with great pleasure, for he knew both parties, and was very fond of Bella, John began to grow absent-minded and restless. He wiped the cold perspiration from his brow; he looked around with a vacant stare, as if in great perplexity; he shifted nervously from one foot to the other; and finally turned very pale, when he was asked if he would "take this woman to be," &c., and bellowing a frantic "*No*" before the question was finished, he suddenly turned away, with a distorting convulsion of his lean body, bolted out of the church at the top of his speed, and made for his wagon as if for his life.

A word from Bella kept the minister at his post, and she went after her escaping fortune, running faster than he; but laughing in spite of herself.

"Go along, get up!" John shouted to the mare; but she shook her head, laid one ear back, and turning her head slowly around, looked at her master, with a sort of grin, as one who would say, "I am acting for your good, though you don't seem to appreciate it."

John gave it up, and was sitting in his seat, a picture of misery, when Bella reached him. After much parley the truth came out.

"Bella," he confessed, "a Van Strom can not act against his conscience: and as I stood before the parson with you, there came into my mind, destroying all my happiness, fresh reasons why a mule is not a horse. After all, you see—"

She thought of an old remedy, and interrupted his logic with the representation that in order to redeem her character, he must go

back and say "yes" the next time, and allow
her to refuse him. As John acknowledged
that it was the lady's place to refuse a gentleman, he agreed to return; but he could hardly
believe his ears, when, after he had said "I
will," according to agreement, she also said "I
will." He started back, and looked at her with
mouth and eyes wide open. It was a critical
moment. She smiled upon him such a winning
smile, that he laughed, embraced her heartily,
and went through the rest of the service like
a lamb.

So, they say, John Jacob Van Strom, Junior,
was married mal gré lui, as the French have
it; and although he was very happy when the
trouble was all over, he little thought that
that was the most sensible action of his whole
life.

With his usual pertinacity, he insisted upon
taking her immediately to the Priory; she
objected, he proved his authority as her husband. As they went through the Park the
old trees frowned on the intruder, and as they
approached the stately house, which was now
to be her home, her courage failed her. At
last she realized what she had done, and what
serious results might accrue. She felt that
the crazy doings of a crazy gentleman might
involve a poor tailor's daughter in disgrace and
misery. True, she held her marriage certificate
tightly in her hand; but she feared lest her
comedy should turn to tragedy, and her farce
change to a curse to both of them. The feverish
energy of her spouse had brought her to the
door of the house, and she plucked up courage
to enter, resolving to crown her coup with
complete success or know the worst.

And when, before old Mr. Van Strom, the
crazy son told the crazy father the crazy
news, her pride upheld her, by the self-con-
sciousness that she was the only rational
creature of the three.

And old Mr. Van Strom did what some
highly intelligent old gentlemen would not
have been sufficiently intelligent to do; he
gave his consent and blessing, instead of trying to undo what could not be undone, or
making worse what could not be mended,
thereby saving himself a deal of trouble,
expense, vexation, and perhaps ultimate remorse, and so making two others very happy
instead of miserable. He embraced his new
daughter-in-law, and John capered about the
room in an ecstasy of delight at his father's
kindness, for he had rather feared the old
gentleman might object. The servants were
called in, and the news announced to them;
the butler looked blank, and the cook made a
face; but they all bowed and courtesied to the
new mistress, who looked resolved to stand
her ground, and not quite so credulous as
certain simple-minded folk who had attempted
to rule them heretofore.

"I think," she soliloquized the next morning, while dressing in a room which seemed a
palace to her untutored eyes, "I think I see
my duty here pretty plainly. My poor husband loves me truly, beyond a doubt, and he
will love me always if I choose. To him I
owe this sudden change of fortune, and I will
repay him by watching his interests, and

caring for him who needs it so much. Yes!
he shall find a prop and a comfort in his wife,
so long as I retain my sound sense and honesty of purpose."

And where was Josephine Van Strom?
Her maid informed her of the news, and her
description of John's wife was not sufficiently
flattering to cause lively joy to the widow.
She was at first indignant, then inclined to
weep and lament; but soon became resigned,
and simply shrugged her beautiful shoulders.

"Here's news, Mrs. Van Strom," Jane
had cried, rushing in without her usual knock,
for Jane was a well-behaved girl.

"What in the world has happened?" asked
Josephine, with some alarm, on beholding
Jane's excitement.

"Mr. John has been and gone and done
it!"

"Done what? Speak sensibly, Jane," said
the widow, expecting to hear of some unfortunate relapse in John's mental condition.
Had he committed murder, arson, or suicide?

"He's been down in the village, mum, and
carted off Bell, the darter of Smith, the tail-
or, and's married her right straight off, and
brought her home, and she be down below
now, mum, a-huggin' and a-kissin', and the
divil to pay, savin' your presence, mum, her
and Mister John and the old gintleman, so
ye'd think they'd all three gone stark mad and
no mistake this time."

Which classic recital had the effect of
keeping Mrs. Van Strom in her room until the
next morning. "Nobody sends for me," she
sighed to herself. "I am not thought worthy
to receive even a wanton hussy, in this
house."

She determined to leave the house immediately, and gave the necessary orders to
Jane and the coachman, both of whom, and
in fact all the servants, were devoted to her,
although they fooled, cheated, plundered, and
at times even insulted Mr. Van Strom and
John Jacob, Junior.

She dressed herself carefully and very
tastefully before leaving her room, and her
mirror gave her courage as it told her how
charming she was. Her curiosity led her to seek
the nouvelle arrivée before taking her leave, so
she entered the drawing-room softly, and, on
discovering a female figure at the other end
of the room, retired, unobserved, into a bow-
window.

"Is this my sister-in-law," she wondered.
"Is this the tailor's daughter turned lady in
two hours? Why she is actually at work.
This at least speaks well for her. Some
women in her circumstances would at once
play the great lady, but here she is dusting
and arranging the furniture. And she is
neither awkward nor homely. Her figure is
comely and her face seems pleasing, though
not handsome. I know some ladies who
would give a great deal for that complexion
and those round arms."

At this moment, the butler, whom Bella
had summoned, entered the room without
knocking at the door, and showing defiance
in his bearing, rather than deference or respect.

"James," said his new mistress, turning

upon him authoritatively, "how long does it take you to answer the bell?"

"Well, ma'am, the cook axed me to—"

"I want you to understand, James," said Mrs. John Van Strom, "that hereafter, the servant who is wanting in respect or attention, will be dismissed *at once*. Do you hear?"

"I have been in the family, ma'am," commenced the old rascal, whining—

"I don't care how long you have been in the family," she interrupted, in the same calm, decisive tone, "but I warn you, that, although I can appreciate an old servant, and will do every thing reasonable to render him comfortable, he must do his duty, or walk off. Now go, I don't need you here, for I have done the work myself."

The servant peered keenly into her face for a moment, finding there nothing but decision and calm consciousness of power, so he made his exit quite humbly.

Josephine, in her corner, opened her eyes at the dignity of this new matron, and could but acknowledge that the butler had well deserved all he got, so she silently complimented Bella, and emerged from her hiding place.

Mrs. John started a little on perceiving her; but as her nerves were not yet fashionably unstrung, she neither shrieked nor trembled at the sudden apparition, but said, with a modesty of tone, which pleasantly contrasted with her manner toward James—

"Excuse me, madam, I did not know you were here; may I ask whom I have the honor to address?"

"My name is Josephine Van Strom," answered the widow. "I am the widow of your husband's brother."

"My sister-in-law," was on Bella's tongue: but she shrank back timidly when she saw no encouragement in Josephine's unmoved face and distant manner. After an instant of hesitation, she again approached and shyly held out her hand.

Josephine's warm heart smote her because of her impoliteness, and she took the offered hand cordially, drew Bella close to her, and with the words, "Yes, my dear, your sister, Josephine," kissed her on both cheeks.

As John had accompanied his father on some errand, the two were left to themselves, and soon after their first meeting they were sitting in Josephine's room, Bella on a low stool at the other's feet, her hands clasped in her lap, and looking up into Josephine's face with admiration and tenderness.

"How beautiful you are, sister Josephine," said the tailor's daughter, artlessly, and how strange it is that the gentlemen have not made you a pet, a dear mistress, a sort of goddess. I can hardly believe it, though you have just told me so."

"And yet it is so, my dear," she answered, with a sad smile, "and for that reason, I am determined to leave the house to-day."

"No! no! no!"

"I must! Although I feel that I could love you dearly and tenderly, my pride has been too deeply wounded in this house to remain for your sake alone, for I have pride, Bella, though it may be wrong."

"It is *not* wrong in you, it would be very, very wrong in me! Do you know that I am half out of my mind? Such a change! A careless, poor girl yesterday, and to-day, Mrs. Van Strom. Why, we children were brought up to regard this house as a fairy castle, a royal palace, every thing that was grand and beyond our sphere. Can't you imagine, then, that I feel like a thief, like a bold and shameless woman to have usurped this place because my poor husband was sufficiently imbecile to take me?"

"You have accomplished the most remarkable feat that I ever heard of," replied Josephine, smiling "but I can not say that what you have done is bad or contemptible. You have fallen in with what some might call miraculous good fortune; but be warned in time against the harshness and unmerciful prejudice you will meet in this new world, which now seems to you all sunshine. This fine society will cost you many a tear—this high station, many a heart-ache; but trust in God and preserve your self-respect. All will be right, and John may thank heaven for his wife."

She kissed her forehead and took her hands caressingly. Bella laid her head on the widow's lap and sobbed bitterly.

"Why do you cry, dear?" asked Josephine. "I did not mean to frighten you, much less to wound you. Look up and take courage. I repeat that I think John has made a better bargain than you have."

"I will be cheerful, and happy, and strong, and any thing else you wish, if you will do me a favor."

"And that is—"

"Will you promise?"

"I will not deny you, if I can help it."

"Remain here. If not for years, stay for months, or, at any rate, do not speak of leaving at present."

"Ask any thing but this, dear Bella."

"Just try us for a little while. *I* am mistress of this house, and my husband and father-in-law shall act like sensible people, I promise you. You are in a strange position; your rights are disregarded; your name, your husband's name is dishonored by the treatment you receive; but if you, beautiful and accomplished as you are, can condescend to let poor me manage affairs—if you will be my ally as I shall be yours—we shall be able to maintain our position together against the whims of our relatives, against the attacks of that society you spoke of, and against all other obstacles. You are no stranger, no guest, no mendicant in this house. It belongs to you as much as to my husband, and I repeat that you forget the name which you bear, if you do not assert yourself. On the other hand, what comfort, what help can I find, but in you? If you are sincere in what you say, you must feel willing to stand by me and to advise me. If I can not coax you, I must appeal to your heart. Can you really pity me or love me, and yet leave me so?"

It was a hard struggle; but Bella's common sense and tact won the day. Josephine had never before viewed her position at the Priory in the light presented by the tailor's daughter. A gentle, loving, passionate, tender woman, she was born to be cared for by others, and when neglected would retreat timidly, uncomplainingly like a wounded bird to its nest, there to mourn and helplessly die. She had never even thought of *asserting* herself, as Bella now called upon her to do, and it was only because the latter's straightforward energy gave her hope and strength, that she finally consented.

"And if the place is sold, Bella?" she asked, after the question was settled.

"You shall still remain with us wherever we go," cried Bella. "The fact is, I shall make John's father sell the place. It is too large."

"You seem to have great confidence in your powers over Mr. Van Strom."

"Yes, I have, though I don't know why, exactly. You will see that the place will be sold before the week is out, provided Mr. Going sticks to his bargain."

"You know about that already," said Josephine, much astonished. "You surprise me!"

"I am a business woman, dear," answered Bella, laughing, "and, I think, much more competent than two certain gentlemen we know of."

At this moment John and his father came in sight, driving toward the house.

"Bella," asked Josephine, softly stroking her new sister's hair, "Bella, tell me one thing, we are both women, you know: *Do you love your husband?*"

"So help me God, I love him dutifully as a wife should," answered the wife, solemnly.

"Then all will be well."

CHAPTER VII.

HOBGOBLIN.

KING HENRY: "You have good leave to leave us:
      when we need
Your use and counsel, we shall send for you."
                                   KING HENRY IV.

SEVERAL weeks elapsed before Mr. Van Strom could bring himself to announce to Mr. Going that he had determined to sell the Priory. Walter fretted mightily at the delay, and favored a second visit to the old man, to compel him to sell at once; but his father felt grave about buying such a costly place, giving a mortgage on it, and sustaining the inevitably heavy expenditures of so large an establishment. Report called him an immensely wealthy man, and his credit was unimpeachable; but what his property would amount to, if his business were suddenly closed, must remain as dubious to us, for awhile, as it was to his friends and enemies in the commercial world of New York.

"If the Priory comes into my hands without any further exertion on my part, well and good," he said to Walter; "if not, we will let it go, and I confess, I shall not feel any the less secure, for *not* owning a princely estate, with a princely mortgage on it."

In the meanwhile our hero was working hard and gaining golden opinions. Already he had proved that his business capacity was of no common order, and it had been noticed and even mentioned to Mr. Going by outside parties. The old gentleman was pleased by the discovery, and liked to hear eulogies of his new clerk. "I must say that it is very gratifying to see a young man winning his way without help," he said to Walter one day.

"Which is not my case," replied the young man, lazily.

"I fear that I made a mistake in smoothing your road too much, Walter," said his father, gravely. "You have never known care, and your energies have never been called upon by harsh necessity. Let us hope that you will not have to face troubles in your maturer life, which will require the energy and elasticity only to be gained by youthful struggles."

Walter made no reply, but echoed his father's wish, in his inmost heart, and listened dutifully and attentively to his words, uttered more seriously than usual. The firm had lost money heavily and steadily for several months past.

Mr. Montant made his appearance in the private office.

"Mr. Going," he said, "a certain Mr. Stilletto and a friend of his, by the name of Muller, are without and desire an interview with you. I understand their object is to propose to you an undertaking, a sort of *scheme*, the value of which it is not my place to determine. But I desire to explain to you that I came across the ocean in company with Mr. Stilletto, and he may possibly refer you to me. Should he do so, believe me it is entirely unwarranted, for I know but little about him, and besides I think I understand my position here, as your clerk, too well to use it for the introduction of strangers to my employers."

"Very good, Mr. Montant," said Mr. Going. "You are quite right to notify me of this, to prevent any misunderstanding. But as I have leisure for half an hour, I will receive them. I like to hear of new enterprises."

"This one," said Montant, lightly, as he was passing out, "has been explained to me before, with the proposition that *I* should bring it before your notice! I would not have done so in this case, even had it been within my province!"

"It seems to me, father," suggested Walter, when they were again alone, "as if Ernest gave you a bit of advice there, in a delicate and inoffensive manner. It will be quite interesting to see what sort of a speculation it is that our noble German friend will not recommend."

The door opened, and two creatures entered whose low bows suggested at once a great lack of good-breeding or of self-respect.

When the two backs had resumed their normal position and the two faces became visible Walter was forced to turn his back to conceal his merriment. Muller's eyes were blinking in an extraordinary manner. He had fortified himself by an extra dose of invigorating beverages before venturing upon the errand. He told Stilletto that he was not abashed in the presence of kings, and much less would he feel embarrassed when business called him to the office of a merchant prince.

"I have before this visited merchant princes. What are they, these merchant princes? They have money, very much money; but not enough to buy for themselves a *friendship* in August Muller's soul. And shall *I*, who stand far above them in education; *I*, who am their superior in every point or phase of intellect, shall *I* cringe before them? Or shall I step up boldly and let them read in my face that I am more than their equal? Let them only hear me speak," cried he, "and if they are not amazed at the force of my intellect, my name is not Muller. I have more brains than these people, and they will see it; they will recognize it; they will, one day, point at me as I pass in the street and say, there goes August Muller, who knows more than we all put together."

"Stop your gas," said Stilletto, nervously. "Your pompous nonsense will turn to meekness unexampled before we are ten minutes older. You will see that money is a king before whom intelligence and education are very slaves."

Stilletto was right, for Muller now presented an incarnation of meekness and timidity. He tried to smile pleasantly; but only succeeded in grinning deferentially, while his long lean body was bent in fawning suppliance, and his face grew redder than potations could have made it. Stilletto, however, seemed any thing but abashed. Indeed, that gentleman's self-assurance was little less than miraculous. He drew up his little figure complacently, and took a deliberate survey of the premises with a critical eye, as though he were upon the point of making an offer for the whole, Walter Going included.

"Your name is Stilletto?" said Walter, addressing the owner of this critical eye.

"Yes, sir," was the dry response; and then the little man, seeing no sign of being invited to sit down, deliberately selected a chair, placed it to suit himself, and sat down.

"Cool," muttered Walter Going.

"Take a seat, Mr. Muller," said Mr. Going, courteously. The great philosopher colored redder than ever, stammered out that he would prefer to stand, and immediately contradicted the assertion by staggering backward and forward in search of a chair, dropping his hat, knocking his head against the desk in picking it up, and, finally, by the interposition of an ever-watchful providence, ran aground on the sofa, one corner of which tripped him as he was backing away from the desk, and he came to an unexpected seat with a violence which cost the sofa a leg. Hereupon the philosopher was taken with a second nervous attack, and had to be pacified with great energy, on the part of Mr. Going, while Walter laughed outright, and Stilletto looked

daggers of vexation and contempt at his miserable companion.

"My friend, sir," said Stilletto, with a sneer, "is a philosopher. He is grand in solitude; but, as you see, rather awkward in the world."

"I think more of a man who is too timid, than of one who is too bold," said Walter, carelessly. "I think it makes a better impression."

"You are right, sir," said Mr. Muller, stimulated into self-possession by his friend's rebuke. "True intelligence scorns the approbation of finery and accomplished manner. True intelligence has been my watchword in life, and I mean to stand upon that platform only."

"To business, gentlemen," suggested Mr. Going.

"Commence, my friend," said Mr. Muller, mildly.

"Don't make a fool of yourself, if you can help it," Stilletto whispered. "Be a man, and speak out. Is this your boasted courage?"

"Well, then," commenced Mr. Muller, taking an imaginary pipe from his lips,—somehow the movement gave him confidence,—"Gentlemen, I stand before a great house! A noble, an affluent house, a mighty firm, based upon high respectability, guided by wisdom, prompted in all its dealings by the mighty intellect of its members, inspired by the principles of integrity and honor, and influenced by that high ambition which sees in the accumulation of wealth but the means of accomplishing worthier objects. To your desire of assisting enterprise; to your ambition to be pillars of the temple of intelligence which this century is proudly erecting; to your appreciation of new and advanced ideas, and to your heartfelt wish for the promotion of the welfare of your fellow-men, do I appeal (though I shall also point out to you an almost princely remuneration), for the assistance which I, August Muller, have come to ask."

The great man looked around for approbation. Mr. Going was leaning back in his chair, looking blandly before him, and balancing his paper-knife, with one hand resting on the desk. Walter yawned once or twice, and said, "Nearly time to go on 'change, father." Stilletto was shifting nervously on his chair and frowning disapproval at the philosopher's prolixity.

"If I understand my friend correctly," he interposed, immediately, "he thinks our undertaking sure to yield an immense fortune to those who will have spunk enough to go into it. I would suggest, Muller, that these gentlemen's time is valuable, and that you may get them to listen to plain statements, but not to half-witted harrangues, such as you have just given them."

"Quite right, my noble, foreign friend," said Walter, approvingly, "I suggest that you take the floor; for if your clever friend does the talking, we shall not soon come to the end. That end, I confess, I look forward to, with enthusiasm."

Walter's suggestion was favorably received,

and Mr. Stilletto told the wondrous tale. So much of it as belongs to this narrative has been explained in a previous chapter.

Between Stilletto's concise and very credible statements, and Mr. Muller's eloquent and enthusiastic interruptions, corrections, and enlargements on the subject, considerable time was consumed. From the beginning of the interview, the firm determined to have nothing to do with such a seedy-looking man as the philosopher, or such an unmistakable sharper as Antonio Stilletto. Yet a' fortune seemed within the grasp of any man of means and enterprise, and, for a moment, Mr. Going felt strongly tempted to say, "Yes, we will go in!" But the twinkling eyes and red nose of the philosopher, his sycophantic smile and forlorn *tout ensemble*, and the uncomfortable shrewdness which characterized Mr. Stilletto, restrained father and son. When the matter had been fully disclosed in all its fascinating, though, perhaps, delusive details, Mr. Going said:—

"Well, gentlemen, this certainly sounds very well, but my business-life has taught me caution. I hardly know you, and know nothing at all of your personal standing."

"As for me, sir," said Stilletto, "I would beg to refer to my friend and traveling companion, Mr. Ernest Montant."

"We will waive that subject," said the old gentleman, with a smile at this fulfillment of Montant's suspicion; "for it is my duty to positively refuse your proffer. The undertaking is entirely out of our line of business, and we do not choose to change. We have given you a patient hearing, because you desired it, but I believe that it was thoroughly understood at the beginning, that we did not hold out the slightest encouragement to warrant the trouble you have taken."

The philosopher's face fell, and it was with difficulty that his friend suppressed his vexation.

"In that case," said Mr. Muller, rising, "there is nothing to detain us any longer. Good morning, gentlemen, and pardon me for saying, as I take my leave, that I am disappointed, even dismayed at my failure to touch a responsive chord in your hearts, which I imagined would throb in unison with my views and ambitions. You will hear again of August Muller."

"God forbid," interrupted Walter, facetiously.

"He is not a man to be utterly disheartened by the failure of his maiden effort. I have laid before you a grand undertaking. I had chosen *you* as my stepping-stone to the exalted position which I am *certain*, yes, gentlemen, *certain* to occupy. You should feel flattered, complimented, and proud of August Muller's choice, for his choice is not that of an ordinary man! You have discarded him, you close your ears and purse against him, look you that the time may not come when you shall *envy* him."

"Fiddlesticks," said Stilletto, angrily, "I must apologize for my friend here, for I verily believe that if he had stayed at home, we would now have been in a very different situation."

"Stilletto," quoth the other, turning grandly toward him, "your remarks can not offend me. Your meaning is too contemptible, and your expressions are too coarse for me to notice."

Stilletto took his hat and walked to the door, rudely pushing Muller out of his way. With his hand on the knob, he looked impudently at old Mr. Going, who had taken up the newspaper, and at Walter, who did not attempt to conceal his merriment, and said, "Good morning."

He was gone; but that last look of his remained. That devilish, mocking "Good morning" rang in their ears some time, though neither Mr. Going nor his son were easily intimidated, the presence of Stilletto seemed to have infected the very air of the room, and recurrently wrought the impression that something repulsive had crossed their path and brushed closely enough by them to leave its mark. After Stilletto's sudden exit, the philosopher quickly wilted; his self-assertion completely left him. Hardly could he remember that his hat was still in his hand. The blood rushed to his face as he turned to wish a good day to the gentlemen, and met Walter's laughing gaze, and muttering an unintelligible something, he rushed out of the room, stumbling over the threshold of the door and nearly demolishing a clerk who happened to be near.

Our hero was to dine at the house in Fifth Avenue that night, and when business was over he walked up town with Walter Going.

"You have all the particulars of this Hobgoblin Mining and Manufacturing Company, you said?" asked the latter.

"Yes," replied the other, curtly.

"What do you think of it?"

"I would prefer to keep my opinion to myself, if you will allow me."

"May I ask why, sir?"

"Because I am your youngest clerk, and I think it would be out of place for me to discuss matters which can only be settled by the firm."

"This is some of your imported German cant," said Walter, impatiently. "Perhaps, in your superior wisdom, you would condescend to benefit me with your ideas, if I were to inform you beforehand, that father and I gave the seedy gentlemen the grand shake, unanimously."

"In that case," replied our hero, calmly, "I have no objection to allow that I think you have done very rightly."

The conversation then turned on other matters until they had reached the house, and, after preparing themselves for dinner in Walter's room, descended to the parlor.

"Jessie is in there," said Walter. "You have my permission to go in and say good evening, while I make a desperate attempt to infuse some system into the waiter's head. By Jove, he is such a dunce, this sweet son of Erin, that, were it not for me, I think he would bring us our claret in champagne coolers and put the champagne on the kitchen range to give it the proper temperature."

So our friend entered the drawing-room

alone. It was a dark and stately room, with bronzes and statuary, rich carpets and costly mirrors, fine pictures and fancy ornaments, carved furniture and massive chandeliers. The blinds were closed to exclude the plebeian light of day from all this luxury, so he could scarcely recognize Jessie Going, until she had approached him, extending her little hand graciously.

She was taller than Josephine Van Strom, and comparatively slender. Her figure was not less graceful and elegant, while her face, set off by luxurious black hair, seemed molded into the most refined and delicate lines of beauty. She was then but in her eighteenth year, and was naturally very lively, lacking entirely that passionate earnestness which was the most dangerous charm of Josephine Van Strom. Jessie Going was called a coquette by some; but she was entirely too good-hearted to go far in that line. A great belle in society, she was still a great home-body, and was entirely wrapped up in her love for her father.

When he first heard the rustle of her heavy blue dress, knowing that she was in the room, he felt half bewitched, spell-bound, and oblivious of all the rest of the world. No matter what doubts and inconsistencies controlled or agitated him when away from her, when in her presence he was her captive.

He took her hand and looked at her with wonder and admiration. In those black eyes and arched brows, in that delicate nose and those charming lips there was no hint of Josephine, and Josephine is forgotten in the presence of this supernaturally handsome brunette.

"I am very glad to see you," she said, in a charmingly musical voice, "for I expect some gentlemen to dinner whom I want you to know."

"Are they fashionable young men?"

"Quite so. One has a gallant mustache and eagle-eyes, and his name is Faro. The other is small, but graceful; dances superbly, and his name is Willy Wheeler. You will have a chance to judge of our New York lions."

"I am not very anxious to meet the lions, neither do I feel in the least inclined to shun their acquaintance," said he, dryly.

"Mr. Faro is very conceited," said Miss Jessie, "but I don't object to that. I like a man to be somewhat conceited."

"Do I suit you in this respect," he asked, smiling.

"Yes, you are certainly conceited, but you are not flat and stupid, like some I know, and therefore your conceit meets with my approbation, which I herewith bestow upon you. But I wish to have a few moments of serious conversation with you," she added, changing her tone and manner; "How is papa's business going on?"

"How little you must know of business to select me, a junior clerk for your informant. Walter will tell you: for, indeed, I have but a small chance to find out. To be honest, even if I had—"

"You would not tell me? That is the old story. None of you consider me competent to receive even a few hints about papa's business. And yet, Mr. Montant, I do not consider this fair, not even wise. I know that I am very young, and utterly incapable of understanding some things *in detail;* but, I think, that if papa and Walter had consulted me upon certain important questions, which I only heard of when it was too late, they would have been better off to-day."

"I quite agree with you, Miss Jessie," said our hero, gravely. "I think that a husband, for example, should always inform and consult his wife upon very important questions of business. I believe that a woman's intuition, in many cases, is capable of great, almost wonderful accuracy and soundness of judgment."

"I am glad to hear you say that, and I am sure it will make your wife very happy to be treated a little better than a doll!" she cried, artlessly. "Yet you will not tell me how papa is prospering; and yet, what do I really desire to know? Whether cotton, or oil, or coal, or hides, or any other nasty thing, is up or down, may be of little moment to me when I am convinced, and convinced I am, that the firm has lost money heavily of late. I see it in my father's face, when he wants to appear merrier than ever. I see it in Walter's restless, irritable mood. I *feel* it," she said, shaking her little head, "and when a woman *feels* the truth of any thing, no assertion, reasoning, or argument, can convince her to the contrary."

"I do not for a moment imagine that any thing has happened to give your father serious apprehensions. Your name is a good one, Miss Going, and so long as it remains intact, there may be fortunes lost under its protecting wing, and fortunes regained by its unbroken strength, without the outer world being much the wiser. I am inclined to think that your father is merely a little troubled about the propriety, at this moment, of buying the 'Priory.' It is a great extravagance, and if you wish to exercise your foresight—you understand me?"

"Yes, and I heartily thank you for the suggestion. The Priory shall not be bought if I can help it! How are you getting along in the office?"

"I am trying hard to rise, and make myself more useful than I can in my present inferior position."

"Walter has told me much about you, which I will not repeat, because it would be a breach of confidence, and besides it might increase your self-conceit beyond the limits which I consider suitable to your character. You have enough already."

Ernest laughed. "You are taking quite a motherly interest in me," he said. "I feel flattered by the attention with which you have investigated my character."

"Seriously speaking, I think that you will be placed in a much more responsible position before long, and here is the point of my remark. I want you to make me a promise. It seems odd to you, I know, for me to ask such a thing; but I have learned to look at you with Walter's eyes; will you make me this promise?"

Our hero looked at her face, all glowing with fixedness of purpose, and felt that he could refuse her nothing: "even a promise of marriage," he thought to himself.

"Let us sit in this corner," said Miss Jessie, with importance. "I do not want *any one* to listen, and leading the way to a sofa in the farthest corner of the room, she continued, with more earnestness in her tone and manner than before."

"Mr. Montant, from various sources I have gathered the knowledge that you have won the good opinion of all your mercantile acquaintances. They are unanimous in the announcement of your *reliability*. Now Mr. Montant, you know that we are a very extravagant family. *I* know what we spend every year, and it worries me. I have thought the matter all over, and this is my conclusion, plain though startling. That no success in legitimate business can support such extravagance, and it must cease or—" she paused an instant.

Ernest did not say a word.

"Your silence tells me that I am right," continued the young girl; "and now comes the promise. If real danger should come,—if ever you should see that the threatening storm must wreck us, and that ruin and dishonor stare my poor father in the face, will you then, at such an hour, remember that we were your first, your best friends in a strange country? Will you stand by us if the world turn its back? Will you devote yourself to my father, save him if possible, sink with him if necessary, even at the cost of refusing the splendid offers that may be made to you to leave him?"

She ceased, breathless. Long concealed excitement, suddenly burst forth, seemed to have changed her very nature.

"One word," said he, scarcely able to suppress his emotion at the spectacle of this beautiful creature pleading so eloquently for her father. "Why do you ask this? What has put such fancies into your head?"

"Intuition, foreboding, call it what you please! Will you promise?" He thought a moment, and then said, deliberately,—

"I promise."

"Thank you, thank you!" she said, holding out both hands to him. "I shall never forget it."

"And I," he replied, looking into the depths of her dark eyes, and holding her soft, warm hands in his, "I shall never forget—my promise."

"Dinner is ready," said Walter, entering, and to dinner they went, where Miss Jessie flirted so outrageously with Mr. Faro and Wheeler, and so completely ignored our hero, that on his way home that night he muttered angrily,—

"I must be mistaken in her! She is a heartless coquette, and no woman for Ernest Montant to love! But that promise I shall keep however it turns out."

CHAPTER VIII.

MASQUERADE.

"Now, this overdone, or come tardy off, though it make the unskilful laugh, can not but make the judicious grieve."—HAMLET.

Two months or so passed by and Mr. Going did not receive any message from Mr. Van Strom, with reference to the sale of the Priory. He had dismissed the subject from his mind, and was heartily glad that the temptation to commit so great an act of extravagance had passed. His daughter, by well chosen hints, and the general tone of conversation had helped his second thoughts on the matter; and Walter, even, moved by the eloquence of his sweet sister, had ceased to mention the subject, when, one day their father came home looking troubled and yet amused at something which had occurred. He handed his daughter a note which he had just received, and she read with a mixture of vexation and merriment, as follows:—

MR. GOING—DEAR SIR:—

I have concluded to cede you my country place, known as the Priory, with two hundred acres of land, comprised in what is known as the Priory Islands, for the sum of two hundred and twenty-five thousand dollars, to wit: five thousand cash, upon signing the contract, the balance of one-third of the whole upon my signing the deed, in cash, and two-thirds to remain on bond and mortgage. My lawyer, Mr. Rivulette has put himself in communication with your attorneys, Messrs. Grave & Paradise, so that the title will be searched at once. I shall call at your office this week to sign the preliminary contract, and I propose to give you possession in one week from this date.

I take pleasure in announcing to you the marriage of my son John to Miss Bella Smith, the daughter of Nehemiah Smith, manufacturer of gentleman's outer garments, in the village of New Rocket. The young and happy couple desire to say farewell to the Priory, in a manner suited to the position my family have always occupied, and you, your son, and Miss Going, are hereby cordially invited to assist at the last festivity at the old place. Your company is respectfully requested, at eight o'clock, punctually, on Thursday evening next, in *fancy dress*.

Yours, respectfully,
JOHN JACOB VAN STROM.

P.S.—I will be dressed as Napoleon the First; will you allow me to suggest that you should assume the costume of old Blucher. I think, as you are driving me from house and home, this would be appropriate. Or Wellington would do as well. Miss Going might then appear as the Goddess of War.

"I can not see my way clear to refuse," said Mr. Going, much perplexed.

"What do you mean?" cried Miss Jessie, horrified. "You are never going as Blucher or Wellington, I hope?"

"Not quite," answered her father, smiling;

"but I suppose I must buy the place, and I think we had better go to the party, provided David Worth will allow us to stay at his villa after the ball."

"But, surely, you don't think any of us had better go in fancy dress?"

"No; we must arrange about that."

"It would be impolite not to comply with the wishes of our host," suggested the young lady.

"I think we had better let Mr. Montant arrange it for us," said her father. "I shall have to send him up at all events, for, although I mean to adhere to my agreement about the place, yet I can not pay him the money until a couple of weeks from to-day. I have no doubt that this will suit him as well."

"I hope he will refuse the condition," thought Miss Jessie; but she was not one of those who talk when the time for words has passed, and so the conversation dropped.

The next day our hero went to the Priory, where Josephine had watched and waited in the true sense of the term. They had corresponded; yes, they were so foolish and imprudent as to correspond; and when they now met they felt as though they had known each other for years. They had another long walk to the shore of the Sound; more conversations on serious and solemn subjects took place, and Miss Jessie Going, by her preference of the gallant Mr. Faro, and charming Willy Wheeler, had accomplished what, perhaps, she did not wish to accomplish, the alienation of our hero, and the opening of the door for a rival to step into his affections.

Mr. Van Strom accepted the propositions made to him; gracefully excused the Goings from wearing fancy dresses, and extended a pressing invitation to our hero, which he accepted with pleasure, and Mr. David Worth, on receiving Mr. Going's note, professed himself delighted at the prospect of entertaining the whole party after the ball. So every thing was satisfactorily arranged, and on the appointed Thursday Mr. Going, with his son and daughter, and Ernest Montant, made their appearance at Mr. Worth's villa. After a jolly reception, and a good dinner, they dressed (but *not* in fancy costume) for the ball, and finally arrived at the Priory at a quarter past eight.

* * * * * * *

The Priory did not present a very festive appearance. The moon was at the full, and perhaps earthly illuminations grew dim in her bright rays; but the windows, certainly, did not seem lighted up brilliantly, the glare from the hall did not dazzle the eye when the door was opened, nor was the ear saluted with heavenly strains of music as one entered the grounds. Perhaps they were drowned by the low moaning of the wind, which was sighing in the trees. It had a desolate tone, as though portentous of a change in the weather, or other mischief; and, hark! there is a strange, unearthly note, sounding near, sounding far off, changing, swelling, dying away—distinct, yet ghostly. The old bell, hanging upon that old elm, is slowly tolling! They heard it as they approached, but comment was stopped, for now they stood in the great hall.

3

One long chandelier, apparently suspended from the clouds, distributed a doubtful luster on the assemblage of Van Strom portraiture, in their moldy frames. In the flickering, smoky light, they seemed frowning upon the unaccustomed revelry below. In the corners and niches of the vaulted ceiling there reigned a confusion of darkness, suggestive of spiders and cobwebs. In one corner of the room a little platform could be dimly descried, on which were perched four American citizens of African descent, fiddling away with such rapidity, and such utter disregard for harmony, that it was really astonishing that the platform could stand up under it. They were shaking their woolly heads as they sawed away, and stamping their feet, rolling their eyes, and showing their teeth, while their shrill voices rang out like the shrieks of agonized demons, as they called the figures of the dance.

"Forwart two! Jemmens to de ri-i-i-ght! All jassay acrosst."

Near the door stood the master of the house, in the dress of the exile of Elba. If the conqueror of empires got his clothing when young, and wore the same suit until he grew stout, the appearance of Mr. Van Strom was historically correct, except that he added to the "little corporal's" taste by mounting a great powdered wig.

John was already dancing at the head of a quadrille. Like his father, he, too, wore a white horse-hair wig, and the miraculous leanness of his body was displayed to advantage by a tight-fitting green jacket, which disdained to keep company with the knee-breeches, which encumbered his lower limbs. His miserable calves were stuffed out to an impossible size; but the plated buckles on his square-toed shoes were his pride and delight. He could not refrain from stealing an occasional glance of admiration at them whenever the dance allowed him an opportunity. He idealized the plain steps which we ordinary mortals take in a plain quadrille, into such swings, and twists, and hops, and shuffles, that he bore an extraordinary resemblance to a deranged frog, or an inspired monkey. His grins would rather incline one to place him among the latter, were it not for an ornament which he wore proudly, and which was a source of anxiety to those who knew him best. This was a real old-fashioned broad-sword he had discovered among the family relics, probably handed down by a certain warlike grandsire, whose portrait hung in a conspicuous place in the gallery overhead, and frowned grimly down on his audacious descendant. He was dancing with his wife. Bella had insisted upon appearing in ordinary costume, and, after a long struggle, carried her point. She appeared unabashed, but nervous and pre-occupied.

"Who is that humpback, dancing opposite Mr. and Mrs. Van Strom?" asked Montant, as they watched that curious assembly, with wonder.

"That is Mr. Paradise, of the firm of Grave & Paradise, our lawyers," answered Walter Going.

"He is joining in with everybody, odd and

absurd as ever," criticized Miss Jessie. Look at him, laughing and capering about, like a deformed goblin. He seems to have left all pride and dignity in his office, as usual."

"And yet he is one of the most clear-headed men I know," said old Mr. Going.

"His hunchback has demoralized and imbittered him to such an extent that he discards dignity, and sometimes even decency, to save himself from entire apathy and utter despair."

"He may certainly thank his deformity for protecting him," said Miss Jessie. "If it were not for pity's sake, he would have received many a sound beating for his insulting way to ladies."

"He would just as lief go into a lady's bedroom as not, without even knocking at the door," said Walter, "and his conversation is so gross that it exceeds all limit."

"And his sarcasm is as bad," added his sister. "He puts in a disagreeable speech whenever he can, and the only way to meet him, or gain immunity from him, is to pay him back in his own coin. I have done so without scruple, and, I assure you, he likes me for it."

Mr. Paradise was dancing with a spinster, who represented Night by the addition to her costume of a bunch of feathers on one shoulder, which might have belonged to a pre-Adamite owl, and a circle of little rents in her dress, through which shone her white petticoat like stars.

Bella's father appeared as Hamlet, in his most despondent mood.

He seemed ready, to be or not to be, any thing that might be desired by the company or by the enthusiastic black fiddlers, if he could only understand what would be required of him next.

To our hero's great surprise, he soon discovered Antonio Stilletto among the dancers, and he was footing it as confidently as though the costume of a Prince of Wales in the good old days, which he wore jauntily, indicated his real social status. How he could have obtained an invitation to the ball was the question. He had expressed his great desire to be introduced into good society several times, and our hero felt sure that some hidden history attached to his presence.

"Who is that lady dancing with the little Prince of Wales," he inquired.

"That is Mrs. Fatman," Miss Jessie answered. "They call her handsome: but I can not see the beauty. She was a buxom, red-faced girl, and the daughter of a baker before she was married. Now, just look at her—thin, and unhealthy, all dress and show, and very little foundation on which to build, I should imagine."

"Birds of a feather flock together," thought he. "If the lady is a *parvenue*, I am not surprised at seeing her with my worthy friend."

"Fatman must be here," said Mr. Going, looking around upon the crowd that by this time had nearly filled the hall. Yes, and a goodly crowd of people it was. The best, the proudest families were there, for Van Strom was a fine old name, and those who did not respect the present generation, had come to pay their tribute to the generations which had lived and died in the noble old Priory, and had not been forgotten.

"Here I am," said Mr. Fatman, stepping up. After he had greeted the party, he added "Everybody seems to know already that this place is virtually yours. I can not help envying you, for your future neighbors are delighted, and anxious to welcome you, with the exception of a few old cronies who prefer the society of cobwebs upon the walls, and cobwebs in certain brains we know of, hey! to life, and youth, and beauty." Upon which he made a profound bow to Jessie.

Our hero soon found his way to the side of Josephine.

"Do you believe in forbodings?" asked the widow, clinging tightly to his arm as they walked apart from the crowd in a comparatively deserted part of the hall.

"Why do you ask the question, Mrs. Van Strom?"

"Because, in my heart, I am certain that something is going to happen to-night. It may be a foolish fancy; but it agrees with another circumstance of no cheerful nature."

"And what may that be," said, he carelessly; for our hero was proof against superstition.

"*The bell rang* last night," she replied, not much reassured. "I heard it in my room."

"It was the wind. Have you heard it to-night."

"No, let us step on the back piazza and listen."

So they walked out through the door into the night and listened. The wind had increased somewhat; but it was warm as in midsummer. For several minutes they hardly breathed, straining their ears to the utmost, when—there was no mistake here—the sound of the bell came to them as distinctly as reality personified. First low and scarcely audible, then with a clear but doleful peal, slowly returning, with terrible regularity. The fatal bell was tolling.

"Let us go in," gasped Josephine, in genuine alarm.

"I am going to see who is ringing that bell," said her companion, resolutely.

"Pray don't—not now. There might be danger," she urged, clinging closer to him.

"Danger or not, I will solve this mystery if possible. I will be back in a moment."

"Stay. For my sake stay," she pleaded, imploringly, with a tone of voice which caused him to look for a moment into her eyes as if he would search her inmost soul for an explanation.

"I can not, for I owe it to my manhood not to be frightened at such a scarecrow as this."

There was no chance for further resistance to his determination, so she said quickly,—

"I will go with you."

"I advise you to stay where you are," he answered, shrugging his shoulders. "If you do not follow my advice, I have at all events done my duty in warning you."

Instead of an answer, she sprang down the steps after him, and they two silently and cautiously approached the old elm on which the bell was suspended. At every step they expected to hear another peal, and even our hero's heart beat faster than usual, while Josephine trembled like an aspen leaf till she could hardly sustain herself. The night was almost as light as day, so bright were the moonbeams.

In a few minutes they saw the bell plainly and distinctly. It was perfectly quiet. Not a sound, not a vibration, not a trace of motion could be recognized. Around was silence and solitude, and it hung there like a dead thing. They returned to the piazza, laughing at their temporary agitation, when suddenly there came another peal, a loud, angry note, which seemed to vibrate through their frames like a shock of electricity. For an instant Ernest stood spell-bound, then he darted off toward the old tree, while Josephine stood with clasped hands, not daring to follow him. He returned in a few moments. No further sound had been heard by either, and he had been utterly unable to find any sign around the mysterious metal.

Josephine shook her head gravely. "What do you think of it?"

"I am convinced it is either a serious joke played upon the family, or the effect of the wind, or the old tree is shaken by subterranean causes. Otherwise, I prefer to disbelieve my senses, to believing in that species of madness called superstition."

"Hush," whispered Josephine; "do not speak so positively. There are powers we must not evoke by defying them entirely."

"And yet I do defy them," answered he, deliberately. "As long as God continues to me the full possession of the faculties he has given me, I intend to use them in spite of all bells and ghosts and goblins, or other creatures of superstition.

They waited some minutes, and as no further sound was heard, they went back again into the house. Supper had just been announced, and a very agreeable change was noticeable in the ceasing of those intolerable fiddles.

The supper-room presented a great improvement over the scene in the dancing-hall. Here, at last, the old splendor of the family shone again. It was not the dining-room, but the large, empty picture gallery, in which the banquet was served. The plate, the glasses, the table ornaments, were magnificent, and the name of Delmonico was stamped more legibly than letters could have written it, on the dishes themselves, and in the style of the numerous waiters, by the perfection of every item, and the correctness of the *tout ensemble.*

The guests, although numerous for a country ball, could each find a seat at this princely table, where the Emperor Napoleon Bonaparte presided at one head of it, and the tailor's daughter at the other. Our hero found himself seated between Josephine Van Strom and Jessie Going. These young ladies had known each other for some time, and conversed freely across his plate, which situation he enjoyed immensely, drawing elaborate parallels between them in the privacy of his own thoughts. The influence of Miss Jessie's sweet presence was over him, and could he, then and there, have had the privilege of choosing his life's partner,

he would have discarded the heart full of passionate love and unqualified devotion, and taken the one not yet proven by the fiery test of life's great struggles, not yet in condition for one to confidently say of it, that it was good, noble, and faithful.

The wine began to circulate freely, and as it disappeared, glass by glass, and bottle by bottle, it came again to view in the suddenly flushed faces and sparkling eyes. To some of the guests, the decanters and dishes, the pyramids of confectionery, and bouquets of flowers, began to lose their distinctive shades, and stagger around the table as if they, and not the gentlemen, were intoxicated. Laughter grew louder and more unmeaning. Conversation became a medley in which each speaker listened only to himself, and the noise and confusion grew louder and higher. There was many a wanton leer in that array of faces, and eyes were glowing in the misty heat of wine. The manner of well-drilled waiters is a fair criterion by which to estimate the condition of the guests. As the latter become noisy and clamorous for a score of things which are not touched when received, they become more mechanical, more respectful, more decorous, and more thoroughly blind to the follies of their superiors.

The revelry increased. There were many country gentlemen present, who had inherited the hard heads of their Dutch ancestors with their appetites, and who did not object to deep potations on an occasion like this, and their willing competitors were some fast young men from New York. You fast young men of New York! It is you, of high-bred families and low-bred tastes, it is you that a City Recorder alluded to, when he said from his bench of justice: "There is a class of young men in this city who vie with each other in setting at defiance alike the laws of God and man."

The atmosphere of the room was growing thick, and the lights turned red and assumed the shapes of drunken goblins imprisoned in the glass-chimneys of the lamps, where before were seen only the patient tongues of flame. The genial Goddess of Plenty exhausted, gave place to the Demon of Debauch, incarnate in the person of Mr. Paradise, who now rose to make an address. It was witty, vile, and reckless, in all its bearing upon subjects of refinement, and it was the signal for the revelry to degenerate into a bacchanalian orgy.

John Van Strom's seat was next his wife. So far he had behaved well, although all Bella's efforts and entreaties to restrain him from drinking to excess had been of no avail. He was all smiles and tenderness for her; but nothing would keep him from excess. Following Josephine, who thought it high time for the ladies to retire, they all arose, but John kept his wife at his side. She looked at him. All his good-humor was gone.

"You stay where you are," he muttered, gruffly.

That gaze told her the truth. His eyes were bloodshot. The expression of his face unspeakably drunken, and, more than this; for, when Bella humbly took her seat again, at his command, she knew that her husband was a raving maniac, ready to show it at any moment.

Many gentlemen, among whom were Mr.
Going and our hero, followed the ladies, who
either loitered about the hall or sent for their
shawls and strolled about the grounds and
gardens on the side of the house opposite the
fatal bell.

"Whither are you bound, Mr. Montant?"
asked Miss Jessie Going, as she passed our
hero on his way to join Josephine Van Strom.

"I am going to join—" Miss Jessie guessed
the state of the case, and interposed artlessly:
"I have something to tell you. Will you
wait here, while I go up-stairs and get my
shawl?"

He hesitated. There was a queer enticing
smile on her face.

"Certainly," he said, and Miss Going swept
proudly up-stairs as if she had done something
great, and fully conscious of having " cut out "
the widow. The latter, being near enough to
hear the dialogue, showed her appreciation of
the incident by turning her back very decisively, while he bit his lips and felt vexed with
her, Miss Going, and himself.

In a few moments the young lady tripped
up to him, enveloped in a shawl, and took his
arm without ceremony.

"What can you have to say to *me*, Mademoiselle?" asked Montant, when they had stepped
out upon the piazza and were marching up and
down sedately.

"The weather has changed. What has become of the moon, I wonder?" said the young
lady.

"Is that all? What an interesting remark
that is, Miss Going!"

"I did wish to see you about something,"
said she, with a certain levity of tone which
displeased him, "but I have really forgotten
what it was about."

"Do you know," he said, gravely, "that you
are too much inclined to tread the path of life
lightly? After your good sense prompts you
to think and act with that sincerity and firmness of which you are capable, you are liable,
the very next moment, to destroy what you
have so well begun."

"Have I shown myself in that light to
you?"

"Yes."

"And may I ask when and in what way?"

Our hero seemed puzzled. He did not wish
to upbraid her for ignoring him and devoting
herself to Messrs. Faro and Willie Wheeler,
at that dinner in Fifth Avenue, immediately
after having appealed so strongly to him to be
her friend forever, and exacted, almost forcibly,
a very serious promise from him. He did not
wish to let her know that he thought her inconsiderate as well as too light-hearted, and
he said, impatiently,—

"With your permission we will change the
subject."

Jessie Going probably knew well enough
to what her companion had referred, in his
thoughts, and there ensued a somewhat embarrassing pause.

"What do you think of Mrs. Van Strom,"
she asked, after awhile.

"I think she is a splendid, noble-hearted
woman, who has not merited her sad trials.

I think she is one of the few who ask from the
world, nothing but love and sympathy, and
who would rather die for a friend than injure
him."

Miss Jessie bit her lips. She was beginning
to understand that this foreigner did not intend
to be a plaything for a girl's whims, and though
conscious of her power over him, as all women
are to some extent, she was a little bit afraid
of him. That speech about Josephine contained a rebuke which he did not care to conceal, and it stung her to the quick.

"Perhaps you would prefer to join the lady
who seems so to excite your enthusiasm," she
said, languidly.

"As you wish, mademoiselle," he replied,
coldly. "I am at your service during your
good pleasure."

"Then let us go in, for the night is too damp
to be pleasant."

These were the last words they exchanged
that evening, and, as he left her to the society
of Mr. Fatman, in the hall, and she turned her
back upon him as if he had been a perfect
stranger, a great bitterness surged up and
filled his heart.

CHAPTER IX.

WHAT THE OLD BELL MEANT BY RINGING.

"Hear it not, Duncan, for it is a knell
      Which summons thee to heaven or to hell.'
                                MACBETH.

IT took but a minute for our hero to find and
join Mrs. Van Strom, and soon they were
walking in the grounds, and strolling through
the flower-garden, with its graveled walks and
artistic box-hedges.

She took his arm, and, after a few minutes
conversation, every trace of jealousy left her.
It is true that she had angrily turned her back
upon him, when a simple word from Miss
Going had proven sufficient to keep him from
her side, and what woman would not have done
so? But when, after a very short walk with
her, he returned, and as she now held possession of him, and he addressed her as warmly
and devotedly as ever, she forgot all but her
great love for him, and what woman would
have done otherwise?

Miss Going's remark on the weather, was
none the less true for its want of originality.
The heavens had darkened and the feeling of
rain was in the air. It was a warm night, and
though the moon had veiled her face, there
were millions of glow worms astir in the
shrubbery, swarming to and fro in sparkling
affection, finding each other by the light of
love. The air resounded with the lively, never-
tiring chorus of katy-dids, and out-doors
seemed the workshop of legions of dwarfish
spirits, each busy in his peculiar way, glittering, chirping, working with indefatigable
energy, concocting magical wonders in Nature.
There! a streak of lightning. Another!
The insects fly about in excitement, the katy-
dids join afresh in a grand allegro, as if the
master were approaching and the little people
were hurried in their work.

The music in the hall ceased, the fiddles lay on the little platform unmolested, for the darkeys were walking into the good things that had been undemolished by the guests. Occasionally a peal of laughter, a boisterous speech-maker's voice, a round of cheers. or a confusion of wanton sound, broke upon the ears of the two strollers, disturbing their serene enjoyment of the most enchanting of nights, alive with all the creatures of a midsummer night's dream.

"What a wondrous, magic scene," said Josephine. "How distorted, almost unrecognizable, these familiar objects around us appear."

"Something is in the wind," said he, absently.

"Yes; and who knows what the next hour may bring to any of us? This grand house may be struck by lightning, and a circle of corpses confront each other in ghastly silence around the table, where they are now challenging the justice of Heaven by their reckless debauch. And, should the storm burst forth, they would still remain there in drunken defiance of its dread powers."

"This is a strange but pertinent fancy of yours, Mrs. Van Strom," he answered, gloomily. "Were their eyes opened, this moment, they would recognize grim death beneath each others' masks of joviality, and with horror they would see that the skeleton is growing in size and strength with every glass they empty."

"Why do men drink?" asked Josephine, sadly. "My experience of its effects on the best and most generous of natures is so sorrowful that I hate the very sight of wine."

"Naturally. But your question applies equally to all the sins committed here below, which are permitted that the righteous may be separated from the vicious in the sight of God and man. These sins are generally an outgrowth of refinement and luxury. *Excess* is the name for them, and *moderation* is the great virtue. I do not believe in total abstinence."

"Why are not all men like you?" said Josephine, warmly.

"Because," said he, smiling, "they have not all been thrown upon their resources early enough, or under such circumstances as to force them to cultivate habitual caution, self-restraint, and firmness of will. Early indulgence breaks their strength of mind, and when the time comes that they need to rely upon it, it shows itself rotten at the core."

"Could you—would you *love* beyond self-control, without reservation, *unconditionally*, and *immoderately ?* "

It was a queer question, and her tone and manner on asking it were queerer. Hesitatingly, timidly, but breathlessly waiting for his answer.

"I do not know. As far as my experience goes—no."

"Look at the fire-flies," said Josephine, dreamily. "Ordinary affections resemble their tiny flickering lights. They illuminate for an instant the dark corners of the foliage around us, fly from spot to spot, staying in none, lighting up the different places they are in for the time, but leave the *entire* scene in darkness. So

with the recesses of the human heart, until the great light comes like a flash; yes, like that flash of lightning which has just darted its livid flame around, illuminating the *whole scene*, the *whole* heart."

"And sometimes, too, brings death."

"Yes. And when it does, God pity the sufferers."

"And you ask me whether *I* could love as you say ?"

"Yes," murmured Josephine. "Tell me whether you can so love. Here in the sight of nature, in its mysterious workings; here in the sight of all its majesty, in the presence of the spirit that governs this hour, tell me if you can."

There was a solemn appeal in these words, not in accordance with her naturally enthusiastic, but timid character. Our hero felt it, and all at once the scales fell from his eyes. Like a shock, the knowledge, the conviction, came to him, and almost overpowered him. Yes, he now knew that she loved him, he felt it in the throbbing of her heart as she clung closely to his arm, he felt it in the trembling of her arm which clung to him as if for life, he heard it in that passionate voice, and he saw it even through the darkness in the wonderful glow of her languishing eyes. With a great effort he gathered his best, his strongest, his purest impulses, and the integrity of his character was prominent in his reply.

"I think I *can* so love. But I do not think it will come to me as a flash; but rather like the dawn of day which is heralded by a faint and struggling ray, to grow by nature's almighty laws, slowly but surely, into the bright and overwhelming beauty of the noonday. That light, Mrs. Van Strom, will not suddenly vanish into the darkness whence it sprang, like your lightning, but it will remain, grand and omnipotent, till the close of life's day, when the night cometh, and we can bid it farewell contentedly."

"Let it come as it may," cried Josephine, passionately; " but when it has come," and she pulled her arm from him and pressed both hands on her tempestuous heart, "there is no power in heaven or earth that can control it."

In a state of agitation heretofore totally unknown to him, he took a step toward her. The lightning's brilliant glare showed her to him, as she stood with her hands on her breast and her face upturned to him—the face of Raphael's Madonna. Reader, if you desire a superhuman hero, close the book here. *Our* hero was human, and, at this moment, all strength of will, all thought of consequences, all scruples, and all presence of mind vanished. His arm was around her; the soft, full, trembling form, as perfect as was ever given to woman, sank into his embrace and she sought, instead of resisting, the passionate kiss which affianced them.

Upon a friendly garden bench, they sat in tender embrace, lost in the intoxication of love. The fire-flies peeped at them, and flew back to their mates in the bushes to tell them what they saw. The katy-dids struck up the old love song. telling the world what the world knows very well; yet is anxious to learn again, a million times, how "Katy *did*" and "Katy *didn't.*" A warmer and more passionate spirit seemed to rule the summer night with loving sway, as though great "Nature rejoiced in the bliss of two of her noblest children."

Called back to a sense of fleeting time, they sauntered back to the house, she lost in him and delirious with happiness; he proud, and joyously excited, and already making plans for the future, and trying to foresee the possible ends of this night work.

They found the piazza deserted, and took the opportunity for a long, parting kiss, and as he held her tightly to his breast, feeling every pulsation of her heart vibrating through his frame, she whispered softly,—

"Ernest, darling, tell me, once more before we part, do you love me with *all* your heart?"

The words seemed to stick in his throat, but he would not hesitate, could not be so cruel as to say "*no*" to her at this moment were it the greatest lie of his life.

"I love you, indeed I love you!" And though at a later day, when, in cold blood he reviews that speech, conscience might tell him he had lied to her, yet when he spoke the words, and received his reward, he thought he had spoken the truth.

When they entered the hall, the scene they beheld startled them considerably. Many had gone home, the ladies that were left, wrapped in their shawls and cloaks were huddled in a corner. Most of the gentlemen, with their hats in their hands, kept close by them as if for their protection, and in the center of the room John Van Strom was dancing a sort of *pas de deux* with his wife. She kept a steady, unflinching gaze upon him, dancing as little as possible, moving closely to him like a snake-charmer, for at this moment John was a manaic on the verge of raving violence.

Mr Paradise, the hunchback, was applauding with a shrill voice, and looked like an insane fiend, striving with Bella for the mastery over this weak intellect, while some intoxicated fools were laughing and dancing about the group, and the Cimmerian Quaternion were fiddling away with accompanying contortions. "'Twas a scene from a madhouse."

"Dance, gentlemen," roared John, his voice rising above the tumult. "Why the devil don't you dance. *Who won't dance?*"

With a shriek and a rush John was left in the center of a wide open space, were his grinning admirers had just stood, his clothes torn, his hair disheveled, his face distorted, and his eyes on fire, brandishing the naked broadsword once worthily wielded by his grandsire, and bellowing like a wild beast.

"Who won't dance? Show me the fellow. I'll have his blood! I'll have his blood any way!"

And there stood his wife, the color all gone from her face, within reach of his weapon. The drunken musicians played faster and faster their fiddles squeaking, tittering, and shrieking as though hell had set loose a band of howling devils.

"Stop those crazy fools," some one at length cried, and when it was done a dead silence prevailed, broken only by the heavy breathing

of the maniac as he stood rolling his eyes around the room, trying to choose a victim.

Bella approached him fearlessly.

"For God's sake, don't;" said some, trying to keep her back.

"If any one has to die by those hands it must be I," was the answer. Then she said, firmly.

"John, give me that sword!"

But it was too late. The wine had intensified him to a paroxysm of fury which defied restraint. A cry was heard as the sword flashed through the air, and the bleeding form of the faithful wife sank to the floor.

Though wounded, she clung to him tightly, and he, maddened still more by the sight of blood, was raging and tearing himself from her grasp, when a little man coolly stepped up behind him, and catching one of his feet, quickly upset him on the floor. It was our acquaintance, Antonio Stilletto, and now, yes, *now*, the gentlemen rushed to his assistance, and John was secured.

Then came the senseless chatter of "what a dreadful thing;" "perfectly shocking;" "he ought to be kept in an asylum;" "poor thing," she's dead;" "what a pity;" "what a shame that he should be at large," &c., &c., *ad nauseam;* but what was that crowd in the corner? Was there to be another horror to mark this eventful night? Was it a visitation on the family, some curse, the fulfillment of some dark prophecy, an atonement for some hidden crime? What was it they were carrying out so carefully, from the place where it had fallen, unperceived in the great excitement. It was dressed in the costume of the great emperor, but the wig had slipped off. It was the body of old John Jacob Van Strom, killed by a stroke of apoplexy.

It had grown late when those guests left the Priory, and they were in a far different mood than when they had come. When the last of the carriages rolled away, a gentle rain was falling as though Heaven would wash away the traces of that night's doings. As the merciful drops rustle through the weeping willows and through the park, the wind sighs in the trees, shaking their heads over the hurrying coaches; there is many a man on whom the voice of Heaven, which called so suddenly upon Van Strom, has not been lost, and many a disconcerted face, many a compressed lip, tells of an uneasy conscience and a heavy heart.

And when the last sound of the departing wheels has died away, the moon breaks through the clouds and looks down upon the house of death, with the willows weeping in front of it, and the old bell tolling a funeral chime. The house lies dark and cold as though hung in crape for the death of its master, and the fire-flies shine no more, and the katy-dids are mute. And the moon looked within the house and peeped curiously around the chamber where but lately license held high carnival. The rats were undisturbed in their disputings over the remnants of the feast, and the instruments of music were lying, still and dumb, on the little platform. And in another room she saw the form of a shattered man, with the blessing of oblivion on his distracted brain, and the bonds of sleep on his boiling veins. The old butler, sitting at his bedside, thinks of the great changes he has seen in the family, and of his dead master, and weeps bitterly.

And peeping through another window she sees the wife of low degree pacing the room. Her wound is not severe, but its pain and the excitement of the evening have kept her from her bed. She is planning out the future bravely, and only sobs when the present distress comes to her mind overwhelmingly.

And below stairs there lies the old man's body, stark and stiff, for him the patient moon hides her face, and the pitying clouds drop tears again.

Josephine has done her part nobly. She wept at first, wept on the breast of the man who will give strength and comfort for her in all her future trials, and then rose and took the head of the household, helping here, directing there, and working wherever work was to be done.

Now she sleeps, and, smiling in her sleep, dreams but the one sweet dream, while her lover watches the body of John Jacob Van Strom, till broad day.

And at last the moon sends a parting glance at the desolate house and sinks to rest. The old bell rings no more, though the morning breezes are coming merrily along. They can not awaken the ghost, the bell finds no life in their fresh breaths, for they herald a dawning day which will bring a change over the Priory.

BOOK II.—FACT.

CHAPTER I.

MARTIN BATES.

"Some sins do bear their privilege on earth."
KING JOHN.

"YES, young man, thirty years in this office! No wonder that every one knows old Martin Bates; but a great wonder that so few people speak ill of him. Long in the service, sir, and prepared to die in it."

And had he not one foot already on the verge of the grave? Several bunches of white hair hung around his well-nigh bald head, and as he sat perched upon his high stool, there was a cadaverous look about him. His high cheek bones protruded in sharp angles, each overlooked by a very light-colored, unexpressive eye. Martin's single fault was chewing tobacco, and he had a very peculiar way of rolling his quid into his *right* cheek whenever he entered a "credit" item in his books, then, with a frightful grimace, rolling it back again to the *left* side when he wrote a "debit." If Mr. Going wished to know whether money was coming in or going out of the house, he had only to look at his head cashier, old Martin Bates, and observe the protuberance on the cheek of that gentleman's square face.

"Thirty years with Going & Son! An errand boy under Walter's grandfather and slowly rising to be the head of the outer office. Do I expect to become a partner? No, sir! Martin Bates was born to ill-luck, and Fortune has kicked him and snarled at him all his life."

The old cashier had taken a great fancy to our hero, and often, after the members of the firm had gone home, he would talk to Ernest Montant, who liked him for his good-natured but melancholy originality.

"You have often promised to tell me of your past life, Mr. Bates," said our hero.

"And so I will, my lad," answered the old man, staring vacantly into the air from his high stool, where he was perched, as usual, in a confusion of angles. "Wait till we find an unoccupied evening, a quiet room, some *good* beef, and a respectable jug of ale. My wants have been modified to a charming simplicity in the course of my life."

"And yet you can not deny that you are still extravagant in some matters," answered Montant, eagerly—"the poor call you *princely* in your charities, and I heard an old woman say you were the best and kindest man that ever lived."

"No more on this subject," said Martin Bates, hurriedly, and blushing all over his sallow face. "It belongs to the Lord of Heaven, alone, with all its pro's and con's."

Our hero looked up in astonishment at his unnecessary vehemence, and equivocal language. He could not imagine what the old fellow meant, so like a wise man, he held his tongue. Through the open window the tedious strains of a hand-organ broke jarringly on their ears. Martin Bates looked up, his face flushed again; this time with expectation. The door opened and in came one of those Italian girls who are a distinct, and not over-respectable part of the city's manifold population. She was pretty, might have reached the age of seventeen and her neatness and evident modesty presented an agreeable contrast to the rest of her class.

Ernest Montant had seen her on many previous occasions, and withdrew, as usual, leaving her alone with old Martin Bates, who was her friend and protector. It did not astonish any one that they conversed in a whisper nor that Martin came to the cash drawer, and got a twenty dollar bill, which he gave to the girl. This had happened before, and, just as before, nobody knew what to make of it.

Weeks rolled on, and Mr. Going had the old Priory put in complete repair, and then the whole family moved out there to spend the summer in their newly-acquired property. The house in Fifth Avenue was closed and became a subject of speculation for the burglars of the city. Weeks rolled on, the business did not prosper as it should, heavy losses had to be met and old Martin Bates chewed his tobacco on the credit side of his face, with a determined air, and an occasional scowl. The Italian girl continued her visits and received so many twenty-dollar bills that Montant wondered at the amount of the cashier's salary which could warrant such liberality. But then Martin Bates was the managing clerk, and with his modest personal wants, he could afford it without a doubt. His preference for our hero increased, and the latter asked himself with wonder how it was that the best, the kindest people so courted his friendship. It is true that he had enemies. Stilletto did not like him, Solomons, the Jew broker, never spoke to him as he did to the rest of the clerks, and Mr. Fatman ignored him in a marked manner, when they happened to encounter each other; but these men and others, belonged to those who had themselves impressed him with dislike, and he could easily imagine that something in his own manner, incapable of hypocrisy as he was, had prevented any approach to cordiality. And, again, Miss Jessie Going had not treated him quite satisfactorily—but had he not the *love* of Josephine Van Strom?

Weeks rolled on, and one evening we find Martin Bates and Ernest Montant at the club of the former. Not a fashionable club. Oh, no! The roast beef was excellent, the ale capital and a good old English cheer prevailed through this retreat for cricketers and English clerks, who here could almost fancy themselves away from New York and once more within the sound of Bow-bells.

"English filberts, my boy!" said Martin, "and some very respectable port. Take plenty of the nuts, they make your plate look cheerful. But what are you doing? Why, man, you must scrape them carefully with that silver knife until they are as smooth and white as innocence itself. There is a soul in a filbert, a true British soul, if you only know how to find it under the rough rind."

"Then I should call some Englishmen *filberts*," said Ernest, smiling, carefully peeling one of the nuts.

"True enough!" said Martin Bates, "Although I would rather undertake to peel a filbert than some of my countrymen. Perhaps even that beast called the *world* has a *heart* under its snarling exterior; but heaven knows I have never found it out. And now let us have another bottle of port and I will tell you a few brief incidents of my life which I have never mentioned, although I have often wanted to tell them to some one."

The waiter was a German, who tried to pass himself off as an Englishman by duly dropping his *h*'s, adding them where they did not belong, and interspersing his few words with "sir," with a liberality which outshone all the waiters of Pickwick. Having dismissed this worthy

Anglo-Saxon, Martin Bates related the following story:—

"I am the younger son of an English gentleman, who lived upon a more ancient than valuable estate, not many hours from London. My elder brother, Ebenezer Bates, the heir of my father's little fortune, the pet of the house, the pride of the family, became a lawyer, saying that wealth could not warrant his idleness. He is a proud, cold man, a strict Protestant, a pillar of the church, bearing a spotless character and standing high in the community."

Martin Bates spoke the last words with scarce concealed bitterness. He paused a moment to compose his feelings and then proceeded,—

"I grew up, an impetuous boy, ready at any moment for a game of cricket, for a footrace, a frolic, or a fight, and my father reluctantly acceded to my importunity and purchased me a commission in the British army. The world smiled on Martin Bates then, my debts were paid by my brother who raised the funds for me without my father's knowledge. I thanked him, and yet I could not love him for it."

"Why?"

"Because he accompanied each gift with a scowl and a sermon. He had no consideration, no sympathy for me, and I saw, only too plainly, that it was just his selfish pride which prompted him to save the family name from disgrace, not brotherly love."

"Mr. Bates," said Ernest, "did you never meet men who, considering themselves much injured by the harsh opinions of the world, nevertheless judged others as harshly? After all, your brother seems to have acted toward you in a manner which would ordinarily call for—"

"Let me finish," interrupted the other. "Heaven knows, he owes all his grand position and good name to those kind acts. I only gave him credit for them. I never balanced any gratitude by such reflections as have forced themselves upon me at a much later period, and, when the time came, I sacrificed myself to save him."

"Now listen. My brother Eben and I, resembled each other to such a degree, that casual acquaintances were apt to mistake our identity. My face is haggard now, while he is still a handsome man; but you must remember that I have sat on an office-stool like a parrot in his cage for the past thirty years, condemned to be a senseless debit and credit machine, while smiling fortune took *him* to her soft bosom and nursed him to a handsome, and vigorous old age. Thirty years ago he was rising barrister of Lincoln's Inn Fields, and I exerted my influence among my fellow-officers to bring clients to him."

"Among others, I succeeded with my colonel, who soon placed the utmost confidence in him, and at whose house he shortly became a welcome and frequent guest. The colonel was so pleased with him, whom he called, 'a man of rare dignity and integrity of character,' that some of his favor even reached me; and though only a lieutenant, without a family title, I also was well received at his house. Now comes the case which shall decide who is the better man. Eben, who has preserved his 'rare dignity and integrity' to this day, in the eyes of the world, or poor old Martin, disgraced, discarded, and condemned to the pillory of an office-stool, for such would I have regarded it thirty years ago when I was a gentleman, and an officer."

Martin Bates paused, and wiped away the perspiration from his square forehead. He had already imbibed freely, and now poured down several glasses of port-wine, like a man who feels suddenly weak and needs a stimulus.

"The colonel's wife, Lady ——, belonged to one of those proud families in England that are descended from some king's left-handed marriage, and feel highly honored by such a record. She was a handsome woman, though already past that bloom of life which ever alone could attract me. I rather admired her for her refinement and dignity; but not a word even of intimacy ever passed between us.

"Imagine my surprise, when, one morning I was placed under arrest, then in close confinement, and finally summoned before a court-martial! I was conscious of neither crime nor misdemeanor; but what was my utter consternation when I read the charges preferred against me! I was accused of conduct unbecoming an officer and a gentleman, in that I had grossly and criminally insulted Lady ——, my colonel's wife. The specifications of the charges related that I was discovered one evening in the garden where my lady had been walking, with my arms around her and attempting to kiss lips sacred to the colonel. Her husband arrived on the scene—at his approach I had fled—and she, breathless with agitation, stated that she had been assaulted by an unknown person, and confirmed the statement by going into hysterics. But the colonel had recognized me, not only by my uniform, but by my *face!* Recognized me with sufficient certainty to be able to swear to my identity.

"At first, I was bewildered, almost to insanity—but finally, my boy—finally the truth struck me like a thunderbolt! Yes, the colonel had recognized the face, though in the twilight. He had recognized my uniform, and *I* knew that *my brother had borrowed one of mine some months previously* for private theatricals, *and had never returned it.* All was now clear. My lady had made a desperate effort at a moment when all seemed lost, and had told a lie to gain time. I saw that this lie would prove successful. At my court-martial she would not be summoned as a witness, and had I accused my brother, all he had to do was to treat the charge with indignant silence, and fall back on his 'rare dignity and integrity of character.' My lady had only to perjure herself and who could doubt that the charge would return to *me* with crushing weight."

"Perjure herself!" cried our hero. "Would she have dared to do that? Could she have unflinchingly faced a cross-examination?"

"Cross-examination!" exclaimed Martin Bates, with a sneer. "How extremely verdant you must be! Don't you remember she was *Lady* ——? Do you suppose that in England ladyships are bantered on a witness-stand like kitchen-maids? And as to her willingness to perjure herself, what else could she have done? Here was her own and her husband's name in the scale against a junior officer's honor; could there be a question that the occasion *demanded* a lie? I may be mistaken, but I felt myself lost, and accepted my doom with as good a grace as possible."

"And your brother?"

"He visited me once. I can see him now, as he stood in my cell. His handsome face, austere and grandly dignified as ever, until the turnkey had left us alone. Then he wept, and begged my pardon—d—n him!"

There was a hardness in his voice that did not please his listener.

"If he repented, and felt for you—"

"Repented and felt for me!" cried Martin Bates, furiously. "He was dismayed at the dishonor which I was sure to bring upon his name; he was trembling with the weight of his guilty conscience, afraid lest I should attempt to show the truth to the world; he was bent upon securing my self-sacrifice by his damnable show of remorse and sympathy. He confessed the intrigue, swore that that meeting in the garden was to be their last; that he was engaged to be married to a sweet girl, whose heart would break if he were discovered, and finally—the villain—implored my forgiveness; and yet I know that had I accused him before the bar, he would have sworn, with two fingers uplifted to God, that he was not guilty."

Montant shook his head, doubtfully. Martin Bates took no notice of the gesture; but continued:—

"I spurned him, telling him that he could not deceive me by his hypocrisy; but I assured him that he might feel safe, that I would quietly submit to my fate. I was court-martialed, dishonorably dismissed the service, and *drummed out of my regiment.*" It was a neat ceremony, by God!"

His passion almost choked him.

"I was a ruined man," he continued, hoarsely. "My friends cut me; no lady would speak to me; but every one pitied my poor brother! Aye, how kind in him to visit his disgraced brother in prison, and finally to give him money to go and hide his disgrace in America. And how natural that the sweet girl to whom he was engaged, did not break off the match on *my* account; but married the kind, the noble-hearted man, with such rare dignity and integrity of character, without heeding what was not his fault—oh, no, not *his* fault, but only his misfortune—which he regretted sorely, but bore with that equanimity and calmness for which he was so duly praised.

"And when we parted, how edifying was his stately, studied kindness, his condescending sympathy, not unmixed with forbearing reproach. How different all this from the craven submissiveness with which he threw himself at my feet in the cell, weeping and groaning as a miserable sinner should do,—only

It was all put on to impose on my soft heart. So I came here a pauper, and old Mr. Going's father took me in his office, and here I am, after thirty years of debit and credit, with the world still snarling at me, as it has done ever since those events happened."

"What, have you not seen your brother these many years?"

Martin Bates never heard or ignored this question, and continued, "He is also in this country. Despite all Lady ———'s finesse, some queer rumors got afloat in London. Heaven knows whether the colonel did not suspect his wife, and cross-question her. Might it not be that my misfortune was the result of a full confession on her part, and a preconcerted plan among themselves to save their spotless names? At all events, they say that when the colonel surprised his wife in the garden, that eventful night, a scene ensued, the noise of which attracted the servants. And yet, I doubt that he prosecuted me under false pretenses. A colonel in the British army, and perjury! No; *that is impossible!*"

"For what reason do you suppose your brother wore your uniform?" said our hero.

"I hardly ever gave it a thought. I do not think that he could have foreseen the consequences; so I suppose that he chose to wear the uniform merely because it fitted him well, and displayed his figure to advantage."

"Is this brother of yours," said Montant, hastily, as if suddenly impressed with a coincidence of names; "that is, are you any relation to Judge Bates, of Massachusetts?"

"Judge Bates is my brother Eben," replied old Martin, drily.

If he had not been absorbed in his own thoughts, Martin Bates could not have failed to notice that this information affected his companion very strongly. Our hero's face flushed —he bit his lips, and endeavored to regain his composure. In a few moments he was able to remark, in an apparently unconcerned manner—

"I understand that he holds a high position in his profession, and is much respected by the community."

"He is a man of rare dignity and integrity of character," quoth Martin Bates, with a sardonic laugh.

"And he has a beautiful daughter," added our hero, almost below his breath.

. "You know him?" asked the old cashier, casting a quick, searching look upon his interlocutor.

"I saw him and his daughter when Mr. Walter Going and I were last in Boston," answered our hero, quickly.

"Did I not understand that he knows my niece pretty well?" asked Martin Bates, slily.

"I don't know the extent of their acquaintance," answered Ernest, composedly. "But to resume our subject," he added, with animation, "I feel at liberty to tell you that you are not quite so kind-hearted in your judgment of your brother, as in many other matters that have come to my knowledge. You are called the most charitable of men. Does this charity only concern your purse? Does it leave your heart, whence it should arise, cold and uncon-

cerned? Have you not sufficient justice to concede that your brother had to consider the reputation of a noble lady, and the happiness of his betrothed; and that he sacrificed your honor only with a bleeding heart? Are you certain that your own behavior did not alienate him from you? Can you deny that after all he did what he could to make up the great wrong which you suffered—not so much at his hands as from cruel destiny? Your own statements exculpate him in a great measure."

"Do you expect me to kiss the rod, like a woman?" asked Martin Bates, with a dark look.

"No; but I am certain that if you approached your brother to-day; if you would seek him in an hour of adversity, you would find a shelter under his roof, and a home in his household."

"Like a stray dog, that would find a kennel in some dirty corner of his barn; and that only because Eben Bates must keep up his character for charity."

"Is it a worthy practice to attribute a man's acts of kindness to motives of pure selfishness?"

"No; unless you know your man as I know mine. But no more of this. I want to make you my confidant, for I am sure you are not one of the world that snarls at old Martin Bates. Besides, I want your aid in a personal matter, provided you feel disposed to aid me."

Ernest was not at all anxious to possess his secrets; but being willing to befriend this old man, left by all, gave him an encouraging nod, as one that would say,—

"Proceed at your pleasure; but at your pleasure only."

"Know then," said the ex-lieutenant, "know then—that Martin Bates, the old fool, is in love!"

The other did not attempt to suppress a smile.

"Smile away, young man, for well you may. Here I am, with gray hair and the experience of half a century to cool my blood and teach me wisdom;—here I am confessing this idiocy to a man not much over twenty, although I am well convinced that *you* would not have sunk so low in the rank of fools as I am. No wonder that I doubt all the world when I have to despise myself."

Did the old cashier *despise* himself only for weakness toward the fair sex? He had used the term in a manner which did not exclusively refer to that particular point of self-accusation.

"You have seen the Italian girl who comes into our office, and receives money from me? She— "

"What? I hope— "

"Hope or no hope," he interrupted. "Her I love, and her I intend to marry."

Our hero was speechless. He simply stared at the old man.

"She is a gentle, good creature, and I want her to comfort me in my last days. I have a little property—a little property," he repeated, as though mentally reckoning the net proceeds, "which I shall make over to her immediately, and then we shall go to Italy. There I will end my days, solaced and attended by her."

"Leave our house?" cried Ernest.

"Yes," said the other, quietly, "and you will have the best chance for my vacant stool. Will you promise not to tell Mr. Going of this until I go? And will you assist me a little in completing my arrangements?"

"Providing I can do so without breaking my allegiance to my employers, yes."

"Of course, with that proviso, certainly," said the old man, intrenching himself behind a thick cloud of smoke.

"Though, naturally, there is no doubt but that my duty to my principals would not interfere with any thing that *you* could desire of me."

"Naturally, no doubt," corroborated Martin Bates, looking up at the ceiling. "And what is more, I will teach you so much of my present duties as will make it convenient for Mr. Going to dispense with my services at any moment. This will almost insure your succeeding me, for no one else will be capable of stepping into my place after I have quietly prepared you for it."

"I don't like that," answered Montant, uneasily. "It will look as if I had been intriguing and planning selfishly for my advancement."

"Not at all," answered the cashier, impatiently. "You are not so slow a man as to hesitate at trifles like this when your success in life is in your own hands."

"But it goes against my grain, and with all thanks to you, I shall not attempt to force Mr. Going into appointing me to a place of extraordinary trust and responsibility."

"Well, then, he must do the best he can after I have gone. I merely tried to save him any inconvenience, when I shall have left him suddenly."

"Why not give him notice now?" said our hero, puzzled and annoyed.

"Because I do not wish to be cross-questioned and pressed to stay, or have this folly of my marriage discovered, and so be turned into the laughing-stock of the office, and perhaps half the town."

"Is the girl willing?"

"Yes; but she is surrounded by a vagabond set of friends or relatives, or perhaps lovers. Among them all I expect to have a hard time of it. Yet, if she does not change her mind, I intend to run off with her in spite of them all, and that is another vital reason for keeping the matter quiet. You know that these Italians are a spying, treacherous set. Already they suspect me of worse intentions than I deserve, and should they hear, as well they might, that I had given Mr. Going notice, they might place her out of my reach."

"And what do you want me to do for you?"

"Have a carriage ready for me to-morrow night, at twelve o'clock, in Chatham Square. I mean to ask them honorably for her hand; but if they refuse to let her go, she will steal out of the house and join me. After I find you, I would like you to see me off at the station, take a letter from me to Mr. Going, and execute a few trifling commissions for me after I have gone."

The old man's plan was so immediate and imperative that his hearer was rather bewildered. Something urged him to accept the service asked of him. His own ways had always been, as he meant they always should be, open and straightforward, and this queer, almost insane freak of the trusted cashier alarmed him. He scanned the old man's face closely. Martin's eyes were unsteady; he had laid down his cigar and was chewing tobacco, rolling his quid from side to side, never leaving it on either the Credit or Debit side, and our hero thought to himself, is money coming into the house, *or is money going out of it?* Although Martin Bates, thirty years in the service, and considered the most honest of old souls, could not be really suspected of embezzling money, yet he thought that question worthy of after-consideration, and not to be dogmatically dismissed.

"This love of yours seems half ridiculous, half fabulous, Mr. Bates," he said, hiding his uneasiness under a smile; "but as long as it exists, I do not wonder at the queer manner in which you mean to carry out your plans for happiness. I will be there to-morrow, with the carriage. Midnight—to-morrow—say at the southeast corner, where Chatham Street runs into Chatham Square."

"Thank you. And you will swear upon the Bible that you will not breathe a word of this to Mr. Going or any one else. Swear that here, and now, if you please."

There was something over-anxious in his tone, as if it had suddenly occurred to him that he should have sworn in his confidant before he intrusted him with so many secrets.

The other thought a moment, and then said:—

"Mr. Bates I am a queer fellow I can only promise this with a reservation, which amounts to this. I will give you my word as a gentleman to keep this matter secret unless my duty to Mr. Going demands otherwise. This clause is so harmless that I hope it will pass as a mere eccentricity, for I can solemnly assure you that I have no doubt that what you are doing is merely something *very* odd. And nothing can be imagined likely to happen between this and to-morrow that would absolve me from my promise."

"Of course not," said Martin Bates.

"Then with that proviso, I here give you my hand and my word as a gentleman."

"Done," said Martin Bates, and they shook hands.

"And now, as the clock has struck nine, I must go and prepare for the party at Mr. Going's. You are not coming?" asked our hero.

"No, I sent a regret," replied the other, and so they parted.

When the old man was left to himself his face changed. With a grim look he asked himself,

"Have I made *another* blunder to-night?"

CHAPTER II.

DEBIT AND CREDIT.

"Screw your courage to the sticking point, and we'll not fail."—MACBETH.

AFTER our hero had polished a little, he made the best of his way to Mr. Going's house in Fifth Avenue. He walked steadily and firmly, every step, indicating a determined state of mind, and surely it was not child's play which occupied him. He had resolved upon undertaking a dangerous task. Dangerous, because it might bring him in the way of committing great injustice to another, and, perhaps evil consequences to himself should he prove to be in error. He ran the risk of losing the respect and confidence of his employers, perhaps of ruining his prospects for life. He might be misunderstood and blamed for over-zealousness, so alienating his best friends or even accused of intent to criminate old Martin Bates from a selfish motive.

Yet he wavered not an instant; had his life been the stake he would have proceeded as directly as he now walked straight to Mr. Going's house, thinking, as he walked of the best method of accomplishing his object.

He reached the house. A carpet was laid from the door to the curb-stone, that the dainty feet of the ladies might tread upon soft dry ground. On either side stood an uncouth assemblage of the curious poor, anxious for a glimpse at the great people. Seamstresses were there watching their own work as it squeezed out of the carriages, swept past, and vanished within the door. Beggars eyed the vision of luxury with hungry eyes, wondering how many loaves of bread this dress or the one yonder would buy. Paupers where there who had once been actors in Vanity Fair, and had now sunk to be mere envious spectators of the gay scene. And the flare of the light within shone queerly upon that crowd, and the music of the dance broke upon their ears like a mockery.

Our hero entered, and after a short sojourn in the gentlemen's dressing-room, came into the parlor. Miss Jessie, as charming as ever, was, as usual surrounded by the proper multitude of admirers. Mr. Faro had just danced with her, and now relinquished his fair partner to Mr. Wheeler, with a suicidal sigh. She scarcely found time to welcome Ernest, and, after a few common-place remarks, ignored him completely. The deferential crowd of admirers saw at once that he was not in high favor with the goddess, and tried hard to look as if they did not consider the new-comer a donkey and a dunce from principle.

Before long our hero found an opportunity to dance a waltz with her.

"Miss Going," he said in her ear, "I must have a few words with you this evening, and as you are very much in demand, I would suggest that you dance the next quadrille with me, to give me an opportunity."

"Very well, Mr. Montant, only don't let it be any thing serious! I don't feel in the humor for it."

"As you wish," he answered, "then we shall not dance the next quadrille."

"Why, yes, we will," cried the young girl. "To be sure, I will be most happy, Mr. Montant," so saying she bowed her readiness to finish the dance with Mr. Faro, who stood by, waiting in delicious suspense as if he looked for an appointment in the seventh heaven.

Montant bit his lips as he turned away. "Humor or no humor," he muttered, "I mean to say a word or two which she may forget if she can."

The quadrille came. Miss Jessie seemed unconscious of her partner, except as an auxiliary machine in going through the figures. In one of the pauses of the dance, he whispered to her,—

"Do you remember a promise which you exacted from me some months ago in this very room?"

She looked at him with apparently genuine inquisitiveness.

"A promise," he continued, gravely, "that I would devote myself, both unflinchingly and loyally, to—"

"Don't speak so loud," she interposed, evidently ill-pleased with the subject. "I do remember some remarks I made. And what can have occurred to remind you of them?"

"I have not come to bother you with such matters," answered our hero, curtly, "I only wish to exact a promise from you in return."

She looked up at him with arch wonder. Fascinated as usual in her presence, his voice trembled somewhat as he continued,—

"Promise me that if from to-night my relations with your father and brother should change; if I should be blamed, and accused of apparently unwarranted acts, you will never doubt me; but believe me, that what I do, is the inspiration of my duty to them, and the conscientious fulfillment of my promise to you, that I would not desert them in an hour of danger *even at my own peril.*"

The figures of the dance separated them before she could reply; but although she flirted with the irrepressible Mr. Faro, and the graceful Mr. Wheeler, she seemed thoughtful and preoccupied. When they paused again, she said, all too lightly to please him,—

"Certainly, I will promise, and I am quite sure that what you do will be all right. But won't you tell me what is this mysterious transaction that makes you look as solemn as an owl?"

"No," he replied, disappointed at her flippant reply, "I am sorry that I can not satisfy your curiosity about business matters. I recommend you to dismiss the subject from your mind. Forget that I mentioned it at all."

"I hope for your—for our sakes, that the matter is not as serious as you seem to think it is. Are you certain that it is not a fancied danger only?" There was some anxiety expressed in the last sentence, and she looked earnestly at him for a moment. Yet he was not satisfied, and only replied, dryly,—

"In all probability, only a fancied danger. The dance having ended, he left her abruptly, but Faro and Mr. Wheeler and their attendant cherubs in swallow-tailed coats, remarked that

Miss Going seemed to have suddenly lost her exuberant spirits to a noticeable degree. Particularly when, after supper, she noticed her brother stealing away from the room and leaving the house in company with Ernest Montant, she utterly ruined their happiness by absent-mindedness, and preoccupation, so that they began to consider the propriety of extinguishing their bright lights by gracefully committing suicide.

"Are you ready to stay up all night, Walter?" said Montant, when they reached the sidewalk.

"I have a bottle of brandy, a brace of pistols, and plenty of cigars," was the conclusive answer.

"Then let us take a carriage."

Reader, have you a correct idea of a night-owl? If not, you have only to hail a hack in New York at midnight, and something will approach you which would furnish an appropriate triumphal chariot for King Plague, were Death to hold a carnival procession. With two skeletons for horses, with two yellow struggling lamps, like wanton, distempered eyes, with a drunken heap of rags on the box for a driver, with an unwholesome noise like the death-rattle of a cholera patient, with the dank odor of the grave filling the interior, and the lining of the seats spotted like the eruptive stage of the small-pox; thus will it lurch and totter up to you, one of a whole legion, not one of which dares to stir out in the light of day, but which prowl about at night only. This is a night-owl.

Directions were given to the driver, and the two gentlemen were soon on their way rattling along as fast as they could be expected under the circumstances.

"And now," said Walter Going, "may I ask where we are bound to?"

"To your office."

"I must confess, Ernie," said Walter, after a pause, "I think it is best that you should tell me all about the circumstances which have brought about this strange behavior of yours. You are not the man to act in this way without good reasons, or I would not have followed you to-night. What do you propose to do at the office?"

"Look over the books," replied he, quietly.

"Whom do you suspect?" asked Walter, plumply.

"I take the responsibility of this little expedition, and you agreed to go with me as a personal favor only, so you can not insist upon an answer. I am not sure of my case, not at all sure, and I run a risk which appears more and more dangerous as I approach it nearer, and full of threatening consequences."

"And why not share the responsibility? If you advise with me, if we work together, then no blame can attach to you. I think you owe it to yourself to avoid this risk if possible."

"I am quite sensible of all you say," replied the other, gravely. "But I have given my word of honor as a gentleman, not to reveal the secret which has led to my suspicions, unless my duty to your house demanded it. So you see it becomes my duty to see with my own eyes whether the secret is to be revealed or not, and for this reason I have called you out to-night, and this it is which forbids my sharing the responsibility."

Walter could not answer this, and his companion vouchsafed no further explanation. As the old coach rumbled noisily through the streets he fell into a brown study. His whole life passed in review before him, and he realized his present position with painful accuracy. He had decided upon a bold lead, and he knew full well that this mysterious way of going about it would tell heavily against him should he prove to be mistaken.

"If Mr. Going hears of it, he will not doubt my honesty of purpose, but he will come to the conclusion that I am a very young and very foolish boy, who, in future, had better accustom himself not to look beyond his daily duties. Now I do hate to be considered a busy body and a spy! And as for Miss Jessie, if she hears of it, she will smile with a mixture of good-nature and pity, and will never respect me."

He thought bitterly of what he had to expect, and how little the purity of his motives would help or excuse him.

"However," he thought again, "there is one woman who will not misunderstand me."

Josephine Van Strom was in his mind. He had not seen her for some weeks, for his arduous duties at the office had not permitted him to make a trip to Massachusetts, where John Van Strom, Bella, and Josephine had settled soon after old Van Strom's death. They had been in constant correspondence, and our hero was comforting himself by recalling some of the glowing words in which she had assured him of her unbounded love for him, when the carriage stopped opposite the tall door, over which the gilded sign "Going & Son," was just distinguishable in the doubtful light of the street lamps.

Meanwhile, all was dark and still in the office. The desk of the old cashier, with its high stool, was standing massive and silent, and if a few little mice were about, they must have already caught the sound of approaching footsteps and have scampered away, for when the gentlemen entered there was not a sound in the room.

The bronze figure of "Justice" holding the scales out at arm's length on Martin's inkstand, had gone to rest long ago, if Justice ever sleeps. Perhaps she had laid down the scales and sword, tired of holding them all day long, and slept with her head resting on them. Perhaps there was a soul in the little bronze, and when darkness prevailed, who knows but what the little image told stories to the mice, describing how Martin Bates rolled his tobacco from one side of his capacious mouth to the other, as he wrote "debit," or "credit" in the books, and how she had watched him many years, and knew him better than any one else, and could tell a secret, oh, a deep secret, only he was such an old friend, she could not betray him unless—unless—

But when the door creaked and two men entered, when the gas was lighted and the two men went to work at something which required books from the safe, and books from the private office, and books from old Martin's desk, the little figure of Justice was standing up and holding out her scales vigorously, with a strange light in her bronze eyes, which shone through the bandage. But there seemed a vigor in the old attitude, and perhaps she would have liked to say: "He is a friend, an old friend of mine. I have known him thirty years; but let him be judged, let him be judged, whoever he may be."

And the flicker of the light danced up and down the polished wainscoting, and peeped into the corners of the room. The mice watched the two men from their holes while they ciphered, and reckoned, and calculated, and compared Martin Bates's accounts, while Justice overlooked the whole proceeding with great interest.

So they sat and worked away, talking in whispers, scribbling and checking off, while the office clock ticked itself to one o'clock, which it struck so loudly as to startle them for a moment, and then to two o'clock which startled them twice more.

Ernest Montant's face was calm, and did not express the agitation of his mind. He knew full well what was making Walter bite his lips and frown; *he* knew why Walter looked pale, and worked in a nervous, fidgety manner. *He* knew how a true man feels when he must play the part of a sneak and a spy, for his own self-respect was fast leaving him over that night's occupation.

"This book will be the last," said he, when the hands of the clock had moved far on the road to three o'clock. "If we find all correct here, as in the others, I will desist."

"You'd better," said Walter Going, in a tone of mingled reproach and weariness. "This whole business puts you in a false light. It was wrong and unwarrantable for you to take all this upon yourself!"

It was our hero's turn to grow pale—pale as death.

After all, he had not realized how bitter, how very bitter would be his reward, should all be found correct, nor how soon he would begin to receive it.

"Your suspicions—" continued Walter Going without looking at him.

"That term is not a just one," interrupted the other, hoarsely. "You don't know that I harbored any, and, indeed, unless the examination of these books should warrant it, which it seems they do not, I should harbor no suspicion of any one. I merely ask you to look over them, and my reasons for doing so are my own and mine only. This was our bargain before we left the house."

"Well; and now that we are as certain of his innocence as I have been from the beginning, are you going to justify yourself in *my eyes* at least, by telling me all about it."

"I do not break my word quite so easily as that," he replied, "I only ask you now to finish this work, and then you may think what you please. Here is the last book."

Walter was checking off the figures as they were called off to him in an undertone, and yawning ill-temperedly over the task, when, all at once, he opened his eyes wider. He did not check off *that* figure. No; how was that?

Could they believe their eyes? Yes, here, at last Martin Bates had made a *false and fraudulent entry!*

They looked at each other in dumb amazement for a moment. The color rose to their cheeks as if they blushed at the manner in which they had made this discovery, and the little bronze Justice held out her scales in a commanding manner, seeming ready to uplift her sword and cry aloud for judgment.

Are you asleep, Martin Bates, dreaming of your Italian bride with whom you are to leave the country to-morrow for a retreat of love and luxury, and all with *stolen* money? Or does a vision trouble your sleep, showing you two men with flashing eyes and busy pens sitting at your desk until the clock strikes five —until it strikes six? Do you notice that one of them has a small piece of paper by his side on which he occasionally notes a few figures? They increase slowly, those figures. Each one is the result of a long calculation; but they increase too rapidly for *your sake*, Martin Bates, for they sum up already to thirty thousand! thirty thousand dollars, Martin Bates; Are not the figures engraven upon your heart, written deep into its tenderest flesh with a red-hot pen, never to be erased, but to bear witness against you before the tribunal of God?

"I think that is all," says Montant, in a scarcely audible whisper, as the clock strikes six, and wiping his forehead—

"I think that is all," corroborates Walter Going, mechanically, and covers his face with his hands. "And now," he added, without altering his position, "now, are you disposed to tell me *all?*"

"Now," replied Ernest, "my duty compels me to give you a full statement, and I am absolved from my promise of secrecy."

"Poor fellow," said Walter Going, feelingly. "Thirty years in the house, and a defaulter. I think that if we were to look back through the books, we should discover that this has been going on for years!"

"It is for you to decide whether an accountant shall be employed for that purpose."

"Let us go and tell my father. It will be hard to make him believe it. Upon my word I expect him to disbelieve his eyes rather than to distrust old Bates."

"And yet he must face the truth. As for me, by the living God, I wish I had been mistaken," said Montant, solemnly.

Walter Going extended his hand, which was taken warmly by the other, and a ray of satisfaction overspread the face of our hero. Yet that feeling could not triumph at the expense of another's guilt and consequent misery, and when they drove back to Fifth Avenue, they were a sad and silent pair.

"I am tired and sleepy and as stupid as a fish," said Walter, as they alighted. "Here it is broad daylight and we have been dancing and cyphering all night. I say, a refreshing trip down town is just the thing after a party, isn't it, especially when it leads to such delightful discoveries?"

"Yet you must listen to my story," said Ernest, for we have no time to lose in sleep."

Walter went up stairs and aroused his father, and while the old gentleman was dressing, the young men refreshed themselves, so that it was still early in the morning when the three met in the library.

Mr. Going's astonishment and dismay were not demonstrative but most painful to the unwilling informers.

"At my age," said the old gentleman finally, in a low voice, evidently much moved, "at my age, boys, a man is not adapted to receive lessons in the school of life. That Martin Bates should be a scoundrel disproves all my knowledge and experience. His motives I can not divine, his hypocrisy I can not fathom, his whole character has become a myth, and yet I have known him thirty years! If he wanted money, even large sums, I would have lent it to him on his word alone. Why could he not borrow, then, even if he never repaid me? That, though bad enough, would not have amounted to crime, for which I *must* prosecute him!"

So true it is that thousands might avoid crime, for in nearly every case honest and open means would secure for them what they so much desire.

Surely, if an employer have sufficient confidence in a clerk, to put him in a position where there is a possibility for theft to a large amount, he would be willing to lend a smaller amount to his employee to save him from the temptation of stealing.

And then our hero told the partners all he had learned from Martin Bates's own lips the night before at dinner, the love affair with the Italian girl included. He went into all the particulars of this last item, concluding with his appointment with a carriage in Chatham Square.

"It may seem unjust to him," he added, " to tell all his personal secrets; but I have no choice in the matter, for I suppose this girl must be arrested too. She may have the money, which may thus be recovered."

Mr. Going nodded assent.

"This morning, at the office, he is to tell me whether he has been able to obtain her family's consent to the marriage. If not, I must, of course, be on hand with the carriage, and we will catch them both at once. In the mean time, of course, you know best how to prevent any further theft, during to-day. I must acknowledge that I think he intended to add to his plunder before leaving; but good fortune—"

"Or rather *your* remarkable energy, foresight, and courage," cried Mr. Going. "Why, but for you, Heaven only knows to what extent this might have gone."

"Mr. Going," said Montant, gravely, "I have been playing the part of a detective policeman, and can assure you that my boyish admiration for the pursuit has been entirely done away by this night's work. I would not steal my way into a man's confidence, and then, saving myself from moral perjury only by a mental hair's breadth, betray him to the retribution he merited, no, not for all the riches of the world!"

"And yet you have done your duty!" cried Mr. Going. "How can I reward you for all this?"

"Dont speak to me of reward," answered the young man, quickly. "For such work as last night's, I don't know of any."

"Will you accept the position of headcashier? I offer it to you. Don't start. I do so, not only because I want to pay you; but because I am convinced that it is important for me to retain your services in a higher place." The old gentleman, seeing that Ernest had colored crimson, arose and gave him his hand, saying, as he did so,—

"As long as I live, I shall not forget what you have done. *I* know that no desire of supplanting him has prompted you. *I* know that no consideration save your warm attachment to us all, could have induced you to run the risk which you did, so I want no overstrained sensitiveness, when I offer you this wellearned advancement. Had Martin Bates died an honest man, last night, and better it had been for him, I would have selected you as his successor, just the same."

Montant shook his head. The pride which drove the bright color to his face at first, was melted by the kind words just chronicled; but he answered decisively,—

"I am very grateful, and under other circumstances should be proud and happy at this distinction. As matters stand I ask you as a great favor to allow me to remain at my present employment until the impressions of this night have left my heart, if they ever will."

"As you wish, of course," answered Mr. Going, much disappointed, and the subject dropped.

Our hero concluded his narrative by showing in a perfectly cool and impassionate manner, that a man who has been drummed out of the British army, can not, as a rule, be trusted implicitly and of course, in the narrative, the name of Judge Eben Bates of Massachusetts was mentioned.

Here Walter became interested in the contemplation of the sidewalk, just beneath the library window.

"You know this Judge Bates, don't you, Walter?" asked his father.

"Yes, sir," was the laconic reply; and Walter began to count the bricks in the opposite house.

"Has he not a daughter, a very charming girl, whom you once pointed out to me in Boston?"

"Yes, sir."

"They are undoubtedly very respectable people, and this disgrace will be very hard on them. Very hard, indeed, on them," mused the kind-hearted old gentleman. In a moment or two he looked up, and said,—

"Boys, we will keep this thing quiet."

"That is what I thought best, sir," said Walter, still looking out of the window.

"If he gives up what he may have left of the thirty thousand dollars, we will let him off and end the matter, without a public show."

"Very good idea, sir," said Walter, and then they consulted as to the best means of accomplishing this end.

Walter Going and Ernest Montant drove down to the office together, leaving Mr. Going at home. During the whole of the preceding evening, while engaged in overhauling old Martin's books, neither of them had mentioned Judge Bates or his daughter whom Walter "knew;" but now they spoke of no one else but this Miss Bates, whom Walter now called *Bessy*, until the carriage stopped at the office door.

They entered the outer office; there stood old Martin Bates already at his desk, and, confronting him, was the little bronze figure, holding her scales in his very face. Truly, Justice had not slept that night.

CHAPTER III.

MR. STUMP.

"Read this and know I know your worthlessness."
KING HENRY V.

"MR. WALTER GOING sends word that he would like to see you in the private office, sir."

So spoke one of the younger clerks to Martin Bates, and the summons was immediately obeyed by the old cashier. When he entered, he found our hero and another gentleman, with his younger principal. Walter immediately arose in a nervous manner, closed the door, and bolted it.

"Let me introduce Mr. Stump to you, Mr. Bates." Whereupon the stranger said, "your most obedient, sir." He was short, quite fat, red-faced, clean shaved, and wore his red hair closely cropped. His eyes were small; but exceedingly sharp, and constantly wandering from one object to another; he was carefully, but vulgarly dressed, and although his round face suggested good-nature, with a tendency to fun, his *tout ensemble* was decidedly coarse.

"Your *most* obedient, sir," repeated Mr. Stump, with emphasis, and took up a newspaper, from behind which he amused himself by taking a mental photograph of Mr. Bates.

"And now that we are all seated, Mr. Bates," said Walter Going, "and as there is nobody present who should not listen, let me ask you at once: *What did you do with the money?*"

Martin Bates started, and his color changed. He looked from one to the other, bit his lips, and did not reply for a moment. Strange to say, there was no dismay, and but very little agitation manifest in his voice when he replied:—

"Fifteen thousand I can account for and you will not lose it. The other fifteen thousand is a dead loss. I can not, will not say, *how*, or *where*, even should torture be revived once more for old Martin Bates's especial benefit—which would not surprise me in the least. As for *you*, sir," turning to our hero, "I am very much obliged to you for the part you have acted; and as for *you*, sir," accosting Mr. Stump, "I suppose I may consider myself your prisoner; and so ends the first scene of the last act of

that great authentic tragedy called 'The Life of Martin Bates.'"

Not until the last sentence did he evince any emotion, seeming to attribute it all to his usual ill-luck, but the last words were given with indescribable bitterness.

"You are wonderful sharp, sir," interposed Mr. Stump, after a pause. "First, to know *what* money Mr. Goin' means, and second, to guess, (and quite right too!) that it was this 'ere Mr. Mountain which fetched you up with notorious genius, and last of all to see right through my swell clothes and reckernize the p'liceman! And all as true as Gospel, sir! You have stated the case in fewer and conciser words than I could myself."

"Has this Italian girl got possession of any large sums?" asked Walter Going.

"Aha!" cried Bates, turning upon our hero with a grim smile, "I see that my friend, according to his word of honor given to me, has favored you with the whole of my personal history!"

Ernest felt the reproach, but said nothing.

"I suppose" continued the old man, sardonically, "that any one having the faculty of connecting two ideas in his mind could name my successor in the office.?"

Montant thought as he turned away, (for defense was useless) that even had he accepted Mr. Going's offer of the head cashier's desk, he would now have resigned it at any cost. He felt that he could not have borne the old man's sarcasm had he consented to profit by his fall.

"I dare say," continued Bates, with biting irony, "that there was a *clause* in that promise upon honor, a loop-hole, through which my highly honorable friend slipped while his accommodating conscience acquitted him of perjury. Of course *gentlemen* can not break their words of honor! How fortunate that this loop-hole existed! He never thought of it until afterwards. Oh, no. *He did not mean to slip through it at the time he insisted upon* putting in that clause in which he promised secrecy *unless* some danger to the firm should compel him to break the trust. What danger has befallen the firm since eight o'clock yesterday evening?"

"Mr. Bates," said our hero, with as much composure as he could muster, "I did not say one word of what you confided to me, until after I had discovered the deficiency in the books. Mr. Going is my witness to this."

"All right, sir! It is of course very just that a man's character should be picked to pieces, and his past history used to criminate him before he has been tried or even heard upon the charges against him!"

"We are ready to hear you now," said Walter, "or we can send for my father, who preferred not to meet you unless you desired to speak to him."

"No! no!" cried the old man, hastily. "Mr. Going has been very kind to me! *I* know that his heart is bleeding from this blow, for it is a blow to an honest man to find that an old friend has become a villain. I would not see him now. I would not accept his pity and forgiveness should he offer it to me, and if he too has turned against me. I could not bear the reproaches of the one who has for thirty years been my only friend, besides your lamented grandfather.''

His voice quavered and broke down, he made an effort to subdue his emotion, but with a convulsive sob, it broke restraint, and he hid his face to conceal his tears.

"Come, come," said Mr. Stump, good-naturedly.

This "Come, come," is quite a by-word with the noble profession of detectives. It is intended to express pity, and to make a show of a soft heart, but its real meaning might be put in these words :—

"Come, come, don't cry, for it's no use, and *I'm* not to be humbugged. Don't make any disturbance or I'll handcuff you—don't waste my valuable time by making a scene. That is quite played out with *me*, I have seen it tried on too often."

All this lurks behind those little words, and much depends upon the tone in which they are said. If spoken in warning accents, and rather stern, they portend prospects of clubbing; but Mr. Stump had a good job on hand, a job which was bound to pay him, handsomely, and he felt that he could afford to be good-natured. His "Come, come," might be translated as follows :—

"My dear fellow, the circumstances surrounding this melancholy event are very touching. They touch my pocket, and your feelings, so cry away and lose my time so much as you think proper."

"Has the Italian girl received large sums?" asked Walter Going, again after a pause, intentionally disregarding the old man's distress.

"She has not," was the reply.

"Which statement is *corporated* by herself," *corroborated* Mr. Stumps, who had wasted time on neither grammar nor dictionary.

"So you have arrested her, too?" asked Martin Bates, raising his head.

"Not at all, sir!" Why you hadn't ought to think me so unpolite! I only had a leetle friendly chat with her this morning."

"Poor Simonetta!" sighed the ex-cashier.

"Poor what?" said Mr. Stump. "The *Eye*-talian gal *I* know of goes by the name of Net Mariner or Meriny, and lives near the 'Dirty Spoon,' in Cherry street, so it can't be the same name"

"It is the same one," said Martin Bates, wearily. Her name is Maria Simonetta Marini, and her father is an organ-grinder."

"I knowed he was a musical man," answered Mr. Stump, somewhat puzzled "but that Net was christened all what your call her, I didn't know. Well she swears she has no money, and cries because somebody won't let her marry you. She's a pretty girl, that Net!"

While rattling away, Mr. Stump has his sharp eyes fastened on Martin's face. The old man seemed rapidly sinking into a state of apathy; Montant could not bear to look at him. Disappointed in love at the moment of apparent success, ruined in every sense; his only friends changed into prosecutors, this

was his situation in the world, the world that had snarled at him all his life.

"And who has the fifteen thousand dollars, which you say we can recover?" asked Walter Going.

"That Mr. Muller, who proposed to sell you his farm in Hocus County. Do you remember when he and Mr. Stilletto came here to lay the project of forming a mining and manufacturing company before you and your father?"

"Certainly."

"Well sir, I advanced August Muller fifteen thousand dollars upon the Hobgoblin farm, thinking it would be quickly sold for an enormous sum, in which case I would have doubled my money, and have repaid you the whole thirty thousand dollars. You may believe this—you may not. Every thing is immaterial to me now!"

There was an utter despondency in his quiet monotonous voice that carried conviction with it.

"And the other fifteen thousand," said Walter.

"I have answered that question before," said Martin, doggedly. The *other* fifteen thousand dollars were taken before I knew August Muller, and it has simply *gone—gone, forever*, sir. If you are wise you will buy that Hobgoblin farm, and carry out August Muller's projects. It will cost you but little more than the lien you will have on it through the money I stole from you. But you will make an immense fortune out of it. This, gentlemen, is all the confession I have to make. You have lost fifteen thousand dollars through me, and I am prepared to serve out the punishment for my crime. The only favor I ask is never to be confronted with Mr. Going."

"And how have your books been kept formerly?" asked Walter Going, with a dark look. "We had no time last night to examine very far back."

"Thirty thousand is *all*, sir," answered Martin Bates. "Of course, I can not expect you to believe my word. *I* have believed gentlemen's words, gentlemen, who were *not* felons, and even then I have been deceived. Nevertheless, I repeat, that up to a very few years ago, your books and cash were kept honestly."

* * * * *

One of the results of the interview just described, was that Ernest Montant felt very blue and despondent, and he accused himself bitterly to the junior partner.

"If my sense of duty is to be so exacting as to turn me into a sneaking busybody, a spy and general informer, and if this is my nature, I believe that earnest, straightforward villainy would win me more respect."

"Perhaps you would have preferred the whole thing to remain undiscovered, and to have had another fifty added to this thirty thousand dollars?"

"You do not mean that question seriously," answered the other, "but I can assure you that I would give much had I baffled him in an open fight instead of such strategy as I have employed against him."

"I will be honest with you," replied Walter

4

Going, with a pleased expression. " I think that, after the risk you have run, no one can impugn your courage. From my own feelings, which were none of the pleasantest, while we were engaged in that night expedition, behind the old man's back, I can believe that it was as unpleasant as dangerous. We would not have done it; but for our duty toward my father, so let us comfort ourselves with the result which shows its necessity."

Montant accepted this conclusion, for his good sense forbade his giving way to over-strained scruples; but, this was another experience in life, and taught him that one's best instincts may so clash with the highest duties as to threaten our peace of mind like the pangs of wounded conscience.

We shall again hear of Martin Bates, and perhaps the old man may appear in a better light. According to Mr. Going's express wishes, his crime was kept quiet, and after the firm had recovered what they could of the thirty thousand dollars, he was allowed to leave the city, to vanish, in fact, no one knowing where he had gone, or expecting to see him again.

It will be remembered that Martin Bates, according to his confession, had advanced fifteen thousand dollars to August Muller, taking as security a transfer of the Hobgoblin farm in Pocus township, county of Hocus, State of New York.

" I shouldn't wonder if it was at Martin Bates's suggestion, that Muller and Stilletto first sought *my* services to induce you to buy this farm," said Ernest to Walter, " and if he then urged them, to call in person."

" Most likely," answered Walter, " for if we had bought it, Bates would have got his money back, and could have repaid us half our loss. Or if Muller had allowed him to double his money, he *might* have refunded the whole amount. This is about what he said his intentions were, I believe. But what do you suppose made him advance this money to Muller in the first place?"

" Muller is a very plausible man, and I have no doubt that Bates thought he saw his way plainly certain to bring him out of his difficulties. I believe he honestly thought that he would double his last venture and then repay the whole."

" So do I; and now we will try to get Muller to sign that farm over to us. I have just received a note from Mr. Paradise, to whom I sent the securities given to Martin Bates, in which he says that they are not in proper shape; that we should have a trust-deed direct from Muller. I think we will let Mr. Stump pay a visit to our noble knight of the red nose, who is probably not the most honest man in the world, and see if we can not frighten him into refunding us the *cash*, instead of saddling us with the property. If we get the farm, I suppose we shall have to build a small factory, and then we may work the thing to advantage."

" I would rather lose the whole amount, than enter upon the most expensive, and most tantalizing of all business enterprises," said our hero, quickly. " And that is, building a factory *outside of your legitimate business!* A

practical man, who works himself, and knows his trade thoroughly, may, in a course of years, see his shanty grow into a huge palace of labor, for he is the soul of his shop, and his shop may grow as the boy into manhood; but if you want to *ruin* a commercial house, induce them to undertake building a factory and go into manufacturing without knowing any thing about the business."

Walter said nothing. Never before had his young friend offered advice or even volunteered an opinion upon business matters, so he was the more astonished at this rapid speech and the energy with which it was enunciated. Though nothing further on the subject was said at the time, he never forgot it, and, in after years, saw the wisdom of Ernest Montant's opinion.

Mr. August Muller was inhaling the aroma of his coffee, sipping a little now and then, and convincing himself that his hand was *not* shaking as he lifted the cup; though the cup certainly *did* shake violently.

His costume consisted of a dressing-gown and smoking-cap, and he was smoking a long pipe, with a tassel dangling from the stem, precisely like that which ornamented the center button of his smoking-cap. The philosopher was pale this morning, and the seediness of his garb did not misrepresent the state of his health and spirits. " I must raise money," he soliloquized. " Yes, money is the only doctor that can cure my complaint, but when you send for him he don't come, having too many patients on hand, I presume, and, when he does come, he does not stay long enough to do much good by his benign presence. This is a very passable simile," he continued, much pleased with himself. " I must write it down somewhere. What a man is lost to thee, oh, thou frivolous world, in August Muller! Does any one know his talents? Has he been brought forward to fame and greatness as he deserved? No, he is allowed to sink lower and lower into slow-killing poverty, and to fade away. Yes, indeed, I am sick, dying! I think half a glass of that fine—" he rises, trembling, from his chair, and gazes eagerly about the room. " I certainly think a glass or two of bitter beer—they brew it quite drinkable in Philadelphia now—Where is it? Has my darling wife—" here he smiled viciously, " has she *hidden* the bottles? Not here—not there." And after looking awhile longer, still in vain, his face changes and he mutters something in which the emphasis falls somehow on " darling wife," " a stout club," and " a good thrashing," in strange connection. He was interrupted by the ringing of the door-bell, and stepped into the hall to admit the visitor.

" Mr. Miller, celebrated as the great philosopher of the present risin' gineration?" asked a little, stout man, with a round, smooth face, in a pleasant voice, as he removed his brannew beaver, and entered the front door.

" If you are not attempting to be witty, sir, you are perfectly correct," answered Muller, grandly. " If you presume to attempt to ridicule *me* I scorn the effort and its author."

" Jokin' is jokin' and business is business," said the little man, soothingly. " Now I have come on *business* and I would like to have a talk with you. My name is Stump."

"Walk in, Mr. Stump, and partake of August Muller's hospitality. Your offense is forgiven. August Muller is easily won over. It is his nature to be easily won over."

They were seated in the little parlor, the same in which, on a previous occasion, the philosopher exhibited his educational practices in the persons of his children.

"Will you have a glass of bitter Philadelphia ale, Mr. Stump?" asked the host. "I do not feel quite well this morning—and—I—"

"All right, Mr. Intellect, I'm agreeable," said Mr. Stump, who was surveying the room and its owner with great curiosity. So the ale was brought by the "darling wife," who had red eyes, as though from recent weeping; but August Muller looked at her with a controlling energy, which had the effect of making her quail and tremble and smile.

"That smile looks bad," thought Mr. Stump. "That '*ere smile*," he repeated to himself with great energy, "means brutal, beastly treatment, and total subjugation of that female, by means of physical force," which eloquent and finely-rounded sentence pleased Mr. Stump to that degree that he smiled himself into the best of humors.

After they had drank their beer, Mr. Stump said:—

"I might make a long introduction and I feel some like it, because the words come to me somehow this mornin'. My head is clear, just the same as yours, which is the result of not having a drop to drink in twenty-four hours or so, I suppose."

Mr. Stump was looking up at the ceiling and Muller scanned his complacent face in vain to see whether this was meant for sarcasm; but he answered curtly,—

"To business, if you are ready. My time is—"

"Exactly," interposed Mr. Stump, pleasantly. "Which reminds me of what my father once told me. Father was a farmer, lived away out back here in New York State. Well, father always said, 'talking is talking, but money buys the land,' and, speaking of land, tell me *what about that money which bought that land, giner'lly known as the Hobgoblin farm, sit-ywated in Hocus County, Empire State.*"

In speaking the last words, his whole manner changed. His round, smiling face grew rigid and hard; his little blinking eyes settled upon the other's face as if they would bore into his skull; and he suddenly leaned forward toward Mr. Muller, to watch him more closely. The latter, alarmed by the sudden change and approach, started back so as to nearly overturn his chair; yet his countenance did not betray any guilty fear, and, after recovering from the slight shock to his weakened nerves, he said, with his old, sickly smile,—

"I can not discuss business matters of such a nature with one, who though a guest at my table, is a total stranger to me. Mr. Stump, I must decline to answer until I have the pleasure of making your acquaintance, as Mr. Toots says in Dombey."

"Well, then, Mr. Miller, let me tell you the whole story in two words, and then we'll understand each other. Listen. There was an old man, one Martin Bates—"

"I do not think that name is altogether unfamiliar to my ears," murmured the philosopher, with a twist of his head as though he would be delighted to hear the sound again.

"Nor *I*," cried Mr. Stump, with a knowing wink. "Well, this old man stole fifteen thousand dollars from his employers."

"Dear me!" exclaimed Mr. Muller, raising his eyebrows in apparent astonishment.

"And you knew it!" continued Mr. Stump, with a friendly nod and smile.

"Sir, do not insult me!" said the philosopher, "I knew nothing of the sort. August Muller's name and reputation—"

"Did not prevent him from selling to this Martin Bates, Esquire, cashier of Messrs. Going & Son, this 'ere Hobgoblin farm for fifteen thousand dollars, when he, the said August Miller, knew that said Martin Bates was poor, and, consequently, could not have raised the *soap* by honest and square dealing." This was said with great determination and in a single breath, after which he favored Mr. Muller with some more friendly nods and knowing winks, and waited for a reply.

Mr. Muller thought a long while and then said:—

"I have studied the law, Mr. Stump, and can inform you, with great certainty, that should your design and intention be to indict me for receiving stolen goods, or money fraudulently obtained, or embezzled—should you attempt to prove this you have *no case!* In the language of the law, you have no case, sir."

"Now listen," resumed Mr. Stump. "After August Miller has obtained this money, he discovers that one of Mr. Going's clerks, Mountain by name—"

"Montant," corrected the philosopher.

"Well, then, Mongtang," continued Mr. Stump, "is a friend of a certain Mr. Staletoe."

"Mr. *who?*" asked Muller, in genuine doubt.

"Mr. Staletoe, or Stealto, or—"

"I presume, Mr. Stump," said the philosopher, patronizingly, "that, in consequence of the failure of those whose duty and privilege it was to watch over the years of your youth, to make your education a specialty, you are rather unfinished, if I may so express it, in your capacity for pronouncing foreign names. I will help you. You mean Mr. Stilletto."

"Just so. Well, you and Mr. Stilletto tried to get Mr. Mongtang to help you to persuade the Goin's to buy this Hobgoblin farm, in which case Mr. Bates would have got his money back."

"And quite an honorable dealing it would have been."

"Yes; but this young Mongtang didn't quite see it in that light, nor wouldn't have nothing to do with you, nor would the Messeoors Goin' see it in that light, nor would they have nothing to do with you when you and Staletoe went and tried it on with them at their office."

Muller nodded.

"But," continued Mr. Stump, "Martin

Bates, Esquire, cashier of Goin' & Son, has been caught."

Muller looked astonished, if not alarmed.

"*He has been caught*, diskivered, sacked, and banished from the glorious land of the free and home of the brave," said Mr. Stump, much affected.

"Well, sir—" commenced Mr. Muller.

"And now," concluded Mr. Stump, "I want you to make out a mortgage of fifteen thousand dollars to Goin' & Son, *immediately*, for value received by you per Martin Bates, upon the Hobgoblin farm, Hocus County, in the township of Pocus, in the great State of New York.

Muller had grown slightly pale. He eyed his opponent steadily for some moments, and then said:—

"August Muller's dealings are straight and honorable; but he does not like to be harassed, or to have impediments cast in his way by the littleness of his fellow-men. My answer, therefore, is this: If the Messrs. Going & Son will promise they have *no case* any way, you know, not to prosecute me for raising this money, I will at once execute the mortgage."

Mr. Stump asked, smilingly:—

"Is the title clear? Is there not a previous mortgage claim?"

"Let me ask you a question first," said Mr. Muller, suddenly assuming a sharp, quick tone, and without wasting his usual volume of words, "you are a police officer?"

"Right, my boy," said Mr. Stump. "My profession is that of a detective, and my home is in Mulberry street."

"Then I can speak openly to you?"

"That you may," rejoined Mr. Stump, pleasantly.

"You do not object to making a penny?" asked Mr. Muller, coaxingly.

"My oath of office does not compel me to starve a family of eight to death, on a salary of twelve hundred dollars a year, and buy good clothes besides," admitted Mr. Stump, frankly.

"How would you like to make a thousand or so?"

"Pennies!" retorted Mr. Stump, scornfully.

"Dollars," replied Muller, with a proud wave of his hand.

"I never lie, unless it is necessary, in business," replied the detective. "I like to make a thousand dollars. I like to make *two* thousand just exactly twice as well as *one* thousand, which is, accordin' to 'rithmetic, as I learned it at public school, when I used to get licked outrajus 'cause my old man was opposed to the schoolmaster in politics."

"Well, it may be two," said Mr. Muller, "and here is the case we must fix up together. There *is* a first-mortgage on the Hobgoblin farm, and Martin Bates only holds a *second* lien; understand?"

"Yes, sir," answered Mr. Stump, who had now regained his natural insinuating politeness, while Muller directed the conference.

"This being the case, it is much better that Going & Son should *buy* the farm out and out, than to hold a *second* lien upon it, which is

never good security, you know, even in the best cases."

"I think that is all exactly so. But how can *I* help you?"

"By preventing them from prosecuting me, which they certainly will be inclined to do, when they find out that I only gave a *second* mortgage for the money which was stolen from them."

"I'll do it. They shan't prosecute you."

"And you can coax them into buying the farm, perhaps?"

"I can do much. Mr. Walter and I have been on a little tear in the little town of York, and we'll go on another. *Two thousand*, you said?"

"That depends upon the price they pay," answered the philosopher. "They must build a factory and buy Stilletto's patents, and they may get rich by it."

"A queer way to get rich, by spending a fortune for the devil knows what," cried Mr. Stump, whose good sense showed him the truth instinctively.

"But they'll make a stock company of it!" cried the philosopher, triumphantly. "They'll sell the shares, and will all get rich, and then the farm, and factory, and patents, and all may go to—"

Mr. Stump finished the sentence with a knowing grin.

"And now, let us calculate to see how much you can make at the best or worst, August Muller," said the philosopher, resuming his flowery rhetoric, "thy star is in the ascendant. Over the hills and valleys of the Hobgoblin farm it shall rise to the zenith, and there remain, a celestial effigy of thine own terrestrial luster, for all time to come. Amen."

"That's what I say, old feller," quoth Mr. Stump, and they began to cipher.

They ciphered away while their victims did not dream it possible for a detective police officer to join hands with crime, and give the protection of his shield to the swindler. And Mr. Stump is not alone, in Mulberry street. He has many associates who do not intend to starve their families on twelve hundred dollars a year. And yet, the newspapers are beginning to inform the tax-payers, and the public generally, that our police excel the European civil guardians, and that the Metropolitan force is composed of as able and honest a body of men, as can be found anywhere.

CHAPTER IV.

LIGHT AND SHADE.

"Poor and content is rich and rich enough;
But riches fineless is as poor as winter,
To him that ever fears he shall be poor."
　　　　　　　　　　　　OTHELLO.

WE must pass rapidly over a period of several months, and will find our friends, the Goings, not only established in their new country house; but long accustomed to it and thoroughly attached to the charms of the Priory.

Our hero had led a steady life, and devoted himself to business more assiduously than ever Mr. Going had not again asked him to accept the vacated post of Martin Bates, neither had he appointed any other clerk to fulfill its duties. He and Walter changed their business habits. Nine o'clock saw them at their office, and one of them, generally Walter, staid until five, and even later, before returning to the Priory, which could be reached in less than an hour by the railroad, not too far to go and come every day. Walter, with many a sigh and scowl, gradually fell into these regular habits of work, and it was principally he, assisted heartily by our hero, who performed the duties of head-cashier.

The old gentleman's face grew care-worn, and his son displayed an energy, born of grave necessity, for the house was laboring through a period of heavy losses and great expenditure. Disaster crowded in from all sides, while the ready cash they could procure was steadily absorbed in a new enterprise of such magnitude that the solvency of the house depended upon its ultimate success.

Messrs. Going & Son had bought the Hobgoblin farm in Hocus County, township of Pocus. They had bought Stilletto's patents and had almost completed a large factory. The construction of this factory had already cost four times the original estimate, and was still only a huge bill of expense; but the *prospective* profits were—unprecedented.

And for this, they had neglected their legitimate, safe business, almost entirely. One of the most respectable houses in the city, they had been inveigled into this wild scheme by such men as Stilletto, Muller, and Stump, and only one man, and he too young to be heeded, had protested against it. When the transaction was completed, Ernest Montant felt that he had no object left, but to do *his* share toward weathering the storm he had so clearly foreseen.

But now we find the family enjoying a day of rest, a glorious September Sunday, at the Priory.

Good luck to you, Mr. Going, presiding over your guests' entertainment. The golden sun streaming in at the bow window and shedding luster around your venerable silvered head the while. The gracious spirit of hospitality is enthroned upon your forehead; kindliness and good-will to all men shine in your eyes, as you survey the good gifts before you, for which you have just thanked God with a few simple, but heart-felt words of grace.

As his eyes wander with satisfaction over the shining plate and sparkling glasses, they send a glance of recognition to each decanter, holding different colored wines, glowing in the light of the September sun, that originally gave them growth and warmth and strength while yet in the bosom of their beautiful mother, the grape. But his eyes rest upon the fairer face of his daughter, at the opposite end of the table, and they exchange a look of love and affection, in which the soul comes forth and gives a new expression to his face. Ah, Miss Jessie, may it be many happy years

before your father's chair stand empty in your sight!

Mr. Fatman, the banker, is here, apparently glorying in his Falstaffian proportions, for he is in a good humor. A dozen times this morning has he repeated that the Priory is a "palatial residence, truly a palatial residence, Mr. Going," and then, to himself, that he would really like to own the Priory, just as if he did not consider it quite beyond the range of possibility that he *should* own it some day!

Mr. Paradise, the hunchbacked lawyer, was also present. His Mephistophelean face wore an expression of epicurian satisfaction, and his remarks were almost polite.

Walter Going twisted his long whiskers and signified his physical happiness by sipping his wine with extra gusto and telling stories of racing, boxing, and hunting, until Miss Jessie begged to be informed if he knew of no subject more generally interesting.

On either side of Miss Going, sat Mr. Faro and Ernest Montant, but to-day she favored the latter so markedly that Mr. Faro was dumb, and wondered in his inmost soul if he were ever to smile again.

Mrs. Fatman, late the baker's daughter, was the only lady present besides Miss Jessie.

The dinner went off pleasantly, and the ladies retired, later than is usual, for Miss Jessie enjoyed sitting with her father and brother while they were smoking, and as for Mrs. Fatman, she became accustomed to man's vices long ago. Finally the two ladies arose and were followed by our hero, who had received notice of a prospective walk in the garden with Miss Jessie, and by Mr. Faro, who had determined to revenge himself by withdrawing his superb attentions from Jessie, and flirting with Mrs. Fatman.

Thus Mr. Paradise and Mr. Fatman were left alone with Going and Son. These two were among the few of the mercantile world who knew of Martin Bates's embezzlement, and of his sudden disappearance.

"What has become of him any way?" asked Mr. Fatman.

"At last accounts, and those reached me only casually, he had gone to Massachusetts on a visit to his brother, Judge Bates," replied Mr. Going.

"I never understood that fellow," said Mr. Fatman.

"I understand him very well," said the hunchback, tersely.

"Then you are wiser than I," growled Mr. Fatman.

"Which is neither improbable nor very complimentary," replied Mr. Paradise. "From their profession, lawyers are accustomed to look a little deeper and read a little further in the difficult book of men's characters."

"And also to investigate the contents of their purses less disinterestedly," returned Mr. Fatman, who knew that his only safety consisted in giving the hunchback a "broadside" whenever a chance offered.

"Quite right," the latter answered, dryly, and not at all displeased. "What a charming repartee! So very witty! Well, I have come to the conclusion that Bates stole the *first* fifteen thousand, to give to somebody else. I am quite certain of it."

The other gentlemen looked at him in inquiring wonder.

"Don't stare at me so," cried Mr. Paradise, ill-humoredly. "I know I'm a curiosity, but I won't be stared at, especially when you want to stare me into telling you what I haven't the least idea of telling any one. So please pass the wine, Going, and don't be ridiculous. I shan't tell you another word."

"I believe you have been my counselor for twenty years, Paradise," said Mr. Going, gravely; "and it occurs to me that we might recover that money yet, if a third party—"

"Twenty years your counselor, and yet I won't say another word about it; no, nor wouldn't if it was a hundred and fifty years," interrupted the hunchback, with offensive sharpness. "If you think that I would withhold the name of this third party when the money *could* be recovered, well and good. In that case you had better take your business away from Graves and Paradise and give it to Van Sachenach, Precedent and Bailiff, that's all."

Mr. Going made no reply. He was accustomed to the usual acerbity of the hunchback, and knew well enough that, could it promote his interest, his lawyer, who was at the head of his profession, would have told him all about the matter without the asking.

Mr. Fatman was less easily satisfied; but as he knew that nothing could open the lawyer's lips when once closed, he snuffed and turned up his nose with disgust and changed the subject.

"How about Hobgoblin, Mr. Going," he asked.

"Hobgoblin," replied the old gentleman, with a forced smile, which did not conceal the nature of his thoughts, "seems to me like a dog given to a poor man. He may be but a puppy at the time, but he grows, gentlemen, he grows larger and larger, and finally eats his owner out of house and home. Now I do not mean to say that I expect to find this creature called Hobgoblin, possessed of such an appetite as to eat me out of house and home; but—"

"I should think not," said old Fatman, leaning back in his chair, and complacently viewing the scene around him. "For a place like this, a truly *palatial* residence, sir, as I have before remarked, is not so easily swallowed."

"And not so easily digested after you have swallowed it," said Mr. Paradise, attentively examining his napkin ring.

"You are right, Paradise," replied Mr. Going, biting his lips. "It is a place which may ruin the financial health of its possessor forever!"

"A palatial residence," murmured Mr. Fatham, *sotto voce*, thinking to himself, "I would like to have it. *I* could digest it, and perhaps—perhaps I *will* have it some day!"

"But as I intended to say," continued their host, "when I bought that farm and the mines, I thought I was only reimbursing myself. It only cost me ten thousand, cash!"

"A mere trifle," said Mr. Fatman, abstractedly.

"A mere drop in the bucket," added the lawyer.

"Right again," said Mr. Going, with another forced smile, "A mere drop in the bucket to what I have paid out on it since! I calculated that I would build a little factory as an experiment, and the little factory has grown like the poor man's dog—grown over my head—"

"Keep your head above it at all costs," cried Mr. Paradise, striking the table with his fist, for beneath all his sarcasm he was a true friend of his client.

"I have thrown so much good money after bad," said Mr. Going, gloomily, "that I may as well try it a little longer. I shall not go too far, rely upon it, and besides, in a short time there will be an income from the sale of our manufactures."

"Yes," cried Mr. Paradise, "and for every dollar that goes into your pocket, two or three, or a dozen, will come out of it. That's *my* opinion.

"Why don't you employ that man Stilletto, Mr. Going?" asked Mr. Fatman, "I understand you have paid him thousands of dollars for his patents, and now you employ another superintendent. I should think he, the inventor, would be the proper man to work his own machinery."

"I can not endure the man," answered Mr. Going. "He is coarse, a libertine, and exceedingly loose in money matters. I acknowledge that his talents are considerable; but you know the proverb, 'He that meddles with pitch is certain of defilement.' His very nature is too foreign to mine to admit of his employment by me."

"Pooh, pooh!" said Mr. Fatman, "Don't you employ dirty brokers and dirty agents every day of your life?"

"Yes—but that is only in isolated cases. Here I will be almost obliged to associate with a man who has not the first quality of a gentleman, neither has he the worthy simplicity and exceeding honesty which alone make men of low degree my moral equals and worthy of my confidence. We have a monstrous undertaking on our hands, and the results may not only be very profitable, but success will couple my name honorably with the advancement of enterprise and civilization. To obtain these objects, you will readily believe that I would bend all my energies and sacrifice my personal inclinations; but, I will not employ a man whose very name is sufficient to bring disrepute upon the whole establishment."

"*I* would employ him if his services were likely to help the business, and I would *not* if they were *not*," said Mr. Fatman, curtly.

There was a pause in the conversation. Every one seemed to be in a bad humor. Suddenly, Mr Fatman cried,—

"I have an idea."

"A miserable one, I'll wager," said the lawyer.

"Make a *stock company* of the whole concern; sell your shares and come out whole and hearty," cried Fatman, without heeding the interruption.

"Limited liability, of course!" sneered the hunchback. "Oh, yes. Capital idea! Limited liability, limited capacity, limited capital, limited attention on the part of one half of the directors, limited understanding on the part of the other half, and limited honesty on the part of the promoters and managers. Finally, very limited success, and not a cent in the end for the shareholder! That is the true *English* for that great national *English* word which you see stuck up on half the sign-boards in London!"

They all laughed; but Mr. Going thought it need not be so in all cases, and Mr. Fatman's idea was not negatived by the lawyer's sharp scrutiny. Finally, they all agreed to meet somewhere in town and talk the matter over more fully.

In the meanwhile, our hero and Miss Jessie were strolling along the beach. The young lady had been talking very seriously, and the old spell was upon him as he watched her in the beautiful splendor of her youth, graced by the mild earnestness of what she had been saying.

"What a wondrous world of variety lies hidden in this young breast," he thought to himself. "Flirting and trifling with the host of her admirers, neglecting, almost ignoring me, she repels me at one moment, only to attract me more irresistibly at another. A husband with a strong will and possessed of her love, would find an endless field in molding her character to what it can and should be. If he could command her emotions and whims so as to call out each in its place, what a delicious treat, what a sweetly interesting life he would have before him; for she would never tire him with a flood of vapid sentimentality. In serious moments all trifling and frivolity would vanish away in the generous outbursts of her great heart, while in lighter moments she would charm, fascinate, and bewitch him by her pretty, harmless coquetry."

"So you will do it, Mr. Montant?" she asked, standing still, and looking imploringly into his eyes.

"I don't know what to say," he answered, unable to bear her gaze. "I feel as if it were a question of manly dignity, and that I ought *not* to step higher over the body of man whom my *craftiness* has brought low."

"I can not understand how a proud man can stop half-way at any thing. If it was not *wrong* to bring a dishonest man to justice, and, perhaps, save my father from complete ruin, how can it be wrong to step into his place and do right where he has been doing wrong."

"What makes you speak that way to me?" asked our hero, perplexed. "It seems strange that you—"

"Certainly strange," she replied, "and, probably it is also forward, immodest, and, it may be, unwomanly; but my love for papa makes me bold sometimes, and I have often uplifted my little voice in business matters. I opposed the extravagance of buying the Priory, although it seems like paradise to me. I also opposed this new

enterprise, this monstrous, ridiculous Hobgoblin factory—"

"Right — quite right," interrupted our hero.

"If some gray-headed old stick could hear us talking," said Jessie, smiling, "he might fancy we were children trying to talk wisely; but I think young people have good ideas, sometimes, as well as the old. But to return to the subject. You once promised me your aid when the time should come. Look in my father's care-worn face, and tell me—has it come?"

He could not answer her.

"You asked me why I spoke thus to you. A woman has no *reasons* for her action. I have confidence in you—*why*, I don't know; perhaps, because I know my father has. At any rate, I want to see whether I can accomplish what I know he failed to do several months ago. He wants you to be the headcashier. I ask you to accept. Will you?"

Oh, that "Will you?" with an encouraging smile, and an enticing toss of the head, and the enrapturing glance of her earnest eyes. Could he resist? Had he, the strong-willed, self-reliant, indomitable man that he thought he could be,—had he so far resisted the entreaty of a friend, and must he yield to the pleading of a woman? He could not conceal from himself that her eloquence, joined to the magic spell of her presence, had melted his strong resolutions long ago, and he consented to her request. She was grateful, and bestowed upon him such little marks of favor and preference that afternoon, that Mr. Faro vowed revenge weere hope seemed dead, and to induce other fashionable people in New York to *cut* the Going's hereafter.

CHAPTER V.

THE GREEN-EYED MONSTER.

"Oh! beware, my lord of jealousy, etc."
OTHELLO.

OUR hero had filled the office of cashier in the great house for but a little while, before the friends and business connections of Messrs. Going & Son knew him and respected him in his new capacity. Naturally modest of demeanor, his calm self-reliance was not betrayed into ostentation or arrogance, and as his manner invited confidence, which was never abused, he soon controlled the finances of the house almost entirely. When he first seized the helm, the finances had never been in a worse condition, yet the credit of the old house soon became better than ever. The Goings were considered *flush* (as New York merchants call it), though they were, in reality, poorer than they had been for many years. Many days there were, when both Walter and his father wore anxious faces as the dreaded hour of *three*, when the banks close, drew nigh; but the new cashier sent Walter away to "go up town," and enjoy himself and leave the bank account to *him*. Walter generally took the advice, trying to cover his admiration with a scowl; but his confidence in our hero was never impaired. And if the large resources of the house would not *always* come to the rescue; if all foresight and management failed to prevent a short period of great strain and alarming pecuniary pressure, there was no one better adapted to step into a neighbor's office and solicit a loan or obtain a favor from the banks, than Mr. Montant, the cashier, for every one liked him, and every one knew that his word was as good as security. It would have looked strange had Mr. Going personally called for favors, for then people would have magnified the importance of the case, while, on the other hand, Walter was not the man for borrowing. So it was that the finances of the house, the bone and sinew of its existence, devolved more and more upon Montant, who, as was his nature, bent his whole mind and energy to the task.

Meanwhile the Hobgoblin factory was growing and still growing, like the poor man's dog; like some financial monster whose appetite for money increases by what it feeds on, never satisfied, ever hungry, and not to be put off. People even began to believe in the wisdom of the enterprise. The outwardly prosperous condition of the house, under Montant's management, deadened all unfavorable reports, and before long Mr. Going was believed to have added another gold mine to those which had yielded the material for the structure of the good old house of Going & Son.

And while the factory is growing and people are talking and the new cashier is doing finely, just as we should have expected from Ernest Montant, we will take another look at the Priory and see how matters are going on there.

A carriage, driving over the bridge, through the park, up to the grand front piazza, with the columns reaching up to the roof and the graceful woodbine encircling and twisting and twining and struggling up along the walls in classic arabesques. Two gentlemen in the carriage and two ladies; two young and pretty ladies, and yet Miss Jessie Going is not there, although the gentlemen we can now recognise as her brother Walter and Ernest Montant.

Miss Jessie was at the door to welcome them; and her father, with the old chivalresque spirit which but rarely looms up in some specimen of the true gentleman, nowadays, stepped to the carriage to assist them in alighting.

"Mrs. Van Strom," he said, as he kissed her softly and affectionately on the forehead, "you are, indeed, a dear and welcome guest here! and this, I presume, is Miss Bates" (as he extended his hand cordially to the other), "whom I also greet most heartily. We owe her kind visit to your persuasions, Mrs. Van Strom, and can only thank you for your friend, madam!"

"Here is the baggage, struggling up the hill," cried Walter, who was in high glee. "It may as well take its time about getting here, for I assure you it won't leave us for a good while to come."

"I am not so sure, sir," said Josephine Van Strom, with a smile. "We must—"

"We must what?" cried Walter. "Return soon? Do not lay that flattering unction to your soul, Mrs. Van Strom."

"I surely do not wish to speak of leaving this spot, where so much is dear to me," answered the widow, and now, the young mistress of the house claimed her greeting with many kisses and welcomes, and they adjourned upstairs, which brought with it a temporary separation of the male and female constituents of the party.

"Who is this coming?" said Walter, as he and our hero were lighting their cigars, preparatory to a stroll to the stables before dinner. "Upon my word it is Faro and Wheeler."

And sure enough, those two gentlemen drove up in a dog-cart, drawn by a tandem team, half smothered with harness.

"Where did you get that coat, Wheeler?" asked Walter, when the new visitors joined them, after consigning their horses to the care of a groom.

"Ah——Pool and Co.——ah——London ye knaw——awfully jolly coat, isn't it? The beastly tailors in this blarsted country can't make a coat to save your life, ye knaw,—ah—"

"Wheeler," said Walter, who could not bear him, "you should not talk that way, or some people might think you were an Englishman."

"Indeed—ah—been told so—look English ye knaw—parents Britishers ye knaw."

"Yes, your parents were English, only they have lived in New York for two hundred years at least," answered Walter, dryly.

"Severe—my friend, severe," conceded Mr. Wheeler, whose great aim and object in life was to be mistaken for an Englishman.

"But never mind, Wheeler," added Walter, "no man of sense will *ever* take you for an Englishman. Let's go into the house, I'm sure you gentlemen must want something to clear the dust out of your throats."

When the ladies had made themselves charming after their long trip (for Josephine Van Strom and Bessie Bates had traveled from Massachusetts that day), they assembled at the dinner-table, and those to whom Miss Bessie Bates was a stranger had an opportunity of examining her closely. A young girl of eighteen. Not so pretty as finely molded, and thoroughly English in her countenance, she was one of those to whom belong curls, and a dress made more for comfort than for fashion. Blue eyes, auburn hair, and features rather placid and classic than piquant. Ernest Montant compared the three at his leisure.

There was Josephine Van Strom, with her golden hair and almost divine eyes; with her superb figure and passionate impulses in every look, every move, every word of her deep alto voice. Madonna and Venus in one.

There was Jessie Going, the picture of a New York belle, all grace and "chic," as the French say. Pretty in every motion, all life and glowing beauty in her black hair and splendid eyes, while Miss Bates, the least attractive at first sight, yet held her own, with her quiet, subdued air, which irresistibly led people to suppose, to use Mr. Faro's words after dinner, that "there must be a deuced deal in that girl!"

"How near alike our names are," said Miss Jessie to Miss Bates.

"Jessie and Bessie," corroborated that young lady with quiet smile of her own.

"And, do you know, Walter has named a pair of horses after us."

Miss Bates bowed to that gentleman, who returned the salute with a queer look straight into her eyes as he said, lightly,—

"Bessie and Jessie are the best little pair in Westchester County!"

"Do you mean us," said his sister, laughing.

"As you wish," replied he, with a comic earnestness; "the remark applies to both. Bessie and Jessie match well, are both very handsome, kind and well-bred. There is but one objection."

"And what may that be?"

"They can not be driven by a lady," replied Walter, mischievously. "It takes a *man* to drive them."

"And a pretty good driver at that, I fancy," added his sister, wickedly.

"I believe thee my child," said Walter; but as Miss Bates was blushing and looking down at her plate, he changed the subject and inquired after her father's health.

"Oh, quite well, I thank you," answered she. "You may imagine he did not like me to leave him, in fact, when Mrs. Van Strom came to me with Miss Going's kind note of invitation, I had no idea he would let me go, and I believe that it is entirely due to Josephine's persuasive powers that he finally gave way. He is so lonely you know, with no one but Uncle Martin to keep him company."

"How is your Uncle Martin?" asked Mr. Going, with a suppressed sigh, which Miss Bates, evidently knowing nothing of Martin Bates' true story, did not notice.

"Uncle Martin," replied she, "is not as well or as cheerful as I have seen him in former times. He is much older, and seems rather broken, and rather as if he had something on his mind, which in reality compelled him to go out of business, though he says it was feeble health which made him resign his position in your office. He always speaks in the highest terms of you all, and I should not be surprised if my visit here were owing somewhat to his influence."

In fact, Walter had been the proximate cause of Miss Bessie's visit. His father and sister were on the point of inviting Josephine Van Strom to the Priory when he suggested in an off-handed manner, that his sister should also invite some young lady for *his* especial benefit, and casually, as it were, mentioned the name of Miss Bessie Bates. Jessie fell in with the suggestion, and thus it happened that the piece of Martin Bates arrived under the auspices of the fair widow.

"Poor John," replied Josephine, to a question from Jessie Going. "is not much better. My sister-in-law has wonderful control over him, even when threatened with the worst

kind of an attack. But his mind, his intellect, his senses seem to be leaving him, gradually. The beautiful scenery around our house has done much, I believe to make him quiet and docile. You know our house is only about a mile from Judge Bates's. Isn't it strange that we should have made neighbors of friends of *yours*, by mere chance, after we left this house?"

"Indeed it is," said Mr. Going. "This is the way in which people are drawn together. as it were by destiny, and re-united when their natures are akin and they suit each other. I have known a connecting chain of neighborhood, marriage and unions of various kinds, join certain families, certain *sets* of people and interweave them in the most remarkable manner. Let us hope," added the old gentleman, with the whole kindliness of his heart "that it will be so, with us assembled here, if Miss Bates will pardon the liberty of such a wish to an old man, to whom years have given the right to speak his mind freely."

Miss Bates colored up and gave him a grateful smile, while Walter looked down and said "Amen," softly; but so impressively, that it attracted attention, and made Miss Bessie redder than before.

"My sister," said Josephine, again in answer to Jessie, "has proved to be a magnificent woman. Although her want of education and low origin were great obstacles to her, she won for herself a warm place in the heart of each one that knows her. She is the most charitable, the kindest creature on earth, and she loves her husband in spite of all the trouble he is, and must always be to her. Any woman," continued Josephine, with animation, "can love a husband who is strong and handsome and smart; but show me the one who can do her duty by the side of a John Van Strom, and she must be a *true* woman indeed!"

The beautiful widow paused, and colored at her own fervor; but Mr. Going, next whom she sat, took her hand warmly, and said, "Mrs. Van Strom, that was well and nobly said."

Montant looked at her. How charming, how superb she appeared, as, filled with her noble sentiment, she shone in all the beauty of her soul. Their eyes met, and as she read in his burning gaze his inmost feelings, she colored again, following the example of Miss Bates. Miss Jessie noticed this occurrence, and put one little white tooth somewhat forcibly on her nether lip, and thenceforward did not make the slightest attempt to entertain the woe-begone Mr. Faro or the disconsolate Mr. Wheeler, though they depended, for very life, upon her smiles.

Of course, the visit of the young ladies at the Priory was prolonged beyond the few days at first specified, and Walter was a great deal in Miss Bates's company. Truly English in her habits, she could keep up with him in the longest walks, and thus excited his admiration anew.

But when they strolled through the garden or park, in the evening, he called her "Bessie," and she murmured "Walter," in reply. although no one else knew of the progress of this affair except our hero, who could also have told that this was nothing new; that it had been going on for months. Yes, and that they were even engaged; but Judge Bates, on one cold and dreary winter's day, objected to the match, and Walter was too proud and angry to ask any questions. Miss Bessie thought that her father, who was a rigid Puritan, given to total abstinence, probably found it impossible to give his daughter to a man of the world, whose very manner showed that he was not a saint. Thus thought Miss Bessie, and as Judge Bates had not fancied the dashing New Yorker from the outset, it is probable that his daughter was correct in her opinion. But another couple are often found in each other's society during that month of October, at the Priory, and they do not seem to care for other companionship. Our hero and Josephine have found each other after a long absence.

"Which seemed longer to me than it could have seemed to any *man*," said the widow, softly, as they wandered along the beach, where the sand lay bleaching in the moonlight, and the autumn wind blew fresh over the swelling waters of Long Island Sound.

"I question it," replied our hero, with a happy smile. "I have been very busy, it is true, and have not been able to write to you as often as I would; but the thought of you has been with all the operations of my mind, and when I have not written as often as I, perhaps, ought, it was because I can not bear to scribble hurried nonsense to you."

They visited the rock, where they had been seated on that bright afternoon in the spring, when they met for the first time. They spoke of their engagement.

"I would be proud and happy to have our love acknowledged before the world," he said, "but I have reasons which move me to prefer, for the present, that we should keep it a secret. You do not doubt my love for you, Josephine? You should not doubt."

"No," answered Josephine, hesitatingly, "not if I were once for all *certain*—"

He stopped her by a rapid motion, seizing her hands, and held her in front of him, while his eyes flashed.

"Do not look at me like that," she implored. "I do not mean—I do not know—oh, I am a foolish woman;" and instead of explaining herself, the fondness of her heart overwhelmed her, and she laid her head on his shoulder. She nestled there for some time and neither of them spoke. Closer and closer she clung to him, and at last he felt her convulsive sobs on his breast.

"What is this, Josephine?" he asked, with evident emotion. "Have *I* occasioned your sorrow?"

"No," she murmured, "but the fear comes over me that I may *lose you!* And if I do," she cried, in agony at the very thought, "God is neither just nor merciful!"

Montant was appalled. His conscience was not altogether clear, and he decided in a moment.

"Josephine, let us declare our engagement at once. Let the whole world know it. I am ready."

She looked up at him, the tears still in her eyes. The old Madonna face!

"And now," he added, affectionately and soothingly, "tell me what has put that nonsense into your head."

She placed her lips close to his ear, and whispered as though even Nature might hear it, and betray the secret,—

"*She is jealous of you!*"

"Who?" asked our hero, thanking his lucky stars that it was not daylight, for his face flushed crimson.

"Jessie Going."

"Nonsense, my dear."

"Say nonsense as long as you please," she answered; "but I tell you the eyes of love can see through every thing! She watches you, she watches me, is absent-minded and pale. When you speak to her, her face lights up with smiles; but if any one else addresses her, she is almost cross. To me she is studiously polite and cheerful; but I can see through it all—see through it all."

Well for you Josephine, that you could not see his face. Well for you that his knitted brow, his firm-set lips are hidden from you by the merciful shadow in which he stands, while he reads your face upturned to his in the full moonlight.

With an almost superhuman effort of repression, he stopped the tumultuous beatings of his heart. Yes he knew it was true! He knew it *now*, although his modesty had heretofore prevented him from reading the signs Josephine now so mercilessly pointed out. Hundreds of little incidents, unnoticed at the time, now came to his mind in a clamorous crowd, each corroborating the other's evidence, each crying out "Jessie Going loves you, and you, fool, have been blind to it."

With a sickening sensation as if some cherished thing were torn from him by the act, he drove away the image which the mouth of *another* had thus brought before him; showing it in enticing proximity, within his grasp, but yet lost forever. With a hoarse voice, which no effort could soften immediately, he said,—

"Let's cut this foolery all short; to-morrow we'll tell the world that we love each other, and then our road *must* be clear!"

After this speech he found it possible to be calm, and they strolled about until very late. Could any man hear her speak, laying her heart open before him with all its boundless wealth of affection; could any man see her, in her beauty, ready to give to him body and soul, and not be reconciled to his lot?

He became satisfied, and she doubted him no longer. Of her own free will she proposed that they should still keep their secret, rather than hasten a public engagement, when he had reasons for postponing it.

And so it happened, that, although his heart had warned him that he was playing a dangerous game, they determined finally to adhere to secrecy. If he had seen as they reached the house at a late hour, if he had heard a window overhead close softly, as they stepped upon the piazza, perhaps he would have had more misgivings as to the proof his heart was to undergo. But had he known that a woman left the window, where she had sat all the evening waiting for *them*, and thrown herself upon her bed and wept bitterly, he would have made his engagement public at once, or renounced Josephine then and there.

But who would have thought it of Jessie Going, the light-hearted belle of the city, the happy young girl of seventeen, who had such a host of admirers?

Next morning broke in a flood of autumnal glory. It was Sunday, and Mr. Fatman and Mr. Paradise drove out to take dinner at the Priory, which, with the two lady guests made up a pleasant party, and merriment ran high. The widow, Miss Jessie, and Miss Bates looked charming, and, for some reason, Miss Jessie was in the best of spirits, flirting with Faro and Wheeler, and exchanging repartees with Mr. Paradise.

So the dinner went off sparklingly, and the younger people went out on the lawn, while the elders talked business over their wine. That day it was decided, in a short final discussion, that Hobgoblin should be turned into a stock company. Further, that Mr. Fatman should be president. Mr. Paradise a trustee, and Mr. Stilletto, manager of the factory, with Mr. August Muller for engineer. Mr. Going was to remain in the back ground, because, as the selling party it was considered advisable that his name should not appear.

"But then," said Mr. Fatman, with fat intensity, "we will go hand in hand, Mr. Going, hand in hand, you know!"

And after Mr. Fatman had delivered himself of that great sentiment he leaned back in his chair and surveyed the room at his leisure, muttering to himself. "A palatial residence! Indeed, a palatial residence!" And then, he added in the faintest of whispers, hardly formed in the deepest recesses of his fat heart, "I would like to have this place! *I may yet have this place!* I THINK I WILL HAVE THIS PLACE!"

"Now it is all settled, and I am glad of it," said Mr. Going, rising. Followed by his guests, he stepped out upon the piazza, where a queer sight awaited them.

Sounds of laughter and merriment reached them from the lawn, where the three ladies and four gentlemen were having a grand jollification as if they were again irresponsible children. Some time previous Miss Jessie had received from her brother a present of two very small and very shaggy black ponies, and they furnished the means for this extraordinary hilarity. At Walter's suggestion they were brought from the stable, hurdles were made of ropes and boards, and a hurdle race was inaugurated, Walter and Ernest volunteering to act as jockeys. Owing to the diminutive size of the steeds, they could not ride them, so each seized the bridle of his nag, and at the word "go," they started, the young men doing their best, and the ponies, excited by the noise, stretching their legs to the utmost. Amid the laughter and shouts of their admirers, they dashed across the lawn—now Walter ahead; now our hero; now Walter stumbles and rolls on the grass, nearly capsizing his pony; but

there! he is up again in time to leap the hurdle, which costs the pony a violent effort, and away they go again after the other. And so they go over the hurdles, sometimes one a head, sometimes the other, till, after a close home-stretch, Walter is declared the winner by a neck," amidst great applause and waving of handkerchiefs. Bets were now made, the race repeated, and the ladies became quite excited over their favorites, so finally a "flat" race, without hurdles, was arranged between Miss Bates and Jessie, which Miss Bates won in fine style, much to her gratification, and to the honor of her pony.

The autumn wind made free with the loose tresses of the ladies, and their faces were in a ruddy glow with the exercise, so that when the ponies were led away there was a healthy, happy air about the whole party, making a pretty picture with their many-colored dresses on the bright green lawn.

Mr. Going stood at the door and watched them for a long time. His eyes passed from one graceful form to another, from one radiant, lovely face to another; but dark and unpleasant thoughts crowded upon him, and silent tears gathered unbidden, as he gloomily fancied how soon this scene of grace and happiness might close or change to one of bitter tribulation. And he lifted his heart to God in silent prayer, that he might be permitted to leave a home like this, *secured* to his children when his time to bid the world a lasting farewell should come.

And again the thought of the dangers now surrounding him, surged through his brain, and a deep gloom overshadowed his soul.

CHAPTER VI.

BORN A VAGABOND.

'What the devil art thou?"
'One that will play the devil."
KING JOHN.

MR. ANTONIO STILLETTO was alone in his room, whose only article of elegance was a large mirror in an ostentatious gilt frame. The carpet shone in a variety of loud colors, but the material was inferior. The furniture had once been fine, but it was now broken and dirty, and the linen on the pretentious bed was soiled. The whole suited well its occupant; as he sat musing by the window, dressed in a velvet coat, which showed only a sad want of brushing, shirt, collar and cuffs nearly black, while his torn slippers revealed a pair of stockings in a most uninviting condition. His hands seemed to beg for soap and water, though his hair had been dyed a glossy brown that very morning, giving his head that peculiarly vulgar, barber-shop appearance, which distinguishes the true New York snob. The room was strewn around with broken trinkets, old combs and brushes, opened letters, half-torn and crumpled papers, some of them very yellow, others of rosy hue and exhibiting feminine handwriting, while here and there was a carpet-bag or portmanteau, which looked as if broken open by burglars and rifled of their valuables, so confused were the heaps of wearing apparel of all sorts and stages of filthiness which appeared at their gaping mouths.

So the room and its contents suited well the man, and his soliloquy was of a piece with the rest. Mr. Stilletto had the blues, and as he racked his brains to find a way out of his present condition, his sharp face wore a look of unmistakable villainy, which might have led a casual observer to imagine that the plans contemplated by him savored of treacherous craftiness. He had not yet been informed of his appointment as superintendent of the Hobgoblin Manufactory, by its president, Mr. Fatman.

"I wonder what reasons the old fool has," mused Mr. Stilletto, meaning, by that complimentary term, Mr. Going. "I wonder what that old fool has against me! He buys my patents and then refuses to employ me to run the factory. And here I am, all the money spent, and no income to keep me alive. Something must be done, and that soon, for here is that old hag bothering my life out, for my board, and I *do* hate to leave these fashionable quarters! I suppose old Muller would take me in again; but what would some of my friends say if they discovered that this house does *not* be-. long to me, as they are fools enough to believe. Tradespeople, women, gamblers, horsemen, and all trust me because they think the house belongs to me, and my debts are of a nature which requires coaxing and some harmless white lies. Still, what fun it would be to clear out and leave them to open their eyes, and rub their noses, and scratch their heads! But it is not time for that yet. No! no! When the time comes to give them the *grand shake*, I know somebody who will make a big haul before he bids an affectionate farewell to this great city of New York! At the same time, what is to be done now?" he asked himself in great perplexity. "Dress myself in style!" was the answer. "Whereupon I shall feel more like myself and show a bold front. Nothing in the world like a bold front when the main army is weak and the enemy strong, though easily humbugged."

So he commenced his process of Adonizing. He washed himself, that is his ablution began with his hands, and—ended there, for the very excellent reason that his hands alone could be seen besides his face, which had already been treated with *eau de cologne* and bay rum at the barber-shop. He next kicked his slippers into one corner of the room and pulled on his patent-leather boots without even giving a thought to his stockings—for who cares what is *underneath* a shining boot in this world of outward display? Then came a search for something which necessitated a general overhauling of portmanteaus and drawers, and a wild scattering of articles which *should* have been consigned to the washerwoman long before. Mr. Stilletto searched and swore, and swore and searched, until the major part of the carpet was covered with the *subsurface* part of his wardrobe.

Finally, he was successful in his search and triumphantly produced a "*dickey*," *i.e.* so much

of a shirt as appears to the public from under a vest, and which only is a brevet shirt. This adjusted to his liking, a paper collar, the surface enameled to resemble linen, was pinned on. Then came some more searching and some more swearing until he found his cravat, of the genius "butterfly," consisting of a piece of yellow satin, ready made into a bow. This piece of false pretence he adorned with a very large California diamond pin, but his pantaloons were immaculate, his vest was simply sublime, and his enormous watch-chain very well gilt (the watch was silver, but kept well out of sight). When he had brushed his velvet coat he was was ready for a promenade.

A knock at the door. Mr. Stilletto paid no attention to it, for he was giving the "finishing touch" in front of the pier glass in the gilded frame. A double knock. Mr. Stilletto, lost in admiration of himself, disdained to heed it. Three distinct, sharp, angry raps. Mr. Stilletto evidently heard them and also recognized the outsider, for his eyes sparkled with anger and his under lip began to quiver. His finely cut mouth could assume a pleasant, almost fascinating smile when he chose; but now he did not feel very amiable.

"I know you are in!" said a sharp, unmusical voice, through the key-hole.

"Why the devil don't you come in, then?" retorted Mr. Stilletto, with a sneer. "You don't suppose I lock my door against such as *you*, do you, Mrs. Hart?"

The door was opened violently, Mrs. Hart stepped in determinedly, stood still, cast her eyes about the room, and slammed the door behind her. Stilletto had not honored her with a look, but continued the review of his toilet at the mirror. Mrs. Hart was a tall, gaunt creature of fifty, with a very yellow complexion, very black eyes, false curls, and a black lace cap. Determination was her forte. Determination spoke in her voice, flashed in her eyes, and marked her manner, as she now took a chair unbidden.

"Do sit down, Mrs. Hart," sneered Stilletto, his back still turned to her, while he watched her through the looking-glass.

"Thank you, I am seated, sir, and, what is more, I intend to keep my seat."

"I think I will change my dress, after all," muttered Stilletto, quite loud enough for her to hear. "These pantaloons are too heavy for this weather."

"I hope you don't mean—" cried Mrs. Hart, bouncing to her feet.

"To use my room when I want to, in spite of an impudent hussy?" asked Stilletto, turning upon her with an ugly grin. "Why, certainly I mean to."

"Your room, is it? Where is my money? It is not your room until you pay your rent, you—"

"No impudence, Mrs. Hart, or you will make me mad, and then I'll break your neck."

"Pay your rent. I want my money."

"Go to hell," said Stilletto, quietly producing his cigar case.

"I won't stand it any longer," cried Mrs. Hart, livid with rage. "You are being the death of me! This room is like a pig-stye.

All sorts of disreputable characters sneak in here to see you and ruin my reputation."

"*Your* reputation!" said Stilletto, lighting a cigar.

"Yes, sir, I am a respectable woman, and my daughter's grown up, and I have respectable people living in my house——"

"And you want me to marry your daughter, and I won't do it," interrupted Stilletto, in the same quiet tone. As his landlady grew more wrathful he assumed an air of unspeakably calm impertinence, though his under lip quivered more and more, and his color changed somewhat in the course of this conversation.

"You lie," shrieked Mrs. Hart, whereupon Stilletto, without moving a muscle of his face, stepped to the door, turned the key, put it in his pocket, and took a heavy walking cane from a corner. Then he sat down in a chair, facing Mrs. Hart, laid the weapon across his knees and continued smoking, staring directly into her eyes. He had queer eyes. Bold beyond description, shameless beyond conception, crafty and cruel beyond imagination, they spoke his real nature in moments like the present.

Mrs. Hart resumed her seat, as if pushed suddenly by a force she could not resist, and, wavering between fear and rage, gave vent to her mingled emotions by the womanly exponent of both, a copious flood of tears. Stilletto, no whit moved by this display, looked up at the ceiling as if he preferred that view to the one before him.

"You almost choked me in this very room once," blubbered Mrs. Hart, "and I have no doubt you would like to give me an unmerciful beating, though I am only a weak woman——"

"Certainly," admitted Stilletto, nodding assent. "'Unmerciful beating' is *good*, and quite appropriate."

"And then," said Mrs. Hart, ceasing her crying and grinding her teeth, "if I had you arrested and sued you for assault and battery, you would bring that nasty Dutchman, that Tombs lawyer, to help you out, and it would cost *me* money instead of yourself. He is the man that wrote out that accursed lease——"

"According to which you lease me this room for a year, so that you can't kick me out as long as I pay my rent every month."

"Yes, and how have you paid it? You refused to pay—I sued you—got a warrant, and when the thing had cost me twenty dollars,—just as I was going to have you 'kicked out,' as you say, and well you deserve it—you paid up! Oh, oh, my heart is broke with you!" and here the woman, who was generally an imperious, self-willed creature, being entirely conquered by her amiable lodger, burst into a piteous fit of crying.

"If you don't stop that I'll choke you worse than the first time."

"Mrs. Hart, who was a powerful woman, and at least a head taller than Stilletto, became desperate at this inhuman threat. She sprang from her chair and seized the first thing within her reach. It happened to be an empty champagne bottle, for Mr. Stilletto and his friends were fond of that beverage, when in possession of sufficient funds to purchase it. With this weapon she was about to make a fierce attack upon him, when loud knocks were heard at the door. With a look of intense malice at the woman, Stilletto jumped to the door and unlocked it to admit witnesses to the scene—which was just what he wanted. Mrs. Hart, comprehending his motives, was incensed to perfect fury, and threw the bottle at his head. He escaped by dexterous dodging, and the bottle grazed the head of Mr. August Muller, the "Dutch Tombs lawyer," of Mrs. Hart's previous sorry acquaintance, who was just entering the room. The philosopher, with a cry of fear, retreated so suddenly that he knocked against the detective, Mr. Stump, who was closely following him, and they both rolled on the floor, while Mrs. Hart stood trembling from the effects of her passion; but appalled by the mischief she had done. Stilletto threw himself into a chair and burst into a peal of laughter.

"Gentlemen," stammered Mrs. Hart, "really, gentlemen, I must beg your pardon—"

"Which I aint a-going for to grant, for one," cried Mr. Stump, in a rage, as he picked himself up and seized her by the arm. "You air my priz'ner, marm, that's what *you* air." At which Stilletto laughed again; nor did the sight of Mr. Muller, unable to recover his perpendicular immediately, cause his hilarity to cease.

Mrs. Hart expostulated; but for a long while in vain. Mr. Stump declared himself to be an assaulted officer, and showed his badge, and badgered the poor woman until Stilletto felt exhausted with laughter, and stepped up, saying,—

"Stump, let me speak to her a moment." He took her aside, and whispered in his most threatening manner:—

"Now look you! You have insulted me this morning. If I let that policeman take you to the station house, you can just bet it will cost you a hundred dollars to get out again; for you know me, don't you? and with my lawyer for a witness against you, I will make you pay handsomely for your impudence to me. But I'll not be too rough on you. You just sign your name to this bill for last month's rent, and I'll let you off. It's only thirty dollars, so don't be long about it!"

"I'd rather go to State's prison, you—" cried the outraged landlady.

"Stump," said Stilletto, "arrest this woman. Muller and I will appear against her to-morrow. 'Till then, she can sleep in the station house."

"Mercy!" shrieked the poor woman. "Mercy! gentlemen. I'm innocent. Oh! oh! the villain—the brute is going to be the death of me!"

"Will you sign?" whispered Stilletto, fiercely.

"No!" cried Mrs. Hart; but when Mr. Stump approached, she whispered a hurried "Yes! yes! Any thing—my life if you like—and you're sure to have *that* in the end;" and thus Mr. Stilletto paid his rent, in a manner at once novel, and highly satisfactory to his purse and his self-esteem.

"And now," said Mr. Muller, after Mrs. Hart had frantically rushed down stairs—a few words from Stilletto had changed the anger of the new-comers into merriment—" I will tell you what brought us here. *It is all right.*"

" What is all right, you idiot ?" asked Mr. Stilletto, impatiently. " Instead of ogling me in that manner, and grinning like a goblin, damn it. I wish that you would explain yourself at once as sensibly as you can."

" *Hobgoblin is all right,*" grinned Mr. Muller.

" It's all a Limited Liability," explained Mr. Stump, wisely.

" A Joint Stock Company," cried Mr. Muller.

" And Fatman is President, and Anthony Staletoe is Manager," added Mr. Stump.

" Do you mean *me,* by that vulgar name ?"

" I do," replied Mr. Stump, " and I wish you many congratulations."

With a cry of joy, Stilletto rang the bell violently ; and after a few more hurried particulars had been given him, the servant made her appearance. With the first impulse of men of his stamp upon receiving good news, he cried :—

" Run around to Delmonico's, and buy me three bottles of champagne : here is the memorandum on this bit of paper."

" Yis, sur ; but sure, sur, where's the money to pay for it, sur ?"

" That's a fact ; I forgot that. Here, confound it, I haven't got any money. Muller, lend me twenty dollars."

" Come to August Muller for friendship, for advice, for sympathy in affliction or in joy ; but come not to him for money, for he has none."

" You are always poor," said Stilletto, with an oath. " Stump, lend me twenty dollars."

" Detective officers are always flush !" answered that worthy, producing a well-rounded pocket-book. " The trade brings it."

" I dare say it does," answered Stilletto, with a sneer, as he took the note from his fat fingers. " Now run, Bridget, and bring me back the change, or I'll wring *your* neck first, and Mrs. Hart's afterward."

The girl left hurriedly, and soon returned. Stilletto threw off his coat, and the three were soon deep in the more detailed discussion of Hobgoblin and iced champagne. Stilletto's spirits rose.

" Now, then, my star is in the ascendency," he cried. " And we will see if I can't make that old fool of a Going pay for what he has done to me !"

The discussion lasted till daylight began to fade away, when Mr. Muller said :—

" At nine o'clock to-night we are to be at the house of Mr. Fatman, the President."

" I will meet you there, but I have an engagement first. It suits me quite well to go, for my engagement is right on the way."

" What sort of an engagement may this be, you wild youth ?" asked the philosopher.

The " wild youth " laughed a coarsely insinuating laugh ; but vouchsafed no further explanation.

* * * * * * *

Mr. Fatman's hobby was, giving expensive dinners to a few very select friends. Although

he knew how to knit his brows, be imperious, overbearing, and pompous to people below him in station, or at his mercy in the course of business, yet few more jovial hosts could be found.

About seven o'clock, of the evening in which he expected Stilletto, Muller, and Stump, to discuss " Hobgoblin," he was entertaining Mr. Paradise, the hunchback, and another gentleman, Mr. Chip, at dinner.

Mr. Chip, familiarly styled " old Moneybags," by his numerous friends and acquaintances, on account of his immense wealth, was a meek little man, and sat at the table more like a tolerated poor relation than a millionaire, whom Fatman was determined to court and fawn upon.

Mrs. Fatman was dressed up splendidly, with her best set of teeth, and newly-arranged false hair—her figure stuffed out and hemmed in, and laced and screwed up to perfection—her eyes sparkling and large, from a judicious combination of belladonna and eau-de-cologne, altogether presenting the semblance of the handsome woman she *had* been ten years ago. She was the only lady present, and was seated as hostess, opposite her liege lord, whose god—his stomach—pressed lovingly against the table, forgetting entirely about the legs, dangling somewhere underneath.

Those poor legs ! A life of gluttony had long ago slackened their muscles ; and yet they had to carry that lump of a stomach from the house to the carriage, from the carriage to the office, and from one desk in his counting-house to another ;—poor legs !

And yet over that stomach there sat a head whose brain had not yet died from overfeeding, a head that was a match for most heads that were based on healthier bodies ; and as its owner entertained his company, this head rolled about on its invisible neck, with a peculiarly good-natured expression.

" Moneybags " was eating with an anxious face, slowly and carefully, being painfully aware of the road to dyspepsia, which he was traveling. When his enemy warned him of its near approach by a nervous pang, he would quickly gulp some olives or *liqueur* or some other delicacy to " help the digestion," which generally results in adding to the misery the morrow must bring.

Paradise was in high spirits, and consequently more impertinent than ever. As his friends did not enjoy a vast amount of intelligence, unless on business topics, he would not deign to sharpen his sarcasm on their dull hides ; but concentrated his efforts on Mrs. Fatman whom he had always hated.

" I am glad to inform you, gentlemen," cried the fat host, " that I have here some English hare which I imported lately. They are capital. My dear, will you taste some ?"

She did taste some.

" Have you not *hair* enough already, Mrs. Fatman ?" asked the humpback, maliciously.

The lady colored a little, but said nothing, venting her anger on a bone of the hare. Paradise, vexed at not having received an answer, returned to the charge.

" Do not bite so hard, I beg of you, Mrs.

Fatman. You might break those pretty teeth
of yours!"

Enraged at this second attack on her weak
points, Mrs. Fatman retorted.

"It is safe enough to insult a lady, when
her husband is not man enough to chastise the
offender."

"My darling," cried Fatman, in perfect good
humor, "if I did, I might break his back you
know, and that would be—"

"Sad," interrupted Paradise, "for my back
hurts when flogged, I tell you. That is the
difference between my humpback and your
beautiful bosom, Mrs. Fatman, *mine is genuine!*"

"By—, Paradise," cried Fatman, who prided
himself on the good looks of his wife. "That
is too much even from you! Remember that
if you rouse me, I might use my powers as
master of this house, and give you more than
you could swallow."

"Well, now, really I do not feel like leaving
this comfortable seat," said the humpback, seriously, "so we will change the subject. Let
us talk about business. Tell me, Mr. Fatman,"
he added, with mock gravity, "what are the
real prospects of the Hobgoblin Company? I
am to own some of the shares you know, and
would sell them if I could get a good price for
them."

Fatman laughed. Old Moneybags smiled;
but an uncomfortable expression came over his
timid face. A few sneering remarks were
passed on the subject, and then it was dismissed with universal levity.

The dinner progressed, dessert was brought
on and removed, and Mrs. Fatman arose to
leave the gentlemen to their cigars.

"Good evening, gentlemen."

"Why do you go so soon, Madam," queried
Paradise. "Is it an appointment with a
lover?"

How is this? Why did she start, turn
scarlet, and dart him a look which was full of
malice? Had his Parthian arrow struck another weak point? In a moment she had
swept from the room. Paradise was taken
aback. This time he had intended no mischief; but his random shot suggested a good
deal of mischief to his fertile brain. He
glanced sharply at the two others, and saw
they had noticed nothing, and then inwardly
chuckled over his new discovery.

Mrs. Fatman went down into the kitchen.
A man cook, and two waiters, who had been
ordered from Delmonico's along with the dinner, were just preparing to leave the house.

"How did Madame like ze deenay?" asked
the cook, pulling off his cap.

"Oh, very well—are you all through?"

"Oui, madame. Zeese man will come in ze
morning to wash ze deeshes. Bon soir
madame."

When the men had closed the door behind
them, Mrs. Fatman turned to a tidy looking
girl who stood by,—

"Maggy; I suppose the other girls have all
gone out, as I gave them leave?"

"Yes, mum."

"Then you can go up stairs to see that the
gentlemen have all they want."

"Yes, mum. *He is in the closet.*" Off she
went, with a serene countenance.

What did Maggy mean? Mrs. Fatman did not
seem surprised or puzzled by the information;
perhaps she had heard that expression before.
At all events she looked carefully around,
opened the closet door, and out stepped Mr.
Antonio Stilletto, quite cheerfully, and as bold,
as ever. Throwing his arms around the
banker's wife, he kissed her again and again,
without ceremony.

But we will not dwell upon the scene.
Stilletto sneaked out, after awhile as he had
sneaked in—as he always sneaked through life
like an evil spirit of darkness, with all that is
contemptible in his character, except cowardice,
for his unmeasured boldness, saved him at
least from that meanest of vices.

Hardly had Mrs. Fatman readjusted her
head-dress and collar, which had suffered some
derangement, when there came a very light
knock at the door, followed almost instantaneously by the entrance of Mr. Paradise.

"I beg your pardon, madam," he said, "I
hope I am not disturbing you." As he spoke
he glanced in every corner, and under the
table.

"What do you mean, sir?" she asked, with
assumed haughtiness, though she could not repress the color that rose to her cheeks, or
raise her eyes to meet his piercing gaze.

"Oh, nothing at all, nothing at all," he replied, in an off-hand manner, entirely unnatural
in him, for his remarks were generally very
pointed. "I only wanted to get some *Italian
nuts,* for the girl up stairs don't know where
they are, and she told us the cook was out, so
I came for them because I happen to know
the little place where they are kept."

Whereupon he advanced to the closet,
whence Stilletto had issued, and procured what
he wanted, while Mrs. Fatman, stood by in
speechless fear doubting in her bad conscience,
that he might know all about her secret. But
no course was left to her but to speak him fair,
while he in his turn was quite polite, which
was a very suspicious sign in him.

Half an hour later, Mr. Muller arrived, and
Stilletto followed him, little suspected of his
previous visit to the house. These worthies
discussed Hobgoblin in earnest with Mr. Fatman, old Moneybags and Mr. Paradise, and made
plans and settled affairs, although neither Mr.
Going or his son had been notified of the
meeting. But then Fatman had said they
were going "hand in hand you know!"

CHAPTER VII.

WARNING VOICES.

"I love, and honor him,
But must not break my back to heal his finger."
                              TIMON OF ATHENS.

MR. GOING, Senior, was sitting in his office
engaged in nothing beyond his own thoughts.
However, they afforded him quite enough occupation; for many matters of great importance
were now presenting themselves for consid

eration, some pleasant, others more threatening.

He was not busy, the firm had not been busy for many weeks; indeed the old and reliable banking and commission business had been neglected since all their energy and means had been concentrated upon the giant enterprise that was to determine the fate of the house and of the family—Hobgoblin.

It may appear strange; but many business men can corroborate its probability from their own experience—from the time that their legitimate business was neglected, barely looked after when it demanded attention, every venture connected with it, seemed charged with disaster. Without fault or special neglect of any particular person, losses continued to come in until father and son, in a fit of despondency, determined to wind up their affairs and devote themselves entirely to the Hobgoblin factory.

Mr. Going sat musing alone in his private room. This manufacturing business required but little office-work, so the old gentleman watched his cashier, who could be seen at his desk in the next room, working away most assiduously. Knowing that but little work was necessary at the time, he became curious, and finally stepped up to him and tapped him lightly on the shoulder.

"What are you so busy about, Mr. Montant?" he asked, smiling. "In these dull times it is quite mysterious to see you so hard at work."

"I am making out a complete statement of the affairs of the house, Mr. Going," replied our hero.

"What for. For me?"

"Yes, sir, for you. I have to ask your pardon for presuming to undertake it without orders; but, in the face of the great change about taking place, I am sure you will be pleased to know exactly how you stand, on leaving the old *régime*."

"On leaving the old *régime*!" repeated Mr. Going, to himself, and after he had gone to rest that night, the dream-god troubled him by putting that sentence into the mouths of hideous monsters, who kept repeating in warning chorus: "On leaving the old *régime*."

"It is all right, Mr. Montant, and I am obliged to you for your attention."

So saying, Mr. Going once more retired into privacy. He felt very gloomy this morning. The office was unusually still and deserted. Besides the cashier, but one clerk was present and endeavoring to banish sleep by making a list of some papers which did not at all require that operation. The vicious clock in the outer office ticked away determinedly and far too loudly to be pleasant. Where was the life of the once great house? Where were the numerous clerks; where, the constant stream of messengers; where, the prosperous, never-ceasing activity, which had made office hours delightful to him? Martin Bates had proved a traitor to him, and in his place sat a man, whom the old gentleman liked; but also, it must be acknowledged, feared a little. Yes, he *feared* him, for he knew that Ernest Montant was bitterly opposed to this Hobgoblin scheme which was swallowing the whole firm. And

Mr. Going, beneath all his self-imposed hopefulness and confidence in the mining and manufacturing company, felt deep in his heart that his cashier *was right*."

A meek little man, in a plain coat, stepped in.

"Good morning, Mr. Chip," said the old gentleman, rising, with great politeness. I am most delighted to see you!"

"Thank you. Busy?" asked little "Moneybags," whose acquaintance we made in the last chapter, as one of Mr. Fatman's guests, a millionaire, interested in the projected Hobgoblin Mining and Manufacturing Company.

"Not at all, Mr. Chip," said Mr. Going. "Just now business is very dull."

"So I see," replied old "Moneybags," looking about him in an uncomfortable, shy manner. "So I see."

There ensued an awkward pause. Mr. Going became aware that there was an object in this visit. Mr. Chip fully aware of that object, but not exactly equal to its fulfillment, was silently embarrassed. He rubbed his thin knees, he coughed, drew his handkerchief, employed all the expedients he could think of to gain time; but finally, was completely at a loss, and sat there staring before him, a most discomfited individual.

"Dull times, eh!" he suddenly said, in a fit of desperation.

"Yes, sir," answered Mr. Going, who was painfully aware of the little man's perplexity. "You see, my old commission business has slackened considerably of late—in fact—"

"In fact," interposed Mr. Chip, seeing that Mr. Going was brought to a full stop, "in fact, you have *neglected* it a little."

"I am afraid so," answered the other, with a sigh.

"And you have devoted yourself to the manufacturing business instead?" asked Mr. Chip, briskly. The ice was thus broken, for this was the subject which he wished to discuss with Mr. Going.

"Yes, sir," said the latter, with another sigh.

"You know that Fatman has got me to invest two hundred thousand dollars in this new company," said the millionaire again, in a hesitating voice, and looking at every thing in the room except Mr. Going, "and I wish to ask you plainly, before we sign the final papers, whether——ahem!——whether——"

"Well, sir?" asked Mr. Going, with a smile.

"*Whether it might not result more to the credit of us both* if we should let the whole thing *go back*. Nothing is signed yet, you know—"

Mr. Going looked earnestly at him for a moment. Something told him that Mr. Chip was not prompted by any selfish motives in coming to him with this new proposition; but he answered, cautiously,—

"I would not entertain such an idea for a moment, had it come from any one else. There is, undoubtedly, a large fortune in this undertaking."

"Yes, as you say—a large fortune," said "Moneybags," absent-mindedly; "of course there is—at least it is so supposed."

"For we can certainly sell the shares in these speculative times," said Mr. Going, in a tone as if he doubted his own assertion very strongly.

Mr. Chip's manner changed somewhat. He turned his eyes full upon Mr. Going, and bending forward a little, spoke very clearly and decisively.

"The capital stock of the company is two millions of dollars. These two millions of dollars are all placed in *my* hands as a security for the advance I make to the company. The two hundred thousand dollars which I advance go toward enlarging your factory, with the exception of fifty thousand dollars which you receive in cash at once. Besides this sum, you receive notes of the company for which no *individual is responsible*, to the amount of one hundred thousand dollars. These notes *may* be paid, these notes may *not* be paid. I decline to be a trustee, preferring to act only as an outside capitalist. As soon as enough stock is sold to repay me my capital, I relinquish the balance and you get half the shares left. It is to be *hoped* that the company will pay me my two hundred thousand, and you your one hundred thousand dollars; it is to be *hoped* that all the shares will be sold, ultimately, in which case you will make nearly a million by the transaction; but we had a meeting at Mr. Fatman's house a few nights ago, and that young loafer Stilletto was there, while you were not even invited to look on, Mr. Going, and, to tell you the truth, I don't like the looks of the whole thing. Shall we withdraw?"

It is doubtful whether Mr. Moneybags ever spoke so courageously on a subject which was not an ordinary business transaction. He was always sharp, concise, and clear when he defined any thing connected with dollars and cents, but he rarely appealed to principles or cautioned any one. With him it was "yes" or "no," and what he had settled in his mind was "signed, sealed, and delivered" beyond appeal; but his better feelings had been aroused in behalf of his old friend Going, whom he had always respected very highly. Had he been a man of moral courage and strength of character he would not have been satisfied with a mere caution. He would have showed Mr. Going *all* that his clear and impassionate discrimination foresaw in this Hobgoblin business, and while denouncing the whole plan in the strong terms it deserved, would have called upon him to keep himself free from the impending danger and possible disgrace.

A powerful, fearless appeal like this, and from such a source, would have decided Mr. Going at once, for already he felt worried, anxious, and distrustful, and the right word in the right place only was necessary to root him to the right spot. But Mr. Chip was too timid and weak to speak that word or to give it weight, so when Mr. Going simply said that, "after all, there seems no doubt that the stock will be sold," and that he was certain Mr. Fatman would really go "hand-in-hand" with him, the millionaire dismissed the subject, thinking that he had done his duty, and after a few trivial remarks took a frigid leave.

Mr. Going had no time to consider well this "warning voice" which had spoken but half its import, before another visitor arrived.

"Good morning, Paradise" said Mr. Going, extending his hand to the hunchback.

"I have that agreement. Will you sign it?" asked the lawyer with his usual abruptness.

"There is no great hurry, I suppose?" said Mr. Going, with a troubled air, taking the papers from his hands.

"If there is any sense in postponing it, you may do so," replied Mr. Paradise, ill-humoredly. "But since you have gone into this thing against my advice, you may as well sign and be done with it."

"Against your advice?" cried Mr. Going, amazed.

"Why, certainly," replied the other, with a sneer, "and allow me to remark one thing which you ought to have learned long ago from its frequent repetition. I know that I am a natural curiosity, but I object to be stared at like a deformed monkey in a show-shop!"

"You can not put me off with your nonsense," said Mr. Going, good-naturedly, "so have the kindness to tell me when and where you honored me with your advice."

"Were I dealing with a school-boy, I might assume the warning-cane and mount gold-rimmed spectacles, but when I want to caution *you*, in respect to your gray hairs, I can not speak so directly. Ridicule suffices to show you the weak points in a clear light without subjecting me to the set phrase of thanks for good advice, which means simply derision or insult, or, at the best, contempt."

In the meanwhile, Mr. Going had found a letter inclosed in the agreement papers, and opened it for perusal. It was penned in a large, firm handwriting, and read as follows,—

"HOBGOBLIN.

"*Messrs. Going & Son :—*

"DEAR SIRS,—Our mutual friend and counselor, Mr. Paradise, will deliver you the contract upon which we have already agreed, for your signature. I beg of you not to delay this last and consummating act, for we are losing precious time. People's minds are speculative at present. There is an almost unprecedented abundance of money in commercial circles. We must declare a dividend very soon, and sell our stock like hot cakes. Rely on me. We will go hand-in-hand.

Yours, very truly,
"FATMAN."

"He is a clever, energetic man," said Mr. Going, considerably elated and quite reassured by the tone of the letter. "I can hardly withdraw with any decency now, even if I wanted to; and I confess that I have as much confidence in this undertaking as ever, in spite of my good counselor's previous advice, and my friend Chip's caution this morning."

"So Moneybag's has been here too?" asked the hunchback. "Now it might look to an outsider as if he and I were anxious to wash our hands in innocence, and be able to say, in case the thing *should* go wrong, 'We told him so before he went into it; but he would not listen to us.'"

This inconsiderate, reckless speech, quite characteristic of the lawyer, struck Mr. Going very forcibly; but he had fully determined to persist in Hobgoblin, and did not choose to worry himself any longer about the final result.

"I will sign these to-morrow morning," he said, "unless I should find some objectionable points in the wording of the document."

"Read it now, and sign it," said Mr. Paradise.

"I do not see the necessity for this great haste," rejoined Mr. Going, calmly.

"I am here now to correct any thing which may be wrong," persisted the lawyer. "Do you suppose that I have nothing to do but to wait upon gentlemen's leisure and to be sent away to call again, like a tailor's apprentice?"

"I have no time at present," said Mr. Going, "and I prefer any way to go over the agreement and contract with Walter, before bringing any possible defects to your notice."

"All right," said the lawyer, rising in his quick, impulsive manner. "Good day. You can send it signed to my office, to-morrow morning, or you can leave it unsigned and throw it into the waste-basket. Fatman, for one, will be very angry, for he wants to go to work at once. Moneybags is ready to pay his little two hundred thousand to-day, and is going to leave town to-morrow, so you see what your obstinacy is going to do for us in the shape of delay."

"Mr. Paradise," answered the old gentleman, with dignity, "I can not be badgered into committing myself rashly in a matter all-important as this. Your attempt to force me into this signature is not calculated to increase my confidence in the wisdom of signing, or in your friendship for me."

"All right, I repeat," answered the hunchback, opening the door. "You had better let the whole thing go, and back out boldly!"

"Your insults I am accustomed to," replied Mr. Going, proudly, "but you should know, from your experience in this community, that no one who respects himself condescends to be offended by them."

"Good day," said the lawyer, spitefully, and slammed the door after him.

"And this is the beginning of this great company!" thought the old gentleman, bitterly. "Mr. Chip comes here with an honest warning and proposes that we withdraw. The result is that we part considerably estranged. Here's Paradise, who spoke truth when he said he had given me proper advice in his peculiar way, leaves me in a manner which may break an intimacy of twenty years. Fatman himself, I suppose, will no longer be on terms of cordiality with me. God grant that I have not initiated my ruin!"

His eyes, wandering in restless doubt and perplexity from one object to another, finally rested upon his cashier, now visible through the door which Mr. Going had opened again when his visitors had departed.

"Mr. Montant!" called the old gentleman. The cashier approached with several envelopes in his hand. His principal motioned him to close the door and then said:—

"Mr. Montant, you know every item of my business affairs, in the firm and out of it. I wish you now to read over this contract and agreement and give me your opinion of it."

He took it and read the title indorsed on the last sheet:—

"Contract between Going & Son and the Hobgoblin Mining and Manufacturing Company."

Without any change of expression, he gave in return three large envelopes to Mr. Going. They were marked respectively—

"Trial Balance," "Schedule of Assets, Commercial and Personal," and "List of Personal and Commercial Liabilities."

"I completed these this morning, sir," he said, calmly, "and I would beg of you to look over them and pardon the liberty I took in making them out. I had a reason for doing so."

Mr. Going looked at him attentively for a moment.

"Mr. Montant," he asked, almost in a whisper, his voice trembling a little, "you have been my confidential clerk, and there need be no disguises between us. Tell me: after the great losses we have had, the heavy personal outlays I have made, and especially after the sums which the factory has absorbed, do these papers show that we are *perfectly solvent?*"

"Mr. Going, unless secret liabilities have been incurred, of which I know nothing, you are solvent, without a doubt," said the cashier, decisively. "I have estimated your personal property very low, and, I am certain, that should you wind up your affairs, you would come out worth, at least, fifty thousand dollars."

"That is, if I sold my houses and my country place?"

"Yes, sir."

"And without that?"

The other said nothing. There was something unspeakably sorrowful in the old gentleman's voice as he said:—

"I need no answer. I knew it long ago. And not a dollar settled upon Je—"

He ceased abruptly. Our hero understood him. In the days of his great wealth he had not provided for his daughter.

"Read that document, Mr. Montant," he resumed, in a changed manner. "I only wish to know whether you find any trivial objections in it."

Later in the day Montant returned the contract with a bland face. Walter had come in, and, as it happened, all three were too busy to comment at length upon Hobgoblin; but before the principals left the office, our hero said to the old gentleman:—

"Will you allow me to pay you a visit in Fifth Avenue, to-night? I would respectfully ask a private interview with you of some half an hour's duration."

"Certainly," replied Mr. Going, in a tone as if he would prefer to say "certainly not."— "Only you know that we have just moved down from the Priory, and you will find the house in disorder. Will you dine with us?"

"You are very kind, sir, but I can not. If you will permit, I will be there at eight."

CHAPTER VIII.

THE LAST APPEAL.

"Look, what I will not,
That I can not do."
MEASURE FOR MEASURE.

THE energetic clock struck six before Ernest Montant laid down his pen and said to himself,—"Through."

He had finished many a trivial task, which, on other days, would not have required completion. He had squared accounts and made memoranda; in fact, put affairs in a condition to be continued by a *successor*. "Who knows but what this may be my last day in this office?" he said to himself before he left the desk, and he took an affectionate farewell of the little figure of Justice, still standing in front of his portfolio.

The little bronze had seen many a face since it first looked upon Martin Bates, long years ago, but upon none had its metal eyes beamed more kindly than upon the young cashier, for this man, at least, had done his duty to his employers and to himself. It was his duty to himself that led him to seek Mr. Going to-night, and little Justice knew it, and held out her little scales toward him affectionately, as if to encourage him. But he felt as if it was bidding him farewell forever.

Our hero took a plain, substantial dinner before he walked up town. A man bent upon important business must be particular as regards his feeding. He wants a beefsteak or a chop, and a mug of good ale, and perhaps a thimble-full of something stronger, that his flesh may not cloud or embarrass his spirit by becoming weak. So, at all events, our hero thought, and so he acted. Starting, then, for his walk, he lighted a cigar, to aid digestion, and proceeded up Broadway.

"I am not quite easy in my mind about this," he soliloquized. "It looks well, don't it, for a mere boy—and he a comparative stranger —to be showing an old New York merchant his duty and his own interest. The result may bring me to grief in more ways than one. What if I should make an ass of myself, besides losing a good place, with first-rate prospects for the future."

But no after scruples could change his firm-set purpose; nor could he argue himself into the belief that he was not acting up to all his knowledge of truth, right, and justice.

As ho ascended the steps in front of Mr. Going's house, a strange desire came over him. A desire to take particular notice of all trifling objects; of the architectural points of the stoop, of the door, of the windows, as if he should never again cross the threshold. He rang the bell, noticing the shape of the knob, and when admitted by the man-servant, he said "Good evening, James," in a tone which would have suited "Good-bye, James," far better. The hat-stand in the hall, the ban-isters of the wide staircase, the few objects he could see through the open door of the parlors—each seemed worthy of his especial notice to-day, and when he was informed that Mr. Going awaited him in the library, down stairs, he counted the steps as he descended, and was surprised to see how high was the ceiling of the basement, and what an extraordinary fine basement it was, as if he had not seen it before.

He found his employer alone, reading the newspapers. As he entered the room he glanced around, and made a rough estimate of the number of books contained in the shelves that lined its walls, and the price they might bring at an auction. But Mr. Going's kind greeting, and invitation to an arm-chair, and a glass of sherry, brought him to his senses, and he gathered his wits to say well and concisely what he had come to say.

"Mr. Going," he commenced, without hesitancy, "my object is so serious that I had better state it at once. I am compelled to resign my situation in your office."

Mr. Going started; but composing himself, remained silent.

"I have left matters in such a condition, that my successor will find no difficulty in going right on. It was to accomplish this that I made out those statements I handed to you this afternoon. Walter knows that my accounts are correct, for he has not left me as much to myself as he did my unfortunate predecessor. I hope there can be no doubt of the purity of my motives, or of my most heartfelt regret at leaving you. I wish to express my gratitude for all the kindness you have showered upon me, and now I have only to receive your permission to leave, which I am sure you will not fail to grant me in a kindly spirit, though my request is sudden and anomalous."

"Quite sudden and anomalous," repeated Mr. Going, with a hoarseness in his voice.

"And yet it is necessity alone that prompts me," said our hero.

"Mr. Montant," said the old gentleman, after a pause, and with that dignity of tone and manner which never forsook him, "we have known each other well enough, known each other as *friends* well enough, to permit an old man like me to ask your reasons. Of course I should be delighted to hear that you can better your condition; but you are yet very young; and as you probably know no one in this city better able or more willing to advise you, I would ask you, for your own interest, to consult me upon so important a step. Still, I do not press this upon you; and if you think best to let the matter rest here, we have nothing to do but part without enmity."

"Mr. Going," said our hero, slowly, "I dare not give you my reasons, unless you—first of all—assure me that you will not be offended. And you can not well promise that in advance."

"I am quite certain that you will not say any thing to offend me."

"Will you then promise me, in the event of my remarks meeting with your disapprobation, that you will try to forget this interview, and, if you think of me at all, remember only the past, striking from your memory the words which I indeed wish to say to-night?"

There was an anxious earnestness in his tone which, perhaps, warned Mr. Going what was coming; but seemingly determined to hear him out, the old gentleman only knit his brows a little, and answered gravely—

"That I can and will promise; I will only think of you as a faithful and most valued assistant in my office, and an esteemed guest at my house. What you have to say, say frankly, and exhaust the subject, that we may dismiss and erase it forever, if we see fit to do so."

"Very well, sir, I will now speak my whole mind. I came here a poor, friendless boy. The world was all darkness to me, and I had nothing but a deep religious principle—to do right *always*—and a strong faith that God would help me. I was, and still am, determined to act according to the teachings of my conscience, be the cost what it may.

"Alone and inexperienced, without a bond of sympathy between me and another being on this side of the Atlantic, I came into your office, and from the first moment you showed yourself, what you ever since have been, the kindest, the most generous of men. You bound me to you for life. This debt I can never discharge; but if ever the time shall come when I can serve you, you shall find me ready and glad of the opportunity."

The evident reality of the young man's sentiments did not fall unheeded upon Mr. Going's ears. Unable to repress his feelings, he said, sadly:—

"And you prove this by leaving me at a time when you know well that I am in need of your help?"

"That help, sir, should be yours were I never to receive a dollar of remuneration; but well and faithfully as I would serve you, I *can not serve* under the Hobgoblin Company!"

"And may I ask, why not, sir?" inquired Mr. Going, coldly.

"I think, sir," answered our hero, after a moment's reflection, "that since we have entered upon this discussion, I had better unburden myself completely, at once and forever, of all that clouds my affection for you.

· "You propose to sell to the Hobgoblin Mining and Manufacturing Company your farm, factory, and patents, for which they will give you only fifty thousand dollars, in cash. You have already expended several times that amount upon the enterprise, so that this fifty thousand dollars does not make your losses good to any material extent. Besides, you hold the company's notes for one hundred thousand dollars. These notes, however, you will soon see, are perfectly worthless. You dare not sue the company for the value of them, should they never be paid, for a lawsuit would be noised abroad, and stop all sales of shares. None of the trustees have indorsed them, and you can only look for their payment to that misty creature—the company. Finally, you pledge all your shares to Mr. Chip for the payment of his loan of two hundred thousand dollars. This money is not loaned to *you*, and yet you have to give security for its repay-

ment. On the other hand, you make over to the company a large amount of merchantable property—buildings, and real estate, and machinery—all of which has a fixed value. You receive therefor, what? Not even these doubtful shares, for they are in Mr. Chip's hands, and if the trustees choose to treat you wrongfully, it is in their power to keep from paying him his money for years, thus depriving you of your stock, while they can sell off *their own stock* at their pleasure. You may say that they have agreed to hold their stock till you and Mr. Chip are paid every dollar; but, sir, you must know better than that; many pleasant little secret arrangements can be made, which will never reach your ears, by virtue of which they can really sell their stock, and yet prove in a court of law that no *actual bona fide* sale ever took place. I have read the contract carefully, and I say that it is a villainous attempt to place you entirely at their tender mercies. But this is not all."

So far he had spoken in a quiet, dispassionate, but most decided manner. In the quietness of the room every word fell with telling effect upon Mr. Going's ear, and impressed itself upon his mind with the irresistible force of sober truth. He felt uneasy and distressed, and at the last sentence looked quickly at Montant, as if to say, "Is it not enough?"

"This is not all," continued the latter, quickly, though without raising his voice. "There is also a moral reason why I *can not* be the servant of the house which allows itself to be inveigled into a complication of such a nature. The public, Mr. Going, will think that the company pays you two millions of dollars for a property which in reality has cost at the most only three hundred and fifty thousand dollars—first cost, improvements, and all. The trustees give you very little cash, and only one million in stock, and the other one million these trustees *put in their pockets!* Now, sir, if a poor tailor or shoemaker invests his hard-earned savings in Hobgoblin, he buys an interest in what has only cost half what he is told it cost. This I boldly brand as obtaining money fraudulently, and I am sure if these trustees were hauled up before a jury, their action would be called robbery. Of course I know that these things are done every day, and by men of the highest standing in society; but, poor and friendless as I am, I decline to be connected with any such operations. If I remained in your service I should only be a hinderance to you, for if any one asked me about this Hobgoblin Company, I should feel it my duty to tell the truth about it, so I should do better to go away."

"At your age, Mr. Montant," said the old gentleman, still kindly, "one is apt to speak quick words hastily. I do not feel offended by your freedom, but I deem it useless to argue the point, for your resolution is evidently taken. And now that we have done with that subject, will you tell me what your plans are for the future?"

"I don't know, sir," answered our hero, sadly, "I had almost hoped—"

"To shake me in my determination to fulfill an agreement into which I entered, verbally long ago, by telling me that my oldest and best friends in business—"

"Oh, Mr. Going!" cried the other, "they will not be friends any longer. From the moment that contract is signed, you will see a change in them all!"

The old gentleman bit his lips. Here his young clerk was certainly right. Had he not already noticed this change in Fatman, Chip, and Paradise?

"I wish," continued Ernest Montant, now pleading his cause with all the fervid energy he could command, "I wish my hair were gray and my head bowed down by the experience of old age, that you might heed my voice! If you draw a line through that hideous page in your ledger, headed Hobgoblin—if you decide to lose every cent it has cost you, you are still solvent, still well off. Then, sir, give Walter —and, let me say it—give me a chance to work for you. With the glorious old name of your house, sir, we can do any thing! I will work as a broker, as a clerk, in any honorable capacity, and I will not ask you for a dollar but what is absolutely necessary for my livelihood!"

The old gentleman was not unmoved by this speech. Its wisdom was not lost upon him, nor did the glowing enthusiasm of the speaker fail to impress him.

"You seem very warmly attached to this house, Mr. Montant," he said, looking him full in the face.

Our hero colored violently. Perhaps he had misunderstood him, perhaps not, but he answered very promptly,—

"I do not quite comprehend your meaning, sir, but I will anticipate any equivocation by assuring you that my motives are in no respect selfish. Even had I ever presumed to aspire to a closer connection with you; even had I been fool enough to hope for a social distinction entirely above my own condition, all such dreams would long since have ceased, for I am at present engaged to be married."

Mr. Going received this communication, made in self defense, with genuine astonishment, but like the delicately refined gentleman that he was, he made a slight bow in acknowledgment of the information, and said nothing.

"At the same time," continued our hero, I would not allow this or any other tie to keep me from serving you, if I could but be allowed to work in the way my inmost soul has prompted me to point out to you. If I leave this house to-night, without gaining my object, I leave it a poor and lonely wanderer, without a friend in the world but a woman as poor and lonely as I am. If I go it is not selfishness, surely which sends me from you—"

"What is it, then, Mr. Montant?" interrupted the old gentleman. "It is stubbornness. Nay, do not interrupt me, for as you have spoken plainly to me, I should think I might express my opinions too. You have scarce attained the age of manhood, sir, and you tell me that what I can sanction, what my good name can agree to is not worthy of your simple co-operation! I can not argue such a point with you. I can only say that such is not my view of the case, and I appeal to the commercial world of this city, whether a young man like you may or may not allow himself to follow where I lead!"

He paused a moment. Montant felt what would be the unanimous reply of the thousands down town who look up to this man with envy, admiration, timidity, or simple respect, and that in their view, he was now acting a very strange part in refusing to be convinced by Mr. Going's kindness and condescension, for it was nothing less for him to listen to such a conversation. But call it eccentric, call it boyish, call it what you please, he stuck to his point, keeping a stern silence after Mr. Going's last words.

"Ernest," continued Mr. Going, in a changed tone and manner, "stay with me! Do not leave me, for if you do, we shall both regret it! I have opened to you my heart and my house; I have treated you as a friend, almost as a son! And now, when I want help, you desert me, and spoil your own career. You are throwing away your best opportunities, and alienating those who should have become dear to you."

Never before had he called our hero by his first name, and there was a something in his voice, that showed that he was growing weak, that he wanted help; that he had leaned upon and cherished this boy, and the loss of him was a pang which he had no longer the power to hide beneath his grand dignity.

Ernest Montant's eyes filled with tears. He knew that argument had lost its power; that by no human means could he prevail upon his venerated friend to give up this accursed scheme, which alone kept them asunder, and he was much moved by this appeal made to his heart. He arose quickly, agitated beyond mere conventionality, seized Mr. Going's hand, and with a faltering voice, said:—

"The time will come when I can prove to you that those last words of yours come home to my heart, and then will I serve you faithfully. But stay with you in this damnable enterprise, I can not. I have seen my father ruined, worse than ruined, and I have sworn to choose a different path in life from that which led him to misery, as little deserved, as you in your kindliness and generosity, deserve the fate which I see gathering like a black cloud over your future. Since we cannot agree, let me say farewell, and believe me when I say that, next my own father, I love and honor you."

He turned to the door. Mr. Going's face had resumed its expression of calm, self-reliance. He arose stiffly from his chair.

"Since it must be, farewell. Shall we see you to-morrow?"

"I think not, sir. I shall stay in New York a few days, and will be on hand should my successor require help or explanation, which, however, I can not imagine he will."

"And about your salary? Have you drawn it?" asked Mr. Going, in his business tone.

"I have addressed a few lines to Walter, asking him to send the amount due me, as soon as he has examined my accounts. Good night, sir!"

"Good night, Mr. Montant!"

Our hero was gone. Mr. Going listened to his quick steps up-stairs, and sank back exhausted into his chair.

"They all leave me," he muttered. "Old Chip, then Paradise, followed by Fatman, and finally, this strange boy! I don't know why, but this last loss seems the heaviest!"

Thoughts fly quickly while the mind is on the wing, and as Ernest Montant strode toward the door which was to close on him forever, he thought bitterly:—

"Accursed be this craving for riches, which distorts honor and integrity. Twice accursed be the evil genius of this age, which leads men to strive for a fortune in a day, or to retrieve lost wealth by *luck* instead of *work!* Thrice accursed be the spirits of wanton speculation, luxury, and recklessness, which are undermining all respectability and clearing the way for King Hazard to hold high rule!"

He reached the parlor door, which stood wide open. He looked in, and there she sat, waiting for him perhaps all this time. There she was, in the beauty of her youth, with her black hair surrounding her marvelously lovely face, with a light in her eyes as she advanced toward him.

"Miss Jessie," he said, hurriedly, "I really did not expect to meet you here."

She was trembling violently; her look, her voice, her gestures betrayed her emotion. "You have been talking with papa," she said. "I heard the voices. You have had a quarrel. You are going to leave us. I know it all."

"You are right, Miss Jessie," he answered, sadly. "I must say, good-bye!"

"And all about Hobgoblin, is it not?" she asked, despondingly.

"All about Hobgoblin," he answered, fiercely.

"Can it not be mended?" she cried, impatiently. "Remember your promise to me! I feel in my heart that all is going on wrong,—all is black, black as night! Remember your promise to stay by papa in the hour of need."

"I keep human promises, humanly," he answered, bitterly. "I have gone the length of my rope. I can do no more."

For an instant, one only, she looked him full in the face with her large black eyes, her color all gone from her, and then she turned away.

"Can you forgive me?" he cried, no longer master of himself.

"Go," she muttered, her face still averted.

"Can you send me thus from you," he asked, in despair, "without a word of kindness, or of comfort, when, God knows, I need it."

No human eye saw her face, as she extended her hand to him without turning around.

"If you mean what you say, *stay*. I know papa has not been unkind to you."

"Indeed, indeed, no!" he cried, "but yet there are differences—"

"Go, then," she repeated, bitterly, at the same time withdrawing her hand.

He stood a moment, concentrated all his will-power in one grand effort to force her to turn her face to him; hesitated, wavered, and then seized his hat, and was gone in an instant.

The sound of the closing front door seemed to rouse her from her attitude of repression. She stood a moment unmoved, then rushed toward the door, and with a love that knew no more control, cried,—

"No! no! no!"

She checked herself. Her own violence had brought her to her senses. She turned round with alarm and dread, and there—there, not five feet from her, stood her father, with his face as pale as death.

With a loud sob she threw herself into her father's arms, and they held each other in such an embrace as would have moved even Ernest Montant, could he have seen it.

The skies were draped in the black garments of the first wintry storm. The streets were cheerless and deserted, while the cold blast and icy-penetrating drizzle suited well the emotions which agitated our hero's breast as he left that house. In one short hour he had again become a wanderer, an outcast from what had been a bright and cherished home to him, just as he had once left the house of his father and mother.

He felt miserable and dejected, absolutely friendless and homeless as the veriest vagrant, and yet he should not have felt so. As he became calmer, there came to him the thought of Josephine. Had he not an asylum then? He who called himself homeless—he who called himself friendless—did he not possess a woman's heart, and possess it *entirely?* Was there not one breast which beat for him and him alone who thought himself *forsaken.* And the more he thought of Josephine Van Strom, the more settled became his purpose to seek her in his misery, and never to part from her again.

CHAPTER IX.

REUNION.

My life upon her faith."
                              OTHELLO.

READER, have you been in the State of Massachusetts, and are the charms of her scenery familiar to you? Have you roamed through the woods and over the hills, along the streams and through the fields, fascinated by those charms of nature that do not aspire to the awful, but content themselves with enchanting one by their soft and smiling loveliness?

On a high bluff which broke the onward course of one of those rivers and turned it aside by a sharp curve, so that the view on all sides was varied and picturesque, there stood a large wooden house, somewhat pretentious in its architecture, and well suited to the grotesque beauty of the spot. This was the home of John Jacob Van Strom, Junior, and had been purchased by him as a retreat where he could live very quietly and modestly with his faithful wife, our old friend Bella, and his sister-in-law the handsome widow.

On an afternoon, late in the fall, an afternoon glowing in the last effort of nature to make the earth beautiful once more before resigning it to the cold embrace of winter, we find the two sisters—for sisters they were—in law, in sympathy, in confidence, and in love, sitting upon the veranda and enjoying the view.

"The village looks charming from here," said Josephine. "The little white houses peeping out between the trees or standing in clusters, scattered over the landscape like innocent sheep in a green meadow, and the church with its belfry and little gothic windows shining in the sunlight, an emblem of sweet simplicity."

"Are you happy here, Josephine?" asked Bella, looking wistfully at her sister. The widow had not changed, only the old expression of Raphael's Madonna came over her noble face oftener than before. And now, as she gazed upon the village, and out into the blue hazy distance beyond, and watched the current of the river as it flowed away from her, this peculiar resemblance to the Madonna was very noticeable. "That river flows to the sea," she thought, "and on that sea there is a certain port, a city of a million or more inhabitants, and of that million I know *one*," and the thought gave her life, hope, happiness.

"Shall I guess what you are thinking of?" asked Bella, gently, stealing Josephine's warm hand away from her lap and holding it in her own.

The handsome widow smiled and colored, but answered in the deep metallic-voice we have heard before,—

"I don't deny it, dear; I am thinking of *him*, but not now, only, *always!* So you see there is nothing so wonderful in my present dreaming."

"Josie," said Bella, softly, "do you think he will come to you soon?"

"I don't know, dear. I am anxious, worried beyond description. He has not written to me in some time, and there was more of business than of love in his last letter. Bella, I think it looks dubious when our lovers write to us that business is so absorbing. It *may* be that business does increase to monstrous proportions; but it looks as though love had dwindled correspondingly, till it has become a mere secondary consideration."

"Very true," said Bella, with a strange smile.

"And I can't feel as confident of his love, as—reliant as—I would like, somehow," said Josephine, with a sigh.

"And so you don't think he will come," said Bella, mischievously.

"What should make him come?" asked Josephine sadly, "He is a beggar and I—"

"And you are the sister of an immensely rich woman," said Bella, in the best of good humors.

"What do you mean me to understand by such a change in the tone of your remarks?" said Josephine, turning her eyes full upon her sister-in-law. "This is the first time that you have ever favored this love affair of mine with encouraging remarks. You used to scold me, call me a rash, impetuous creature, and tell me that I ought to be ashamed to bestow my love so soon, and prate away about my attractions and fascinations, which, practically, do *not* lay the world at my feet or even the smallest part of it!"

"Is *he* not even a small part of the world?" asked Bella, merrily. "You strange woman! To love a man who is nobody. He is not a part of the world? Oh! Josie, is he an angel?"

Josephine leaned over to her and gave her a warm kiss.

"Now just hear this," continued Bella, in the same tone. "This woman is trying to make me believe that she does not know how beautiful and bewitching she is."

"Scoff away," said Josephine, laughingly.

"I am going to speak seriously now," rejoined the tailor's daughter with a sedate face. "I have come to the conclusion that you two love each other sincerely and truly, and my majesty is graciously inclined to favor the match."

"Have you news from him?" asked Josephine, quickly. Her face colored crimson in an instant. She aproached Bella, put her arms around her, kissed her, and with tears already starting to her eyes, repeated in passionate entreaty,—

"Have you news from him? Tell me; oh, tell me. Do not keep me in this suspense. Something tells me you have!"

"I have," answered Bella, calmly.

"Then tell me—oh, how can you be so cruel!"

"Do you think he will come to you soon?" asked Bella, looking slyly aside from where they were sitting.

Josephine, whose intuition told her instantly that something was coming, became suddenly pale, a vague fear possessed her heart, and almost stifled her voice as she gasped,—

"Is the news bad. Tell me, for heaven's sake. I can bear it. Is he—"

"Sit down, you little goosy, and compose yourself," answered Bella, smiling, "for you may as well. He wrote me that he was coming on here."

"Thank God, cried Josephine, tears of joy and gratitude streaming down her cheeks. "But why didn't he write to me?"

"Because he had a vague idea that I was a sensible, honest woman, and he first wished to be informed whether he had any rivals to fear, or whether your heart was still all his own, so that he might receive it at your hands without a hinderance."

"*He, rivals!*" cried Josephine, clasping her hands, over her face, "a hinderance, between him and *my* heart!"

Touched by the earnestness of her exclamations, Bella now approached, and kissed her warmly.

"Tut, tut," she said, "I understand you now and I am satisfied. Compose yourself, for he may be coming soon."

"Soon?" cried Josephine, radiant with joy, "Tell me, tell me quickly, darling, when is he coming?"

"You must not speak so loud, Josie," answered Bella, with a bright and happy face "for some one may be listening," and again she cast a sly glance behind her.

Josephine followed the look. The form of a man had emerged from the house, and now stood a few feet from them. She started to her feet, looked at him for a moment, and with a cry of ecstasy, rushed into his arms.

"My darling, my own lover!" was all she could mutter, as she nestled her head upon his breast and wound her arms around him, holding him in a passionate embrace, as if never again to release him.

He could not say a word. He had heard the latter part of their conversation, and all his sorrows, doubts, and fears vanished in the presence of *such love* as this woman had confessed for him. The gallant tailor's daughter, she of low degree, but high and noble mind, stood by with moistened eyes and a smile so bright and happy, that it lent radiance and even beauty to her plain face.

"I have you! I hold you! whispered Josephine, still clasped tightly in his embrace

and half delirious with joy. "Will you, can you again leave me, darling?"

"No," said Ernest Montant, kissing her upturned lips and drinking in the luxury of love in the looks they exchanged. "You may take me as I am, cast away by the world; forsaken and alone, a wanderer and a stranger to all but you."

"And me," said the tailor's daughter, softly.

"Bella," cried Josephine, in the fullness of her heart, extending one hand to her, while, with the other, she still clung to him, "as I pray for all that I need and receive, so shall I pray to God, all the rest of my life, that he may bless you forever!"

"Amen," said our hero, solemnly, and the three sat down together and watched the sun sinking in the west, and the moon rise softly over the hills. They talked of all that friendship and hearty good-will gave them in common, until Bella said that she had to go in and see her husband. So at last the lovers were left alone to enjoy the beauty of the earth, this glorious night, and the bliss of the heaven which was in their hearts.

BOOK III.—FELONY.

CHAPTER I.

JOHN VAN STROM MAKES HIS WILL.

"Be comfort to my age! Here is the gold:
All this I give you."—As You Like It.

ALL hail to the woman that can make a loving study of her husband's imperfections! All hail to the *worker* where others would *weep*; for she will find pleasure where others would only reap bitterness!

Bella Van Strom loved her husband, not poetically, not romantically, but with the whole integrity of her honest soul. Her great trials had wrought a great change in her character. She had been a wild, ambitious, venturesome girl; but when her last and greatest madcap freak, her marriage, as recorded in the early part of this book, had forced her to face such consequences as the fatal masquerade at the Priory, her gratitude to him who had made her life more than she had ever expected it could be, and her sense of duty developed traits of character heretofore unknown, and, as we have seen, she bravely did what she could, becoming the most devoted of wives, the most careful of nurses, the most faithful of friends, and the most conscientious manager of her husband's affairs.

As she had risen, so her unfortunate husband, John Van Strom, declined, sunk into

perfect subserviency to her stronger organization, became like a doll, seemed to have no intellect of his own where mind should compete for the mastery. Yet John had not lost his mind, but, by the time we again meet them, Bella had succeeded in gaining complete control over it, repressing its mischievous outbursts, while encouraging all that was left him of reason and sentiment. Nor was she afraid of a return of the frenzy of intoxication to which we have seen him subject, for she had invented a harmless but effectual remedy, in case entreaty was too weak or circumstances too unfortunate, to prevent his inebriation. She provided herself with a harmless narcotic which she mixed in a glass of wine when he insisted on taking too much, and so stole away his senses while she watched by his side until he awoke, a weaker and a wiser man. But these occasions grew more and more unfrequent, and we find them a most peaceable and well-behaved couple, "the gray mare proving the better horse," as John, in his more lucid moments, knew perfectly well, and admitted with a contented laugh, for he loved his wife, and, unlike many people of more wits, was not ashamed to acknowledge her superiority.

The day after the arrival of Ernest Montant at Van Strom's, they were a merry party at the breakfast table. John, presiding as host, presented no very imposing or dignified appearance, but he was cheerful and comparatively bright in his mind. Our hero noticed that he had grown much older in his face since his father's death, and really, to judge by his scant and fast-blanching hair, his sunken cheeks, his sallow complexion, the wrinkles that seamed his face and surrounded his shapeless mouth, he might have been considered an old man. Though much thinner in flesh than ever before, and though he stooped very much, he rarely complained of bad health; while Bella was too much occupied in watching his mental improvement to see that, judging from externals, she might expect to be a widow before many years had elapsed. John had no idea of the true state of affairs between Josephine and his new guest, but, as he really liked them both, it seemed the proper thing to chaff them all through breakfast; which the handsome widow, radiant with beauty and sparkling with joy, accepted very graciously, to the evident enjoyment of Bella and our hero, so that John, delighted at his success, felt highly pleased with every one else. He called Josephine "my dear sister," and our hero "my esteemed friend," and his wife "my darling girl," and was so lively and amiable that, before breakfast was over, Bella had tears of joy and gratitude in her eyes.

After the meal was concluded, Josephine and her lover decided to take a walk, leaving the master of the house alone with his wife, thus giving Bella an opportunity which she had eagerly watched for—a chance to talk half an hour with him, while he was in the best possible humor, on a subject of great importance.

They were sitting by the window. She was leaning her head on his shoulder and had taken his hand, while an expression of cheerful contentedness softened his worn features.

"John," she said, after thinking in silence a few moments how best to approach the subject, "John, I want to talk business."

"Talk any thing you like, Bella," he replied, kindly. "Upon business, any how, I can answer you in a manner worthy of your great talents and intelligence, for I know something about business."

Now, although he said this with a childish pride, it was not untrue. Notwithstanding his shortcomings on other points, John was what might be called a naturally shrewd business man, and in matters where dollars and cents alone were concerned, he rarely went wrong or was deceived.

"Well, then, John, you know that you are very rich!" said Bella, without changing her position, and speaking in a certain affectionate and soothing tone to which he could listen for hours without becoming wearied.

"Yes," said he, "I would not be surprised if I could sell my property, real and personal, for something over two millions of dollars. That is, my mortgages, my railroad bonds, my houses in town and my place here, besides my silver and your diamonds."

"Which I never wear," said Bella, laughing. "But never mind that, I appreciate your kindness just as much. Well, now, John, I wish you would make a will."

"What for, Bella? We have no children;

Oh, if you could only have a boy to inherit the old name and all this money!"

"You know that is impossible, John," replied Bella, gently, "so let us be thankful for such happiness as God has given us, without hankering after the impossible."

He said nothing.

"Will you make your will, John?" she asked, after a pause.

"I don't see what you want with a will, I don't mean to die, and the property will all go to you anyway. Do you want me to die right away, and do you want to be sure of the—?"

"John," she interrupted, seeing that he was growing ill-tempered, rapidly, "John," taking both his hands and catching his eye, in an imploring, kind but steady glance, "you don't mean what you say!"

He looked at her a moment. Even to him, those eyes full of tenderness, spoke convincingly, and his rising choler was exorcised. He took her to his heart and held her there in a long embrace which reassured her.

"I want you, John, to leave half of all your property to Josephine!"

He stared at her in utter bewilderment, but she continued, quietly,—

"You know how your father treated her all his life, and finally left her penniless, although the widow of his first-born. Will you make up for the error of your father? This is the reason why I want you to make a will. You have made her a small allowance now, and I can not for the life of me see why she is not entitled to half your father's estate. Mind I don't ask you to give her any thing now, unless—"

"Unless what?" said John, slightly bewildered.

"Unless she should marry!" said Bella, slyly.

"Well, when she gets married, we'll talk about it," said John, assuming a business tone, "and I can not see why I should leave her any property in my will, because if I die—nay, don't be distressed, I am talking business now—if I should die, then you can give her what you choose, you know."

"But I would rather have it the other way," said Bella, "because she is *entitled* to her portion, and I would much rather she should receive it at *your* hands than from my charity. I would give it to her any way."

"Well, it is all the same, one way or the other" rejoined John, slightly impatient.

"Yes, dear, but is it not *right* for you to do as I say? John, remember that we must all die, and do not leave an act of justice undone when opportunity offers you the chance to do it."

"And do you think, Bella," asked John, simply, "that we can die the more easily for doing what is right?"

"Indeed I know it!" she replied, fervently.

"And have I always tried to do right by you, Bella?" he asked with a trembling voice and quivering lip. "You know that I love you dearly, but have I always tried to do right by you?"

"You have been nothing but kind, and generous and noble-hearted to me," she answered, weeping, "and I shall pray to God all my days to reward you for it!"

Again for some time they were silent, but Bella, as she held his poor weak head to her bosom, prayed an earnest prayer, a prayer of faith and hope, that she might see the day when the darkness should be lifted from his soul, which in moments like the present one seemed not far distant, and from that day John seemed more docile and manageable. In the meanwhile, before that interview ended she carried her point, and after lunch (which they eat alone, the two lovers being still away in heaven knows what part of the country) a messenger was dispatched to somebody who lived within half an hour's ride, and two hours later a tall form darkened the doorway of the library where John and his wife awaited him. It was their legal adviser, none other than ex-Judge Bates, the brother of the disgraced and discharged cashier of Messrs. Going & Son.

He was reputed the handsomest man of his age in all the country round. Very tall and well proportioned, his imposing figure was well sustained by a stateliness of manner almost too aristocratic for a citizen of this free and democratic country. He wore no beard, his features were finely cut in a noble mold, his complexion exceedingly delicate, piercing black eyes and long snow-white locks, falling down to his coat collar, intelligence enthroned upon his lofty forehead, austerely dignified, calm pride, and self-reliance in every gesture, and every slow spoken word of his clear ringing voice; this was Judge Eben Bates of Massachusetts.

"Judge," said John Van Strom, after the usual greetings, "I have asked you to step up here because I want to make my will."

"I am at your service, sir," answered the lawyer. "Do you wish your wife to be present?"

"I think the law does not prohibit her attendance?" said John, sharply.

"Not that I am aware of, sir." So they proceeded to business, John had prepared a list of his property, and divided it equally between his wife and Josephine Van Strom. Judge Bates, at this point, opened his eyes as wide as his dignity permitted and glanced sideways at Bella with strange and irrepressible wonder at her happy smile.

"According to this document, sir," said Judge Bates, sonorously, "your wife receives only half your property."

"Quite right, old gentleman," said John leaning back into Bella's arms, which awaited him.

"Quite right, and very satisfactory, sir," corroborated Bella, tersely.

"Before it escapes my memory," said Judge Bates, laying down his pen (for he had been taking notes), with apparent indifference, "I would beg leave to interrupt you a moment. You remember that matter of fifteen thousand dollars, which you were good enough to advance me upon a second mortgage upon my house?"

"A *second* mortgage, sir?" asked John, quickly, coloring with sudden astonishment. "I thought it was a *first* mortgage."

"I told you distinctly, sir, that I had already given a first mortgage on my house to another party," said the old lawyer, in a tone of injured innocence.

"I did not understand it that way, sir," rejoined John, sharply. "You said that you were about paying off a mortgage which had become due, and out of respect to you, I did not have the county records examined!" and John would have said more had not his wife nudged him to control himself. Ever sensible to her admonitions he stopped here, though his face betrayed his angry feelings on the subject.

"I am astonished at your misinterpretation, sir," answered Judge Bates. "That first mortgage is going to be paid off and you may consider yours a *first* mortgage with impunity, I used the term *second* for the sake of adhering to the present *legal* condition of the case!"

"All right," said John, ill-humoredly. "Let us resume our business."

"You do not wish to leave *any thing to any one else?*" asked Eben Bates, pointedly, peering out from beneath his bushy white eyebrows at his client.

With a woman's quick intuition Bella thought that he was fishing for something to be left to him—perhaps fifteen thousand dollars to pay off his own mortgage, and at the thought she could hardly conceal her anger and loathing for the old lawyer, in spite of his white hair and venerable countenance.

"Nothing to any one else," said John, dryly.

"Now please to name your executors," said Judge Bates, resuming his pen without betraying any feeling of disappointment.

"For executrix, Bella Van Strom, my wife, for executor, added as an assistant and adviser to her, Ernest Montant of New York."

"How do you spell that name?" asked Judge Bates, between his teeth, as he bent over his paper to write it down; and after it was correctly written, he said—

"May I be permitted to ask, considering my many years and professional experience, who is this Mr. Montant? Considering my position as your solicitor, sir, I think it my duty to advise you to appoint some lawyer, one in whom you repose trust and confidence, to the all important office of executor!"

"Mr. Bates," answered John, quickly, "you may either write out my last will and testament, or you can leave it alone. I have not asked any counsel from you, and if you think you can push *yourself* into this position of executor, you have got into the wrong box with me, I assure you."

"Such words as those you have spoken, sir," said Judge Bates, with an angry flash of his black eyes, "are unbecoming for you to utter, or for me to hear! I trust my age and reputation will sufficiently protect me from such vile accusations as you have taken the liberty to express. Were it not for the respect I have for your old name, and the memory of your father, I should certainly leave this room at once, never to return."

Again Bella had to interfere, and make peace between them. As the old lawyer was not really anxious to make good his declaration of war, and John's rising temper was easily repressed by her experience, she succeeded. The consequence was that Judge Bates exhibited once more his better nature, and John regained his good humor, even inviting his late opponent to stay to dinner, which the old lawyer gladly accepted. And so John Van Strom's will was made.

"I am really glad to accept your invitation," said Judge Bates; "for my daughter Bessie is not at home to-day, and I am miserable without her company."

"Your brother, Mr. Martin Bates, is at your house, I believe," said Bella, carelessly.

"Yes, ma'am; but he and I have never been of the same tastes or dispositions. I gave him an asylum at my house because he was poor and friendless. I will always extend hospitality to those who are in need; but sympathy and affection can not be bestowed from a mere sense of duty upon objects of general charity."

Josephine Van Strom and our hero came home to dinner. The blush caused by fresh air and exercise was on her cheeks; certainly it was *only* the blush of healthy exertion out of doors. Maybe her face unconsciously betrayed the raptures of love which had been hers this happy day. Bella alone knew the real cause that made her eyes brighter, her cheeks redder, and her expression so radiant with happiness, for their engagement, their love was not as yet promulgated. So, when Bella winked at Josephine in her mischievously sly manner, the fair widow could not choose but blush, while Ernest Montant vainly endeavored to conceal the fact that he was in very high spirits, and mightily proud of some new thing. He soon found an opportunity to take Bella aside and whisper to her:—

"Good luck, sister-in-law! I am poor, and deserted by nearly all my old friends; but to-day I feel able to fight the whole world!"

Here John Van Strom came up with Judge Bates, and introduced the gentlemen to each other. When this little ceremony was over, the old lawyer turned to his host, with a look of astonishment, at the evident youth of the appointed executor, and asked:—

"Is it possible that this gentleman is Mr. *Ernest* Montant, sir?"

John Van Strom looked a moment at our hero, as though to be sure of his identity; then placing both hands behind his back, answered, with a decided bow and decisive tone, "Yes, sir."

The old lawyer did not seem inclined to court the acquaintance of John Van Strom's executor, *in futuro*, and Ernest Montant, although much impressed by the noble appearance of the old gentleman, was not the man to make advances without encouragement. All the more did Judge Bates devote himself to Josephine Van Strom at dinner, bestowing upon her a hundred little marks of attention and gallantry, which she, being in a very good humor, received very graciously. Our hero muttered,—

"Hang his extraordinary politeness. If he were twenty years younger, upon my word I'd

be jealous. Of course gallantry in old gentlemen is very well to a certain extent, but I rather think Judge Bates carries it a little further than any one else I ever saw. Positively, it seems to me more like foppishness."

And then Martin Bates came before his memory's gaze, as he had sat opposite him in the English club-house, when narrating the scenes of his life, given in a previous chapter; and with the voice of the old cashier still ringing in his ears, as he execrated his heartless brother, he gazed upon the judge's innocent face, and said to himself,—

"This is the man who is accused of betraying his brother,—this man, with every mark of high-toned dignity,—of having permitted that brother to suffer a terrible disgrace for crime which *he*, this white-haired emblem of virtue and honor, had committed. Is it possible? Did Martin lie?"

And as he contemplated the stately figure before him, and noted the expression of the noble face, he doubted no longer but that Martin had indeed lied.

CHAPTER II.

TWO BROTHERS.

"I know her answer."
"What?"
"She will not."
"The fouler fortune mine, and there an end."
TAMING OF THE SHREW.

WHEN Martin Bates left the office of Going & Son he felt as though every door was closed to him that might have led another to competence or support, and wandered around the city like an accursed spirit.

Several days afterward Judge Bates, all unconscious of his brother's ill-fortune, was sitting at tea with his daughter, at his own house, in Massachusetts. Miss Bessie, only child of his first wife, whom he had married in England, under the circumstances related by Martin in his confidential mood, to our hero, assumed the duties of housewife. In these duties she was assisted by an old housekeeper, well-bred, and deeply attached to the family. No wonder, then, that Miss Bessie's father was loath to encourage her marriage. No wonder that when Walter Going paid his addresses to her the old lawyer was glad to find in the young gentleman's acknowledged recklessness, rather wild manner, and loose views, a valid excuse to oppose the match. But reason proposes and love disposes, and the two had secretly reached the relationship in which we have seen them at the Priory; in fact, they were engaged without her father's knowledge, or slightest suspicion.

Judge Bates was the most rigid observer of moral principles in the village, and said a long extempore grace before each meal. In this exemplary devotion he was this night interrupted by a ring at the front door. The servant entered with a perplexed face.

"An old man outside, sir. I don't know who he is; sure he don't look like a gentleman, and not like a blag-gard, saving your presence; and he want's to see the Jidge, ma'am." So Judge Bates forgot the half-finished grace, and went to the door.

He staid away five minutes, ten minutes, half an hour. Miss Bessie had tea removed. She then sat down by the fire—still necessary in the evening, though by the calendar it was almost summer—and listened to the storm which was howling around the house, and rattling in the chimney. Still her father did not return. A horrible feeling of anxiety came over her; but she did not deem it prudent to go and search him out; so, still she waited and listened. It seemed to her that there were unwholesome voices in the air; a vague presentiment of evil possessed her; by degrees she grew nervous, and finally decided to go and see what was keeping him so long; but as she arose to go to the door, it opened, and her father appeared, pale and agitated. He was not alone; an old man followed him, with tottering steps, who, without speaking a word, or raising his downcast eyes, seemed to grope his way to the fire, and there crouched, shivering. Bessie looked at him with a strange awe. His sunken eyes, his attenuated features, his shreds of uncombed gray hair, his trembling limbs, his shabby coat, wet with rain, his whole appearance repulsive, frightened her; but there was something familiar in it all. She stood, affrighted, gazing and wondering, until her father, who had regarded the stranger with a cold, disdainful look, broke the spell by saying, sternly:—

"This is your Uncle Martin, Bessie, of whom I have sometimes spoken to you. You can make his acquaintance to-morrow; at present you will oblige us by leaving the room, for we have business of importance to discuss."

She advanced a step as if to welcome her uncle; but Martin Bates did not look up, or seem to be aware of her presence. So she timidly left the room to spend the rest of the evening in fear and anxiety, and then to bed, to dream of Uncle Martin, in the most horrible manner, for he appeared to her in the most un-uncle-like shapes, and oppressed her with the most ingenious tortures of dream-land.

Judge Bates took a seat opposite his brother, and both stared silently into the fire for a long while until the servant brought in a bottle of brandy and some hot water, which she placed upon a table between the two and left the room.

"I had to send to the village for this," said Eben Bates, ill-humoredly, "for not a drop of the vile stuff is ever kept in my house, sir."

"I would not have asked for it, brother, were I not chilled through and totally exhausted. Although I habitually use spirits, yet I respect your abstinence."

"Which should be made law!" said Judge Bates, sternly. Martin nodded demurely.

"You are celebrated for all the virtues," he said, slowly, still keeping his gaze fixed on the fire. "Whether you have true charity in your heart, is a question between you and your God!"

"We are judged by what we do," answered the elder brother. "I have devoted myself to the promulgation of high moral ideas."

"Promulgation by force?" queried Martin, in a low voice.

"If necessary, yes!" "I would make total abstinence a law! At any cost I would make slavery illegal! I would—"

"Stop; would you break the chains of the slave, knowing that he would die under the operation?"

"Dead or alive, slavery must cease to pollute this free soil!"

"The liberty of the grave," said Martin. "Do you know, Eben, I sometimes doubt that you have true charity, true love for poor humanity?"

"I am a man of principle!" answered the other. "My life is devoted to religion and to the improvement of the public morality."

"And how about the correction of private immorality?"

"I wash my hands of it. Let those who fall from grace look to themselves!"

"Eben," said Martin, impetuously, "what I hear from you is the cant of religion based on heartlessness. We can dispense with the mask when we are alone, for I know you well. You speak of charity? You may subscribe to the meeting-house and abolition societies; you may be at the head of the poor-houses and prisons; but I know you would have turned your poor brother away from your door this night had you been sure the world should never have known it."

Judge Bates's dark looks were confirmation strong enough; but he said with some vexation,—

"You come to my unpolluted house branded as a thief! If the world knew of your crime, surely, I could not have subjected myself to public disgrace, by giving you aid and comfort under my own roof."

"Eben," said Martin, deadly pale, but very calm, "did I not steal that money for you? Did you not receive the fifteen thousand dollars out of my employer's coffers?"

"It seems so, indeed; but at the time I did not know that it was stolen! I had fifteen thousand dollars ready to repay them, which I borrowed of John Van Strom upon a mortgage on my house."

"At last," said Martin, with open contempt, "at last you have forgotten yourself, and show your true character. In other words, you provided yourself with money to repay me in case I should tell people you received it, and owe it to Mr. Going. But since it all remains on my shoulders, you never mean to restore what you have received!"

"Put it in that light!" cried Judge Bates. "Make me give my last penny away, because you gave me—it was not a loan, sir—because you gave me some money once upon a time! Tell every one the secret! Make me a pauper, ruin me, drive me to the grave, and blast my daughter's happiness for ever! It would not astonish me in you!"

"Eben," answered Martin, solemnly, "do I deserve this, after having sacrificed my honor for you these two times, first in England, and then here, when you wrote to me that you *must* have money?"

"The old story," said Judge Bates, who was fast losing his dignity of speech and manner in the conversation. "Thirty years ago, you and I were boys. I committed a piece of boyish folly; had an intrigue with your colonel's wife, and by a strange combination of circumstances, you were suspected in place of me. You had nothing to lose but your commission, while I was engaged to be married; you goodnaturedly consented to leave the world undeceived. Luck was against you, and you were condemned to a great disgrace, and yet you charge me, thirty years afterward, with your misfortunes. It is absurd!"

"Be it absurd," said Martin, drearily. "At all events this is a strange version of that story. I have suffered for your sins ever since we were at school, and I only wonder for what purpose you, with your high position at the bar, required money so badly as to induce me, poor fool, to steal it for you! With the first five hundred you asked of me, came a most earnest appeal to my brotherly love; but the more I sent, the more you wanted, until with that and my own extravagance, I became pressed for cash—went into speculations—lost more, and finally *stole* money to make it up! You owe Going & Son fifteen thousand dollars, Judge Bates!"

"And I tell you that this is a falsehood, sir. What I wanted with the money, is *my* affair; and, as I never promised to repay it, I would like to see the court of justice which would give decision against me!"

"Eben," cried his brother, "when people are thoroughly dishonest, they always have the *law* in their mouths. But be that as it may, I have served you all my life, and the consequence is, that the world has always smiled upon you, while it only snarls at me like a wild beast, and shows its teeth at every step I take."

"Do I snarl at you and show my teeth?" asked Judge Bates, in a changed tone. There was a soft affection shadowed in his voice, a kindness and persuasive unction, whose value with a jury he well knew. Was he now more sincere than when in the exercise of his profession? God and he only knew; but Martin was moved by the simplest show of sympathy from his elder brother—moved to tears.

"Oh!" he cried, "this is the voice, Eben, which appealed to me in the barracks prison thirty years ago. Against the voice of nature I have no weapons, and I belong to you, body and soul, when you approach me thus. Let the world go. I love you, Eben, and you can reward me for all I have suffered by an hour of kindness!"

The old man bowed his head and wept.

"Let us be friends, then," continued the elder brother, in the same smooth, caressing voice. "Take my hand, Martin! I will not forsake you. Live in my house, and call it your home for the rest of your life."

And old Martin Bates, broken-down in body and spirit by the consequences, not of an *evil*, but of an almost crazy transaction, took the proffered hand, the hand of the man that owed

him every thing, caught it eagerly as though it were the greatest condescension of some superior being.

So the two old men, each queer in his way, and together exemplifying how craftiness can take advantage of brotherly love combined with a weak character, sat late into the night speaking of various subjects. Martin was all confiding, all affectionate. Eben reserved all his secrets, and his manner toward his brother soon fell back into the stately dignity, for which he was so celebrated. Their heads were white; whether they thought of death, and after death, the judgment, or, from other reasons, they henceforward lived in apparent peace and happiness, Eben displaying a high-toned kindliness to his brother, Martin sinking each day into a fixed melancholy, each day shrinking together in body and soul.

He would sit mute and lost in vague thoughts for hours, and at such times his face wore the livid hue of death. Like a thing half-defunct already, he moved ghostily around the house; but he was most affectionate to his niece, Bessie. How little did she dream of the character of his thoughts toward her; how little could she interpret his soliloquy when she saw his lips move silently; and how distressed and terrified she would have been had she heard the words formed by those pale lips,—"God, if a *felon's* prayer can find grace with thee, let her *father's* sins not be visited upon her innocent head!"

*　　*　　*　　*　　*

A few days after our hero's arrival at John Van Strom's house, Judge Bates appeared very much pre-occupied one morning, and partook of his breakfast without a word for any one. He was dressed with such care that his daughter remarked it, and asked, smiling,—

"Is there a great law-case on hand to-day, papa, or, are you going to make love to one of your numerous lady admirers?"

To which "papa" replied with a monosyllable, and remained intrenched behind his stately reserve. As it was such beautiful weather, he did not order his carriage, but told Bessie, with a ceremonious kiss, that she need not expect him before evening, though he might return much sooner, and then he strode out of the door. Bessie went to the window and followed him with her eyes, as he walked, tall and erect, toward Mr. Van Strom's house. He was so lost in thought that a beggar-woman on the roadside failed to attract his attention. His handsome face, his snowy-hair, each seemed to have received particular attention this morning, and never had the handsome old gentleman looked handsomer.

Active, and in full possession of his bodily strength, he covered the distance, some three miles, within an hour, and rang the bell at Van Strom's door. The servant informed him that Mr. and Mrs. Van Strom were out; but when he looked through the open door, he saw Josephine with a book in her hand sitting in the drawing-room. An expression of satisfaction overspread his countenance, and he stepped in quickly. She arose and held out her hand; he looked at her for a moment with undisguised admiration, struck by her charming appearance in a morning dress, with her golden hair fallen about her in loosely-gathered braids.

"Excuse my appearance, Judge Bates," she said, in her deep, melodious voice, "I am hardly presentable."

"I am too old for compliments, madam," he answered, "or I would assure you of the contrary. Do I find you alone?"

"Yes, I am sorry to say. Bella and John have driven out, and our guest, Mr. Montant, went to the village about some business, I believe."

"Mrs. Van Strom," said he, after they were seated, "I am delighted to meet you alone, for I want to speak to you on a matter of some importance."

She looked at him expectant.

"I am fifty-seven years of age, and I have a grown-up daughter," said Judge Bates, slightly flushed, in spite of his determination to appear at his ease. "I have a name second to none in the State, and the question is, whether I can still call myself young enough to harbor any thoughts of marriage."

Not dreaming of what this was the peroration, she answered naively,—

"I think, sir, that you are younger than most gentlemen of forty, and although I don't feel competent to give any valuable opinion on a matter of such importance, I should say that there would be nothing extraordinary in your marrying again. But why ask me such a question, sir? Do you contemplate—"

"I do, Mrs. Van Strom," he answered, redder than before, because he thought he was sure of his case. "And let me plead my cause like a man, old enough to be your father, and not like a young and fiery lover, for that I can not be. I believe you are without means, I know at least that John's father did not provide for you, and I do not suppose that John has settled any estate on you, since his father's death. Therefore I have hopes that you will incline a favorable ear to the offer I have come to make to you to-day. I will give you a home, a good name, and all the love that is left in my old heart. If you will think of it, let reason and prudence urge my suit, and be assured that I have all the affection for you that is requisite to make you happy. Remember that you have experienced the happiness and the misery of marrying a man whom you loved, but whose character was not yet formed, and who disappointed you in the end, and consider that it may be most advisable for you, in your condition, to form an alliance which may make up by safety, peace, and a happy home, for the lack of an intensity of love which I am not fool enough to expect."

He paused. She had listened with growing astonishment, and colored crimson; not from what *he* thought agitated her, but from shame at having hastily made a speech which could not fail to encourage him to speak out. It took some time for her to regain her presence of mind, so the Judge gained the opportunity to plead his cause; but when he finished, her answer, as the reader may imagine, caused Judge Bates to leave the house, a thoroughly disappointed man, and Josephine, when she

was left alone, cried a little, but laughed a little also. While she was thus innocently amusing herself a wagon drove up. It was Bella and John returning from their drive, and *mirabile dictu!* the same yellow mare, Bella, that had dragged John into his marriage, was she, that John was now leading to the stable, followed, at a respectful distance, by the groom who had been in waiting.

"What is the matter, Josephine?" asked Bella, as she embraced her sister. "We just met old Mr. Bates walking rapidly away and looking much agitated. Has he been here?"

Josephine answered evasively under her sister's sharp scrutiny and close questioning.

"I believe he has been here."

"And what have you been talking about?" pursued Bella.

"I promised not to tell," answered Josephine, innocently, whereupon Bella sat down, opened her eyes as widely as possible, and burst into a peal of laughter, in which Josephine could not help joining.

"So he actually proposed? Did you accept him?" and again Bella gave way to her merriment.

"I never could keep a secret!" cried Josephine, in dismay. "The harder I try the sooner it is discovered! Well, since you have guessed it, he told me that since he was rich and I was poor—"

"What?" cried Bella, very earnestly, all of a sudden. "He told you that since you were—"

"Poor—" repeated Josephine, "and—"

"The villain!" muttered the tailor's daughter. "I can see *now* what he is after." ·

"What do you mean, Bella?"

"What do I mean?" she cried, in a rage. "I mean that he has just drawn up John's last will, and that he knows, as well as I do, that John has left you very rich. That's what he wants to marry you for!"

The news that she would be rich some day could not but fill the widow's brain with the brightest and happiest thoughts, for her lover came to her mind in an instant. She had not expected it. Her innocence in worldly matters had made it easy for her to accustom herself to the thought that the Van Strom property was never to benefit her, and, so far, her wildest hopes had not reached beyond a wished-for loan from John to start her future husband in business. This news, therefore, well-nigh overpowered her; but, before she could realize it, the door opened and our hero entered. With a cry of joy, she rushed into his arms and they had a good long embrace.

"Why did you stay so long, Ernest?" she asked, when she could free her lovely lips from his, so as to speak at all.

"Couldn't help it, baby," replied he, but the conversation was always apt to proceed under continued interruptions, until they could so far accustom themselves to the delight of being together as to speak like sensible people,—and then Josephine imparted to her lover the good news, that she was a "rich woman, and all was now clear before them."

"However that may be," he answered, "I do not desire to investigate matters which belong to the future, especially as it is my intention to rely upon my own strength and labor *alone*, accepting what may, in the course of kind providence, be in store for you, as a gift of fortune unlooked for."

CHAPTER III.

THE ITALIAN GIRL.

"Plots have I laid, inductions dangerous."
KING RICHARD III.

OUR esteemed acquaintance, Mr. Antonio Stilletto, found himself called to Boston and decided to make the journey in company with his faithful ally, the great German philosopher, Mr. August Muller, and also a young lady, dressed in black and secluded from the vulgar gaze by an impenetrable veil. When this worshipful company found themselves at the New Haven depot in New York, Stilletto made arrangements with the conductor for the exclusive use of one of the compartments of the new-fashioned cars, paying therefor somewhat toward that official's house-rent.

So they soon settled themselves comfortably, in anticipation of the long ride before them, Mr. Muller in one corner of the back seat, Mr. Stilletto in the other, and the veiled lady couched upon the front sofa, seemingly regardless of appearances.

Mr. Muller's philosophy teaches that it is a needless expense to shave when traveling, and as he considers himself a traveler, from the time he makes up his mind to start until he arrives at his destination, his growth of beard does not improve the appearance of his thin red face or conceal the perpetual sneer. Mr. Stilletto's chin is, on the contrary, just from the hands of the barber, his whiskers are dyed a jetty black, and a beautiful color; not the hue of youth, not the blush of health, but the rosy tint of "rouge," graces his sharp face. In fact, he has made an exquisitely-vulgar or vulgarly-exquisite toilet, and his shining silk hat and his immaculate gloves are calculated to attract attention. Go where he may, written plainly on every inch of his bran-new exterior, are the words—"Here goes a snob."

These two worthies are smoking, and upon the vacant seat between them recline two bottles, whose appearance seems to please Mr. Muller, for he steals an affectionate glance toward them with his little blinking eyes, and the restlessness so noticeable in his movements would fully justify one in expecting the question which has been assuming to itself shape and words in his classic brain, voiding itself thus:—

"Why is it that railroad-traveling makes one so thirsty?"

"Because," answered Stilletto, "one happens to be a drunkard, and a coward besides, who seeks excuses instead of coming out boldly and acknowledging the fact."

"Stilletto," began Muller, proudly, sitting bolt upright, "my standing and intellect—"

"Please don't," said Stilletto, disdainfully.

"Take your drink and stimulate yourself into a reasonable frame of mind if that is possible. I have something to say to you."

The train had now left the suburbs of New York, and was dashing along on its smooth and firmset path in the open country, noiselessly enough to permit conversation in a half undertone.

Muller took the bottle, uncorked it, almost filled a cup which he produced from his pocket, and cocking his little eye at the veiled lady, cried, "Here's a health to all good lasses!" The lady took no notice of his politeness, nor indeed had she appeared conscious of. the existence of her fellow-passengers since she had first settled herself in her corner.

"Now, then, Muller," commenced Stilletto, "the Hobgoblin enterprise seems to be a failure, hey? The company is now fairly started; but while under Mr. Going's management of the factory, there really were some profits realized, yet under my management and yours, things go wrong."

"Because you, my young friend, have not yet arrived at the age when we leave off all the pardonably easy ways of youth and attend to business."

"It is true that I have a good deal of fun, and have not confined myself altogether to that accursed factory. True, the foremen have cheated us, paying large wages to men that have done no work. True, my inventions and patents are not what old Fatman thinks they are. But then—"

"But then," put in Mr. Muller, with an abstracted air, "we expected to make money anyhow, even under these untoward circumstances, yet we have not made money."

"And we want money."

"Precisely so," corroborated the philosopher with an approving nod. Whereupon a silence ensued as if their intellects required rest, after the laborious task of reaching this conclusion.

"Mr. Going," continued Stilletto, after a pause, "has made a mistake, and is daily adding to the proportions of that mistake. He holds the notes of the company to a large amount, and has pledged his shares in it to Mr. Chip, old Moneybags, you know, as security for the money lent to the company. Now, if the company fails to meet its engagements his notes become worthless and old Moneybags gets his shares. So you see, in helping the miserable concern along, hoping to bring it into a condition where his claims upon it would be met, he has just thrown good money after bad."

"You state the case clearly, and with acute comprehension seldom found in one of your tender years, and therefore I find it the more astonishing."

"Take another drink, Muller! you deserve one after that," said Stilletto.

"Proceed," said the philosopher, after having helped himself most liberally.

"Fatman," continued Stilletto, "has been obliged to invest some money in Hobgoblin, though sorely against his will, and the trustees have likewise had to lighten their purses having found out that, after all, a trustee, even though it be inconvenient, is expected to do something for the company that has purchased his great name to deceive the public with, so these have all bought some shares in addition to what was presented to them. Finally, oh great philosopher, every one will be the loser by Hobgoblin, though as yet nobody knows it but old Fatman, you and I, and Mr. Going. At least, if the latter don't know it now, he soon will, when his notes become due and are not paid. Then he will fail, Hobgoblin will suddenly be *dead*, the trustees will open their eyes and retire in disgust, and among the shareholders there will be weeping and gnashing of teeth."

"Your prophecy is accurate and to the point; but will they not make an effort to sell the shares at the Stock Exchange, and inaugurate such a speculation in them as to enable us all to realize before the final death of Hobgoblin ?"

"That is only a chance. In the meanwhile we can not sell our shares, and having both been very extravagant, you as well as I, *want money*."

"Precisely so," repeated Muller; and again there was a silence.

"I am sorry for Mr. Going, after all," said Stilletto, in a sincere tone.

"My young friend," said the philosopher, grandly, "God has instilled in our breasts the instinct of self-preservation by which alone we exist, though it must be confessed, to the detriment of man and material around us. Therefore I beg leave to vary your words somewhat in clothing the sentiments of my soul and will say, *I am sorry for ourselves*."

Without replying to these sublime words, Stilletto said, in a quick and altered manner,—

"But we will get money where we are now bound to."

"So you told me ; but—how ?"

Stilletto was about to explain something which, to judge by the working of his countenance exercised his brain mightily, when he suddenly checked himself, and with an expression of doubt and distrust turned to the veiled lady. He had noticed, out of a corner of his sharp eye that she had altered her position slightly, and he saw even through her thick veil that her dark eyes of unusual luster and penetration were at this moment turned upon him. In a half-annoyed half-angry tone, he asked her abruptly,—

"Simonetta, do you want any thing to eat or drink ?"

There was a strange constraint in her tone, as she answered, not very promptly,—

"Non ho capito ciò che mi hai detto, caro mio."

"Don't you really understand English, Netty ?" again inquired Stilletto, only half satisfied.

She merely shook her head, and told him in Italian, that since he did not choose to address her in her native language she was unable to understand or answer him. Stilletto was now satisfied, and after a few remarks exchanged between them in Italian, the lady turned her face away and seemed to settle herself for a nap.

"I can hardly bring my mind to believe

that she is deceiving you," said Muller to Stilletto. "I know that when that poor misguided creature, Martin Bates, was courting her, she had to teach him Italian before he could make much headway in conversation. Strange and incomprehensible fancy of an old man like him to propose honorable marriage to an organ-grinder's girl ! And I believe, from my knowledge of the man, yes, I am certain that he was sincere. And then to have been circumvented at the last moment by her friends !"

"No, Muller. She had promised to meet him at Chatham Square, where he was to have a carriage in waiting, on the night of the very day his rather funny little transactions in Going's were discovered by that beloved friend of mine, Earnest Montant."

"What about him ?" asked Muller, who noticed that Stilletto showed malicious propensities on pronouncing the name of our hero.

"I have an old grudge against him," said the little man, "which old grudge may be settled in a new way in New England, where I expect to meet the gentleman. But to return to the girl opposite (she is asleep!); it was I who kept her from meeting Martin Bates. She did *me* the honor to prefer me to him, and the fierce *brother* who served as a mysterious and ever invisible bugbear to scare Martin, never existed, except in the person of *myself*. We loved each other then already," added Stilletto, with a coarse levity.

"But," said the philosopher, "let me ask you how a gentleman of your standing and prudence can expose himself to the merciless attacks of this gossiping, scandal-loving, and unjust world, by carrying his—well his mistress all over the country with him ? I must confess that August Muller, as husband to a sweet and pure wife, and as father to an innocent and growing family, can barely tolerate such company, and would not have tolerated it had you previously apprised me that the lady you intended to escort, was Simonetta Marini, the daughter of an organ-grinder, and your—"

"I want amusement," said Stilletto, carelessly, "and as far as the injustice of the world is concerned, I do not understand what you mean. If any one is sharp enough to recognize in my pretended *sister* the real character of that lady, I can see no injustice in his saying so where and when he chooses."

"How if Mrs. Fatman should hear of it ?" asked the philosopher, slyly.

"I don't care a snap," was the impatient answer. "Women must have cause for jealousy, flying into passions, bursting into tears, and considering themselves dreadfully injured by us men before they go crazy over us, as they should."

Before this cool speech, when the name of Mrs. Fatman was mentioned, the veiled lady started as if something had disturbed her sleep. But then she *was* asleep, of course ! And even had she been awake, *she* could not understand a word of English—had she not said so, and was it not true ?

Is it possible that even the shrewdness of Antonio Stilletto has been deceived by a woman? Is it possible that Simonetta Marini the outcast Italian girl, *does* understand English? If so, she has heard words which may fill a woman of her character with such hate as to employ the arts of a demon, poison, or a dagger to revenge herself.

"My dear friend," resumed the philosopher, "you have enticed this girl away from house and home. You have betrayed her, and intend to discard her when you become tired of her. I am certain you are her seducer."

"I hope so," said Stilletto, boldly.

"And do you not fear her friends? These Italians are insane in their revenge, and quick with the dirk."

"So am I," answered Stilletto, who, as we have seen, was not a coward. "But, old fellow, I have done wonders in my time, by what you, in your philosophy, might call 'brass,' and how could I have achieved it if my courage had been tamed by that most disheartening feeling, called the fear of consequences?"

"Then, you stick at nothing?" asked Muller, in a tone of undisguised awe.

"How does that follow?" asked Stilletto, with a sneer.

"Because," replied the great philosopher, "when you fear no consequences, what is there to keep you from all manner of crimes when you can gain any thing by their perpetration?"

"My conscience, I suppose," said Stilletto, languidly.

Muller looked attentively at him for a moment, and failing to grow wiser by attempting to read *that* face, he gave up the argument with a sigh, and took some more whisky.

Both drank freely, and it was not until darkness closed in that they fairly entered upon a discussion of what they expected to do in Massachusetts. The names of Judge Bates and John Van Strom, of old Martin, and of Ernest Montant, were frequently mentioned, and Stilletto's plans thoroughly ventilated. Whether she understood English or not, every word of the conversation reached Simonetta's ears; whether she understood English or not, her black eyes flashed fire, underneath her veil. She did not move a muscle during that conversation, but had darkness and the veil been lifted from her face, even the courage of a Stilletto might have failed him at the sight of her clenched teeth and flashing eyes. But then she does not understand English! Whether or not, her hand has clutched the dagger she wears in her bosom; and thus the three passed the greater part of that night in the train, which is steaming, and flying, and rattling through the darkness which lies over the lovely landscapes of New England.

CHAPTER IV.

MARTIN BATES PUZZLED.

"Now I see the bottom of your purpose."
ALL'S WELL THAT ENDS WELL.

JUDGE BATES's residence, like most of the villas in the vicinity, was situated on a hill, and surrounded with gardens, orchards, arbors, and groves, the whole inclosed by a stout, rough stone wall. This wall, in front, was of dressed stone, to correspond with the façade of the house, and a handsome iron gate admitted one to a wide, straight gravel walk, lined on either side with arbors, leading to the front door.

The sun was setting at the close of a brilliant day, when the two brothers, Eben, erect and stately, Martin, half crouching by his side, lingered near the gate on returning from a walk through the distant fields.

"Eben," said Martin, as they strolled along and into one of the arbors, where the shadows of night had already stalked in under the somber roof of foliage, "Eben," said the old man, mournfully, "does it not seem incompatible with the wisdom of God that there should be even one existence on earth which is not only a burden and a weariness, oh, so inexpressibly tiresome to the one who should enjoy his life, but to every one else around him. Yet this is my sad case. Sometimes I have a foreboding, a presentiment that the eternal Providence has spared me for another task in life, that I am still to be a useful tool in the hands of fate. If this be so, if my work here be not yet complete, chance must direct the affair, for I no longer possess any energy. I am fast rusting away and sinking into that complete apathy which is akin to death."

"Your life, Martin," answered the old judge, in a kind, almost tender voice, "has been a most useful one. You have saved a brother from the punishment which the sins of former years had called down upon his head; you have enabled him to become a good man and a useful citizen, and to hold his head high in the community, occupying a proud position, indeed!"

"But, Eben," replied Martin, thoughtfully, "you are still in the toils of some dark mystery. To this day I am ignorant of the purpose for which you required the money I obtained for you by crime. How can you, therefore, hold your head high while this matter can not bear daylight?"

"This point, Martin," said the judge, coldly, "was long ago settled between us as forbidden ground. I can not explain. Your crime was not my fault. I asked assistance from a brother. He procured that assistance in his own way. Do his ways therefore become mine?"

Martin sighed. Oh, the power which that strong, proud man exerted over his weak-minded but affectionate brother! Like the dog that licks the hand that lately struck the cruel blow; like the slave, who clings to his master whose fetters weigh him to the ground, so this strange creature, Martin Bates, loved his terrible brother.

A footstep on the walk,—some one humming a song, and the brothers, looking out from the arbor to see who the intruder could be, beheld a little man, strolling along, smoking a cigar, with an air as if he owned an indefinite number of other rural residences infinitely superior to this one. The sun was now some time at rest, and the stranger approached them closely before they recognized him.

6

Judge Bates, with an altered manner, stared hard at the sharpface and shiny hat, as though he doubted the testimony of his eyes, but the disagreeable, bold voice that now accosted him, settled all his remaining doubts, and he started back with an exclamation of dismay, only half concealed by apparent indignation.

"Good evening, Judge Bates," said our worthy friend, Antonio Stilletto. "I have been looking for you all over the place."

"Have you, indeed?" muttered the old man, between his teeth.

"Ah," continued the little man, "I see my old friend, and your dear brother, Martin is with you. How do you find yourself, my dear Martin," taking the old cashier's hand by force, and shaking it with an air of impudent familiarity.

"*You here again*," gasped the judge, still unable to control his vexation.

"Yes, my dear Judge," answered Stilletto, apparently in an excellent humor, "and *of course* you will ask me to take a walk with you just outside the gate, and *of course* old Martin here will excuse us, and *of course* I will not stay to supper with you although you press me so kindly to do so, and, in short, you will, without the slightest doubt, do your best to accommodate your welcome guest."

Eben seemed irresolute. Here was a moment in which the net that had entangled him for years, seemed capable of being torn to shreds by one bold action which only required courage, for his reason had long ago pronounced in its favor. Then, weak irresolution with her thousand doubts and fears for the future, disarmed his reason, and he knew no longer what he would or would not. He glanced around him; he loved his gardens, his walks, his flowers. He looked toward the house on the hill; it was a monument of his high respectability; and a ray of light from one window fell upon his agonized eye. He knew whose window it was; he knew his daughter Bessie was there, and he loved her! With a quick, impatient gesture, he bade Martin await him, and strode rapidly toward the gate, while Stilletto followed him with swaggering, rapid strides, noiseless as a cat.

Martin remained rooted to the spot. He had not been aware that his brother knew Stilletto, whom he remembered well as the projector of Hobgoblin, and disliked accordingly. While he thus stood, bewildered and alarmed by doubts and fears for his brother, his eye fell upon a white object upon the ground.

"Stilletto surely dropped it out of his pocket," he soliloquized. "He is the most disorderly vagabond I ever saw, and I am sure he'll ruin some grand scheme yet by some act of petty carelessness." So musing, the old man stooped and picked up the object, which proved to be a small package of papers, and instead of calling to the probable loser, who, with Eben, was just at the gate, Martin quickly concealed the bundle in the inner pocket of his coat, with a feeling of some satisfaction, for now, he doubted not, the mystery of Eben's life in America was to be solved.

From a feeling of caution and the possession of a bad conscience, he looked around and listened attentively to be certain that his action had not been perceived; when, hark! a noise as if of a rustling dress in the arbor. He held his breath and heard it again close to him, and yet the darkness concealed the moving object from his view. Cold perspiration stood upon his forehead, not from bodily fear, for Martin Bates would long ago have welcomed danger of life; but now he feared lest he had been seen to take the papers from the ground.

Again he hears the rustling of the dress against the foliage of the arbor, close to him, and the crunching of the gravel on the walk under a light, hasty footstep. Suddenly he beheld a dark object flitting by, and with a bound he gained the entrance of the arbor and barred the way out.

With a suppressed scream, a woman dressed in black recoiled from his very arms. There was light enough, now that they met face to face out of the shadows of the dark arbor, for them to recognize each other.

"Martin Bates!" she exclaimed, in surprise.

"Simonetta Marini!" cried Martin, wonderingly.

"Perhaps the good God has made that we meet," continued the Italian girl in quick passionate accents. "I am not your enemy, Signor Bates, I am your friend if I may be it."

"Friend!" cried Martin Bates, bitterly.

"Praise the virgin who has saved you from the misery of calling me your wife," answered Simonetta, in her hurried, vehement manner. "Your gray hair should have bleached with thoughts of wisdom and not the passions of youth, for the two go not together."

"I like to hear you speak again, Simonetta," cried Martin, "your half Italian-English used always to soothe my misery."

The girl seemed newly agitated by Martin's speech. After a moment's hesitation, she approached him, and laying her hand upon his arm, said in a whisper,—

"Will the best friend of my life make me a promise?"

"What is it, Simonetta?"

"Never tell that I speak English."

"Why? all your friends know it!"

"All that are my friends in New York, yes. But one man, he that can look into woman's soul and hear the talking of her heart, he has been blind and deaf with me. He thinks I do not understand a word of English, and he has spoken words in my presence that are burned into the flesh of my heart, to stay there till I die!"

Martin began to understand. With a questioning gesture he pointed to the gate, and by her assenting nod knew that she referred to Stilletto.

"And what has he to do with you," he asked, eagerly. "Has he—?"

"Yes," she answered fiercely, comprehending his hesitancy. "Yes, *he has*, and he must die for it!"

Martin felt a deathly sickness coming over him. He had loved this woman truly—and now—and now! And that brute Stilletto, too!

"You have been to me a kind and generous friend always," continued Simonetta. "To your kind sight my innocence of thought was seen though my dress was rags, and you believed in me. Never did you approach me with baseness of man; but it had to come as a snake in the night. And when I pray to the Holy Virgin now, I only ask her for vengence."

"Hold ! Simonetta," cried Martin, appalled; "by your religion, which is mightier than ours, I warn you from further sin."

"He has beaten me," gasped the girl, in answer. Martin shuddered.

"Beaten me cruelly," repeated the furious woman; "but that is not all. Blows do not sting like jealousy. Will you promise not to tell that him I speak English?"

"Yes, yes !" muttered Martin. "But what are the secrets you have learned through his imprudence."

"When God's time comes you shall hear all. There are steps coming this way. They are returning. Away with you. I must return to him !"

"When will I see you again ?" whispered Martin; for by the closing of the gate, some one was approaching.

"When I want you I will find you. You forgive me ?"

"In heaven, poor girl, I will, on earth it is impossible," answered Martin Bates, tearfully.

"We are friends in this one cause ?"

"I do not know what it is," answered Martin, bewildered, "but I suppose I shall find out." And he thought of the papers he had picked up.

Simonetta glided away as though she had melted into the surrounding darkness, and he now saw his brother approaching with an unsteady, wavering step. When Judge Bates perceived Martin still waiting, he mastered himself and walked firmly as ever.

"I have been keeping you long, brother ?"

"I have beguiled myself with my fancies," answered Martin, as they sauntered toward the house together.

"You ask me no questions about that man, who came so boldly into my premises, and whom I followed so readily, " said Eben, casting a sharp, suspicious glance upon his brother.

"I believe," said Martin, solemnly, "that your business with that men belongs to you two, and God, only."

Eben was silent.

"And why should men pry into secrets that do not concern them. It may be, that should I lift this veil of mystery, the disclosure would blind my moral sight for ever !"

Still Eben remained silent; but Martin heard him breathing heavily, as one that endeavors to master his emotions, and when they reached the house, Eben said in a hoarse voice —

"Go in and talk to Bessie, make her happy, for my mind is heavy with care this evening. I will be in directly."

Martin paused. A vague fear crept through his nerves.

"Eben!" he cried, tears rolling down his withered cheeks, "Eben!" taking his brother's hand, "God keep you from any thing wicked ! Come in now, I am afraid to leave you alone."

"Fear not," answered the Judge, quietly. "Do you think that I would heap disgrace upon my name and family by committing suicide ?"

Martin, reassured by the import of the speech rather that the droll, almost jocular, tone in which it was spoken, obeyed his brother's request without another word.

"He will not heap disgrace upon his name," he muttered, as he entered the house. "He will *live*—live a life of hypocrisy ! As long as the world can not look on his *real* face, distorted by the anguish of guilt, as long as it only beholds his *outward* face, where virtue and dignity sit enthroned, so long he will bear up, so long he will be as happy as God will allow him to be. I will leave him to recover the mask which is intended to be gazed upon !"

Martin soon retired to his room. He locked the door and closed the window blinds. By the light of a solitary candle he produced his half-stolen treasure, those papers he had found on the walk in the arbor. If one could only have seen him ! His cheeks were even more sunken, his hair scantier, and his complexion more ashy palo than when we first met him confronting the small but ominous statuette of Justice, at his desk in the office of Messrs. Going & Son. The light of his gray eyes was unsteady, but now as he read the first words of the captured documents, he seemed to shrink into himself with a feeling of awe that made him shudder in that dismal room where he sat alone with an overburdened conscience, and only the dim and flickering rays of a candle to illumine the title page.

THE MANIAC'S STORY.

So Martin Bates read the story which forms the opening chapter of this book, and as he went on, his interest rose to intense fascination, as if there was a mystic link which connected him with the strange confessions of the lunatic Count of Unkstein. The spirits of the Black Forest seemed to fill the air of Martin Bates's lone room; the gradually increasing mania of the count, affecting his eyes and ears, until he actually beheld a material wolf's head in the countenance of his once beautiful wife; the precision with which the apparition of the black wolf and the spectral reproduction of that awful tragedy in the woods were depicted; the terrible earnestness of the whole account, and the evident wish of the maniac to prove that he was perfectly sane, and telling the unvarnished truth, all these elements combined to make the crazy story assume a superhuman aspect and similate the truth. Martin's few locks of thin hair uprose in horror, large drops of perspiration hung upon his wrinkled brow, though he was chilled to the very marrow with overpowering, causeless fear, and he would have given much had he never seen the manuscript. Even the dead paper, after he had finished reading and had folded it again, seemed inspired with an awful individuality, as though especially sent from the kingdom of spectres to appall human kind.

Who could have written it? The penmanship was feminine, regular, very distinct, and very small. No date or author's name appeared, to give a clue; no testimony save the bare fact of its existence, told of its production; yet there it was, a living, speaking thing, when once opened.

It took some time for Martin's nervous agitation to subside sufficiently for him to answer the question that kept recurring to his mind, "What has all this to do with Stilletto?"

For a few moments he was strongly inclined to think that it had nothing to do with him or any other human being, but had fallen into his hands through the agency of some evil spirit. But what is this on the floor? What! more papers thrown into Martin's path by—Heaven knows who? He picks it up. It has evidently dropped out of the manuscript he has been reading, between the leaves of which it has been carelessly left. It is a letter, unsealed, and addressed to Judge Bates. Martin read as follows:—

" *Copy of letter written to Eben Bates.*

"I inclose you herewith a copy of the MS. which will show you that I am in full possession of the facts regarding the earlier history of your lovely Countess of Unkstein, which lady has the honor of being my mother. Other papers (such as letters from you to her, dated thirty years ago), and her own written confessions, must establish the fact pretty thoroughly that I am your beloved son; but, also, that when you did me the kindness to father me, you and my worthy mother most unaccountably omitted the marriage ceremony.

"Now I think that a father is expected in this world to support his children, and I am happy to inform you that I am very extravagant, so as to afford you plenty of opportunity to practice that heaven-born virtue called generosity.

"Understand me thoroughly. I am a gentleman, but in reduced circumstances, and you know what men will do when they are reduced. If you do not pay me ten thousand dollars within six days from this, I shall proclaim to the world that you, the high-toned, pious judge, have an illegitimate son living in New York, and I can not imagine that a gentleman of your wealth should think that a large sum to give to your own son.

"I expect an answer to-morrow, and remain,

"Your obedient son and servant,
"ANTONIO STILLETO.

("Which name I adopted because you had not the kindness to leave me reasons to prefer any particular name!")

"Now I see it all!" exclaimed Martin Bates. "This letter is dated three years ago to-day. This whelp is—must be—really Eben's son. And now—now," continued the old man, pacing the room and rubbing his forehead, "I remember a rumor that Eben had an intrigue with a German or Italian countess on the Continent. This must have been about thirty years ago, and this woman doubtless was the unfortunate but villainous wife of this poor German nobleman."

"There is not a doubt left," continued Martin, in soliloquy, "or why has Stilletto such an influence over Eben? And I can see plainly that this terrible living punishment for an old sin, is the cause of Eben's pecuniary embarrassments. From what I know of that brute, he is capable of tormenting any one to the very confines of the grave for money. And this ten thousand dollars demanded so boldly three years ago, was doubtless but the preliminary to greater requisitions.

"Three years!" he mused. "Has not Stilletto been to Europe since then? Yes; but he is just the man to make a pleasure-trip at the expense of my poor brother! Poor Eben," cried Martin, beating his forehead with his hand, "how the grace of your body has defiled the grace of your soul! Who would recognize in the noble judge, the former rake, the liar, the hypocrite, the remorseless egotist, that I know he was! I say poor Eben — *I* that have suffered more than any other human being by his deceit and selfishness—I that have lost all for him—honor, virtue, peace of mind, forever more! Yet notwithstanding all this, I love him still, and would die for him!"

"How strange," he continued, after he had calmed himself somewhat, "how strange that Stilletto lost these papers, copies of those sent my brother three years ago. Thus does Providence spoil the nets of villainy by letting one thread break—and, lo! the whole is destroyed. This planning, cunning, cruel devil, this fiend, Stilletto, is, by the direction of a merciful God, born with one great failing—carelessness, want of order. The consequence of a small, thoughtless act, such as carrying these papers in the same pocket with his pocket-handkerchief, the dropping them at my feet, spoils all his calculations.

"But how does it spoil them? How can *I* help Eben in this dilemma?" he asked himself, in sudden perplexity. And though he could not immediately answer these queries, he laid awake for the balance of the night thinking about it.

CHAPTER V.

HAND-IN-HAND.

"This cunning cardinal,
The articles o' the combination drew
As himself pleased."—KING HENRY VIII.

HAPPY the man who owns the ground upon which his house is built, and the house itself, from the foundation to the roof as an unencumbered property, for only then may it be called his home in the fullest sense of the word.

Mr. Going, as we know, was the reputed owner of two homes—one in town, and one (the newly-acquired Priory) in the country. But were they unencumbered? No: that first and greatest underminer of a man's personal solvency, a *mortgage*, rested like a curse upon the Priory, and vitiated the anxious mind of the merchant with every enjoyment of his beautiful country-seat. Besides this, a mortgage had long since been placed upon the house in Fifth Avenue, so the old gentleman was really in a doubtful and false position. Did he own his houses? Yes: the world thought so; envy proclaimed the fact—malice mentioned the extravagance—and yet, in his communings with himself, he could not say, "This property is *mine!*"

The office of Going & Son seemed to grow more desolate and become more forsaken as relentless Time advanced with steady, measured stride, removing a veil here and there, and developing matters as they approached their consummation. He touched the old business of the house and it turned to nothing but an empty name, the office no longer presented a scene of well-regulated activity; but rather the unwholesome, mysterious bustle which precedes the consummation of a great undertaking, an enterprise upon which hangs reputation or disgrace.

The little figure of Justice on the cashier's desk still held out its scales at arm's length, though the dust lay thick upon it in the ghostly luster of the setting sun, as it peered through the windows and then departed with another day, leaving one day less of the few which would accomplish what was but a question of time; one day less of weary endeavor and self-mocking hope; one day less of morbid energy and despairing strife to avoid what Mr. Going felt in his inmost soul *could not be avoided.*

Yes, the house must fail! Like a ship whose every timber, to her very keel, is rotten and worm-eaten, the firm must founder and go down in the troubled waves of the financial storm that rose higher and higher, breaking over its fast shattering hulk.

Fatman had gone hand in hand with them until they were fairly launched on the sea of destruction.

"Mr. Going," said Mr. Solomons, the Jew, on entering the office one morning, to find father and son in gloomy, indolent reverie, staring on the void that now reigned upon their writing desks, while at the further end of the outer office, a lonely clerk was perched upon a high stool like a melancholy crow on a withered branch.

"Mr. Going, sir," said Mr. Solomons, taking an unproffered seat, "Hobgoblin is *sick*. Fatman got it on the board, you know. I bid for it every day to keep up prices, but it amounts to nothing but *wash* sales."

"What do you call wash sales?" asked Mr. Going, rather sharply. "I should very much prefer that you would divest your language of your stock-board slang when you come to talk to me, and use terms calculated for the comprehension of a plain merchant."

"Wash sales," answered Mr. Solomons, "are sales made for show, you know. Instance, Hobgoblin is called at the board. All brokers present; I offer twenty-five; Walter, quick as lightning, you know, *takes it.* Folks think stock sold. Papers quote, Hobgoblin

twenty-five. After board closes, I go to Walter and say, 'Walter, this is *wash*,' you know, which means the stock *ain't* sold. I don't pay twenty-five for it. But in the meanwhile, if an *outsider* offers twenty-five or twenty in the board, Walter takes that, too, and the outsider *has to pay*. Do you see? In other words, we keep up a fictitious market to rope in the greens! Understand?"

"I understand," said Mr. Going, showing in his tone and manner the humiliation and disgust that he felt; "and I would give a great deal if I need never hear of such transactions in connection with my affairs!"

"Pooh, pooh!" said Mr. Solomons, pityingly. "But I wanted to tell you that Hobgoblin is very sick. Dying fast, sir, is Hobgoblin. Folks beginning to see that two millions is rather a large capital for a company owning nothing but a factory, which stops work pretty often, and a few acres of mining lands, which nobody knows the value of, only folks begin to wonder if the whole concern could have cost more than fifty thousand dollars!"

"Mr. Solomons," said Mr. Going, with an effort, "I am not very well this morning, in fact my head does not feel strong enough for a business talk."

Walter looked up at his father. The old gentleman's face was haggard and mournful in the extreme. His son could there read the pain, the anguish, inflicted by the broker's frivolous remarks, and with his old brusqueness toward Mr. Solomons, he said:—

"You better go and sell a thousand shares of Erie for us, and hurry up about it, too. We have had enough of your twaddle about our own stock!"

"Erie! Yes, sir. Now there is a stock worth talking about. Erie closed at twenty-five last night, sixty this morning, and Files & Banker made a million, old Scudder lost about as much, and busted! I'll buy you Erie at fifty-nine and half-buyer three, or I'll sell you at fifty-nine and half *cash!*"

As soon as Hobgoblin yielded the floor to Erie, Mr. Solomons resumed his accustomed flow of language, becoming quite enthusiastic, and this change Mr. Going noticed with a feeling of great despondency as a proof that his cherished Hobgoblin had sunk very low in the estimation of such men as the broker, who will praise the most worthless stock as long as there is a shadow of a chance of inducing the ignorant public to deal in it.

When Mr. Solomons had left the partners once more alone, Mr. Going said to Walter,—

"If the company does not pay us the notes which mature to-morrow, we will have a hard day, my son. I do not see how we can manage to get along without that money."

"They *must* pay them," cried Walter.

"That is the question," answered the old gentleman, sadly. "The notes are given by a limited corporation. Not a trustee, not an individual is responsible for them. And we do not dare to sue the company for payment, lest the whole enterprise tumble about our ears, and all our stock become valueless! And still I think we had better make an end of every thing. If the company does not pay us, suspend payment ourselves; make an assignment and let the trustees answer for their conduct before the public and the law courts!"

"Father," cried Walter, "how can you speak that way. We must not suspend! It would break your heart!"

The old gentleman involuntarily looked up toward heaven and laid his hand upon his heart. Was it not broken already? Was not his calmness that of despair? Walter did not perceive the agony to which that quick gesture bore witness, for he was pacing the room like an imprisoned wild beast; still protesting against suspension and trying to persuade himself that this step would not be necessary. The clerk brought in a letter. With a foreboding of evil the old gentleman broke the seal:—

"HOBGOBLIN.

"*Messrs. Going & Son:*—

"Dear Sirs,—I regret that it is necessary, in my capacity as Treasurer of the Hobgoblin Mining and Manufacturing Company, to notify you that it will be impossible to meet the notes of the company, which fall due to-morrow, at maturity. After much trouble and the exercise of powerful influence we succeeded, as you know, in getting Hobgoblin added to the list of stocks, which are sold at the board of brokers. I have no doubt that Mr. Solomons, whom we selected as the fittest party to manage the sale of the stock, has already informed you of the total failure of the enterprise at the board. We can sell no stock, and we hold no funds to pay off the notes you hold. I am sorry to be obliged to further inform you that we begin to see what an exorbitant price we have paid for the Hobgoblin. You are much to blame for having attempted to make such an enormous profit out of your manufacturing enterprise, and we have more to complain of than you. However, we will still go hand in hand and endeavor to make the best of a bad bargain. Unless you commit the very evident mistake of suing the company (in which case *all* of us would be heavy losers, for the stock would sink at once to the value of waste paper), I still offer you my aid, and we will fight it out, going hand in hand, as I mentioned before. Yours, truly,

"FATMAN."

"Hand in hand to the devil," cried Walter, in a rage.

"Compose yourself," said his father, trembling like a leaf.

"Father," said Walter, beside himself, and walking up to Mr. Going with tears in his honest eyes and a husky voice, "Father, I swear that Fatman shall suffer for this before he gets through with us."

"In the meanwhile we are ruined," said the old gentleman, with unnatural quietness of voice and manner.

"Can we not work through?" asked Walter, composing himself.

"Yes; but I feel as though an honorable failure were better than a dishonorable solvency. I know a man whose advice I would like to have just now." This last sentence was not addressed to Walter, but was spoken almost in a whisper, as though he were communicating with his own thoughts. Yet Walter's attentive ears heard the words, and he said, abruptly, as usual:—

"I know whom you mean; but Ernest Montant is not worthy your regard. He left you, his benefactor, at a time when he knew that you required the best of help. No clerk, no employee, that has a spark of honor left, deserts a house in the time of severe trial, such as we have experienced, and, if he should do so, it is often a black mark against him in the business world. We only humiliate ourselves by regretting his loss!"

"No, Walter," answered his father, sadly. "He was right. In his mind the events which are now crushing us were clearly foreseen, and his prophecies have come as true as Scripture. He knew that mere seamanship could not save a rotten vessel, and he left our undertaking, not our friendship, for, should a time come when we need his aid, he will stand by us as of old. But this accursed stock company must cease to exist before we can again stand clear and unsullied in the eyes of good men or even in the light of our own consciences, so let us take the bitter pill at once, Walter, let us—fail." The last word cost him an effort. It almost choked him.

"This Fatman!" cried Walter, rising to his feet again as his anger returned,—

"To dare to write us such a letter. He is indeed perfidious," said the old gentleman, picking up the document to peruse it again.

"After telling me again and again," continued Walter, "that those notes would certainly be paid, he now, at the eleventh hour—"

"The notice is too short," said Mr. Going, dolefully. "I have never heard of such doings before. It seems as if his intention was to lure us on into feeling perfectly secure and to strike the blow when it was too late to ward it off!"

"Perhaps he wants us to suspend payment, so as to throw the blame of the Hobgoblin failure upon us," said Walter.

"I can not see the reason for his treachery," said Mr. Going. "It may be the inborn hatred which naturally exists between a blackguard and a gentleman!"

It was but rarely that Mr. Going permitted himself to use violent or inelegant expressions; but his just indignation spoke in the last sentence, as well as the proud consciousness of his own superiority, which he did not care to disguise.

"'We can sell no stock, and we have no money to pay the notes you hold,'" quoted Walter, between his teeth, as he was re-reading Mr. Fatman's letter.

"It is perfectly outrageous," said Mr. Going. "As if they had not received *merchandise* for those notes! And then to dare to tell us that they have paid too much for the property!"

"Nothing but those shares, which seem valueless, or very nearly so."

"Wasn't it *they* that insisted upon issuing two millions of shares, so as to enrich themselves, I should like to know?" said Walter, bitterly. "Wasn't it against our opinion, advice, and warning, that they, who now accuse us, attempted to realize these immense profits? And now, when they find out that their designs upon the public are of no account, they refuse us our money and throw their own villainies into our faces for an excuse!"

"I have deserved it," muttered Mr. Going. "I was warned. Chip, Paradise and *others* warned me; but I could not believe that they were right, and now I must suffer the penalty!"

"But, father," said Walter, resuming his seat, "we must not fail. Whatever we do, whatever we may have to sacrifice, let us keep up our good name."

And although the old gentleman heard a warning voice, in his heart, which told him that a man who is not solvent has no right to keep his state a secret,—although his experience told him of hundreds of houses that had made honorable bankruptcies, and so preserved the respect of the community, which soon brought them back to better fortunes,—yet the sound of his good name was too precious for him to insist on coupling it with that ugly word, and he yielded to his son.

He yielded, and the anxiety of every day through which they had to struggle increased; they no longer knew, experientially, the meaning of undisturbed sleep, or peace of mind. And thus the two merchants kept up the tottering firm at all hazards—at all sacrifices; through weeks of disheartening toil, through months of thankless endurance, through periods when all seemed lost, and only miracle could save them, only to remain in the midst of a never-ending battle with fresh uncertainties and agonizing doubts, to enter upon new labors without end; and all this to keep alive a phantom, a creature of the mind, a reputation undeserved, an honor based upon deceit. And, at the same time, they knew that they were only postponing the catastrophe. All these horrors, agonies, and labors, for no other purpose than *postponement*.

And during this season of trial what of the gay life which had filled the halls, and enlivened the grounds of the stately old Priory? What had become of the grand magnificence of the house in Fifth Avenue, and what was the condition of our dear friend, Miss Jessie Going? Did she know what was passing in her father's office? Did she know the trials of his mind? Let us see what the envied belle of New York thinks in her youthful heart, though she betrays no sign in her gay exterior.

After the day's toil, the throng of working men and women moves away from that part of the city where their daily bread is earned,—their daily bread, and perhaps not a penny to spare for years,—away toward their homes, to sleep until the morning light shall bring the unwelcome summons to another day of labor. But few of these elect to choose the more fashionable thoroughfares for their daily walks, the majority preferring those streets more suited to their station; streets which connect their homes with their workshops, in one unrelieved line of mediocrity. But the few who do venture on a timid walk past the domains of wealth, stare at the palace-homes of that class of humanity which, by its superiority to their own fondest dreams or aspirations, seems so far beyond them as almost to partake of the divine.

Doubtless, then, there had been many hungry and covetous looks cast upon that mansion in Fifth Avenue, where Miss Jessie Going, on this bright Indian-summer afternoon, is watching the passers-by, from the window of her room.

"Who lives in this splendid house?"

"Mr. Going, the great merchant."

"Immensely rich, I suppose?"

"Immensely rich—yes (with a sigh).

"Has he a daughter?"

"Yes, one (what an neiress!); and they say that she is more beautiful and accomplished than any other young lady in New York. She is the reigning belle."

The speakers might have been poor working girls.

Two gentlemen, of unpretentious appearance, are walking home on the other side of the street. No one imagines that they purposely avoid passing that envied house; yet it is so. Mr. Chip and Mr. Fatman, the two millionaires, no longer wish to approach the house of their former friend. Miss Jessie, at her window, recognizes them at a glance, and with womanly pride, retreats for a moment from view, that she may not appear to seek recognition, since it is evident they no longer seek it. She lowers the blind, and when thus in the solitude of her room, her face and manner are relieved of all constraint. On the side of her bed—that virgin sanctum whither she has often retired when her heart beat high with an exultation too strong to be exposed to the scrutiny of society; where the brightest and fondest dreams—sleeping and waking—have beguiled her; where her tears have fallen, gently, joyously, or bitterly, according to their cause—there she sits, with her hands in her lap, and her hair disheveled, misery in her face and a void in her heart, while her young and inexperienced brain is in a whirl with a thousand agonies.

Ah, now she realizes the truth! The world has turned against her father. His friends have fled with his wealth, and now enemies lurk in every corner. The truth is not yet known by all. The decaying skeleton of what was once the great house, the great family, is closed yet from general scrutiny; but a few have lifted a corner of the covering, and peeped under, and those few show in their faces what they have seen. *Appearances* are still kept up, fostering envy, but better envy than that treacherous, smooth-tongued, villainous thing, called *sympathy*. How can any one sympathize with her? Who but she knows that each hair of her father's venerable white head is an inestimable treasure, to be sacredly guarded? Who can feel, as she does, his humiliation, and the harshness of his fellow-men, by which all his strivings to save the integrity of his name, and to secure the welfare of his children, is met?

And when she tries to be cheerful and to comfort him with a world of love, he looks upon her with pity—an expression that would move a brazen image to hot tears, a gaze that is harder to bear up against than would be the bitterest complaints.

"If it were only over!" cries the young girl. "How these articles of luxury by which I am surrounded mock me. I feel as if the fiends animated the finery of this house; as if the bronzes and pictures sneered at us; as if each piece of gold and splendor were a grim mockery, selected by fate to sentinel our misery! Yes," she cried, passionately, "misery, unmitigated misery, is all that life has now in store for me. Perhaps, if the worst were over, I might smile when Heaven granted me a ray of hope or an hour of pleasure. I have seen ragged children in the streets laugh merrily, and even beggars look happy; but this tormenting, maddening condition of uncertainty, and the undefined dread of the future galls every joy, and is, indeed, too hard to bear! The afflictions heaped upon me in my prime of youth are annihilating hope—and creating a *bitterness without end!*"

But youthful vitality revolts against despair, such as was enveloping her meditations, and with the intention of changing her train of thought she approached the window once more, gazing out upon the little piece of dark gold blue sky over the house-tops yonder. That sky reminded her of many an hour of happy exhilaration. She thought of the fields and woodlands glowing in the bright colors of autumn; where the wind blew fresh and the air was luxurious; and the memory of many a face and many a happiness lost forever now (so she thought, poor child), crowded upon her.

Many a face! Was it not rathe *rone* face? She pressed her hands to her heart,—to her heart which enshrined but one image, and yet was desolate, because the image was only a blighting shadow of a happiness once shown to her, to be only too soon removed. Her imagination places before her the form of the man she loves. All her sense of admiration for the beautiful and the graceful do homage before it; all her thoughts of what is good and noble crowd around it; and, from the depths of her inmost soul, the Genius of Love arises and places upon its head a crown of glory; and thus it stands before her mind,—and her mind tells her that he belongs to another.

She sinks upon the couch and buries her beautiful head in the pillows. Let us draw a veil over her weak moments, when utter despair conquers maidenly pride and dashes reason and hope to the ground, until, in a calmer mood, she raises her eyes for the comfort, which, since earth is dead, heaven must accord her

On her knees, praying for her cherished father, imploring the divine grace by all that is good and sweet on earth and holy in heaven, and crying to God, that in his mercy he would heal her heart, half-broken,—thus for the present, we leave the envied belle of New York.

CHAPTER VI.

GOING, GOING, GONE.

"How goes the world, that I am thus encountered With clamorous debt—"
                                    TIMON OF ATHENS.

THE Priory is sold; Mr. Christian Fatman has bought it, and Mr. Going has submitted to the publicity of his comparative poverty only after many an ineffectual struggle. What necessarily had to come, sooner or later, occurred in the following manner :—

On a December day, marked by the first snow of the season, Mr. Going and Walter were occupying the dreary quiet of their office, in moody silence, when the door opened. A fur coat, loaded with snowflakes, entered, and, after unbuttoning itself and opening its wings, graciously permitted the exquisite Mr. Solomons to step forth into the outer world.

"This is a rare favor nowadays," said Mr. Going, greeting him. "I am much afraid that Mr. Solomons, like the rest of the world, does not fancy paying visits to this office, since it is known that we have suffered severe losses and are retrenching in all directions."

"Mr. Going," answered the Jew, "that is not deserved, sir; and to show you that it is not deserved, and that I don't mean to deserve it, I have come to propose a great business to you." With these words he produced a card and handed it to the old gentleman.

"How is this?" asked Walter, moderately astonished, "'NATHAN SOLOMONS, AUCTIONEER'? So you have left the stock business, hey?"

"I have. No money in it. If you lose, you pay; if you make, nobody pays you. Money is tight when you're hard up, and when you have any, you can't get seven pershent. Losing business, sir; all credit and no cash."

"Well, sir," said Mr. Going, with a smile, after they had seated themselves, and an awkward pause ensued since the last sentence of Mr. Solomons' valuable wisdom. "As it is easy to perceive that you have business to propose, speak it out."

"Our mutual friend, Mr. Fatman—"

Here Walter muttered an oath which startled the late stock-broker so considerably, that Mr. Going had some trouble to persuade him to continue his remarks.

"Well, sir, Mr. Fatman sent me here," ejaculated Mr. Solomons, coloring violently.

"For what purpose?" said Mr. Going, coldly.

"To see whether you would not—"

"Speak, man!" cried Walter, impatiently, as the broker stopped once more in utter confusion.

"Would not.—" Here he actually stammered.

"Another pull, my man, and you'll fetch it!" cried Walter, laughing at the sight of the Jew's helpless confusion. He was shifting about on his chair as if it was uncomfortably hot for him, and his face expressed mingled reluctance and fear. Finally he seemed to collect all his energies for one grand effort and almost shrieked out,—

" Fatman wants to know whether you'll sell him the Priory for two hundred thousand dollars, cash!"

Mr. Going shrank back from the words as if he had received a blow, then he sat up very straight in his chair, and was about to answer, when Walter, whose face had suddenly assumed a very grave expression, extended his hand to Mr. Solomons, and said, warmly,—

" You're a good fellow, Solomons. I see that you have a heart and the honor of a gentleman, or you would not have felt that just hesitation in making us a proposal, which, coming as it does from the man to whom we owe our misfortunes, sounds more like a taunting insult than a mere business proposition."

" My son has spoken my sentiments," interposed, Mr. Going, " and you may tell Mr. Fatman the answer you received!"

Reader, does it not seem strange that in the course of the next hour after this answer to the Jew's proposition, the Priory was sold, through Mr. Solomons, by this high-toned gentleman, to Mr. Fatman, for two hundred and ten thousand dollars ? If you think this seems unnatural, remember the power of money. Messrs. Going & Son, though not yet bankrupt, in the eyes of the world, were, at this time, poor men; and if we reflect upon the sore needs of the firm we shall not wonder that these two men sacrificed their inclinations, conquered their pride and stretched a point of dignity in accepting this offer from a contemptible · enemy. And it so happened that the Priory was sold.

Mr. Solomons remarked in the course of the interview, that he had undertaken this negotiation at the earnest solicitation of Mr. Fatman, and also because he felt satisfied that it would be for Mr. Going's interest to accept the offer. Of course the private transfer of real estate is not an auctioneer's legitimate business; but since Mr. Fatman did not wish to purchase the furniture of the Priory (except the carpets and fixtures, which had been included in the sale), Mr. Solomons now suggested an auction of all the rest, which he had no doubt would realize a handsome sum. Since the house in Fifth Avenue was completely furnished, and the storage of valuable furniture was not advisable, this furniture could be of no service to Mr. Going. After considering these suggestions of the Jew, Mr. Going had another sharp struggle with his pride, and they agreed to that also.

" Are you going home, father ?" asked Walter, when evening drew on. Mr. Solomons had disappeared long ago, and the old gentleman, rising from his desk with a deep sigh, had called the solitary clerk to assist him with his overcoat.

" Not immediately," answered Mr. Going, evasively, moving toward the door.

" There is one comfort," said Walter, after a pause, during which both reflected upon the fact that on this eventful day neither had any inclination to walk home in company with the other, as usual, and that by silent and mutual consent they had got rid of each other. " One great comfort," said Walter, lighting a cigar,

and making ostentatious preparations for writing letters which only existed as an excuse for remaining at the office until his father had left. " A *wonderful* comfort, which consists in the fact that Fatman, besides assuming the mortgage which John Van Strom still holds on the Priory, will pay us enough *cash*, as Solomons says, to settle a lot of villainous private debts and small business accounts which have accumulated, and leave a good sum besides to meet coming obligations."

" Temporary comfort, Walter," answered the old gentleman, turning to the door. " Private bills will accumulate again, business debts will press upon us, and *we have no more Priories* left to sell ! Good night. I hasten to break the news to Jessie."

He was gone. " Straight home after all," thought Walter, " so we. prefer to entertain each other, separately, this evening. Well, let me see—" and he went into deep calculations, appropriating in advance a much greater portion of the proceeds of the Priory than he had at first expected would be in immediate requisition.

In breaking the news to Jessie, Mr. Going found an easy, even a joyful task, where he had expected a distressing scene. Nor is Jessie Going the only American girl that carries a brave and noble heart, under the mask of frivolous love of pleasure, and reckless coquetry.

At the first timid and sad hints about the possibility or desirability of a prospective sale, Miss Jessie threw herself into her father's arms, and cried cheerfully,—

" Out with it, papa ! You have sold the dear old Priory, and you are afraid your little daughter will be distressed about it. Let it go, darling papa, furniture and all. Yes, and this house too, and every thing else except contentment and poor me !"

Her father's face was radiant with joy. He pressed her to his heart, while in their mingled tears was sealed anew the compact of mutual love and trust, whose value is most appreciated in the hour of adversity.

When Walter returned home that night, his father and sister were in such excellent spirits that he found courage to inform them that he had received a very good offer for the four bays, the harness for driving four-in-hand and the accompanying carriages. It was at once agreed that the offer should be accepted, and Miss Jessie, so far from expressing regret at this new sacrifice, became quite jubilant and insisted upon Walter's company that night, to a ball, which, under other circumstances, she would not have consented to attend.

" I want to find out who are my friends, when every one knows that we are poor," she said, and the time was not far off when it would prove her happy lot to discover that under the world's vanity, there is a current of real excellence, whose presence the cynic denies because through his prejudice, he remains only half informed on the subject of human nature.

When the day of the auction sale arrived, a large crowd gathered at the Priory. Many came from the neighboring families who had not yet moved to town or who lived the entire year in the country, and many purchasers from the city had been induced to attend the sale by Mr. Solomon's glowing advertisements in the daily newspapers. Dame Rumor had also gratuitously advertised the sale, telling far and near that Going & Son—the great firm—had been compelled to sell their celebrated country-place, and that, on such a day, the furniture, which was quite princely for a citizen of a republic, would be sold to the highest bidder at public auction.

Miss Jessie had insisted upon attending at the sale; but when she and Walter were treated like strangers by the horde of vandals which had invaded their home,—when they had to pick their way through the confused heaps of furniture, now piled up into "lots," and she recognized many a cherished object, and many a household god now dethroned and strewn about like the corpses on a battle-field,—when she heard Mr. Solomon's voice shrieking and yelling, and rattling away, as if he were possessed by a demon, as he rapidly sold off to the highest bidder many a thing become priceless to her from associations,—when the unceasing "Going, going, gone!" smote her ear with increasing pain, and Walter made a grim joke on the analogy of their own good name, to the irrepressible refrain of the auctioneer,—when she finally *realized* that here a home was being desolated and demolished, cruelly stripped of the cherished though inanimate companions of many a happy hour long past,—when these reflections pressed themselves upon her consideration her spirit broke down, she felt that she was being driven away from a happy home by that yelling clown of a Jew, and she hurried her brother away from the scene. Like a fugitive, she sought a retreat in that house where she had once enjoyed all that comfort and luxury can command, and there she found none. From the inquisitive gaze of strangers she again fled away, and this time found shelter in the same summer-house where Ernest Montant had first conversed with Josephine Van Strom, long ago. As Walter's presence was needed elsewhere, he left her there in the still powerful beams of the winter's sun, and there, protected by thick shawls, she found an hour of solitude and contemplation.

She was disturbed by some one's approach, and a respectful voice said:—

"I have been searching high and low for you, Miss Going. I have something to say to you, and, if you will allow me, I will say it here."

Miss Jessie lifted her eyes and beheld before her the elegantly attired form of Mr. Wheeler. We must remember that he and Mr. Faro were two gentlemen distinguished for their wealth, fashionably good standing in New York society, and intimacy at Mr. Going's house. Both of them had often excited our hero's deep contempt and animosity by their inanity and claims upon Miss Going's preference, claims which were honored with a sincerity of which we are well able to judge.

Mr. Wheeler then lifted his hat and for one gracious moment exhibited to her delighted gaze his exquisitely-dressed hair, parted exactly in the center and nearly touching his eyebrows, since his noble forehead had been molded very low by "dissembling nature." At all events, there he stood, his mustache-crowned lips parted, and his eyes dilated, while his delicate right hand entertained its white fingers by allowing them an unrestrained freedom in pulling and twisting his whisker.

"Miss Going," he said, still at a respectful distance, "Faro told me—"

"Well, what did Mr. Faro tell you?" asked Miss Jessie, the slight tears with which her gloomy reflections had moistened her black eyes, giving place to a coquettish glance.

"He advised me—in fact—"

"Did he advise you to stop short in the middle of every sentence, Mr. Wheeler?" asked the young lady, laughing.

"No—no. But he thought that since my uncle died—" explained the gentleman.

"What a dismal subject!" cried Miss Jessie.

"Well, now, it isn't dismal, at all," said Mr. Wheeler, with a grin.

"Why, Mr. Wheeler!" cried Miss Jessie, in amused wonder. "Who would have thought you so heartless as to make merry at your uncle's death!"

"No, but it isn't that."

"Well, then, what is it?"

"He left me a great deal of money, Miss Going—and—in fact—Faro thought—"

"Mr. Wheeler!" said the young lady, somewhat alarmed by his continued grins and the incoherence of his language, "I sincerely hope that your newly-acquired wealth has neither turned your brain nor made you a victim of that *disgusting* habit—drinking, you know." Having said this with due emphasis, a pause ensued, during which the young man rolled his eyes around desperately, as if in search of some relief; but none was forthcoming, the silence was becoming unbearable, and he finally found courage to reply, looking at any thing rather than the person addressed:—

"It isn't that at all, Miss Going, but you see the Priory is sold."

Miss Jessie nodded, an intimation that she had heard something of the kind before.

"And—you see—Faro thought you were poor!"

It is impossible to describe the grimace which accompanied this happy delivery of his inmost thoughts. His listener, however, was very much startled by the remark, and the suspicion of what was most likely to follow only increased her amazement.

"Mr. Faro is perfectly correct. I *am* poor."

"And, therefore," continued Mr. Wheeler, apparently addressing the ornament on the roof of the summer-house, "and, therefore, Faro thought—that—that since I was rich and —you were poor—" The perspiration stood in beads on his face, he trembled violently, and, with a convulsive effort (now that he could not retreat), he gasped out,—

"Faro thought that, since I love you, and you were poor and I rich — in fact, Faro thought that if I asked you to marry me, you would do it." He retreated a step as if horrified by his own speech, and stood before her with eyes fastened upon the ground, the picture of complete confusion, muttering to himself, "Well, if it's all wrong, I have put it off on Faro, anyhow!"

But Jessie Going felt no inclination to laugh at him. With a woman's correct intuition, she recognized and appreciated the kindliness of heart which was prompting this man to offer himself to her, and she was too good and kind and gentle, not to feel very, very sorry for him! In the opinion of every one, Mr. Wheeler was a fop, and was called a fool by many. What little brains he possessed were seldom exercised except on petty affairs of amusement or dress, yet it seems that he had a large heart beneath his immaculate shirt-bosom, and it is an open question whether he was not more prompted by generosity, in this offer of marriage, than by pure selfishness. His simplicity (oh! how very simple, reputed men of the world are at times) led him into this error, but his noble intention made him worthy of consideration. So thought Miss Jessie Going as she heard the ludicrous utterance of Mr. Wheeler's feelings, and instead of derision she gave him pity. It is hardly necessary to say that she refused him, but the manner in which she did it proved her soul as true as steel and her heart to be of pure gold.

In spite of the severe disappointment, in the course of a long conversation, she succeeded in soothing him considerably. Before they parted, she had brought him back to common sense, and to his great astonishment he soon found himself in a smiling, good humor, and as happy as if Faro had not played him this trick.

On the whole, however, the effect upon Miss Jessie was very beneficial, for although she was very sorry for Mr. Wheeler, yet she was gratified at the thought that *such* friends were to be found among her least-esteemed acquaintance, and as she had learned to esteem Mr. Wheeler more than she had thought possible, her views of the false world that had educated her were correspondingly elevated, and she felt new energy and new confidence in herself and her fellow-creatures.

Miss Jessie would not release Mr. Wheeler, and he accompanied them back to town, while the whole trio were in far better spirits than Walter had expected they would be after saying farewell to the Priory.

*　　*　　*　　*　　*

" A palatial residence—it is indeed a noble place—a *regal* place, Mr. Paradise," said Mr. Christian Fatman, to the hunchbacked lawyer, as they sat down to the first dinner in the newly - furnished dining-hall. Mr. Fatman rubbed his hands delightedly, and looked around the table. Mrs. Fatman sat opposite him, and the rest of the company of ladies and gentlemen were all from the city, and had joined in a midwinter excursion into the country for the purpose of doing justice to the sleighing, skating, and hospitality which they had been promised by their host.

As usual, Mr. Paradise had to make a disagreeable remark.

" Well, Mr. Fatman," he sneered, " if it is a *regal* place, you certainly did not get possession of it by *kingly* means!"

An awkward silence ensued. Each one looked at Mr. Fatman, and then at Mr. Paradise, and then at his neighbor, finally, concentrating his attention on the good things before him. Mr. Fatman looked very uncomfortable, but did not conclude to take up the gage of battle.

When the old port wine was brought out of the closet, the door of which looked crusty and like port wine, as Walter Going had noticed when they first visited old John Jacob Van Strom—when the wine was brought on the table, and had been poured out—Mr. Paradise arose and gave a toast:—

" To the late owner of this noble house. May our present host prove as kind and hospitable as my old friend Going; and when he fails may he be *hoisted out* by as sharp practice as was measured out to Going!"

But then Mr. Paradise was deformed, and pity gave him license to make disagreeable speeches. *He* had long known that Mr. Fatman had set his heart on obtaining the Priory, and understood perfectly well all the maneuvers he had used to satisfy his desires. And now the lawyer grudged the success which had crowned the rich man's schemes.

CHAPTER VII.

SO FAR, SO GOOD—BUT, HOW NOW?

" Thou wrong'st a gentleman who is as far
From thy report as thou from honor."
CYMBELINE.

WINTER had come with frost and snow, bringing desolation to nature, and ice-cold chills upon all the North. The airy situation of John Van Strom's house gave freedom for the December gales to play their storm games upon the trembling frame of the building, and although Bella had the means and the taste to make the interior comfortable, the voices of the wild blast without put a damper upon her fireside as well as upon those not so well defended, and the proposition of moving to town for a few months of winter enjoyment was often advanced, and more and more favorably received· John's moods had lately assumed a more melancholy turn, and as his wife watched him, crouched by the fire and staring vacantly into the dancing flames on those dreary winter nights, she felt sad and oppressed.

It was generally in the cosy dining-room, and with a great wood fire roaring merrily, that the married couple spent those winter evenings in the quietest manner, and with a tinge of irrepressible melancholy, while the lovers, Josephine and our hero, after diligent search, might have been discovered snugly ensconced in some corner, screened from observation and existing, during those precious moments, for and in themselves alone.

But they did not forget their duties as guests, in return for the hospitality and kindness which they received, and they were always ready for a game of whist, or to engage in any other amusement agreeable to their simple host. They also made it a point to keep up

John's interest in ordinary matters, by conversing freely at the table and elsewhere upon topics of general interest—discussing questions of the day and commenting upon the latest news. Thus they were seated together one evening, John, for once in a good humor, with Bella on the sofa near the fire, his arm wound lightly around her substantial waist, and the lovers opposite in a more demonstrative attitude of affection. No longer was their engagement a secret, and John had given his consent in terms of most extravagant approbation and delight.

"I have advices from town to-day," said our hero, "and I am sorry to say that I hear bad news of my former employers, Messrs. Going & Son. It seems evident that they are struggling hard to avoid what can not be avoided, instead of making an honorable retreat from their lost position, acknowledging their defeat, but saving their honor."

"Has Walter written to you?" asked Josephine, turning her face toward him, for, we may as well admit it, her lovely head was reclining on his shoulder, while his arm encircled her figure, not quite so lightly as the arm which embraced Bella.

"No, dear," answered Ernest; "some one one has written to me whose confidence is too sacred to be revealed, even to you."

Josephine was satisfied, and resumed her former position in entire acquiescence with his better judgment.

"Mr. Van Strom," continued our hero, "far be it from me to presume upon meddling with your affairs; but I was sorry that you did not send an agent to bid on the Priory furniture. By the way, why could you not have repurchased the old place? It was sold for less than it is worth at any moment."

"I have no money," answered John, seriously. "Do you suppose I am rolling in wealth?"

"Really, I never investigated the subject," answered Montant, with a quiet smile.

"Honestly, haven't you?" asked John, eagerly, and fixing a sharp look upon his guest.

"It would have been contrary to my character and habit of mind had I done so," answered Ernest, with some dignity; and as Josephine nestled closer to him as he spoke, he pressed her tighter to his breast.

"Mr. Montant," said John Van Strom, after a pause, "I hope and think you speak the truth, and as that is my opinion, I, to-night, invite you to leave those disagreeable lodgings in the village, and come to live altogether with me. If I thought you were hankering after my money, like everybody else in this accursed world of greediness, I would hate you; but as I believe you are honest, I love you. Take my advice and marry that girl there as soon as possible. *Marry her*, I say. John Van Strom tells you to MARRY HER, sir," he continued, with great energy, "and that same gentleman means what he says!"

"I accept your invitation, with gratitude," answered our hero, looking into Josephine's face, as it was turned to meet his gaze, all radiant with loving entreaty and hope and happiness, "and as for marrying this girl here, I mean to do that very thing in less than two weeks; that is, unless she objects."

"Of which there is great probability," interposed Bella, laughing.

"And now, sir," continued John, with dignity, "let us talk business, in spite of the girls' listening. They'll find it all out, any way, you know."

"Do you think we would, Josie?" asked Bella.

"If it is to be interesting," answered Josephine, "I don't so much mind listening; but if it is going to be dry and long-winded and horrid, I would rather be excused."

"Well, sir," continued John, without heeding the interruption, "you are, I believe, poor."

"Your belief, sir," answered our hero, good-naturedly, although firmly, "is entirely wrong. I am the undisputed possessor of nearly two thousand dollars, and I have brains and arms fully capable of more than supporting a wife. If you call that poor, our ideas on the subject differ. I ask no one's assistance, because, in the first place, I don't need it, and secondly, the idea of assistance is distasteful to me."

"But," cried John, in some excitement, "just because you do not ask it, I am going to offer it to you! How much capital do you want to go into business?"

"I thought you had no money!" said our hero, laughing.

"Nonsense! Tell me how much you want!"

"Upon my word, that is hard to say," answered our hero, cautiously. "Wait till I have a business, and then I will tell you. It may be any imaginable sum that my future business will warrant me in borrowing, or it may be not one cent."

"But I want it to be something," cried John, angrily. "Do you think a Van Strom can be put off in this contemptuous manner, sir? Do you think it is *nothing* to have me, John Jacob Van Strom, make you such an offer? I will not be contradicted in this way!"

Bella gave our hero an anxious, pleading look, for John was working himself up into one of those fits of passion which she still feared and strove to avoid; so Montant, catching her meaning, said, quickly,—

"You misunderstand me, and although I can not mention a sum at present, I promise you that I will call upon you at an early day for what I may require."

"And that will be *something*," persisted John. "Not a few hundreds, nor only a few thousands, mind you!"

"It will be quite enough, I assure you," replied our hero.

"And you will stay at my house to-night, and remain until you marry that girl?"

"I will, with great pleasure."

"And you will marry her this month?"

"Here is the bargain sealed," replied Montant, laughing, and kissing Josephine's lips. John gave vent to an exclamation of enthusiasm, and running like a child to Josephine, kissed her on both cheeks.

"Good-luck to you, sister-in-law!" he cried, in the best humor. He then rang the bell, and upon the appearance of the same old butler who had been "in the family forty years," he ordered a bottle of champagne. When he had composed himself somewhat, he said, with that singular acuteness in judging himself which often characterizes people of contracted intellect,—

"I am astonished at my liberality, to-night, because, even though I am a fool, I am close in money matters and shrewd in business. I am the last man to take out my purse; but when I once have confidence in a man, he might rob me of my last dollar, and I would give the last as readily as the first. This comes from my stupidity, I suppose, which allows me only one idea in my head. But that idea, sir," and he struck his fist on the table, "that idea, sir, must be carried out, sir, at all hazards!"

Hereupon the toast of the new couple was pledged in a merry bumper, and John heaped the most affectionate attentions upon Bella, showing so much sprightliness and loving kindness, that tears of gratitude and happiness stood in her honest eyes.

A ring at the door-bell interrupted this friendly and interesting family party, and the unusual event of a visitor to the lonely country-house at this unpropitious hour (for half-past-eight had been announced some time before by the pretty little French clock) could but create a sensation of half-anxious curiosity as to the character of the one asking for admission.

"Mr. Stilletto, from New York!" announced the old butler, who, to his disgust, was compelled to answer the hall-door; which duty, he opined, belonged to "ordinary waiters," but not to such as he.

Not one of our four friends failed to experience a sort of disagreeable sensation at the mere sound of the name. They all knew Stilletto. Our hero knew him intimately, as we have seen, and the others, since the evening when Mr. Fatman introduced his *protégé* into "good society," to the infinite gratification of the *protégé*.

"I must beg pardon for this late call," said Mr. Stilletto, with perfect self-reliance, as he greeted the party. "Good-evening, Mrs. Van Strom," bowing to Bella, entirely too low to be in good taste. "Mr. Van Strom, your most obedient, sir,"—"Madam" (to Josephine) "I see you are as beautiful as ever; and Montant, old fellow," shaking hands with our hero, and affecting a very cordial intimacy with him, "I am glad to see you; but of course (with an insolent leer which was intended for shyness), that might have been expected." Josephine, for whose benefit this refined speech was made, turned away with an expression of intense annoyance, and all but John treated the intruder with marked coldness, from the very beginning.

With an acuteness worthy of better motives, Stilletto saw at once how matters stood here, and if any one could have read his heart, it would have been perceived that the situation was entirely satisfactory to the wily Italian—for what reasons, remains to be seen. He had not displeased John, though he might well

have feared lest he should. He was a disagreeable object to the ladies and to Montant, —this he had foreseen, and he did not care a straw about it. John's excellent humor had opened his simple heart to the ready welcome of any one, and he had not brain enough to detect the innate coarseness of the unexpected guest.

But the favorable opening presented to Mr. Stilletto's maneuvers, was not allowed to remain unimproved for a moment. That he had some object in view was especially apparent to the quick perception and sound judgment of Bella Van Strom, and she had not watched his cat-like movements around the room, his cunning ever-watchful looks, his alertness and sharp speeches, for many moments, before she said to herself: "This man has an aim in inflicting his vulgarity on us. He is entering upon a planned series of operations, and I would give much to know what it is all about."

Stilletto strained every faculty of his fertile brain to entertain John Van Strom. He flattered him and drew him out until John commenced to talk loudly about his own affairs and make a complete fool of himself. But he had an attentive and obsequious listener, and not until he had exhausted his stock of weak, though pardonable conceit, and had come to the end of his conversational powers, did Stilletto talk more than his fascinated host. Then he commenced to tell anecdotes which aroused John's mirth to the pitch of boisterousness, until the ladies, annoyed and thoroughly disgusted, rose to retire. John bowed them out, much discontented at their coldness and scant courtesy toward Stilletto; but the latter, when the three gentlemen were left alone, quickly restored him to good humor, by showering praises upon Bella.

"Montant, old fellow," cried the Italian, "I see you are at home here! How hospitable you are, Mr. Van Strom. But then there are reasons—of course, good reasons!"

Our hero gave him a look which should have cautioned him somewhat, but he went on:—

"You have not re-entered business, have you, Montant, since you were discharged—beg pardon—I mean since you fell out with Mr. Going?"

Our hero did not answer a syllable; but with compressed lips kept his eyes fixed upon the fellow with a strange light in them, which should again have warned Stilletto; but either he welcomed a possible altercation, or his natural courage made him defiant, for he went on, in a sneering, insulting tone,—

"Is it not pleasant for broken-down men to find friends to sponge upon? I wish poor Stilletto could find a great gentleman to feed and lodge him for months at a time, with a beautiful, near relative of that same great and *rich* gentleman, to marry into the bargain."

In an instant Montant was on his feet. For one moment Stilletto seemed doomed to a terrible visitation of a just wrath, and the livid palor which suddenly overspread his face, as he made a hasty movement behind the table, showed that the flashing eyes, the furious tremor of Montant's whole frame, had not escaped his notice. But at the right moment our hero mastered himself, though only after a severe struggle, and saying, between his teeth,—

"Thank your stars that this is not my house," strode to the door, and left the room.

"His house!" snarled Stilletto, more incensed by the fright he had suffered, and by the contemptuous tone, than by the import of the words he had just heard. "I dare say he thinks it is almost his already, intriguing pauper that he is. I do not pretend to offer any advice to you, Mr. Van Strom, but it was very kind in your guest to say that this was not his house! A stranger might have supposed from his general manner that he was master here already!"

The manner in which John had borne himself during the quarrel, showed how well Stilletto had studied the ground before provoking the quarrel. His most sanguine expectations had been realized, and that, not after weeks of careful strategy, but on his very first visit. He had dared to throw the gauntlet of defiance at Ernest Montant, and John Van Strom had taken sides with him. What could follow, but that the two ladies would take Montant's part, discord would reign between Montant and the ladies, against John. Then was it not within the range of probability that John would need an ally, and by proper management, why should there not be a firm alliance between the "great and *rich* gentleman" and Antonio Stilletto?

Yes, John's fickle, unstable mind, worked upon by the cunning remarks of the intruder, had instantaneously changed against our hero, the man upon whom, but half an hour previously, he had lavished every manifestation of friendship and good will. Stilletto had made a masterly attack. He had opened the way to John's good will by amusing him, and then, when he had gained his confidence, launched into his weak and impressible mind the poisoned arrows of suspicion, upon which base the crafty villain designed to erect the superstructure of his intrigue.

John Van Strom had not only failed to resent the impertinences offered to his guest by Stilletto, but had maintained a dogged silence, which encouraged the bold offender. John, however, seemed satisfied when Montant had left the room, and said,—

"Let us have a social glass of wine, Stilletto! We can be merrier without that solemn chap's companionship.

"Come, sirs, let us drink,
   While the glasses chink," &c.,

he roared, at the top of his voice, as if possessed by some demon, while he filled both glasses to the brim, and emptied his at one gulp. Stilletto was not slow in following his example, and another bottle of champagne having been called for, the new friends became more and more charmed with each other. Such an acute general as the Italian had proved himself, would not lose this golden opportunity for defaming the character of Montant, and he accordingly put in many severe and cutting remarks about that gentleman, until, at a late hour, good or evil fortune brought the latter into the room.

He had just left Josephine and Bella, to whom he had complained, in a manly, dignified way, of the manner in which John had permitted the almost incredible insolence of Mr. Stilletto, and he informed them that he would not consent to remain under their roof that night, unless amends were made to him for the insults he had received. To Bella's sorrowful prediction, that such a demand would only lead to general discord, our hero quietly assured her that he would bear the consequences alone; that his action was dictated by his manhood and sense of honor, and he remained deaf to their entreaties for peace. "I think I need not ask him for the privilege of marrying you, my dear Josephine; and I am quite sure that I am independent of him, or his pecuniary assistance, as I told him very distinctly."

So he came back to the room where the new friends were enjoying themselves, and immediately upon encountering their more curious than pleased glances, informed them of his errand.

"Mr. Van Strom, after recovering from my momentary anger, I have returned to ask you, as host here, whether you will kindly hint to Mr. Stilletto, that in choosing the protection of your roof, from which to safely attack me, he has made a mistake; and that in insulting me, he has insulted you—my host; and that you require an apology made to me at once."

Instead of answering, John, with a malicious grin, turned to Stilletto and said,—

"Answer, friend."

"Do not open your lips!" cried our hero, trembling with the rage which was fast gaining the mastery. "Not a word from you," he added, between his teeth, turning so squarely upon Stilletto, that the latter, borne back by that fiery glance, recoiled to the very wall. "Not one word, at your peril!"

"Well, then," cried John, with a red face, and flashing eyes, "I'll answer you——"

But at this moment Bella appeared at the door. She had no sooner cast one look at her husband, than she was at his side. Half a year ago he might have cast her from him in contemptuous fury, as he had done at the Priory; but she had not made him her study and sole object in life without gaining more power over him than she then possessed. Power of what kind? Call it magnetism; call it cunning; call it will-power, or love, or the influence of one human soul upon another; but it was a power sufficient to lead him out of that room, in spite of the mad attack that was upon him, and which in another moment would have carried him beyond control.

White as death, his under-lip quivering, as we have seen it before, Stilletto stood, his eyes flashing forth a world of hatred, confronting our hero in the impotent fury of a chained dog. He knew that he had no chance against *that* man, as he stood with his arms folded, his eyes riveted on him, his breast heaving, and his lips drawn tight, in the effort to be calm; but Stilletto's evil genius drowned his prudence in the mad boiling of his Southern blood, and although his physical instinct kept him from attempting violence, his ungovernable tongue hissed these fatal words,—

"Where is *your* hussy? Why don't she come and take you up-stairs?"

The words had hardly escaped his white lips, when every fiber of his mind and body thrilled with fear for the consequences. An arm of iron was upon him. Blows that knew no moderating restraint showered upon him, marking his villainous face and body, and he felt himself dragged through the hall, knew that the front door was opened, and with a quick succession of parting blows, he rolled down the steps upon the grass, in front of the piazza, and heard the door close behind him, leaving him alone with darkness, and no inconsiderable amount of pain, from the punishment received. It took him some time to recover any thing like composure. His first thought was to ring the door-bell, and ask for his hat, which had been forgotten in his hasty exit; but he did not dare to confront that man again. In the midst of his dismay, and mad vexation, and pain, and confusion, he remembered that at the first onset he had given up his life as lost; but that our hero had suddenly ceased his blows, and contented himself with kicking him out like a dog, evidently desiring to spare his life. So Stilletto came to the conclusion that he had got off pretty well, all things considered; and thinking to himself, "the next time he might finish me entirely," he sneaked away from the house, out into the road and darkness, with thoughts that will be understood when we see to what actions they brought him.

In the meanwhile, our hero had sunk into a hall chair, exhausted, not by his physical efforts, but by the frenzy which had mastered him.

Yet he felt relieved, and when one or two frightened servants appeared, he laughed and told them the circumstances in a few words. Josephine had heard the noise, slight as it was, for Stilletto had not called for help, he belonged to a more dangerous class of dogs than those that bark. The widow had retired; but, hastily throwing a wrapper around her, came down stairs, pale and frightened at all sorts of dangers which had suggested themselves to her imagination. Her lover caught her in his arms, and reassured her. Bella now appeared from her room, which was situated in another part of the house.

"What happened?" she inquired, anxiously. "I heard noises, though John only asked who had left, when he heard the hall door closed. I can imagine all," she added, looking attentively at our hero. "You have treated the fellow as he deserved, and he left *alone* instead of with you, as I told my husband to keep him quiet. I am very glad indeed that the wine had somewhat blunted John's sense of hearing!"

They then held a council of war. At first our hero insisted upon leaving the house that night, as usual, and going to his lodgings at the village hotel. But the earnest prayers of his fair friends prevailed upon him to remain, lest Stilletto, who might be lying in ambush for him, should seek his revenge by striking at his life from some dark corner.

So he spent the whole night in the dark parlor, without closing his eyes in sleep, thinking over the occurences of the evening and of all the possible consequences; and at the first peep of dawn he left the house, whose host, but a few hours previous had offered him unbounded hospitality, with the firm resolve never to enter it again.

CHAPTER VIII.

GREAT SUCCESS.

"I'll pour this pestilence into his ear."
OTHELLO.

MR. STILLETTO had laid out a grand and comprehensive plan of action, with a definite object in view.

Although unexpected success, as already stated, had crowned his first interview with John Van Strom, it was not pride that now inspired him as he strode rapidly along, entertaining himself by violent gesticulations, hurrying through the black night away from the scene of his late degradation and well-merited punishment. Without his hat, and his coat torn, his whole attire and his hair no less disordered than was his mind, by the sudden violent stop put upon his promising intrigues, he sought among the scattered buildings of the village, the house were he and Mr. Muller had taken up their quarters, and whither we will now precede him, and pay a respectful visit to the great philosopher.

Oh, for philosophy and a pipe! What a great man Herr Muller thought himself as he allowed the fire in the stove before him to irradiate its rays of heat upon his lean body? How disdainful of all other worldly wisdom than his own, was the egotistical sneer on his lip, and how compassionately he mentally regarded that poor humanity which did not appreciate his grand philosophy! But with all his superiority, there was one tender spot in that great soul, there was one weakness, a strong weakness, and it took the name of *beer*. Beer it was that enlivened the companionship of his pipe, beer it was that changed the roaring of the storm out doors into soothing music to his ears, and it was beer that beguiled the time of waiting for the return of Stilletto, who had gone through the rain and wind to pay his first visit to John Van Strom and to play the first move in the game those two acute intellects had planned out.

The room in which they sat was one of a suite which they had hired in an uncomfortable summer boarding-house. The furniture was uncomfortable in shape, while imposing in color, the walls were bare, and the lamp dim. In a remote corner the Italian girl reclined on a lounge, mute and motionless. She hardly ever addressed her conversation to Muller, for she hated him. In fact she hated most people, and especially herself.

When the lights in the village had all disappeared, and honest people had gone to bed, there they still remained in perfect silence, with nothing but their own reflections to break the dreary monotony of the storm without, until they finally heard a noise at the door, and rapid steps in the hall and on the staircase forwarning them of the arrival of Mr. Stilletto.

Muller, with his usual dignity, did not change his position, or even turn his head when his chum entered. Simonetta being "in the sulks," as Stilletto would say, did not seem aware of his presence, until he cried, angrily,—

"Can't you look up, you cursed fools? Here I come half beside myself with fury, and you dare to run the risk of turning it to madness! Look to your rotten bones, you drunken devil; and you, hussy, in the corner, come out into the light or I'll leave my mark on you!"

Simonetta remained motionless until he addressed her in Italian, when she arose and went toward him reluctantly enough. Muller now deigned to turn around, and raised his eyebrows, while he took a survey of Stilletto's condition.

"Sit down," he said, deliberately, pointing to a chair. Stilletto, upon whom exhaustion and vexation began to have an effect, obeyed.

"So he beat you, I see," said the philosopher, crossing one leg over the other, and lighting a fresh pipe.

"Who beat me, you drunkard," snarled Stilletto.

"Mr. Stilletto," replied the other, loftily, "August Muller can not, must not, will not condescend to be insulted by the vulgar epithets suggested to your vile lips by your innate coarseness! Fit your tongue to my dignity, sir, and we will further discuss the accident which has befallen you, if I may judge by your disheveled hair, your bleeding countenance, and withal the vehemence of your manner."

"The English of which is, I suppose, that I look as if I had got a good thrashing. Well, it is true."

"Candor graces the hero and removes the stain from the coward," said Mr. Muller, with a sneer.

Without regaining his temper, Stilletto related what we already know of his visit to John Van Strom. Muller's face brightened with an unwholesome satisfaction as he heard of Stilletto's success—that the seed of discord had been already sown in that quiet household, and that, at that moment, the Italian probably stood higher than any one else in Van Strom's confidence. Stilletto's ejaculations of hate, and threats of revenge, with which he accompanied his narrative failed to disturb the serenity which beamed from the philosopher's countenance, and when all had been told, and Stilletto, worked up into a snarling fury, finally ceased, exhausted, Muller answered,—

"All is well, my worthy friend! The campaign has opened gloriously."

"The devil it has! That—"

"Don't waste your time on eloquence," interrupted Muller. "Revenge thou shalt have. Be patient and wait till the time comes."

"How shall I have my revenge?"

"Not by dirk or dagger—not by suit or libel—not by any of those mad proceedings by which people heap additional trouble on their stupid heads! Be calm and we will consult."

"But revenge I will have, even to his death," cried Stilletto.

"Well, we'll try to have his life for it," whispered Muller, mysteriously. "But not by murdering him! Oh, no!"

"I promise to be quiet and wait patiently, if I can be certain that he will have to drain a bitter cup for this."

At this moment Stilletto happened to glance at the Italian girl. She had taken a seat near them and was gazing steadily upon his face. There was a something in her look that did not suit him, and he told her, angrily, to leave the room. She compelled him to repeat the order in Italian, and then slowly rose to obey. With a defiant air, she was passing through the door, when he, dying to revenge himself on somebody for his hurts, ran after her and actually kicked her.

It was more the insult than the violence of the blow that sent the blood to her face, leaving it an instant after, deathly pale. Her eyes flashed, her lips quivered, and with a quick movement, her hand sought something hidden in her bosom. Stilletto knew her, and recoiled a step, searching for the weapon he was accustomed to wear concealed about his person, but, with an exclamation of fear, he discovered that it was lost. She did not draw, however, but turned away and sought her own chamber after darting one look of scorn and hatred at him.

"I promise to wait patiently if I can be certain he will have to drain a bitter cup," she soliloquized, repeating his last remark. "That fool! He knows what revenge means, and swears his soul away to obtain it, and yet he is not afraid of me."

"I have lost my dirk!" said Stilletto, when he had closed the door upon her. "I must have lost it in the fight I had up there, for I know I grabbed it."

"Then it must be in Van Strom's house now," said Muller, sagely, and meeting no contradiction, the philosopher added, thoughtfully,—

"None but an idiot disdains to use the little incidents which chance throws in the way!"

We shall see before very long what resulted from this dirk left in Van Strom's house and will leave these two to prolong their consultation, which did not treat exclusively of holy subjects, to the small hours of the night.

*   *   *   *   *

After this Stilletto frequently repeated his visits to John, and a change came over the household at Van Strom's. The mental condition of poor John, approaching to possession of perfect reason, reached to a state of gloom, varying with irritation. Dark thoughts and evil suspicions, oppressed him too palpably to escape the anxious solicitude of his faithful wife, who now saw reason to fear that the results of her unflinching energy, constant attention, and intelligent treatment would be lost entirely. Her husband, whom she had accustomed to regard her in the spirit of an obedient, confiding child, became sometimes perfectly obdurate to all her best timed and most skillfully contrived blandishments and counsels. He even repelled her attentions as he had not done since the dark days that had now nearly passed away from her memory, and at such times, his look and manner warned her of actual danger. In former paroxysms, his sullenness or anger were only momentary, evincing no malice whatever; but now his monomania was too well defined to be nameless. The demons of distrust and suspicions, galled him and fevered his ill-balanced brain, constantly gaining strength from him who had first planted those devilish passions in his soul. He thought that he had been blind before, and knew not, poor fool, how utterly perverted his sight had now become; that he thought he perceived what did not exist at all; that he was stimulating every faculty by frantic efforts to detect what only existed in his own poisoned imagination; while, at the same time, he could not recognize that the devil, in human guise, was his teacher.

Stilletto's plan, that this poor, rich man should suspect his wife of being leagued with Montant and Josephine in designs upon his money, had succeeded marvelously well, and much sooner than he had hoped for. Intelligence and bravery are closely allied in human nature—men of small intellect are cowards! John had not the courage to confront his wife with open accusations; but he distressed and offended her by ill-humor and petty insults, and availed himself of every opportunity to wound her by malcious hints too coarse to be misunderstood.

"John," she said, one morning, when breakfast had been removed. "John," she repeated, struggling between tears and well-founded anger, "I can not pretend not to see the recent change in your tone and manner to me. It would be a strange woman that would not seek an explanation. I ask only for justice. As your wife, as a lady, I ask for kindness and love from you. You have banished Josephine from the table by your rudeness, which you no longer care to restrain. Where is your manliness, your chivalry, that you can not a treat a lady, a guest, your own sister-in-law with respect, while you know that she can not yet leave your house! I have borne in silence what I have tried to attribute to some passing eccentricity—but, I must speak plainly at last, as your loving, faithful wife always, and also as a woman determined to preserve her own dignity."

It was true that John had become so pointedly insulting in his remarks to Josephine, intimating no less than that her lover was a needy adventurer, intriguing for pecuniary gain, that she refused to meet him any more, even at meals. When his wife had concluded, John had not the hardihood to reply angrily. Distrust and cowardice are awkward companions in a man's mind, and forced him to sullen and obstinate silence like a spoiled child. Bella's power was great, and she knew it well; but with a pang of despair she felt that she had to fight against a concealed foe, and that her straightforward appeal fell upon a ground all undermined by treachery and fiendish cunning. So successfully had Stilletto prepared him against scenes like this, which he had foreseen must occur between the husband and his wife, that with the little Satan's teachings fresh in his mind, he turned a deaf ear to her, determined not to be deceived and coaxed over though, at the same time, he was morally powerless to give expression to his distorted sentiments.

The door-bell rang. With an ill-tempered scowl, he rose in silence, like a whipped cur, to leave the room.

"John," said Bella, agitated, in a pleading tone,. "my heart tells me that something evil is approaching. If Mr. Stilletto is at the door, do not see him. For the love of God and your poor wife, my dear, dear husband, do not listen to him."

This earnest pleading, amounting almost to an agony, penetrated his soul. For a moment he wavered; for a moment he looked at her like a penitent child; but as she was about throwing her loving arms around him to secure her, as yet, doubtful victory, the door opened—Stilletto entered, and, as if his presence dissolved at once the newly-woven tie between them, Van Strom recoiled from his wife's embrace, and welcomed his visitor with a grin of delight.

With a low moan bursting from her anguished heart at this her latest and most lamentable defeat, Bella stood for a moment motionless, and then dropped into a chair and averted her face from her cruel enemy.

"Good morning, madam," said Stilletto, with unmistakable impertinence of tone, casting upon her repelling attitude a glance of unspeakable impudence, which revealed his whole nature. "I trust you are as well as the bright look on your face would seem to indicate, this morning."

As Bella did not choose to notice him in the least, John, still without the courage or desire to upbraid her, took Stilletto by the arm familiarly, and led him out of the room and away from the house.

Hours elapsed before Bella left the seat at the window in which she had taken refuge, thence she watched her husband walking, arm-in-arm with the Italian, away across the fields toward the village.

"He is taking him to his lodgings, doubtless," conjectured Bella. "There they will ply him with drink and thus prepare him to believe all kinds of falsities. Where can I find counsel? where can I look for hope or for help in this terrible danger? I am seeing him being ruined, body and soul, and I, his wife, am powerless, powerless as a stranger, to rescue him from his peril!"

"A change must come," she sighed, despondingly. "This can not go on forever. A change must, *must* take place!" and a hundred times that day did her prophetic soul re-echo the words, "A great change will come, may come soon, and God grant his aid when it is at hand!"

* * * * * *

"I tell you what it is, Stilletto," said John, as the two ill-assorted friends crossed the fields, on their way to the village. "I tell you that my wife is not like other women; she's different. I had a talk with her this morning and, I must say, she don't talk as if she had a guilty conscience!"

"Guilty conscience!" said Stilletto, shrugging his shoulders. "I don't see that a person must needs have a guilty conscience for trying to obtain what all the world covets. I do not say, or pretend to say, that your wife, who is a splendid woman—"

"You are right!" cried John, much gratified. "A splendid woman is Bella!"

"I do not pretend to say," continued Stilletto, "that she would use foul means to accomplish her object. What wrong is there in marrying a man for his money and then devoting herself to him as she has done? No harm that I can see! She has earned what you paid her in advance. And it is all right and proper!"

"But I tell you she loves me," said John, faintly.

"Of course she does, and faithfully. Does not the dog love his master who feeds him? Indeed, he is devoted to his owner; but, had any other man bought him, he would have loved that other just as well. Such, also, is human affection, and, say what you please about disinterested devotion. I assure you that the rich and powerful are the masters, and the poor are their most affectionate and devoted dogs."

That he dared thus to speak to the husband about his wife, without fear or compunction, showed the influence of Stilletto over Van Strom, which can only be accounted for by his remarkable knowledge of all that is weak and bad in human nature.

"It is plain enough," continued Antonio, in a nonchalant tone, little demonstrative of his anxiety to finish the work (so well begun!) of poisoning John's mind. "It is an old story, yet some people shut their hearts to the moral of it. A rich gentleman, in a moment of thoughtless weakness, allows himself and his fortune to be won by a poor and low-born girl,—and, would you believe, that this same gentleman oftentimes will tell you, with every appearance of sincerity, that his wife married him for love! Pooh, Van Strom! Childlike trust and perfect belief in the holiness of human motives, are not adapted to this practical and merciless age!"

The reader can imagine what strategy of the tongue had been accomplished before this plausible fellow could venture upon speeches like this; how complete his power over Van Strom, before he could be certain that the latter's wrath (never entirely asleep) would not turn upon the accuser, instead of the accused.

John thought that he had just been awakened to the true state of affairs. His narrow, though not obtuse, intellect immediately remembered a hundred circumstances, which seemed, under the searching philosophy of Stilletto, to favor the conviction that Bella (as well as Josephine and Montant, whose verdict had long been sealed) was only a calculating, greedy wretch, feeding on him during his life, and anxiously awaiting the moment of his death, to take entire possession of her prey.

"I do not blame Mrs. Van Strom," said Stilletto, with calculating urbanity. "On the contrary, I think it would be wrong to charge her with any more than human wickedness! True honesty, true friendship, true love, even Truth herself, have all vanished from the earth! Look at the scene which occurs on the death of a rich man! How those he loved forget their hypocritical tears, in their wrangling over his property! How his very memory becomes but a barometer of his wealth, and how the grief of his bereaved relatives is only a copy of his last will, by which any fool can read to whom the property was bequeathed. When the best men are poor, they are strangers in the world; then how can a rich man believe in the existence of a love for him that is not dependent on his money!"

Thus holding the first place in conversation, taking the lead, and endeavoring to destroy the holiest and best attributes of human nature, by crafty insinuations of Bella's guilt, Stilletto employed the duration of their walk from Van Strom's house to the place where he and the philosopher had taken up their abode. Mr. Muller received them with a stateliness of manner, designed to disguise his delight at Van Strom's visit; for August Muller could not condescend to fawn and cringe before any man, not even the highest upon earth, though, just then, Van Strom was the man of all others whom he most desired to welcome.

"Mr. Van Strom," said he, motioning him to a seat, with the air of an ass seated upon a throne, "August Muller bids you welcome, sir, welcome as a *friend*, sir, and, I tell you, that but few have attained that title. August Muller, sir, can not offer you princely hospitality or luxury, for the reverses of life have humbled him to the station of expounding the law, which means poverty."

"I never heard that before," said John, rather puzzled.

"Because, in your station of life, Mr. Van Strom, you have only met those lawyers who make the world's wealth their scene of operations, taking care of the property of the rich and appropriating the 'pickings' with modest but inflexible persistency. But August Muller's ambition soars above the counting of gold! His brain belongs to *justice*, planning by night and pleading by day, to rescue persecuted innocence from the clutches of the law. This is my profession, and, though it leaves me poor, it is building me an eternal monument in the hearts of those I have saved and restored to light and life!"

"Most of whom should be in State's Prison instead," was on Stilletto's lips, but he thought of his visitor, and contented himself with a sneer and a meaning look, only perceived by Muller.

"Well, sir," said Van Strom, rather nervous on his chair, and doubtful whether to be favorably impressed with Muller's harangue, or to be put on his guard, "you promised some testimonials of your character and standing before I employed you as my attorney."

"Here they are, sir," answered the other, producing a bundle of letters. "Here are the tributes of the Atridæ to Nestor, the voices of the Romans in favor of Cicero!"

"I don't understand you," said Van Strom, a little nettled. "Let's to business." One of the letters was from Carrions, recommending Muller as a reliable, even eminent man in his profession. Now, Mr. Carrions, with all his merciless shrewdness in business, was not a likely man to give a character to a pettifogging "Tombs lawyer;" but Stilletto and Muller, by more wonderful than unfrequent maneuvers, had gained his good graces to such an extent, that he could not refuse the letter now before Van Strom. This, with others not less undeserved, removed all doubt in the poor gentleman's mind, and he could but consider Muller a very respectable man.

"Well, then, we will proceed to the drawing up of my new will," said John.

"Stilletto, withdraw," quoth Muller, with a pompous wave of the hand.

Mr. Stilletto obeyed, and when he was recalled, after the elapse of an hour, Muller's face was radiant from another cause than beer, and the instrument was then properly signed and witnessed.

"And you understand that the suit against that rascal, Eben Bates, is to be pushed vigorously?" asked Van Strom. Stilletto started at these words, but a look from Muller restrained him, while the lawyer immediately volunteered an explanation.

"Mr. Van Strom, Stilletto, has loaned Judge Bates fifteen thousand dollars, upon a mortgage on the judge's dwelling-house. It now appears that another and prior mortgage exists, which makes Mr. Van Strom's security almost worthless, and my esteemed client has authorized me to associate myself with some first-class practitioner in the Massachusetts courts, and bring a suit against the judge for false pretences. That, now most clearly proved scoundrel, also drew up Mr. Van Strom's will, which is now set aside, made null and void, by this document. Is is a great document, sir. It rends asunder every thread of a most adroitly-woven intrigue, and bears the stamp of justice and wisdom.

"Well, I'll go now!" said Van Strom, somewhat abstractedly. He felt nervous and half unsatisfied, and now that the deed was done, something told him that he might have made a mistake; but Stilletto's influence over his weak mind prevented him from drawing back, and taking further time for consideration.

Stilletto accompanied him from the room. Without asking any questions about the will, he enjoined the strictest secrecy by the most convincing arguments his slyness could suggest, and boldly accused Bella, and Josephine and her lover, of having plotted together against him ever since his marriage.

Feeling tolerably certain of his dupe, Stilletto then returned to Muller, who received him in an ecstasy of extra beer and intensified volumes of smoke. Antonio now heard what he knew very well would never have come from John Van Strom unaided by the philosophic lawyer.

"You, my friend," cried Muller, "you and Fatman and I are trustees of this immense property. Bella Smith, the tailor's daughter, receives one-third only, and the rest is left to lunatic asylums and other charitable institutions. August Muller, sir, instilled into this man's heart, the highest principles of charity, and he has left his property nobly."

"A third is too much for Mrs. Van Strom," growled Stilletto.

"Would you have me risk all, by attacking the impregnable position which his dear wife holds in his affections?"

"All right, then. Nothing for us, hey?"

"Ten thousand each for our valuable services as trustees; that's all," said Muller.

"That all, hey?" asked Stilletto, with a truly satanic expression. "But of course it is an honor to be trustees!"

"He wanted to make it more," said Muller, "but I entreated him not to do so. I told him that to prove our disinterested friendship, with the honor we attain, is worth more than mere money."

"We will take care of his property, won't we?"

"We will, sir."

"And that of the widow, too," cried Stilletto.

"Which widow?" asked Muller, sharply.

"Oh, she is not a widow yet!" sighed Stilletto. "I wish she were."

"For her sake, I join in the wish," answered Muller, with benevolence, puffing away at his pipe. "He can not make her happy, and it is pure charity to wish he were dead. But now I will depart to seek my associate in the suit against Judge Bates."

"How about Montant, the superseded executor?" hissed Stilletto, detaining him. "How about my revenge?"

"All in good time," said Muller, and having now worried on his overcoat, he left the house.

The interview with Van Strom and the above conversation took place in the front parlor, which was separated from the back parlor by a sliding door, closed when Van Strom first arrived. When Mr. Muller set forth on his professional mission, Stilletto walked to this door and opened it. His movements were always quick and noiseless, and as he had not tarried in approaching the sliding door, he opened it almost simultaneously with the philosopher's farewell sentence.

He stood motionless—Simonetta was in the room, and his experienced eye at once convinced him that she had been listening, though she had made a hasty retreat, the instant she saw the door move. Stilletto's eyes darted fire. Livid, trembling, frenzied with rage, he stood like a tiger ready to spring upon his victim, his head and chest bent forward, his under-lip quivering, and such madness in his face that the girl, in turn, changed color, seriously alarmed.

"You have been listening! What did you hear? Confess!" hissed Stilletto, in a voice she hardly recognized.

"Nothing! May the Holy Virgin forsake me——" she faltered and stopped, arrested by the expression of that demoniac white face before her. With a benumbing sensation, she read in the amazement on that face what she had done. *She had spoken English!* At this moment she gave herself up as lost, she knew he would kill her. In a moment of terror she had betrayed her secret, shown him that she knew, that she *must* know many of his secrets; that though she had loved him, she had never trusted him; but had acted a double part to gain power over him. She knew that there was no hope of his mercy.

His fury, violent enough to fetter him for a moment, soon burst forth. He made a rush at the door, to lock it. She knew that if he succeeded, her life was lost. Mortal fear breaks the paralytic spell of despair, she reaches the door before he does; she is in the hall; he seizes her hair flowing behind and drags her to the ground. Foaming at the mouth, every feature savagely distorted, every muscle swelled to iron strength, he beats her unmercifully, while with agonizing cries she struggles to make her escape. Finally she manages to reach the hilt of her concealed dagger with one hand; the steel is bare, the point is toward his heart, he forces it from her hand, but in the struggle for its possession she breaks away from his grasp.

Great philosophers are apt to be absent-minded in small matters: Muller has left the door open. With one last piercing cry she rushed out of the house and fled away across country as if pursued by the furies.

Stilletto found pursuit unadvisable (for several laborers were in the field at work, in the direction she had taken), so he took a position at one of the windows whence he could watch her course, and contemplated the situation. His anger subsided, and, singular contrast, he began to feel sorry for her, and to wish it never had happened.

"Such forms as her's are not intended to be thrashed, after all," he muttered, "and yet I would have killed her, if she had not got away! She has saved her life and my neck from a hempen cravat!" He thought of her deceit, of his unaccountable obtuseness in not suspecting that she understood English, during his constant intercourse with her. He remembered their first meeting, and how it had astonished him that she could not speak the prevailing language, how he had hardly credited it, but had finally believed, it to this day. He admired her for her craftness and self-control, and now that she was gone, he told himself that he had almost loved her.

"The only woman in the world that I ever really loved has been a lurking enemy, a spy upon all my actions," he continued, bitterly, and with this reflection, he threw away the last regret for her loss. The fierceness of his anger returned, in some measure, and it is certain that the treachery of this woman made even such a wicked man worse than he had been.

The brutality of his nature, awakened by his cruelty to her, took a firmer hold of him than ever, after he had cast away all his former affection for her, and when he left the house soon after, for the purpose of dogging her steps to see what mischief she might be up to (for did she not carry his secrets and an Italian woman's revenge in her heart?), his

determination might have been correctly expressed by those terrible words of Gloucester:—

"And since I find I can not prove a lover,
I am determined to prove a villain!"

When August Muller returned, he found instead of Stilletto, a few lines left for him by that gentleman.

"See no one. Hold on to the will at all hazards. Get our money and portable valuables together and wait in the house or in the neighborhood till I return."

So the great philosopher waited.

CHAPTER IX.

CROUCHING FOR THE SPRING.

"Time, thou anticipat'st my dread exploits;
The flighty purpose never is o'ertook,
Unless the deed go with it."—MACBETH.

WHEN John Van Strom, in company with his delightful friend, Stilletto, left his wife to solitude and the discomforts which mark a household immediately after breakfast has been removed, Bella found herself in a more than unhappy mood. The routine of housekeeping, so satisfactory to all womanly women, failed to divert her mind from anxiety, and she soon found her way back to the window and passed through one of those hours in life when we realize our utter helplessness, and appeal to God for aid and comfort. A complication of dangers and sorrows was crowding around her; she saw her husband ensnared in the nets of a fiend, her cherished sister, in a most humiliating situation, and her friend Montant, thwarted in his hopes and enterprises; Josephine's happiness and very existence jeopardized, and all because a contemptible villain had wrenched from her the influence over her husband which she had attained as the reward of her unbounded devotion to him and her unfaltering persistency in serving and watching over him.

As John, returning from Stilletto's, passed by the stable on his way to the house, the same old coachman who had once driven the carriage that took him to be christened, approached him with a dismal expression. John's heart was filled with apprehensions, which, after a few words, culminated in great grief. They reached the stable-door. Open it softly, you old servant, enter with an awe-inspired tread, bereaved master, and let your sorrow speak but in whispers, for the presence of death is here. Stiff and cold, felled to the earth by quick and cruel disease, John's adored mare lies in her stall. Her wondrous spirit has gone to await him on the road to heaven, probably with the faithful intention of dragging him up to St. Peter's porch in some spirit chariot. Good-bye to your ladyhood, poor Bella! Your eccentricities have been exceeded by your fidelity, and John Van Strom forgives them all and bemoans your good qualities. Your memory will be more honored than that of many human beings who live and pass away unappreciated by men that probably think themselves sages, compared with John Van Strom.

But John, in his simplicity, bewails his loss, and great, honest tears trickle down his homely face. His mind and nervous system had undergone many trials since his acquaintance with Stilletto. His wavering reason had not been perverted without many a torturing doubt and fear, and his temper, leading him on to crazy haste of action, had destroyed his peace. Utterly at war with himself, despondent, stung by remorse, still unyielding in his morbid tenacity, and withal, as weak in mind and body as a child, it took but some definite emotion, such as the loss of his mare, to unstring him completely. In this condition he entered the house to find his wife still at her window, staring into the void of her thoughts in listless dejection.

He sank into a chair, and a sob burst from him, which startled Bella into a consciousness of his presence, for she had not heard him enter.

"What does this mean, husband?" she asked, rising from her chair and approaching him.

"It means that I have lost the only thing I loved on earth. My mare is dead!"

She stopped short. This was too much. At first hot anger, even hatred, surged up from her heart, and choked her utterance, but they gave way before the utter misery wrought by his idiotic ingratitude and cruelty, and regaining her seat she sank back into it and burst into tears. He misunderstood the cause of her emotion entirely, and said, softly,—

"That's right, my love. Weep for her, for she was true to me, and now poor John has not a friend left in the world."

She came to his side, she knelt by him, she encircled him with her arms, and laid her head on his breast.

"And have I not been true to you, John, and am I nothing left to you?"

"You have, indeed, you have, Bella," he answered, somewhat incoherently, not resisting her embrace, and laying his hands on her devoted head. "And you see it was she that won you, it is to her that I am indebted for my darling wife, and that made her holy to me." Still his wife clung to him.

"Bella," he continued, almost in a whisper, "a strange feeling possesses me. It seems to me as if my head was free from confusion and my thoughts clear. Have I not been an idiot all my life, my dear wife?"

There was something in his simplicity and soothing tone that made Bella's heart swell with regained hope.

"Answer me, Bella," said John, drawing her toward him with a bright smile, which broke like a ray of light through all the heavy clouds which had darkened his soul. "Answer me, Bella, have I not always been an idiot?"

She was on his knees, and through tears of happiness, looked in his face. And though he bore marks of the strain of his mental disorders, yet at this moment, the bright, intelligent light of his eyes cast an appearance almost of beauty over his countenance. She saw it, and knew for the first time, that she was capable of loving him more than the nurse loves the child intrusted to her care, more than the coldness of mere duty demanded. This sudden awakening of a hundred new voices in her heart, this precipitate happiness nearly overwhelmed her senses, and in passionate accents she assured him of her love. His face grew brighter and brighter, and they exchanged vows and pledges of an affection, which, in many an hour of bitterness, she had considered but a mocking farce, the enactment of a blasphemous lie. Finally, he said to her,—

"Now, Bella, since we have found more in each other than we have ever sought for, I wish to speak to you on a grave subject. Be assured that I shall speak plain, common sense to you, for my past follies seem revealed to me as if by a miracle. That dear old horse must have been a minister of heaven, ugly as her form was—for she first got me a wife, and then died just at the right moment to bring me to my senses."

"Dear wife," he continued, when they were seated side by side, "I hope that a foreboding, which is strongly impressed upon me now, is part of my late distraction; but I fancy that I am not to live long. Therefore (it is only a fancy, dear wife) it becomes me to use the few hours still remaining to me to set my house in order. Oh, that I had a son to inherit and keep alive the old name of Van Strom!"

"Don't talk that way," answered Bella. "Do not demoralize yourself by a morbid contemplation of death. I am not so weak as to shiver at the mere sound of that word; but I thank heaven that, so far as my husband is concerned, it has no meaning for me! John, I have a hope which tells of many happy years in store for you and me; and who knows but what, in the mercy of nature's Omnipotent Master, a time may come in which you will have to set in order a larger household than this, which only numbers your poor but loving wife!"

She kissed him affectionately, and then said, archly,—

"What did you say to me? You had something practical on your lips, when you launched off into those dismal fantasies which I do not choose to encourage."

His countenance fell, and his thoughts seemed to grow unpleasant, but he replied by asking the plump question,—

"Bella, no matter how much you love me now, as you say you do, but did you not marry me for my money?"

This was entering upon dangerous ground, and she quickly summoned all her wits to her aid; for, knowing very well that here was a great opportunity, she determined to gain the day over all the powers of darkness which disputed her mastery over him; and to lose no time about it either. Her intuition prompted her, and she immediately replied:—

"When you came, a stranger, to our door, I only gratified my ambition by accepting you. I hope you do not think your good looks captured me; do you, dear?" she added, laughing, and stroking his stubborn hair; "although, I must confess, you look quite handsome this morning. But when I first married you, I certainly took you for your money, please your conceit!"

John laughed outright. Mr. Stilletto, so far the woman has the best of it; only it was not your intention that she should have a fair chance.

"Now, hear this," cried John, putting his arms around her waist, "she acknowledges herself, the saucy little witch, the very thing which that scoundrel tells me she is doing her best to conceal."

"I know the scoundrel you speak of," cried Bella, fixing her flashing eyes on him, "and I mean to have *my* say now!"

"And yet," interrupted John, with suddenly-knit brows, "your own words indorse that scoundrel's accusation."

"Listen to me, John," said Bella, very earnestly. "Did you marry me for love?"

John was puzzled.

"Well," he answered, "I thought you were good-looking, had a good figure, and, on the spur of the moment, I took you. But, of course, I did not love you as I do now."

"And I," rejoined Bella, dryly, "thought you were so-so, and rich, and I took you on the spur of the moment. But, of course, I did not love *you* as I do now! We are quits, my dear!"

"But, Bella, what have been your feelings since then? Have you not plotted for my money, and hoped for my death? Have you not intrigued, and joined others, to take advantage of me? Do I not owe your attention and fidelity to my fortune? Answer, woman!" he cried, almost fiercely, "and justify yourself if you can."

"That I will," she answered. "You ask me whether you owe my love to your money? I answer, that if love can be purchased with money, God in heaven may also be bought, for God is Love. Buy a woman, body and soul; but you receive your purchase with love, the holiest attribute, left out; save her from starvation—deliver her from torture—take her soul out of the jaws of destruction, and, although she can thank you with her life, if you need its sacrifice, yet the bestowal of her *love* rests with God alone."

He made no reply, and she continued, solemnly raising her voice,—

"As regards the charge of intriguing against you, in league with your sister Josephine and her lover (don't think I am too dull to comprehend the whole of this vile calumny), I ask you to consider, for a moment, the baseness of those that accuse me. You lend an ear to the scum of humanity, you listen to the venomous slurs of a man, whose soul is a spring of villainy, and whose very breath is corruption; but, John Van Strom, I am your wife! You hope, some happy day, that I may bear you children, and, when you swore to love and honor me, you made my name yours, my honor the honor of your family, of your home. Name, home, family, yes, even Christianity itself, and all our civilization, all our respectability, are founded upon marriage, and your wife is the corner-stone of your house. Reposing entire faith in her, you preserve your own dignity and integrity. Let me beg you, then, not to heap shame upon yourself, not to degrade yourself by allowing a greedy vagabond to dispossess me of your heart,—your heart, John, which is mine, which, to-day, I have received anew from the merciful Father of us all, to hold and keep forever!"

She threw herself into his arms, crying like a child. John Van Strom held her tightly to his breast, and there was no more question as to her truth in his mind. He confessed all he had done that morning, and, she helping him to comprehend the craftiness of Mr. Stilletto, he resolved promptly to baffle the plotters against his peace without an hour's delay.

In the meanwhile, as we already know, Mr. Stilletto had quitted the house in the village, honored or dishonored by his sojourn and that of the great philosopher, for the purpose of watching Simonetta's movements.

Between the house of John Van Strom and the village, the contour of the landscape, marked by bold undulations, was of a somewhat wild character. Ravines and rocks obstructed the road, forcing it into curves hard by perilous descents, and cutting into the hillsides, whose crumbling walls endangered the safety of the thoroughfare. It becomes necessary for us to pay some attention to a particular point on this road, where a footpath led over a steep hill, around the foot of which the road lay in a long curve.

The slope of this hill had been selected by the scanty Roman Catholic part of the neighborhood as a site for a modest little church or chapel, which, small and unpretending as it was, had its share of the ornamental and sensual, so peculiar to Rome, in the shape of an audacious plaster-cast caricature of the irrepressible Virgin, standing in a niche on the façade next the road. It was, however, a pretty little chapel, in a romantic spot, half-buried in the pines which studded the hill, and yet not quite shut out from the view of the surrounding country.

The day, which had begun so brightly, changed its mood in the afternoon. It had been unusually warm for December; but now Heaven began to knit his brows and closed his golden eye. The winds awoke and began to chase the multiplying clouds, and a chill was felt in the air, foretelling heavy weather.

The pines which sentineled the lonely chapel shook their heads and rocked about with wild gestures; but there was a creature of flesh, beneath them, prostrate before the effigy of the Virgin, not heeding the warning voices of the approaching tempest which moaned in the tree-tops, unconscious of all save her own misery. On her knees, and praying to the Holy Mother with the fervor of despair, Simonetta Marini long remained perfectly absorbed by the horrors she had so lately passed through. She knew not that she was watched, but, had she scrutinized one of those somber groves, she might have seen, with terror, a pair of vicious eyes, whose piercing glance was riveted on her. After she had undergone Heaven only knows, what agony of soul, and derived, Heaven only knows, what comfort,—she arose with the energy of one in whom resolution has been born of despair. The thick, heavy tresses of her raven hair were her only covering, her simple dress, all torn and fluttering in the wind, her only shelter, as she descended the hill with hasty steps, and, gaining the highway, hastened on toward her destination without a backward glance.

"By Jove," quoth Stilletto, stepping out from the trees, "she is handsomer than ever. I am afraid I was a fool to lose my temper, and her, together! A man should not get angry at a woman's treachery. Had I been wise, I would have paid her a great compliment on her smartness, and flattered her a little, and so I would have saved all."

Thus did Mr. Stilletto reason with himself, keeping the object of his watch in view the while, following her cautiously, and not surprised when she took the direction toward Eben Bates's house. "As I thought," he muttered to himself. "She is going there to get old Martin Bates to help her mar our whole affair. One of them, or both, or all three (if they can frighten my dear father into joining them), will put in an appearance at John Van Strom's house, not many hours hence. Then will come a great assault on his better nature, Madam Bella in the heat of the battle. They will show him what a black devil I am, and what a legion of holy angels surrounds him. Then comes a scene, Judge Eben Bates penitent and forgiven, by John, *may be;* Bella and her constituents reinstated in all their lost power; Simonetta sainted even in this life having acted the part of the virtuous sinner, who saves a world of trouble by timely reform; and the drama will close with an affecting tableau of virtue, generally triumphant. John grinning in the center, Bella weeping on his neck, that cursed dog, Montant, laughing in his sleeve, and poor Stilletto left out in the cold, with John's latest will more lately revoked, an August Muller clearly showing by all philosophy that the miscarrying of our plans is entirely my fault, to comfort him. But wait, ladies and gentlemen, I'm not dead yet!" From the crest of a hill he gained a view of the judge's house, and saw the Italian girl, like a flitting shadow in the distance, open the gate, and hurry up the path to the door.

"Now, what shall I do?" said he. "Judge Eben, even if he is persuaded to side with them, can not harm me very much. No: the real danger lies with John, and to him I'll hasten, and prepare him for the attack."

As he crossed the fields on his way thither, it blew so hard that he could scarce keep his feet, frail little monster that he was. He passed many hamlets, and saw the horses brought in from their work with their manes and tails streaming in the wind. Although it was not raining yet, such a blast filled the air that the anxious faces at the windows told him the inmates feared for the safety of their roofs. It was growing dark fast, though the afternoon was still young, and the mad clouds seemed ready to discharge themselves but for the violence of the hurricane, which chased

the very rain so fast along, that not a drop reached the ground.

"This will be a queer night," thought Stilletto, making laborious headway, while the favorite cloak he wore on his shoulders, made frantic efforts to escape from him and elope with its lover, the wind. "A queer night," he repeated, and the awful roar that greeted him from the woods as he approached the litte chapel, which he had to pass, on his way to Van Strom's house, seemed to chant an angry "Amen" to the sentiment.

"What is this? Were it not for the color of the horse, I should say, that here comes John Van Strom, driving to the village in his light wagon! Strange that he should be out; but, although his yellow mare must have turned gray or died, this is certainly he."

He was not in error. Apparently in danger of being upset by the violence of the wind, John was driving along, and being hailed by Stilletto, stopped his horse.

"Has Bella turned gray?" asked Stilletto, with a sneer.

"She died this morning," answered John, unconcernedly, which astonished the Italian still more, and he wondered at the change apparent in John's whole manner. His gloomy and awkward eccentricity seemed to have left him, and there was a wide-awake intelligence in the glance that met Stilletto's little eyes.

"Where are you going," asked the latter, impudently.

"To the village to see that lawyer. I want Bates to be prosecuted at once, for what I begun this morning must be finished, cut and dried, before the end of the week!" He spoke with suavity, and seemed to consider this frank explanation a duty to a friend.

"But it blows hard enough to make one ride on the clouds," cried Stilletto.

"You should know that what I do, I do quickly!" answered Van Strom, looking to his horse, who would not stand quietly in that wind. "Will you jump in?"

"How I would like to go; but I dare not leave that girl unobserved," thought Stilletto. "No, I thank you," he answered, aloud, but be careful; you are alone, and it will be dark when you return!"

"I have your dirk with me, which you left at my house some days ago," answered Van Strom.

"Have you?" cried Stilletto, quickly. "Then I wish you would give it to me! I will make you a present of this one." Here he produced Simonetta's handsome weapon from his breast pocket. "The one you have, was given to me by my dear mother, and I hate to part with it."

As there seemed nothing unreasonable in this, John exchanged weapons.

"Does your dear wife know that you are armed?" asked he, carelessly.

"She handed me the dirk herself," was the answer.

With some trivial remark, they parted, John letting his horse have his own way, and saying to himself:—

"It was a good idea to treat him politely. He has no suspicion that I am going to the village to make a legal and thoroughly competent instrument that will revoke my will of this morning. I am glad he did not come along, for I would have been obliged to get rid of him some way, or else to postpone what should not be postponed."

Stilletto turned back and entered a little country hotel which lay on the road to Judge Bates's house. Men and women were sitting around the stove, and talking about the fearful gale that was blowing. Being not very far from the sea-coast, there were many relatives of mariners and fishermen among the people who discussed the danger of such a hurricane, "and blowing right in shore, too," with troubled looks, and hearts heavy with fear for some friend or relative.

Stilletto asked for something to eat, but when it was served, his under-lip, that great indicator of his mental condition, quivered so that he could hardly perform the task. After swallowing a few morsels, he again set forth toward the village. Near that part of the road before described, where the little chapel crowned the hill among the trees, he paused on noticing that a streamlet in a ravine crossed the road, being bridged over by a few timbers rudely laid, and planks placed crosswise over them. He stooped to examine this sort of bridge.

"It is easy to tear up one of these planks," he muttered, "and if some one should do so, and if some one should drive by in a dark night, the horse would probably step into the hole and break his legs." After having assured himself of this fact, he went on in his soliloquy :—

"So far, John is evidently all right." He little thought that the interference of Martin Bates and the revengeful accusations of the Italian girl were no longer necessary to undo his intrigues, which seemed to him so wonderfully successful.

A clatter of hoofs reached his ears, and he was delighted to recognize old Judge Bates riding along at a rapid pace, little heeding the wild storm.

"Hold, father !" cried Stilletto, jumping in front of the horse's head, and seizing the bridle. "Dismount, for I have to confer with you."

The horse shied at the flapping coat worn by the little man, and Judge Bates came near losing his seat. This did not improve his temper, and although, after a moment's hesitation, he did alight, he accosted Stilletto furiously,—

"How dare you stop me on the highway, you high-handed bandit ! Had I fallen from my horse, I would have had you arrested for waylaying—"

"Stop," cried Stilletto. "Don't cry shame on criminals, for you are going to add another crime to your list before many days are over ! I want to see you very particularly, and how lucky it is that I meet you by chance. You have been at the village to see Van Strom's great lawyer, August Muller, trying to stave off the suit which is pending against you for raising money under false pretences, to wit," he added deliberately, "pretending to a capitalist that a mortgage on which he advanced

you money, was a *first* lien upon your property, while, in reality another mortgage on the same property was in existence. Am I right ?"

"You barefaced, brutal scoundrel ! For you only did I commit this crime, and from what I learned to-day, I shall probably have to suffer for it."

"Look here, father. If you could make John Van Strom die, *by accident*, and could make me trustee of his estates, having power to stop or compromise that suit against you— would you, to save your honor, make a false oath ?"

The handsome face of the old judge was flushed with riding in the wind ; but the blush that now suffused it seemed as if all the blood in his body had mounted to his head. What he then and there spoke, confronting his fiendish son while the storm was raging around them, while the wild voices of nature drowned their own, and the blast chilled them to the marrow,—what he said and then revoked,—what he swore and then gainsaid,—how he struggled and then succumbed, —all this must be left to oblivion, as each word that escaped their lips was snatched away by the fury of the winds and hurled away to empty space. But, on their parting these words were heard,—

"I will do it because I must, but heaven grant that you get no opportunity !"

The judge did not know that it was growing darker very fast, that it was beginning to rain, or that a night was coming when the elements were to exhibit their foulest behavior. He was only conscious of a tumult in his breast and a darkness in his soul which was never to know the dawn of day again.

His horse took him home on a run, more anxious to reach it than his master, and the latter was somewhat relieved to find that Martin had gone out, leaving word that, if it should rain hard he might not return that night. They also told him that a strange woman had called for his brother, and that they had left the house together. Eben scarcely heard the latter intelligence, but pleading exhaustion he retired early, though he knew he could not sleep; though he knew that he was doomed to watch this dreadful night, and to wait for morning, without closing an eye. And so Judge Eben Bates waited.

CHAPTER X.

THE MURDER.

"Yonder's foul murder done."
                                       OTHELLO.

"I WILL move to town next week," said Mrs. Van Strom to herself, when John had left her to have his horse (alas no more the gentle and clever Bella) put to the carriage. "I will certainly move to town," she repeated, seated by the fire and enjoying the warmth of its cheerful blaze. Had she not reason to be happy ? More than happy—she was grateful to heaven for having given her a husband she could love, for one she could only pity. Now, since John had been reborn to reason by what might almost be called a miracle of mental development, now, since in her own heart also a new day had dawned, now she realized the immense difference between loyalty and love. Loyalty, the noblest issue of the mind—love, the very life of the heart.

Oh, what a happy day had she spent! John had been affectionate and reasonable. Was not that enough to make a wife love her husband? How many women in the wide world could say this moment: "My husband has been amiable and reasonable all day?" And now John had gone to undo with one stroke of his pen, all the machinations of her enemies, and the great change that she had hoped and prayed for, had come to pass. Josephine was saved, restored to her lawful inheritance, and a future spread before her which was almost too glorious to be believed entirely.

"I will move to town next week!" said Bella, for the third time, "I can stand a good deal of country life, but when the wind blows so hard as to shake the marrow of my bones, I would rather be excused from living right on the top of the highest hill in the country. Doesn't it seem as if some calamity was piling up over our heads? These fearful noises, this appalling commotion outdoors as if heaven and earth were being hurled at each other to form a new chaos! I wish John had come back again."

She listened. The dismal howl in the flue and the confused roar of the storm without, alone gave answer to her listening ear. A hundred times she imagined that she heard wheels. It was but the battering of the rain against the windows, or a fresh blast gaining strength in the distance to sweep down upon the house with such a mad violence, that the very earth seemed to tremble with the exertion of holding the foundations firmly in their places, to save the tottering masonry. Bella grew restless, then fearful, and finally, appalled by nameless apprehension. Perhaps the blessedness of to-day was too much for fate to allot without admixture; perhaps the cruel gods would wrest from her this very night what they had given with mocking kindness; perhaps heaven had vouchsafed to John one ray of its glorious light, only, as it were, on his death-day—perhaps Eternal Justice would enhance her punishment for a giddy deed, by showing her a happy change in that which she was to lose, that her loss might be the heavier.

Her nervous system, usually so firm and so impassive, gave way to an excitement she had not known before. Her discomfort assumed imaginary shapes. Was John dead? Was his body distorted by the pangs of death, lying somewhere out in the black night, feeling no longer the storm which rages round him, hearing no more the voice of the elements? "John, John!" she cried aloud, jumping up, and clasping her hands. "John where are you? Speak to me! Give me some token of your presence, speak but one word!" But as she listened, the only reply was a hollow moan of desolation, which arose far, far away,

and swelled as it came nearer into a fearful howl, striking the house as if it would sweep it from the face of the earth.

But what is this? She feels that some one is approaching the house. The bell rings, she rushes to the chamber door, delighted, "John, John, where have you been so late, husband?" escapes from her lips before she can see who is at the door. There is no response; but the old butler comes half-way up the stairs with a face as long as a barometer, indicating foul weather, and says:—

"Mr. Bates, ma'am, Mr. Martin Bates, and a young woman with him, ma'am, as I doesn't know, and doesn't want to know, if you please, ma'am."

Bella immediately descended to the parlor, and there found Martin Bates, and a woman dressed in black. Too nervous to pay much attention to what they had to say, she hardly noticed the careful recital of Martin Bates, occasionally interrupted by the vehement ejaculations of the Italian girl; for she knows all; knows of Stilletto's artifices—Muller's nice calculations,—John's temporary hallucinations.

"I do not desire to hear my husband's weakness enlarged upon by those that are not friendly to him," she said proudly. "What you have told me I know, for I am the wife of John Van Strom."

Martin Bates sits at the table where the lamp burns, fretfully, as if the storm had frightened its strength and vigor away. The face of the old man is more haggard and death-like than ever, and if you look closely at his dull eyes, it seems as if death had cast a forerunning shadow over his soul, and his features are shrunken and corpse-like. The Italian woman sits in the shade, and though her face can not be seen, the very air around her trembles with her suppressed passion, and her voice, when she speaks resembles the subdued voice of a charmed fury.

"As usual, my kindness is returned by ingratitude," said Martin Bates. "I have disclosed the plans of a devil to you, showed you the brutality of a hog and the viciousness of a monster, yet you shut your ears to the counsel of a friend."

"My ears, old man," cried Bella, "are wide open to hear news of my husband! I have watched for him until I am nearly distracted. With him, I fear neither devil, beast, nor monster. If he die, let the whole world surrender to Satan, I don't care!"

"He will murder him!" hissed Simonetta.

Bella turned fiercely upon her. "Do you wish to call forth curses on your lips, with your foul prophecies? Haven't you known all this and held your tongue until he cast you off —until he ceased to keep you as his dear mistress, and most likely, willing accomplice. Your vengeance, not your honor speaks, young woman; and had I known all I now know, John would not be out to-night. I have been listening for the sound of his wheels while you were telling your story, and did not gather more than half of what you said; but now, all at once, I see the whole danger. He has gone out alone into the night to save a miserable fortune. God knows I would willingly pay my last dollar to see him home again in safety."

The door opened, and Josephine appeared, Bella rushing toward her and threw her arms around her. "Josie," she cried, "save me from these people!"

"Why, Bella, you must be seriously sick," answered the widow. "I never thought you could be agitated like this. What! my strong, self-reliant sister carrying on like a child! What is the matter?"

"I am worried about John," Bella whispered in her ear.

"How absurd," answered Josephine. "It is only just dark, and he can not get back so quickly. Besides," she added, with a calm smile, "Ernest is returning with him, you know."

Her soothing, confident tone did not fail to have an effect on Bella. With a manner no one would have thought her capable of she turned to Martin Bates, and said:—

"Mr. Bates, the night is more than dangerous for travelers. Think not that because I spoke hastily, I have forgotten the duties of hostess or the teachings of hospitality, and let me entreat you and that lady to spend the night here."

Another ring of the bell prevented Martin's reply. Bella flew to the door and there stood still as if turned to marble. White as a sheet, she held her hands to her heart; something, God only knows what, had given her a shock. Josephine rushed to the hall door. Bella heard a smothered bustle, confused, but hushed voices reached her ear. The front door was opened wide—they were carrying something in. A word—a whispered word—was spoken; but had it been breathed by a zephyr in the midst of the Great Desert, her ears would have caught it. With a low moan, she sank senseless into the arms of Martin Bates, who bent over her with a face like living death.

*   *   *   *   *   *

John had finished his business. The will was "made, signed, sealed, and delivered" safely, and the friends were reconciled. John and our hero climbed into the light wagon to drive back to the house, which Montant did not intend to leave again until he should take his bride with him. Premature darkness covered the road and made it almost undistinguishable.

"I wish we were at home," said John.

"So do others besides us," answered our hero. "The horse can hardly face this terrible gale. In such a night, folks should stay at home in mere gratitude for having a home to stay in."

"In such a night," said John, "the angel of death rides upon the clouds, and frightens away the angel of life."

"In such a night," continued our hero, to kill time, "love seeks his mate and people bless the warmth of their hearths and hearts which keeps out the blast."

"In such a night," said John, "human misery cries out to heaven and despairs at the angry answers."

"And religion bends the knee and trembles before the power of God."

"In such a night" continued John, in a hollow voice, "heaven and hell sweep close to the earth."

"And Nemesis watches for victims."

"It is easy for a man to die in his bed when God calls him away, but I would not like to die when all is dreary, and bleak, and desolate around us!"

"Hold!" cried our hero. "Is that a man by the roadside?"

Was it a specter that danced across the road, making the horse stop and snort with fear, or was it a weird shadow of the night which had flitted by under the trees. Surely a hundred spirits seemed hovering about; but this was a man.

"He is gone!" said our hero, who had drawn a dagger which John had given him, he being the better man to carry it, "but I am certain it was a man standing close to the wheel as we passed. When the gale rips up the ground it sounds as if there were steps behind us and beside us; but my eyes are good and I will trust them, even when I know that my other senses are deceived."

"There are voices in the air," cried Van Strom. "Perhaps they warn us of danger. I wish we were home."

Ernest Montant seconded the wish in his inmost heart but they had slow work before them. The horse struggled bravely against the piercing rain and the terrific gale; but on the slippery, undulating ground, little more than a brisk walk could be obtained. Suddenly, they both felt a shock, and, before their eyes, the horse seemed to sink into the ground. A strange and supernatural cry chilled their hearts, and made their hair stand on end.

"Great God!" cried John, "this is an evil spirit's voice."

"No!" cried Montant, jumping to the ground, "I have heard that cry before. It comes from our poor horse. I am afraid he has broken a leg."

They examined the struggling brute, and found that his leg was indeed broken, as our hero had surmised. He had stepped into a hole where a plank had been removed from the little bridge we know of, and there had snapped the bone of his leg.

"Here is foul play," cried Montant. "We do not know who may be at our backs. Let's leave the horse and trudge on. We are not far from home!"

"Look!" said John, pointing up the hill by the roadside. "Isn't there a light in the old chapel?"

The reader knows the spot where this accident had befallen them. Right above them stood the Roman Catholic chapel, and by one of those strange phenomena of a stormy night, it seemed indeed as if a light shone from it.

"It does seem so," answered Montant, possessed with a fear, a nameless dread that he could neither account for nor shake off. "Hurry up—come on. If this means murder, I shall sell my life dearly!"

"Lord have mercy on my soul!"

Wild was the cry which accompanied these

words, the last that John Van Strom uttered in this world, a cry that burst from a heart laid open by a foul blow. He fell—a man was struggling with our hero over his body, the assassin broke away almost immediately and fled through the woods as if already pursued by the avenger. The leaves start from the ground and flee after him—he hears pursuing steps in their rustling. The shadows of the night crowd around him and lay a hundred traps for his perdition; but he clears them and rushes away. On, away, with the foul deed on his heart, with the stamp of murderer on every line of his face wherever he goes, with the ghost of the murdered man linked to him for all eternity. Flying with him—sinking to the ground with him when he falls from sheer exhaustion—talking with him when he soliloquizes—dining by his side when he eats—laughing at him when he forces a smile, but not sleeping when he sleeps. No, no, never sleeping to give the murderer rest until Eternal Justice has been satisfied.

The furiously raging storm sends the fallen leaves in all directions from the spot where the corpse lies to proclaim the deed of horror. The trees hear of it and shake their heads, moaning aloud, so that the few remaining birds start from their sleep with horrid, monstrous nightmares. A ghost sweeps through the house where Bella is watching, and in its presence the flame of the lantern over the gate expires with a ghostly grimace like the last quiver of a criminal on the gallows.

The wind tolls the bell on the little Roman Catholic chapel as if a shadowy congregation were summoned by that funeral knell to sing the poor soul to rest, and strange sounds come forth from its gothic interior. Perhaps, far off at the Priory, the wind is tolling that old monkish bell at this same moment in honor of the last Van Strom, as it did at the death of his father.

From the thousand dumb witnesses the news ascends to the skies, and the moon parts the ragged clouds to see if it can be true, and looking down suddenly coats the little chapel with silver. There in the middle of the road, right near the house of God, half buried already in the mud of mother earth, which will soon claim his body wholly,—there with his face all white and limbs distorted, lies the body of poor John Van Strom, each lineament softly visited by the tender rays of the moon, with Stilletto's dagger in his heart and its hilt glittering in the silvery light.

BOOK IV.—FORTUNE.

CHAPTER I.

CHRISTMAS.

"This was my lord's last hope, now all are fled,
Save only the gods."

TIMON OF ATHENS.

"GRAVES & PARADISE" had been the style of that great law-firm years ago, and their old clients still spoke of them as "Graves & Paradise;" but with the increase of business the name of the firm had lengthened until the time we pay them a visit at their office, it read "Graves, Paradise, Stubbs, O'Brien, & Cianini." No wonder the old clients adhered to the short and convenient "Graves & Paradise!" Messrs. Stubbs, O'Brien, and Cianini were gentlemen with bald heads and stentorian voices, whose pomposity somewhat exceeded their wisdom; but they performed the bulk of the labor, while Messrs. Graves & Paradise, only attended to cases of great importance. It was a triumph presaging success for any client to obtain the personal attention of Mr. Paradise, and a poor mortal in the labyrinth of the law might well allow the hunchback's insults could he but enlist in his cause the falcon eyes of that mind, the serene power of that intellect and the might of that eloquence, which could sway the hearts of the jury, and win a case despite the judge on the bench, justice or equity.

On Christmas-eve, a quiet, solemn fall of snow filled the air, and the reign of darkness was disputed by the brightness of the flakes, as if mysterious light were descending in shreds to the earth, giving a holy luster to the white robe with which the heavens were decking her for the great holiday.

Nine o'clock had sounded from all the town clocks, and still we find Mr. Paradise in his private room, in Wall Street, bending over documents and books, and, in spite of Christmas-eve, studying out the intricacies of a great case, apparently forgotten by friends and family on this great occasion of universal rejoicing. The tall book-cases along the walls look dark, for the room is large, and the two students' lamps on his writing table only illumine the papers immediately before him. The lawyer's face wears a peculiarly sinister expression. Papers tied up in bundles, and papers lying loose, papers written and papers printed upon, papers of all sorts and sizes and shapes, surround him in an apparently confusing chaos. Heaven should be kind to him, who has to unravel all their intricacies, yet there is one word, plain and bold, heading each one of them—that word is "Hobgoblin."

On his right, "Hobgoblin" awaits him, on his left, "Hobgoblin" asks his attention; behind his back, "Hobgoblin" stands out in impudent relief. "Hobgoblin" confronts him in a hundred different handwritings; it meets his eye at every turn, and flows mockingly from his pen when he commences to write. His sharp, sallow face, his piercing black eyes, his homely mouth with the bitter sneer set in withered wrinkles, show plainly in the circle of light cast by the lamps, while darkness crowds around him, and ugly shadows dance attendance on him, and sit upon his crooked back. Thus, like a master goblin banished from the Christian world, and concocting some horrid scheme of mischief, the great lawyer spends Christmas-eve working up the defence in the great suit of Going *versus* The Trustees of the Hobgoblin Mining and Manufacturing Company.

A knock at the door. Mr. Paradise takes no notice of it. Another, and a third, with the same result, and the visitor, perhaps, accustomed to the lawyer's manner, considers the notice sufficient and enters.

"What do you want?" asked Mr. Paradise, gruffly. He has not turned his face toward the intruder; but knows that it is old Smiles, the most faithful and the most dismal of servants. Smiles, in the days of his youth, thought he would be a lawyer, and to that end commenced reading law and copying law. Upon abandoning the reading as hopeless, he had "copied law these thirty years, sir," a statement which unfailingly drew tears from him whenever he told any one his story; but finally he had changed his condition of semi-starvation and the profession of law-copyist, to become special attendant, door-keeper, messenger, and factotum of a lower grade, in the office of Messrs. Graves & Paradise. Thus, from the funeral of his ambition, though it left him in perpetual melancholy, arose an humble post of ease, good pay, and comfort, in his old age.

"I crave your pardon, sir," said the sepulchral voice of Mr. Smiles, from the dark depths of the room; "a lady wants to see you. She is veiled in black, she has come through the storm in the night, alone and unprotected. It is a case of—of—in fact it must be a case of murder or crim—"

Mr. Paradise would have interrupted him sooner, but he was for once, very much astonished at the announcement, and the ejaculation which now escaped him, was instantly followed by another still more significant of amazement, when the lady, "veiled in black," having followed upon the heels of Mr. Smiles, stepped into the circle of light which fell from the students' lamps in the center of the room, and presented to the astonished gaze of the hunchback, a graceful figure robed in heavy mourning.

"You may well be surprised at seeing me here at this most singular time and hour," she said, in a rich, deep voice, which trembled with agitation, "but I drove to your house in Washington Square, and was there advised to look for you here. I must see you at once upon business of such importance as no earthly interest can divert me!" and she took off her veil.

"Mrs. Van Strom!" cried Paradise, quite bewildered, "you are the last person I expected peeled out of this black husk. Smiles, leave us."

"And bid the carriage wait—two hours if necessary," added Josephine Van Strom. "I will pay the man well for it."

"What in the world gives me this honor, Madam?" asked the lawyer, not very respectfully. "You have hunted me out in rather an inopportune moment, and I have not the time to gratify women's whims on Christmas-eve, which should be a time of respite even for lawyers!"

"Mr. Paradise, I am past being offended at your insults, past heeding any one's anger," said Josephine, having sunk into a chair near him. "I have come to you on a matter of life and death, and though it be Christmas-eve, I want your services instantly, for you, I believe to be the fittest person to help me. Here is your retainder or retaining fee, whichever you call it."

Mr. Paradise glanced at the thousand dollar bill she had placed upon his table, and then at her. In her face, beautiful as ever, he saw the traces of such suffering, that he relented; and settling himself for a patient and most thorough hearing of the case, he returned her the bill, saying, with a touch of respect in his voice,—

"Take it back for the present. We will first hear what you have to say."

She received the note again, half unconsciously, and crumpled it up nervously in her soft, white hand; but before she spoke again, the color rose to her cheek, and her eyes were downcast.

"Mr. Paradise," she commenced, timidly, yet determined to lose no time in entering upon the subject, "I have laid myself open to your censure; nay, placed myself at the mercy of your ridicule, in coming to you alone at night, and in this strange manner; but there is one in danger, who, perhaps, has no other friend than me."

"*Friend!*" repeated Mr. Paradise, with an involuntary relapse into sarcasm. "I assume that this friend is of the masculine gender, and wonder whether your legal adviser may be informed of the nature of your attachment. Is it platonic?"

"He is a friend," answered Josephine, with that gentle majesty so peculiar to some women, "to whom I am betrothed."

There was something in that simple answer which touched the humpback, and he said:—

"Well, well, don't be offended, but let me know the trouble."

"He is accused of *murder*." She stopped as if the word choked her. The lawyer gave her time to continue.

"He is in prison at this moment," continued Josephine, hoarsely, "and, as I verily believe, I am his only friend on this continent, the duty of saving him devolves upon me. You," she added, with a sudden change of tone, "are the man I have selected to defend him.

You, I believe to have more ability than any one else, and upon you I call in the name of God and Justice, to rescue the innocent!"

Her eyes more eloquent than her tongue looked beseechingly into his, and the plaintive, entreating gesture with which she half arose from her chair seconded the appeal which her soul made to his, in a manner that was not lost even upon Mr. Paradise. She saw her answer in the compassion which took the hideousness from his face; she read encouragement in the luster of his dark eyes as their looks met, and she inwardly thanked heaven that she had discovered the *heart* of that deformed body, so that more than professional pride would inspire the defender of her lover.

Paradise, like many men habitually cynical, disliked to exhibit any tender emotion, and although the woman's intuition saw that he was moved, his manner did not betray it.

"Give me the papers relating to the case," he said, in a business-like tone. "I see you have a bundle of documents there which undoubtedly contain the affidavits upon which the warrant for his arrest was issued. Is it so?"

"Yes, sir, here they are."

"Then be kind enough to sit by the fire, there, and don't speak a word until I have looked in to the case."

Turning around she saw what she had not before noticed, a bright, pleasant fire roaring away in a grate near the attorney's table, and moved toward it as she had been bid.

"What a Christmas!" she murmured, sadly. He heard the words and looking up, said in a voice of sardonic bitterness:—

"This is a sample of the only Christmas I ever knew! The world calls me a cynic, and an ill-tempered monster; and what else could have been expected? Born into this world where a fair exterior successfully hides interior foulness, what excellence, what beauty of mind or soul could find appreciation under this lump of deformity, this shapeless shape, this masterpiece of hideousness, this offense to every sense of beauty, this monstrous mistake of nature, this disgusting, appalling creation of a wrathful hour in heaven!"

Josephine was speechless with surprise. She had known the hunchback for years, without ever hearing but one pathetic speech from him, and that was addressed to a jury. Just as on that occasion, his eyes now shone with a luster which shed a glow of beauty over his face, and his features inspired by the fervor of his powerful mind lost their repulsiveness.

"It is very well," continued the hunchback, with less vehemence, "for other people to call me hard-hearted, stoical, and malicious; but I have never known a sympathy above that contemptible way of hinting, 'I am better than thou,' called pity, no not since I was born. I have had to fight my own way over all obstacles with this detestable load of homeliness to back me, and as you see me this Christmaseve; alone, and without a tie to call me to my home, thus have I spent every day of my existence!"

"But, I think," replied Josephine, warmly, "that you could have found one creature to afford you consolation for the enmity of the whole world."

"I know what you mean," said the hunchback with intense bitterness. "You think there might be a woman I could love, who would love me, hey?"

"The man who can command the judgment of twelve honest men can easily win a woman's heart. You are not homely when you address a jury, Mr. Paradise."

With a shrug of his shoulder he turned his back upon her and began in earnest to examine the documents which she had brought him. She could catch a glimpse of his face from which all trace of his recent emotion had fled, leaving the sneer and wrinkles which proved they were permanent beautifiers.

She stared into the flames which danced up from the glowing coal in fantastic shapes; she saw the coal wast away into pale ashes and fall a disorganized mass. She heaped on fresh fuel with her own hands, but the lawyer did not notice the noise. Frequent glances showed her how deeply he was interested in her case. At times he would think a moment, make a note with his pencil and fall to reading again. Anxious as she was to hear an opinion, a decision, her good sense made her hold her tongue with patience. Sometimes, when he frowned, she fearingly longed to ask him what danger had presented itself to his mind, and again, when he, by a slight nod of his head, signified his satisfaction, she could have fallen on his neck and kissed him for the encouragement. He seemed totally oblivious of her presence, but she saw how he was scanning every portion of the evidence against her lover and she forgave him, even blessed him for it. Blessed him from the bottom of her heart, and prayed for him, her comfort in this hour of need, that God would remember his friendship for her and bless him with contentment. "Contentment," she thought. "If I were a man and had his giant mind, I would not exchange it for the charms of an Adonis, and my songs of love to women should be more powerful than the music of Orpheus."

And as she once more gazed into the orange depths of the fire, she thought of the inestimable happiness which gladdens the earth this wonderful night, and of the untold misery of those passing these hours harassed by the pangs of sickness or poverty. She had journeyed from Massachusetts that day, she had traversed the endless snow-fields in the country, had seen the sun take a golden farewell of the country homes, where happiness awaited old and young, and her thoughts flew to a prison, within whose desolate walls there was incarcerated the one being on earth whom she loved and adored. Many agonized tears fell from her eyes as she thought of him, without whose memory she treasured no thought, without whose image her heart was empty and desparing, and without whose love her life was utter death.

But she summoned up courage as she reflected that she need not despair. So surely as God lived her lover would be saved; for to her mind a doubt of his innocence was a blasphemous doubt of God's integrity.

Visions of the misery on earth, of dingy rooms, haggard faces, sickness, and death, and the appalling anguish of mothers who can not appease the plaintive cry of childhood for bread even this hallowed night;—poverty in all its horrible shapes crowding the streets and cursing the illumined palaces of the rich with hungry covetous glaring at the bright windows.

There came to her a vision of sin; of women dressed in silk, with wanton faces painted into a similitude of freshness. She thought of the hearts heavy, on such a night, with the loss of innocence; of the millions of lonely tears which wash away the gaudy paint, and of the terrible remorse which comes all too late,—so late that it has to seek solitude to escape ridicule in that *demi-monde* which has cast away the better half of life and soul. And the eyes of her mind penetrated prison walls and watched the agony of crime detected, and heartily she pitied every wretched prisoner for being unable to "trust in God and fear nothing," as her lover could.

And as the lawyer still was reading and making notes, her own life passed before her; the Christmas night of her childhood, when every pulsation of her youthful heart told only of joy and pleasure; a vision of Christmas trees and candles, neither brighter nor more beautiful than the happy faces which crowded around; remembrances of her solemn happiness, when, on this great festival of all Christendom, she first pledged her troth to her husband, and the holy exaltation which filled her maiden heart, as she bound herself to be a wife according to the teachings of that Christ whose nativity was then celebrated. Then she thought of the joyous day when her child crowed in her arms, and the world and life seemed to her one endless blessing.

The fire was smoldering away into ashes, and, as the last glow expired on the crumbling heaps, she thought of her husband, of her child, long buried—ashes to ashes; and of herself, left a lonely widow, with naught but two graves in her heart until new life came to her from the mercy of God—new life, new love; and, though she was sad this night, faith in God made harmony between her sweet and bitter thoughts.

As the ragged and black and broken surface of this polluted earth is often made clean and smooth and beautiful by old Winter's festive white robes, so the holy spirit of Christmas descended upon her bruised and wounded soul and she prayed fervently that "Peace on earth and good will toward men" might be realized as fully as "Glory to God in the Highest."

She lost herself in what might be called a trance of devotion, which is not often experienced in our churches. Her surroundings melted away, the dingy room expanded to a temple of worship, and her immortal soul, unfettered, brought sacrifice of prayer and thanksgiving to the Father above. In her ears a chorus of angels chanted a Christmas carol; with the swelling of the joyful music she felt that something united her heart with a countless number of other hearts, lifted up to the Divine source of all good in adoration, and deliciously intoxicating to her devout soul was the exultation of being at this moment one step nearer heaven. A sharp though calm voice broke in upon her ecstasy and brought her to herself.

"I am done," said the lawyer. She did not immediately answer. When he approached her he found her weeping.

"Leave your tears at home, when you come on such serious business as this," said Mr. Paradise, coldly. She came to her senses at once, and, taking a seat at the table, showed him a resolute face, though full of intense anxiety.

"Mrs. Van Strom," said he, "this is a *very* serious case. His life is in danger."

He was startled by the expression of her face. Not a vestige of color was there; but, through her eyes, he could look in and see the wound she had received by the sudden thrust of those words.

"But then," she gasped, "can you, *you* think for a moment that—Oh, God—no!"

"No," he answered, promptly. "I do not for a moment think that he is guilty. The evidence is cooked up by some great master of cunning, though, and unless we can find more flaws in it than I can discern at present, we hardly have a case!"

"But, merciful Heavens! how can he be in danger while he is innocent?"

"We will save our time for business," he answered, "and leave out philosophical puzzles. This master mind. Do you know who is its happy owner? Is it the little Italian, Stilletto, whose affidavit fills up so completely this prettily-arranged testimony? It is, hey? I can see by your angry face, at the very sound of his name, that I am right. Now, be a sensible girl, and tell me all you know of this fellow, since he honored your part of the country with his presence. I know a good deal about him already, from his connection with the Hobgoblin company, and this knowledge may help us considerably. Proceed."

His unpassionate, practical manner helped her to gather the powers of her memory, while the terrible danger, which seemed to threaten, made her calm and concise in her account. She told him about Stilletto's visits to John Van Strom, how he had stolen into his good graces, and had finally prevailed upon him to make a will, appointing him and Muller executors. How Bella had brought John back to his senses, so that, on the day of the murder, he had gone to the village, determined to undo the intriguers, and had succeeded in completing a document, in which he divided his fortune equally between Bella and herself, and reappointed Ernest Montant to be executor.

"Hold on, there!" interrupted Paradise. "Stilletto did not know that this last testament, which upset his intrigues, had just been consummated at the time of the murder?"

"He could not have known it."

The lawyer once more referred to the documents. "I see here that the strongest affidavit is that of Antonio Stilletto. He says that he heard the accused expressing strong enmity, and distinctly threatening the murdered man. One remark is quoted: 'If I can only get his property safe, I don't care how long the poor fool lives.' If we can not impugn Stilletto's

veracity, we have a dangerous case. But the most damaging point in the testimony is the dagger which was found in the breast of the deceased. This dagger is absolutely identified with the one given Van Strom by his wife, when he drove to the village that day, and as Montant, according to the testimony of the lawyers in the village, received this dagger from John, and returned with him in his wagon, the circumstance amounts to almost positive evidence against our client. True," he continued, half to himself, while Josephine listened in an agony of doubt and fear, commencing to realize what she had heretofore refused to believe, that there was real, tangible danger for her lover, "it appears evident that a third party must have removed the planks of the bridge, while they were in the village, for Van Strom had driven over the road with safety in the afternoon, and found Montant in the village, and they remained together until returning. Is it likely that Montant could induce Van Strom to stop the wagon, while he alighted and removed the planks himself?

"Unlikely it does certainly seem, but with Stilletto's testimony, which establishes a motive, strengthened as it is by the fact of Montant's full acquaintance with the contents of the will he had just seen completed, and then that confounded dagger evidence, and the indisputable fact that Montant is the only person *known* to be present—I tell you, the district attorney has a rare case of circumstantial evidence. Short, not complicated, and delightful to all parties except Mr. Montant."

Josephine's distress was mastering her senses; for a moment she thought her reason would leave her; but, making a giant effort, she asked, desperately:—

"Will not his character, his name, his high tone and spotless life, help you?"

"Yes, it will, and I do not give it up at all yet!"

He sat musing awhile.

"Who do you think is the murderer?" asked Josephine.

"Do you expect a *lawyer* to answer such a question?" he asked, with a sneer.

CHAPTER II.

"ARE YOU GUILTY?"

"I fear thou play'dst most foully for't."
MACBETH.

THE reader will remember that the Italian girl Simonetta Marini fled from the savage wrath of Stilletto upon being discovered at the folding-door after the conference between that worthy and Mr. Muller. We have also seen that from the direction taken by Simonetta, the Italian correctly foresaw the warning which reached Bella through the agency of Simonetta, and it has been related how John was won back by the love of his wife to confessing the foolish acts of changing his will at the instance of Stilletto and Muller, and to his former friendship for Ernest Montant. Impetu-

ous as usual, he had at once started off to the village to seek our hero and an honest attorney to remedy his grave error without risking the dangers of delay. On his way thither his conversation with Stilletto reassured the wily Italian, so that he only feared the interference of Simonetta and her friend Martin Bates, who he fully expected would discover to Bella the existence of the will John had made at his instance, in which case Bella's influence upon her husband to undo what he had so madly committed, was a matter to be feared.

When Martin and Simonetta went forth into the wild night again, after having disclosed the intrigue to Mrs. Van Strom, still ignorant of the death of her husband, they were filled with bitterness against themselves, each other, and all the world.

"So sure as the night is bleak and the storm is mingling the heavens and earth," cried the girl, "this man will cause my death. Ah, that he might come now and tear my heart from me in an instant; it would be far better than to live a life like a hunted beast! Never will his fiery eyes lose sight of me; his serpent steps will glide after me wherever I go, till fearful watching for his coming will drag me down to death by slow degrees."

"Oh, Simonetta!" cried Martin Bates, dolefully, "why did you reject the love of a man who sought you out from the filth of the scum of New York to elevate you to a position of comfort and respectability?"

"You!" cried the girl, angrily, "you talk of comfort and respectability? I know from what those two vile sneaks have said to each other in my unsuspected hearing, that you are a robber, a base falsifier of the truth, and a villain as bad as they! How dare you call heaven's curse upon your white hair by reproaching my loathing for you? Your folly alone can excuse your wickedness, you sensual, old fool!"

"And is this your thanks for my friendship and kindness, you ungrateful, foul, and sinful wretch?" cried Martin. "I loved you when the world spit in your face—I helped you when heaven turned away from you—I respected you when society pointed its finger at you and said, 'There is a creature of shame!' And now, since you thus return my affection which indeed was the full measure of human folly, we had better part company forever. Go forth into this dark night alone and unguided, for you have rejected your best friend. Return into the darkness from which I would have rescued you, and henceforth be to me a thing dead and passed from memory!"

And with these cruel words he left her, turning abruptly away toward his brother's house, where, before long, he first heard of the murder.

Simonetta found herself alone in the wild, tempestuous night, forsaken by the last friend she had. She stood on the dark road, exposed to the blast which seemed near to sweep away the whole surface of the earth. Scarcely could she keep her footing, and she knew not where her steps were tending, nor did she desire to again enter a dwelling inhabited by that hated race called human. But she had not been

brought up under the kind influences of home and friendship, nor had her dreary experience accustomed her to dependence upon companions. What would have driven a creature of delicate mold to complete despair only intensified the bitterness of her fierce nature, steeled by the experiences of her hardening life. She resumed her way without an aim or settled plan, except a vague determination to be, henceforth, not a wretched creature of misery, but hardened, bold, shameless. The night, filled with the howls and shrieks and dismal moans of the gale, was not so dark, nor was the rage of the elements so infuriated as the thoughts which chased every vestige of decency from her heart. Suddenly, as she was mentally surrendering body and soul to the fiend which seemed let loose upon the patient earth on this fearful night, while she was groping her way, she knew not whither and cared less, she felt that some one was behind her, and approaching rapidly. Frightened, she turned quickly, and just escaped a collision with a man who was hurrying along the road. Had the darkness trebled in intensity, and the raincloud madly flying along overhead shed a hundred drops for each one, had the deafening, blinding, confusing hurricane, summoned a world of additional force, no fury of the elements could have hindered the instinctive recognition of *those two* as they now met.

The wild shriek which rose to Simonetta's lips was instantaneously stifled by a sharp and cruel blow, and as a grip of iron closed on her throat, she heard a hissing voice she knew too well :—

"Out with your dagger! You or I, this time!"

She had no weapon with her; but even if she had, she did not possess sufficient courage or presence of mind to use it. And as she felt herself growing giddy, the blood filling her head near to bursting, the voice of her heart cried to the Virgin for mercy and pity, and death stood before her dulling eyes, ready to grasp her in another instant.

Whether reassured by her being unarmed, or whether some other impulse checked his fury, Stilletto suddenly relaxed his hold, allowing her freedom enough to breathe, and then drew a dirk, forced its point with a knowing thrust, just through her dress, until a terrified shriek announced that it pricked her breast, and said, quickly,—

"I don't want to kill you. I'll forgive you all if you'll swear to return to the countess immediately, and never tell that you saw me this day—never repeat what you know about John Van Str—"

He paused, and, for a second, her intensified senses told her of a shuddering which seemed to run through him, and relax his hold on her throat so materially that she might have escaped, but that she was spellbound by terror.

"About that will, Muller and I made out to-day," he continued, "or about any thing that has transpired to-day."

"I promise—I promise!" she gasped. "Let me loose. God help me!'

But the wily Italian was not to be pacified by a mere promise, and he continued,—

"I want you to bind yourself by an oath which will send your soul to hell if you break it!"

And in the midst of that terrible night, to the accompaniment of the moans of the wind which seemed to come from men in agony far, far away; in the midst of that night's unfathomable darkness, Simonetta repeated after him words of such dreadful import as would seal the lips of a superstitious soul, close as the tomb. When the appalling formula of that oath had been spoken twice over by the half-crazed girl, Stilletto, feeling quite certain that she would never break it, just as she, in her Romish superstition, was certain in her own heart, that she never could break it without being struck dead to the ground, Stilletto, satisfied, released her, and said, more lightly,—

"I forgive you all the harm you have done me, Nettie, and if you want a friend, come to me! So you will go straight off to the countess, and stay there, will you ?"

"Yes, yes, I will."

"Here is money to take you to New York." She took it. It seemed to burn her hands, and with a sharp cry she flung it from her.

"What is the matter now ?" he exclaimed, fiercely.

"I don't know," replied the trembling girl. "It burned me! I am sure it burned me! Holy Virgin have pity on me!" and she burst into a fit of tears. He, trembling violently himself, tried to soothe her, but it was of no avail. She pushed him away, and crying more bitterly, sank to the ground in a fit of hysterica. For a moment he stood irresolute; perhaps he was moved, perhaps he would have liked to stay by her, perhaps he wanted such a friend as she might still prove; but stronger motives drove him onward."

"She will keep her oath," he muttered, "and she is smart enough to take care of herself any way. Farewell, remember what you have sworn to me," he cried aloud, and hurried on through the darkness, leaving her to the mercy of the elements, and also to the mercy of their Ruler. The soft moon broke through the clouds and looked down on her, just as a half hour previously she looked down upon another shape, not writhing like hers, but stiff and motionless, not half a mile distant. At this first sight the Queen of Heaven had veiled herself in horror, yielding the supremacy once more to the wild storm; but now she held her sway, and when Simonetta returned to consciousness the world lay bright before her, the skies were starry above, and she could look up for consolation and be answered by the rays of hope.

* * * * * * *

But the grounds upon which Martin Bates brooded until he entertained terrible suspicions against his brother, were partly known to himself alone. The whole of his knowledge and suspicions were as follows:—

Josephine has told us that Ernest Montant was arrested on the charge of having murdered his friend, John Van Strom. Martin

Bates, from his acquaintance with both parties, was convinced that Stilletto was the guilty man, and nothing would have prevented him from putting his own worthless self into jeopardy, by making the accusation publicly, without out any evidence to sustain the charge, had he he not noticed a certain change in his brother. Eben was restless, nervous at times, confined to his room by illness. When the affidavits upon which Ernest Montant was arrested, reached the Judge's hands he showed them to Martin. With great care he dwelt upon the conclusiveness of the preliminary evidence, and although he paled visibly, when he read the Italian's testimony aloud to Martin, yet he enlarged upon it with great legal precision, and tried to show his brother how it seemed impossible that Stilletto could have accomplished such an extensive and intricate statement had it been perjury.

"Where was Stilletto at the time of the murder? Oh, I forgot he was here!"

"Yes, at this house," answered Eben, quickly.

"Strange that no one knew it," said Martin, with a thousand distracted emotions in his heart.

"He was here. That is enough. I can testify to that, again in court," answered the judge, calmly, but paler still.

Martin said no more, turning away to think, heaven knows what.

The date of the trial of Ernest Montant, for the horrible crime of murder had now been fixed, and was not many days distant. Martin Bates became gloomier and sadder all the time, waiting for fate to prepare his last task on earth, the duty for which his life had been prolonged. The tragedy had made a terrible sensation. Not only the neighborhood, but the whole country was aroused, the detectives from the great cities were at work, the bar was in a flutter of expectation, and prominent among the attorneys who had been engaged, stood Mr. Paradise (who fortunately was a member of the Massachusetts bar) to conduct the defense of the accused. It was generally understood that the trial would go hard with the prisoner, but the activity of the detectives and the extensive employment of spies, private agents, and attorneys showed that some person of means and influence had befriended him.

As to the prisoner, Montant, immediately after the murder, he had accused Stilletto of the deed. He swore he had recognized him—he described the dreadful occurrence with startling circumstantiality, and on his affidavit Stilletto was arrested. But by the testimony of Judge Eben Bates, who swore to Stilletto's presence at his house, before, during, and after the time when the murder must have been committed, an alibi was proved so clearly that he was immediately discharged. Then came Stilletto's affidavit regarding threats made by Montant, against John Van Strom's life, the circumstance of Montant's charge against Stilletto began to look as if he had desired to shut the latter's mouth by putting him in jeopardy, the undeniable fact that Montant was the only person known to have been present at the murder, and, finally, tho

testimony concerning the dagger, with other circumstantial evidence, all combined with singular fallacy to make up the situation which had inspired Mr. Paradise with the most serious apprehensions. As Martin Bates thought it all over, he trembled, not so much for the life of a man who had not shown himself to be a friend of his, as for the probable escape of the real criminal, who, he was positive, was Stilletto, in spite of his brother's oath, proving the alibi.

"If that oath was false, Eben is accessory," soliloquized Martin, and while he was torturing himself about this question, he received the following letter, postmarked, New York, and written in Italian by the Countess, for Simonetta herself was not mistress of the pen:—

"SIGNOR MARTIN BATES:—Will you be so kind as to favor me with a call on the day before the trial. Ask the countess, who is writing this for me, if I am within, and if she says yes, wait for me by the great stove in the dancing hall. I shall come there by eight o'clock in the evening. If I may be absolved from an awful oath I will show the world where a certain person was, at a certain time, and the lies that have been told will be blown to the four corners of the earth. If I can not be absolved from this oath, human kind shall no more know Simonetta. Try not to seek me, keep the officers away from my path. At the first sign of pursuit I will fly away beyond their reach, where I can spend the rest of my life in better ways. I know all the evidence that has appeared in the newspapers, and it is all false, but unless God commands me to break my oath I must let it stand. Remember that no friendship, no relationship should prevent bringing the real murderer to justice. Murder strikes at the core of life, whence friendship and love arise, and necessarily severs them.

"SIMONETTA."

After the two sleepless nights which followed the receipt of that letter, Martin put to his brother that dread question which heads this chapter.

He had made up his mind to steal away from the house, the next morning before daybreak, go to New York and confer with Mr. Paradise or any other of the counsel for the defense, that he could readily find before going to see the Italian girl. As he was retiring to his room, his heart sank with the fear that he might not again see his brother until——He stopped at Eben's door. He heard his brother's voice low, moaning in agonized prayer. He opened the door noiselessly. There was the stately judge, a pitiable wreck of manhood, on his knees, in anguish, as if tortured by an accusing conscience.

Martin laid his hand on his shoulder.

"Brother, dear brother," burst from the old man, in faint accents, "tell me what is troubling you! I know your secret. I know Stilletto is your son, and that it was he for whom I brought you the sacrifice of my honor. If he has forced you into denying your knowledge of his crime—if he has drawn you into—perjury; if he has made you his assistant, his tool, his accessory. Oh, for God's sake! tear the diabolical net of lies which has been spread for the life of an innocent man, throw yourself upon the mercy of man, law, and God, and confess."

Taken unawares by the sudden interruption, Eben had needed time to recover himself.

"Martin," he said, furious with shame and confusion, "you are no longer addressing your brother, but Judge Eben Bates."

"Then I charge you, Judge Eben Bates," cried Martin, with flashing eyes, "you, who have preserved your dignity by my crimes, you, who have purchased your honor with my shame, I ask you, in the name of the Judge whom no affidavits can pervert, I charge you on your immortal soul, in the name of truth, life, and death, by heaven and hell, and the eternal God, to tell me, *Are you guilty?*"

Judge Bates stood grandly towering. His face showed more of death than of life. Only one motion did he make, no syllable passed his firm-set lips. He pointed to the door. The majesty of innocence offended, or a giant at bay?

Without another word, Martin retired to his own room. "No friendship, no relationship, should prevent bringing the real murderer to justice," he quoted from Simonetta's letter, as, a few hours later, he quit the house, never to enter it again.

CHAPTER III

"A PERFECT STRANGER."

"When fortune in her shift and change of mood
Spurns down her late beloved, all his dependents,
———Let him slip down,
Not one accompanying his declining foot."
TIMON OF ATHENS.

THERE is an intoxication, an egotistical satisfaction, a luxury in the excess of grief. The condition of overwhelming frenzied suffering brings with it an elation, during which the strong man calls upon his manhood and his religion to bear him up, and his spirits revel in an intensity of feeling and a depth of thought which raise him into closer proximity to God.

But when we have to face slow, lingering tortures; when we have to live through tribulations which do not engage our whole mind, but give us breathing spells of treacherous happiness, only to be succeeded again and again by lower descents; when these trials are of a nature to destroy pride, self-reliance, and strength of purpose; when we see those depending upon us, whom we love and cherish, and find ourselves powerless to help them,—then do we suffer a thousand pangs in one; then do our multiplied afflictions break down our strength and blight our life, and Hope and Faith die a lingering death. Such is the downfall into *poverty!*

Do you see that old man, with but the remnants of grace and beauty, walking the streets of New York? He has lost his wife in the prime of manhood, and his God helped him through that agony; he has seen two children die in his arms, and he recovered from the shock with unbroken faith; he has known false friends, but his belief in human nature was not shaken. *Now he is poor,* and, in his old age, he has to taste the bitterest gall; he is poor, and now only does he hang his head and succumb to grief.

Thus do we find old Mr. Going, his name still untarnished, though a thousand tongues heap suspicion on it, his credit not yet forfeited, though virtually gone, his house, the good old house of Going & Son, still standing, but rotten and tottering, so that the whole cruel world can see its decay. Thus he goes forth one morning, with a face where grief and shame have set their seal, with a step which has become feeble and wavering, with a heart broken long, long ago—to borrow money! Yes, to *borrow.* Heaven knows what that word means to an honest man, when he no longer applies for an accommodation, or asks a favor, but has to beg it as a charity!

He goes to seek Mr. Chip, "Old Moneybags," as he was called by half New York. Oh! the sigh which escaped the old man, as he entered the banking-house, with the clerks bustling about, and an intimation of wealth and solidity pervading the very air of the stately counting-room. It was so with him once!

He asks for Mr. Chip, and, upon sending in his name, is informed that Mr. Chip is busy; but will see him in a few moments. He takes a chair and waits humbly.

"He has dined at my table," soliloquized Mr. Going, "and, although with the exception of Hobgoblin, we have had no business transactions together, he can not refuse me."

Finally, he was admitted to Mr. Chip, who received him with studied politeness, an expression on his thin, fishy face the while which might have meant, "I would be delighted to see you, were I quite certain that you did not come for money."

"Mr. Chip," said Mr. Going, in an unsteady voice, "I have come to ask you a question."

"I am bus— that is, I am at your service, my dear sir," answered Mr. Chip, nervously; adding, with a sudden inspiration of decisiveness, "I hope it is not about Hobgoblin! I have resigned my trusteeship in the company, as you know very well, and I really must decline to enter into any conversation on that subject."

"It is not Hobgoblin," said Mr. Going, quietly. Mr. Chip wheeled around on his chair, like a weathercock, and examined the ceiling as if he had never seen it before.

"Well, what is it?" he asked, growing fidgetty.

"Mr. Chip," said Mr. Going, trembling in every limb from timidity and humiliation; but proceeding, because he *must,* "you know that I have lost my fortune. Still, I am, I hope, not a bankrupt, and when I now ask you to kindly loan me a few thousand dollars, to make my family comfortable—to make my family comfortable," repeated the old gentleman, in a thick voice, "I can assure you that I will repay you, and I must also confess that I need this assistance very much—very much, indeed."

The human race has produced brutes,—heartless, cruel, savage creatures,—but there are many hardened felons, who, had they possessed the money, would have spoken cheeringly to Mr. Going and helped him willingly. Mr. Chip was reputed to be an accommodating man, an easy-going, rather good-tempered fellow. Hear him answer:—

"Mr. Going—ahem! I am sorry, very sorry for your difficulties—but why do you come to *me* for assistance? To me, *a perfect stranger? A perfect stranger*," he repeated, with emphasis, so as to express, with all the refined cruelty of which this cold age is capable, that the world of selfishness, which is composed of wealth, had cast him out, that he was now an unknown, unpitied stranger, and that he was thrown to the mercy of God knows what!

And yet, Mr. Chip was not a harsh man. The word stung Mr. Going to the quick. At first, an angry rejoinder rose to his lips; but the pain of the rebuff, the cruel thrust at his noble heart, took the last remnant of strength from him. For a moment he thought of the bitter lesson he now, in his sixtieth year, had been taught; he remembered how often this man, that called him stranger now, had enjoyed his hospitality, and he became proudly aware that the creature was not worthy a reply. With a cold "Good morning, sir," he moved to the door.

"Wait a moment, Mr. Going," stammered Mr. Chip, seriously discomfited, "I did not mean to offend you, sir."

"You did not offend me, sir," replied Mr. Going, with a bow.

"But, just wait a moment," cried Mr. Chip, in some alarm. "If it must be done, we will try to arrange—only—you know—I am sorry that I myself can not—just now."

"I believe that I did not ask you a second time. My first request you have answered with a single word. Good morning."

He left Mr. Chip in as uneasy a frame of mind as possible from so trifling an occasion. The little millionaire had not intended to be harsh. His narrow views could not take in the misery which the mere uttering of the request caused the old gentleman, much less what had brought him to that necessity. Could he have correctly interpreted the expression in that plaintive bright eye, could he have understood the language of that haggard though still handsome countenance, had he reflected upon the sanctity of those silver locks, upon which the hand of Heaven was now so heavily laid, perhaps he would have acted differently;—and perhaps he would not.

Mr. Chip had occasion to meet Mr. Paradise that day. The lawyer, whom every one disliked, and who had wrung respect for his ability from the scoffing world by sheer power of intellect, was a liberal, off-hand man in money matters. Mr. Chip related to him the circumstance of Mr. Going's visit.

"The old man never knew how to borrow," said the hunchback, laughing, "and fortunately for him it was no great loss heretofore. I like people who do not know how to borrow, and I have half a mind to go to the old

gentleman and help him out from sheer friendship."

He was a man that *might* have assisted Mr. Going in the hour of his need—but then again he *might* have changed his mind, for money means treachery personified all through this world. And it happened that Mr. Going, sick at heart, did not renew his attempts to borrow; and it also happened that Mr. Paradise, although a liberal, off-hand man in money matters, forgot all about his generous impulse, and *did not* assist his old client, from whom he had received a fortune in fees, and through whose patronage he had acquired a great portion of his practice and standing.

When Mr. Going reached his office, he found Walter awaiting him anxiously. On this paltry sum of a few thousand dollars, depended a world of vital issues, embodying the safety, comfort, and serenity of the family. When a man is harassed for money, he is in no condition to grapple with other questions, even though vital to his future welfare. One look at his father, showed Walter, only too plainly, that another effort had failed, that another humiliation had been undergone, and that another day had been sadly inaugurated for them. Without asking a question, or subjecting his father to the additional sorrow and vexation of discussing what had happened, Walter put on his hat, and with a defiant swagger, left the counting-room. In an hour he returned with so much money as was actually needed; but how he had obtained it, what desperate efforts had been required to wring the small sum from the merciless multitude of friends, that were friends no longer, how much sacrifice of pride it had cost, and how he had been obliged to screw his courage to that unnatural sticking-point, vulgarly called "brass," no one ever could learn from him. When Walter Going left the office to saunter up town, he met Mr. Solomons at the corner of the street. The Jew looked as brightly polished as ever, but his diamond buttons, his watch and chain had disappeared.

"Solomons, what is the matter with you? Where are your diamonds and your watch, hey?"

The sad face of the stockbroker and auctioneer gave sufficient answer. His sallow countenance was drawn to that length and had assumed that expression which in human physiognomy denotes extreme depression. Walter had not seen him for some weeks, having been so entirely occupied with his own troubles that the doings of others necessarily escaped his attention. Therefore he had not known that Mr. Solomons had lost all his money, and indeed many times more than he had ever possessed.

"Mr. Going, sir," said Mr. Solomons, "I am ruined. I was an ass. I did not stick to my regular business, went speculating again, *ay vollaw law raysoultaw!*"

With a smile at the Israelitic French, Walter said,—

"Why don't you end your sentences with *Cash* any more, Solomons?"

"The day of cash is done," answered Solomons, dolefully. "*Cash* is dead, it has taken wings and fled. My diamonds and watch are learning Hebrew."

"Doing what?"

"Learning Hebrew at the house of an esteemed countryman of mine. I mean that they are pawned."

"Well, let them rest," said Walter, laughing. "We are well met; being both poor, we are good company, and I propose that we walk up town together. You see the great thing is that neither of us will be afraid that the other will borrow money from him! How delightful, and how much more comfortable that is than when a rich man and a beggar meet!"

Mr. Solomons explained that he was completely ruined, and absolutely without credit at any shop, hotel, or restaurant. He lived "by the grace of God," as he said, but how he managed to keep from utter destitution, he was no more able to relate than any student of social science can account for the existence of thousands like him.

As they walked up town, Walter realized, with a disagreeable sensation, that his situation was more analogous to that of Mr. Solomons than he would have desired.

"Let us cross over the street," said the Jew, when they had got pretty well up Broadway.

"Why?" asked Walter, following him.

"My tailor lives hard by," answered the other, "and I have secret reasons which impel me to avoid his door."

Solomons laughed, but Walter did not.

"*My* tailor lives right here," he said, "but I have not gone so far quite yet, as to be afraid of him."

"Do you owe him a bill?"

"Yes, what of that?"

"How long has it run?"

"About a year."

"Do you expect to be able to pay him in the course of this year?"

Walter bit his lips. "I hope so," he answered.

"Well, so did I *hope*, a year ago," rejoined the Jew, dryly. "But my hopes proved vain, and let me tell you my proud friend that if you do *not* pay him, you will shun your tailor's door next year, as I do mine to-day."

Walter would have been angry, but he had not the heart to take offense at this shrewd and unanswerable piece of philosophy.

"Let's take a glass of wine, Solomons, and drop the subject," he said, sharply.

"With pleasure," answered Mr. Solomons. "But not in there," he added, pulling his friend away from a door he was on the point of opening. "I owe that fellow money, and don't want to be seen."

"Solomons," cried Walter, "It is not respectable to be in debt all over town."

"Is it respectable to be hungry and thirsty, and see your clothes wear to threads? I tell you, sir, this town owes me a living. I have spent thousands with these traders, and they can afford to trust me a few hundred for a year or two."

"Then why don't you tell them so, and keep out of the disgraceful position of shunning them."

"Because they would not trust me at all if I explained to them. Tradespeople are a mysterious set of characters. They form a study for a man, and he must know how to handle them."

"God keep me from that science!" cried Walter.

"That science has kept me alive," answered the Jew, quietly; "and live I must and shall, in spite of all your high moral ideas! Besides, I do nothing dishonest. I mean to pay them some day. The worst of it is that I cannot economize! I can get a Delmonico dinner and a bottle of claret on trust; but if I stopped in a Bowery cellar and begged for a bit of bread and cheese, they would kick me out. By the way, I want to go in here to buy a cravat."

"Never mind," said Walter, "I have no time; it is late."

"Is that the only reason?" asked the Jew, scrutinizing his face.

"None of your business," answered Walter, angrily. "If you are so anxious, let us go in."

They entered the gentlemen's furnishing store. One of the proprietors of the establishment immediately stepped up to Mr. Going, and, rubbing his hands, said, what a fine day it was, and inquired why he had been such a stranger of late.

Walter, under the continued observation of Mr. Solomons, turned red, and after displaying considerable of nervousness, said, with an effort,—

"Muggins, I owe you a bill. Let me know how much it is, and I will write you a check."

Mr. Muggins, all smiles and politeness, brought forth his account, and the check was given.

"Aha!" said the Jew, when they had regained the street. "So I was right in suspecting a *reason* for your unwillingness to enter that shop! But what a lucky man you are to be able to write him a check!"

"Solomons," said Walter, gloomily, "I will confess to you that my check is not good until we make it so, by a deposit to-morrow."

"Then you were a fool to give it. The idea of allowing a fellow like that to put you to such inconvenience, or even danger of considerable annoyance!"

"The bank will pay it, of course, good or not," answered Walter, vexed with himself, and all the world. "But you are right; I should not have given it."

"Cheer up, my dear fellow," said Mr. Solomons, soothingly, "I am a thousand times worse off than you; but that does not change one fact, which, with your permission, I will state frankly. You are on that sort of a road to poverty where nothing but a large amount of ready money can save you."

Walter thought of those words long after they were spoken, and with a heavy heart was forced to admit their truth. A few months longer of this state of affairs would reduce him to Mr. Solomons' level, and that was not respectability.

Miss Jessie awaited her father and brother at home. They were still living in Fifth

Avenue; but it appeared to them as if they enjoyed the fine residence only as tenants, simply tolerated out of charity by those who owned the heavy mortgages which had long ago been given upon it.

She received them with a smile,—a smile that was born from a day of tears—a smile so forced and unnatural that it was not reciprocated by her father. The old gentleman had not laughed for months. His whole face was changed, she thought, and she felt as if she would have given all she possessed in the world to see once more a happy smile upon it.

No more friends at that hospitable board. No more cheerfulness in that house. Thus they had lived through the heavy days, in gloom, anxiety, and misery, and for what was it all? Was there any visible cause? Surely, the poor work-people, who daily passed the house, did not dream of this, yet the curse of poverty was upon them; and its fangs are keenest where least apparent.

"Jessie," said Mr. Going, when dinner had been removed, and Walter had strolled out, "I hear that Paradise is engaged for the defence of Ernest Montant. I hope and trust that he will procure his acquittal. I can not imagine that he is guilty."

"I know he is not," answered she, brightly and cheerfully.

Her father, astonished at her tone, looked at her closely. Our hero's name had not been mentioned between them since that day he had left the house, after making his last appeal to Mr. Going, when the father had read in his daughter's face the story of her love and struggle. Like a wise man, he had determined to let her fight alone, where no help could avail, and, until this instance, Montant's name had remained unspoken by mutual consent. He was, therefore, astonished at her open and hearty answer, which, although so confident, of the prisoner's innocence, yet showed none of that confusion he had feared would overcome her. He, however, continued without betraying his astonishment,—

"I most certainly agree with you, and I am glad you think so well of him."

"He is a good, fine fellow," answered Miss Jessie, unhesitatingly. "And I like him as a brother. I suppose there is no doubt about his engagement to Josephine Van Strom?"

"I think not. It was she that employed Mr. Paradise, Jessie," continued the old gentleman, drawing nearer to her, "do not think that I am desirous of forcing myself into such of your confidences as even a father can not share. But I must confess my astonishment that you can speak with such nonchalance of these things, and—"

"I know what you mean," she answered, with a smile. "I had a foolish fancy once; but the great cares and great anxieties belonging to the practical, have quite satisfied my *ideal* requirements."

Mr. Going kissed his daughter, and he sighed, though he was glad to hear it.

"Do not despair, father," said Jessie, lovingly. "If my plans of a cottage in the country, and a total change in our manner of life, are carried out, all will be well. As for

me, do not believe that an evanescent attachment can make me unhappy any more. I only hope and pray to see you free from care, and as for our friend, I am certain he will not suffer for a crime of which he is innocent. I can pray for his welfare, for he is true and noble—but nothing more to me.

CHAPTER IV.

STRANGE CONVERSATIONS.

"How much had I to do to calm his rage!
Now fear I this will give it start again."
HAMLET.

BELLA VAN STROM'S grief was terrible. It never gave her a moment's respite. She paced up and down the piazza of her dwelling while the snow and the thaw rendered the garden paths unpleasant, for she could not endure the idea of sitting down quietly in the house. She watched the sun as it sunk into the embrace of the gilded hills, and lighted up the winter landscape with dazzling splendor. To her the world was empty. She had withdrawn within herself, and had dropped a black veil between herself and the outer world.

Well might that world envy her and wonder at her "luck." She had married an idiot for his money—the idiot was dead, and the money her's. All the pleasures of the earth lay before her, with plenty of good, handsome, well-bred fellows, apt to like her well enough and her fortune better. And yet her grief was terrible!

She had learned to love that idiot before he died.

Bella is walking up and down the piazza, heedless of the wind which is beginning to blow sharp and cold as evening shadows stretch over the country. A carriage drives through the gate up to the house. A lady in black alights and runs up to Bella. She throws back her veil and kisses her; Bella returns the kiss affectionately, but without enthusiasm. Josephine's nature demands enthusiasm, requires warm impulses. The hasty, joyous words which trembled on her lips, die away and she recoils a step:—

Josephine (half-timidly, half-angrily). "Pardon me, I forgot that we are sisters no longer."

Bella (quietly). "We are sisters *in law*, Josephine, and sisters in affection as well. I never gave you reason to doubt it."

Josephine. "Where there is a change in manner, there must be a change in the sentiments which dictate that manner! Ever since that awful visitation of God's wrath which widowed you, and desolated my life, you have treated me like a stranger."

Bella. "No. But I feel as if we two should let Time and Truth do their work before we force each other to profess a contentment and pleasure in each other's society which can not really exist until the shadow which stands between us now is removed."

Josephine. "And what have you done to

remove it? Have you taken that interest, have you shown that anxiety, have you acted with that sisterly love which you have just professed?"

Bella (calmly). "I have done my duty. As your fortune is not yet available to you, I have, by my own free will, out of my private purse, supplied you with the means of procuring for your lover the best defense in the country."

Josephine. "And have you given me your advice—have you stood by me, that am so weak, with your strength and power of mind and will? Oh, it is cruel to find that when you most need them, your best, your only friends grow cold as ice!"

Bella. Josephine, I love justice well enough to see justice, and nothing but justice, done. I have love for nothing else until time and nature restore me to a semblance of my former self."

Josephine. "You suspect him of being guilty?"

Bella. "I suspect the whole world and yet suspect no one. I have aid for the accused, that his cause may be so protected as to insure impartial justice. I have zeal to assist the law in all its just prosecution; but I have pity for no one until his innocence becomes as clear as that sun now saying good-night to us."

Josephine. "Oh, how hard it is for a woman to be alone."

Bella. "*I am alone—forever!*"

Josephine. "And is this the sisterhood to which we are pledged by our holiest resolves? Do not our destiny, the name we bear in common, the sympathies which have interwoven our very souls, teach us to seek comfort in each other, to bear up and strengthen each other now that we stand apart from the whole world?"

Bella. "My grief is selfish. It will endure no helpmate. I have to fight a sacred battle, and no human eye may profane it by any intrusion."

Josephine. "Did I so spurn you from me when you came to me at the Priory a frightened, miserable being, not knowing where to turn for a word of encouragement, a ray of sympathy, a look of love! Oh, I see that I was mistaken when I said to myself, 'Poor John's intuition has got him a nobler wife than all the wisdom of the wise could have selected for him. Really, we know the human heart only when the hour of trial brings it out in its true light!"

Bella. "What would you have me do? Condole with you, before I can *know* that a heavier blow is not in store for you? I will save my consolations till then. Do you expect me to speak sisterly words to you while a specter stands between us, whose ghastly wounds cry to Heaven for retribution? Do you think I can weep for you, while my own tears are petrified, making my heart cold and heavy as lead? I have not yet shed a tear for my own loss. When I see the guilty man brought to justice, I shall be clear in my conscience, and then, perhaps, God, in mercy, will vouchsafe me tears."

Josephine. "You wrong yourself—you wrong *him, me,* cruelly; oh, how cruelly!"

Bella. "I wrong no one. I am ice-bound in a remorseless mission of duty. That will I fulfill, though each unrelenting step should crush a world. I feel as if that alone could give me peace; I feel as if that alone could restore me to the favor of heaven, from which I am now shut out. That accomplished, I feel that I could be a woman once more and weep, while now I am but a cold, dead instrument, animated by the god of vengeance to fulfill his purpose."

Josephine. "This language is unwomanly, unchristian, ungodly, and unworthy of your better self."

Bella. "Yet so you find me now. Come into the house. Although I can not keep you company, you will find hospitality. I have no merit in that; the house belongs half to you, half to me. Through my instrumentality you have recovered the one-half of the Van Strom fortune which belongs to you. In this I have done my duty, and claim no praise for it. Only when I continue henceforward to do my duty, I will not be upbraided."

Josephine. "Bella, God help you and me! What do your words mean? Do you—can you suspect me?"

Josephine, utterly unstrung, burst into a passionate fit of crying.

Bella, with a look of amazement, said,—

"This, at least, I was not prepared for! Fool that I am, how have I conveyed such a meaning?"

She assisted Josephine into the house, and reassured her, when the latter had become somewhat calm.

"I call Heaven to witness that the faintest idea of such a cruel wrong was furthest from my mind. Compose yourself on *this* point any way, and rest assured that I will help you as I did before, though I can not counsel you. God grant that the day may soon come, when I shall be able to make atonement for my harshness to you, but I can not do so now—not now. There is nothing in my heart that speaks against *you*—no, indeed! But I am become a stone and I can not speak even to you as I should. So let time develop the change I know must come over me, living or dying, and till then bear with me, and hope that you will regain your loving sister ere long. Good night."

She kissed the weeping woman and disappeared.

Josephine, though somewhat comforted, spent many hours of sleepless sorrow, bewailing the awful phase her sister's grief had assumed, but her thoughts would still turn back to her lover and to the grave doubts Mr. Paradise continued to express. So near the trial, so very near—only a few days!

And now we will leave her and listen to what two gentlemen have to say, who are troubled almost as much as she, though from slightly different causes.

We left our highly philosophic friend, Mr. Muller, waiting for *his* friend Antonio Stiletto. He could wait; he knew how to wait, which is a great science. He had plenty of beer and tobacco, and the flight of time was to him only the source of a majestic contentment as he smoked his pipe and drank his beer.

But when noon had faded away into evening, when night put in her black appearance, accompanied by such a tempest as threatened to disturb the balance of this mundane sphere, and, finally, when the beer and the pipe, those two mainstays of true philosophy, began to pall upon the palate, and taste bitter from unlimited abuse, then did the philosopher almost lose his serenity; he began to wish that Stilletto had kept his marching orders in his pocket, and, to his shame be it confessed, swore great polysyllabic oaths, in German, at the Italian.

When finally a ring at the door sounded clear and startling, and when Stilletto made his appearance, dripping wet, shivering and shaking with extraordinary excitement and a sort of wild look in his eye, Mr. Muller felt a vague instinct of repugnance, and wished, as we often do in life, that the person whose advent was so much desired had staid away indefinitely.

Muller. "Where have you been?"

Stilletto. "I was at Judge Bates's from three o'clock till now. Just come from there. What is the exact time?"

Muller. "Nine o'clock."

"From three till nine, from three till nine," repeated Stilletto, mechanically, and finding it a difficult and thankless task to start any further conversation, the two friends went to bed in the worst possible humor. Muller was too lofty to ask why he had been kept waiting, all ready to start at a moment's notice, and felt injured at Stilletto's silence on that subject, while the cunning Italian was afraid to say any thing near the truth, for fear of betraying his night's work.

We find them again, some time after the murder, and after Stilletto had been arrested and released upon proving an *alibi* by Judge Bates's testimony.

The philosopher was enjoying the solitude of his room and the anticipation of the glorious success of their scheme, which would come to light as soon as John Van Strom's will should be admitted to probate, when Stilletto burst violently into the room and seriously disturbed his equanimity, by conduct worthy of an escaped bedlamite, while he explained in accents hardly intelligible, from excitement and oaths in all languages, that John's will had been opened, and that it utterly demolished and ruined all their fond hopes, and further, that the will which they had so cunningly got out of him was canceled, revoked, and made worthless, in the most positive legal language that could be employed, and all this by a will made in the village on the afternoon of the day of his murder. A will which complied with the minutest requirements of the law, without a ghost of a chance for them if they undertook to dispute it.

Muller (dejectedly). "The great boss devil is against us."

Stilletto (almost foaming at the mouth). "Nonsense! I know who is at the bottom of it all. Those two women worked upon the idiot and he confessed to them, the cursed fool, what I was moving heaven and earth to keep from

their ears until I had—" Here he stopped short, and, growing pale, scrutinized the philosopher's countenance, as if anxious to see whether he showed any suspicions of what he was about to confess in the madness of his temper. But Mr. Muller was simply paralyzed and livid from this most unlooked-for news. He could not speak, but sat as if a thunderbolt had descended upon him on a clear, sunny day.

Stilletto (pacing the room). "But there is money enough yet in the country for a smart man, and, although we can not now hope to control millions, I mean to get enough though I have to tear it from the jaws of hell! Revenge is the word! One of the dirty wenches is a widow already, the other shall see her lover hanged, unless Antonio Stilletto becomes crazy over night!"

Muller (in utter despair). "Thus does Destiny bring us within sight of the goal, thus she dazzles our eyes and captivates our souls with a foretaste of what we covet, only to snatch it from us at the eleventh hour. I shall go teaching school!"

Stilletto (sneeringly). "With your sentiments I'd turn priest."

Muller. "No, no! I can train the young and budding mind and rear a full glorious plant of human intellect. I can humble myself and starve for that purpose; but I can not serve in the ranks of bigotry or hypocrisy. Reason is my god and I am her priest. Take a note of it, young man,—thus speaks August Muller."

Stilletto. "Thus speaks an ass, who has done me more harm than good all the time I have known him."

Muller. "Young man, your intellect is but a small degree above that of the brute, and your impulses are on a level with your intellect! Do not make yourself ridiculous or provoke my just wrath by such foul language!"

Stilletto. "Go to hell!"

Muller (pale with rage). "I wish I never had met you, you villainous, mongrel dog! Another word, and I will proclaim to the world what I know of you."

Stilletto hesitated a moment. There was a dangerous flash in his treacherous eye; he made a movement toward Muller, so threatening, that the latter recoiled in terror, but suddenly checking himself, he remembered that if his relationship to Judge Bates should come out, his father might, in a moment of despair, say some thing about that *alibi*, which would be very undesirable. True, it is not pleasant to confess the crime of perjury, but when a man is once thoroughly disgraced, he generally unburdens his whole conscience to make a clear breast of it.

Stilletto (coldly). "Neither you nor I can afford to quarrel, so stop your nonsense. I have nothing against you; but your senseless chatter about philosophy vexes me at times. Let us consult about the next thing to be done."

Muller. "August Muller is easily won over, especially by a friend. Let us pledge this new alliance in a bumper of malt."

Stilletto. "Well, take it down until you burst yourself, if you want to: but excuse me."

Muller. "To-day I was subpœnaed for the trial as a witness, and I don't regret it. I like to talk in public, for a man of superior mind should not always remain unnoticed. In my testimony, sir, I mean to argue—"

Stilletto (interrupting). "I tell you what you'd better do. Make up your mind to say as little as possible—only 'yes' or 'no,' when they will be sufficient. Paradise is engaged for the defense, and if you give him a chance, by talking too much, he will make you say things that will astonish you when you see them on paper afterward, and hear what a nice thing he will make out of them in his pleading. No, no! The great point is, that you and I must not contradict each other, and to prevent that, we must talk it all over between ourselves."

Muller. "But the truth needs no preparation before it is given in evidence."

Stilletto. "I say it does."

Muller (thoughtfully). "My friend, do you really think that this countryman of mine, this lad whom I once came near taking to my bosom as a friend, this intelligent, well-born, and educated person, whom August Muller, yes, sir, *August Muller* received at his house?"—do you—can you think that he is really guilty?"

Stilletto. "We will see at the trial whether he is or not. I hope he'll be hanged, that's all."

Muller. "I hope not, if he is innocent."

Stilletto. "You have promised me my revenge upon him, remember. Now that I have a chance, I mean to improve it."

Muller. "Do not speak thus. The utterance of such sentiments is an ill omen."

Stilletto, (turning pale). "Do you believe in omens?"

Muller. "Yes, sir, for philosophy teaches us that there is a mysterious connection between the past, present, and future, and that great events are often foreshadowed in a hundred trifling occurrences."

Stilletto. "And do you believe in dreams, too?"

Muller. "Yes, sir. Sleep presents two aspects. One is the near approach to death when the mind slumbers with the body; in the other, the mind freed from the grossness of the body, becomes etherealized, and travels through the land of spirits, accomplishing mysterious wonders. Spiritualism, my friend, will grow into a great science, just as astrology was the mother of astronomy, and alchemy the predecessor of chemistry."

Stilletto. "You always have your mouth full of big words, but their meaning is either hackneyed or utterly absurd."

Muller. "I tell you dreams have a relation to the past and future."

Stilletto. "I don't care if they have. If I believed in them, I should be scared out of my wits, for I have had vile ones lately."

Muller. "Who do you think *can* be the real murderer?"

Stilletto (jumping up). "What do you mean by asking me such a question? If you dare suspect—Well, well, Muller, don't mind me, I am going to New York to-morrow to see the countess, and will not be back until the day of the trial."

The philosopher was delighted to hear it, for in truth Stilletto frightened him terribly.

Stilletto. "By the way, do you know that Stump is in this part of the country. I have seen him several times. He tells me that he has made lots of money, and from an old liking for the business, he has just taken a look into this murder affair. He has some relatives here whom he is visiting. If I had not seen them myself, personally, I should be almost afraid that he was hired by the defense to—to—"

Muller. "To what? Why should you be afraid? Now that I think of it, he has been here twice during your absence, and I had a long talk—"

Stilletto (frenzied with rage). "The devil you did? You drunken old idiot, why did not you tell me so before?"

Muller. "Because, whenever we meet, you indulge in such gusts of temper, and assail me with such invectives and threats, that I forget to tell you trifling news, being altogether engrossed with solicitude for your peace of mind, and always fearing lest some hasty mood of yours may breed an eternal breach of friendship between us."

Stilletto's lynx eyes rested long upon the philosopher's face, and he relapsed into a gloomy silence, during which he seemed to be reflecting and weighing something in his mind with great attention.

*   *   *   *   *

Mr. Paradise did not lose an hour, nor did he overlook the most trifling aspect of the defense he had undertaken. Josephine had parted from him that Christmas-eve with grave fears, and yet the hunchback, his heart moved for once, had endeavored to reassure her, rather than to lay the fullest stress upon the dangers that threatened Montant. Before the lawyer thought of his night's rest, he had written several notes, intrusted to the particular care and despatch of Mr. Smiles, and intended to summon immediately to his aid such assistance as he knew, from his great experience, the affair demanded. One of these letters was addressed to Mr. Stump, our old friend and ex-detective; and sure enough, the next morning, though it was Christmas-day, the little man with the short hair and dumpling proportions, made his appearance in Washington Square.

Mr. Paradise received him *en deshabille,* and not in a very encouraging humor.

Paradise. "Stump, if you will see that the next room is empty, and then lock the door of it, I will talk to you."

Stump (obeying with alacrity). "Thank'ee, sir."

Paradise. "Now, Stump, I hear that you want to re-enter the secret service.

Stump. "Yes, sir. Being as I didn't agree with the gentleman that owns my grocery, so he has now shut down on me, and shut up the shop."

Paradise. "You mean you did not pay the rent, you vagabond, and your landlord kicked you out. Is that it?"

Stump. "Just as you please sir."

Paradise. "And since you want to re-enter the service, I suppose you would like me to use my influence with the police commissioners in your favor?"

Stump (grinning sweetly). "Indeed, I would be proud of it, Gov'n'r."

Paradise (curtly). "We'll see. You know a man by the name of Stilletto?"

Stump. "Antony Staletoe? I know him, as if we'd been raised by one hand."

Paradise. "Have you read the evidence in the Van Strom murder?"

Stump. "No, sir."

Paradise. "Read it, then, while I finish my toilet."

He handed the necessary papers over to the little man, who read the affidavits quickly; but with that prompt insight which he had acquired in his profession.

Paradise. "What do you think of it?"

Stump (rising to go). "Nothing."

Paradise. (amazed). "What do you mean, sir?"

Stump (doggedly). "Nothing."

Paradise. "Explain yourself, or take the consequences."

Stump. "I'll take the consequences, sir. I said *nothing.* I mean *nothing,* and NOTHING will I have to do with this case."

Paradise. "For the last time, *Why?*"

Stump. "Because Antony Staletoe is a friend of mine, and if it's so as you want me to dodge him, as I can see plain you want me to, I'll say this. Police commissioners or no police commissioners—sitoowation or no sitoowation, I won't dodge a *friend* that's always treated me square."

Paradise. "Stump, you are a sharp fellow for guessing just what I want of you; but you are obtuse in another direction."

Stump. "What does that word mean, sir?"

Paradise. "It means that you have told me something I did want to know—your opinion of the case."

Stump (aghast). "I expressed no opinion of the case, sir."

Paradise. "You have as much as told me that you think Antonio Stilletto murdered that man, and that Judge Bates committed perjury when he swore to the *alibi.* What else made you think of dodging Stilletto, and what harm can you do your *friend* if he has done no wrong?"

Stump (admiringly). "You are the greatest lawyer in the country, sir."

Paradise (disdainfully). "And since it pleases me to employ *you,* and no one else but you, I herewith assign to you all that interesting work which consists in laying, spying, and tale-telling, which you call *dodging* your friend."

Stump (very decidedly, and again rising to go). "And I, sir, with all respect and regard for you, must say I can't do it, and what's more, I won't."

Paradise. "Stump?"

Stump. "Sir."

Paradise. "How about Hobgoblin?"

Stump. "About what? Oh! you mean—"

Paradise. "Yes, I mean to refresh your memory a little on certain joint transactions which you engaged in with that German drunkard, Muller, and your *friend* Stilletto."

Mr. Stump looked first puzzled, then frightened, and finally resumed his seat, demurely, and looked foolish. Mr. Paradise proceeded to do as he had promised, viz.—to recall to his mind the fact that he had been connected with Hobgoblin, in a manner which had better not be inquired into (which the reader may remember was detailed in book I). When the lawyer had proved that he had been remarkably well posted on that affair, and known the parts taken by Martin Bates, Muller, Stilletto, and Stump, the latter gentleman looked crestfallen, but his admiration for the lawyer increased.

Paradise (firmly). "And now, all I have to say is that you will do as I bid you. I can employ no regular detective, for I am afraid Stilletto is sharp enough to penetrate any disguise, while you are his *friend,* and besides, quite sharp enough to manage it."

Stump (despondingly). "Well, sir, I'll do it; but I swear it is the meanest, most sneaking, villainous act of my whole life! To dodge a man's friend what he's borrowed money from!"

Paradise. "I'll pay you well for it, and we will make the bargain as soon as you receive my instructions. You must start for Boston to-night."

Stump (meekly). "I'll do it, sir."

Paradise. "And you must look sharp."

Stump. "If I must do it, I'll do it well, sir."

*　　*　　*　　*　　*　　*　　*

The day before the trial had arrived, and Mr. Paradise was just preparing to leave New York for the scene of action by the afternoon train, when the door of his private office was opened violently by a man, followed by the astonished servant. The man was old and bald, and bony, and breathless with haste. "I came here on an inspiration," he gasped. "Thank God I find you!"

Paradise (staring). "Martin Bates?"

Martin. "Yes, and here is something of more importance than old Martin Bates."

The lawyer glanced over the paper which Martin handed him. It was Simonetta's letter, with a translation appended, to which Paradise referred from time to time. His face brightened.

Paradise. "Why there is more hope in this than in all the eloquence of a Demosthenes! Do you think she saw Stilletto about the time of the murder?"

Martin. "I am certain of it."

Paradise. "Now sit down here and tell me *why* you are certain of it. If we can upset your brother's *alibi,* the whole case falls to the ground, and Montant and Stilletto change places. But hold on a moment, Stilletto is in town."

Martin. "Aha! Then we will want help at the countess's to-night, or at least we will have to play a sharp game if Stilletto happens to be there."

Paradise. "So I think. I will send for Stump at once. He is our man."

CHAPTER V.

THE COUNTESS.

"My hair does stand on end to hear her curses."
                        KING RICHARD III.

THEY were a queer couple, crouching close to the large fireplace in the dance hall of the Italian boarding-house.

And this was the countess, the ignoble proprietress of the ignoble den, with a yellow turban crowning her wrinkled wicked face, and her vicious black eyes gleaming like will-o'-the-wisps in a dangerous swamp.

And by her side, Stilletto, his demoniac face unmasked of hypocrisy—that was useless here—and yet not open and honest, for that it could not be. The conversation was carried on in Italian.

"Well, my son," said the countess.

"Hold on a moment! Do you know it has often occurred to me that you are not so certain about this mother and son business!"

"Ain't I," chuckled the old hag. "A man may never be sure that he has fathered a child, but the mother that bore it—no mistake *there,* sweetness."

"I can't say that I am proud of my ancestress, though you claim to be of noble family. A nice place *this,* for aristocratic people," said Stilletto, glancing around the room.

The dull light of the leaden day did not add fascinations to the coarsely-painted walls or the queer, many colored paper ornaments adorning the ceiling. There was that about the room which reminds one of the seediness that follows upon dissipation.

"Wait till the lamps are lit," said the countess, following his eyes, and noticing the impression made upon him.

"Yes," answered Stilletto, with more truth than grace, "the lamps will be lighted, but to-morrow this same damnable shabbiness will come out again and again and again, until the rotten shanty falls to pieces, just like you, my lovely mother!"

"Well, it's true," said the countess, with an oath, "it does seem strange for *Angelica, Countess of Unkstein,* to be what I am."

Stilletto did not appreciate the touch of sentiment and remorse that spoke in her words, and dejected tone. "Do you know," he cried, "that I have in some way lost that sweet little autobiography of your lamented husband?"

"What! the *Maniac's Story!*"

"Yes, along with the copy of some letters I wrote to my father. I must have dropped them, some months ago, when I called upon the honorable Judge in Massachusetts."

"You always were a careless, harum-scarum dog!" said the countess, with more pride than derision.

"No wonder I'm a dog, being born of a she wolf."

"Don't say that! By the Virgin! I shudder when I think of that crazy man in the Black Forest, and read his half-reasonable story."

"You've led a queer life, mother!"

"Yes, yes. The difference between Baden Baden and the Fourth Ward is considerable! I was a good enough girl when I first saw the count. He was a sinister, half-cracked man then, but he was rich. God help me forget the years I spent at that castle in the Black Forest. A dreary, lonely spot it was, a morose half-spectral husband to make it lively, ha! ha! Still I liked him well enough, and when, on returning late one night from the hunt, he recoiled from me as I met him at my door, thinking, idiot that he was, I had turned into a wolf—"

"Well, mother, I'll be cursed if you don't look like one at times!"

"Do I?" snarled the countess, showing her teeth savagely.

"Don't!" shrieked Stilletto, in genuine alarm. "You know I can't bear that look. I don't blame the count for seeing the bloody brute stick right out in you!"

"You damned, crazy vagabond!"

"Now, don't, and talk reasonably."

"What shall I talk about?" asked the countess, with a bitter expression on her vicious face. "Shall I describe to you how I was an innocent girl once? Shall I tell you that I had a happy home and have experienced the old story of virtue, love, sin, despair, all in due rotation? Would you like to know how I became your mother? Well, after the count died in the asylum, I had some money and some respectability left. I met your father, Eben Bates, who was making the tour of the Continent to allow some British scandal to grow cold in his absence. He left me a wretch, dishonored and forsaken, expecting to give birth to his child. That child turned out to be a hideous monster. That child was called *Antonio Stilletto.* After giving you an education, and discovering that you were a born vagabond, sharper, and thorough scoundrel, I brought you to America to pester your father, who had taken his wife to this side of the sea to escape the consequences of his actions in England. What wonder that, in spite of all the money you got from him, I found myself as poor as a rat when my own money was gone! No wonder you allowed your mother to sink down to this filthy profession, for you are a dirty, greedy, cruel brute, and you know it."

"Well, I suppose I am," conceded Stilletto, soothingly.

"What villainies you have committed during your travels and behind my back I can never know, nor any one else, for a cur like you will be a mystery to his own mother and to the whole world forever. I wouldn't be surprised had you murdered Van Strom yourself, you unconscionable, cold-blooded, hellish dog!"

Stilletto had suddenly grown a sickly yellow.

"Don't say too much, mother," he cried. "I have always helped you when I could, and have often come to you for advice like a dutiful son; but I won't have such words as those! Mind—I'm dangerous if you rouse me!"

"So is a cowardly, carrion-fed hyena; but

there is no fight in him when he meets his master. Just try to bite me, you—"

"Hold—I say! I have made up my mind not to get mad, but don't tempt me! Let us be friends, mother, and tell me how to act at that trial to-morrow. Come, come, I'll treat to a bottle of wine if you'll be reasonable."

The countess relented, and after she had filled the glasses, threw one dirty-stockinged, slip-shod foot over the other, leaned back in her chair, and said, affably,—

"After all, I have some pride in you, and if you tell me all about your scrape, I'll tell you what to do."

"In the first place, where is this girl Simonetta?"

"What's that to you?"

"I want to see her."

"What for? Isn't it enough that you seduced her, then kept her from marrying that good old fool Martin Bates, and then got her into—God knows what scrapes, down in Massachusetts?"

"This is a tender spot in your shriveled old heart, mother."

"Yes—and it always will be. Look through this ward; see the drunken dogs and sluts, the thieves, murderers, and scabby reprobates of all kinds, and I'll tell you something the police don't know, and the charity folk don't dream of. They all have a tender spot. Now, then, my tender spot is that girl."

"Damn her!"

"That's a blessing on her," said the countess, almost devoutly, and her face assumed a kind, half-tender expression. "She was poor when I first knew her. Her father, the organ-grinder, was a servant in our house in Italy, long, long ago. He lived next door here, and when he died, I took her entirely under my protection."

"A nice protection," sneered Stilletto. "I had a hand in it, mother."

"So many more curses, on you, then—but that is passed. You have ruined her and prevented that marriage—"

"Martin Bates is a thief; but I suppose that's what you looked for in your darling's husband."

"Thief or no thief, he is a kind-hearted man."

"Enough of him. Where is she?"

"What do you want of her?"

"I want to make sure that she won't turn against me to-morrow."

"Ha! ha! ha!" laughed the hag, with such demoniac glee that Stilletto shuddered.

"What are you laughing at?"

"Because, fool that you are, you have let out that she can turn against you if she wants to! So you're in a scrape about that trial, are you, my precious chick? How smart to tell me so!"

"Mother! or, rather, hellish old hussy that you are—"

"Ware!" she cried, flaring up. "Though they call me the countess, only as a nickname, I have more power than many a duchess! I am queen in this neighborhood, and I won't be the first queen that saw her son hanged for insulting her!"

"Where is she?" demanded Stilletto, livid and trembling with rage.

"I won't tell you!"

"So you know?"

"Yes, and she's safe from you."

"Don't go too far," said he, hoarsely, advancing toward her.

"None of those looks. They won't do here!" cried the countess. She drew a dirk and retreated a step in defense. At the same time she stamped upon the floor, and in an instant Stilletto saw a vicious, dogged fellow by his side, whose broad shoulders and dangerous eye told him that he was foiled.

"Ha! ha! ha!" again laughed the countess, with a more hideously, shrill voice than ever. "Your tricks won't do here, my pet. Teach your own mother to play points, hey? Get out you white-livered, black-souled, ill-begotten, murderous hound, or you'll be sorry for it!"

"You'll suffer for this if that girl comes to the trial to-morrow," snarled Stilletto, and left the house in impotent wrath.

*   *   *   *   *

The lamps were illuminating the flimsy ornaments of the dance-hall, and shedding an artificial glare upon the painted faces of the girls in short dresses as they hung around listlessly awaiting the company which had not yet arrived.

The shriveled old mistress of iniquity, the countess, sat by the great fire and smoked a cigarette. She was expecting some one with a nervous agitation she strove to conceal. When the old clock struck the hour viciously, the expected visitors, punctual to the minute, entered. One was a withered old man, in a shabby coat, his square features working excitedly. We know him by the name of Martin Bates. The other, a short, old gentleman with a flowing white beard, we can not recognize but the countess sees through the disguise in a moment.

"Mr. Stump," she says, quietly, in English, "all them air masks of yourn are played! That's what they be. Played!"

"Keep steady, melady," replied Mr. Stump. "Keep steady to-night, and stand by us, or by —you'll make an enemy o' mine, an' of all Mulberry street besides."

"Where is the girl? Where is Simonetta?" inquired Martin, hastily.

"What s that to you?" retorted the woman, sharply. "They don't want to hang you to-morrow, do they?"

"No; but I have determined to save the innocent, at all hazards; even should it cost a brother's life, and I mean to leave no stone unturned."

"A new character for Martin Bates."

"Where is the girl?" persisted he.

"In her stockin's, I s'pose!"

"Now, mistress melady, countess——" began Mr. Stump.

"Hold your noise!" interrupted the mistress, "or you will make me hold mine, that's all. Before we go any further, I want to tell you something, Martin Bates. You say that you want to rescue the innocent, although it cost a brother's life, or happiness, or virtue, or honor, or what you may call all the cursed things.

Now, what harm has that brother done to you to make you act so?"

"The harm that he has done to me is as nothing—"

"But the harm he has done to *me* is something," interrupted the hag, viciously. "Do you know who I am?"

"No—but where is the —"

"Let me finish. I want you to know that I'm a *real* countess, though my noble count *did* go mad, and though I *am* more of a wolf than some people might think if they read a certain eloquent description of me, which he wrote in a Dutch mad-house before he died."

"You don't mean to say—" cried Martin, in astonishment.

"Well!"

"Are you—can you be the Countess of Unkstein?"

It was the hag's turn to be astonished.

"What do you know about Unkstein?"

"I found a paper. Stilletto dropped it in my brother's garden. I read it—can it be?"

"Oh, you found the paper," said the countess, again resuming her disdainful tone. "Give it back to me."

Martin had not allowed the paper to leave his pocket, and he handed it over mechanically. As he did so he stepped close to her. She looked up at him, and with a snarl, showed him her teeth. He recoiled, terrified, and staring at her, cried,—

"I think the maniac was not all wrong!"

The countess laughed a peculiar chuckling laugh, and said:—

"Now I'll tell you something else. If Eben Bates is shown up as a perjurer, he is a broken man. You lose a brother, *I* lose a lover;" and again she laughed in a manner resembling the bark of a dog.

"What! are you—?"

"Yes, I am."

"I begin to see the truth! You are the same countess with whom my brother had an intrigue on the continent, thirty years ago, and—but what else are you, for heaven's sake?"

"Stilletto's mother," she said, quietly.

"And you have set him on to extort money from his father?" cried Martin, fiercely.

"Just so."

"And you are the torturer that tormented him till he left the path of honor and virtue, and became what he is?"

"Yes, my dear."

"You have been the evil spirit of his life, working through the instrumentality of his bastard son," continued Martin, livid with rage, becoming more and more excited by his own invective and her cool replies. "You are the ugly, foul nightmare, that has banished sleep from him, and you have poisoned his life until it became saturated with the pestilence of your own black soul."

"Don't talk so loud, brother-in-law; the girls will hear you," replied the countess, lighting a fresh cigarette.

"You have distressed and harassed him, driven him to despair. Look at the result, you—hellish slut!"

"I'm looken at it," said the countess, with a yawn, crossing her legs, as she leaned back in her chair." I'm looken at it; and I say, he hasn't come down enough yet. So we'll bring him down to-morrow. He has brought me to what I am."

"A lump of filth!"

"Exactly; and that's what he has got to come to before we are even. Blood for blood, you know, brother-in-law."

"Don't call me by that name again," cried Martin, beside himself with fury.

"Why hear this! Because Eben did not marry me, as he promised he would, is that any reason why you are *not* my brother-in-law, Martin, dear?"

"Well, call me what you like. You have dragged me, too, down to destruction. Do you know that I stole money to help Eben in his troubles, and that my perdition is on your soul,—if you have any?"

"Well, if it was'nt, it would be on some one else's! Nobody can tell me that a man'll steal unless it's *in him!*"

"Enough of such plagues as you!" cried Martin. "I'll not go to the trial to-morrow. Let the innocent suffer, but you shall not succeed in your designs against my brother."

"Allow me," said Mr. Stump, "allow me, in a mild way, to interrupt this much interestin' and pious confabulation. May I ask your ladyship how it is as you knows so much about this 'ere murder, and about the honorable judge's lying perjury?"

"I'd as lief tell you," said the countess, languidly. "Simonetta has told me more than both of you, and all the lawyers in the land, know. You only *guess,* while I *know* all about it."

"So she has broken the awful vow about which she wrote me?" queried Martin.

"I made her do it. I got a priest to absolve her, for ten dollars, and spent the money willingly. I might as well have been there, so well am I posted on all that happened. The girl saw my dear boy just about the time that the crazy Van Strom was killed, so this Stilletto, son of mine, was *not* at his father's house that afternoon. You may draw your own conclusions."

"But this will bring your son—your own son —to the gallows," cried Martin.

"He's been a disobedient, burdensome, white-livered whelp; so I've about concluded to let the father hang the son, and the son send the father to State's prison or suicide, I don't care which. I am sick of the whole tribe."

"Can you expect mercy in heaven?"

"Leave me alone," she replied, with more animation. "A queer story might be told of how I changed from an innocent girl, in an Italian home, to the old hag, keeping the lowest den in New York. But the story has all happened, the change has taken place, and damn all those that helped to kick me down."

"Oh, God!" murmured Martin Bates, "canst Thou look upon such as these and not blush at thy handiwork!"

"Don't blarstpheematize," admonished, Mr. Stump, shocked at Martin's ejaculation.

"But to come to business," said the countess, in a whisper. "My son, Stilletto, Martin's precious nephew, paid me a visit this afternoon. He seemed afraid of the girl—he tried to get at her through me."

"Did he succeed?"

"No: I love that girl."

"Where is she?" again, asked Martin, entreatingly.

"Up-stairs. I am afraid to let her come down, for I'm never sure of my dear son's whereabouts."

"I'll take care of her," said Mr. Stump, with the majesty reflected from the law. "I have ten men outside. We'll see her all safe."

"After all, the police is a great institution," cried the countess. "But ain't it queer that the life of that gentleman, who is accused of the murder, should be saved just because a creature like me wants revenge upon a son and that son's father! Is that the way innocence should be saved?"

"No," replied Mr. Stump, blandly; "innocence in this case is saved by the circumspection of—"

"God," said old Martin Bates, fervently.

"Of the *Police*," corrected Mr. Stump, and then he added with some heartiness,—"I have not been an officer all my life for nothing, Missus Countess, and I see that I can trust you. Now there is a lawyer by name of Parydise up town that is the shrewdest man born. He has paid enough to surround this 'ere house of yours with picked men, and not a mouse can leave it *nohow*, without that mouse is diskivert. Now you know the ward police all know this Netty Merino, and in case she ain't produced, we'll have her out by force. *I* never axed you where she was, did I? Why? 'cause I knowed she was here. I never meant to go up town to watch for my friend Staletoe. Why? 'cause he started for Bostin four hours ago. Now, then, I have told you all about it because I think I can trust you, and I've throwed off all disguise, and here I be a tellin' the truth for oncet."

"But suppose she refuses to go with you?" asked the countess, ill-pleased.

"We'd kidnap her and gag her, and make her go, though it cost Mister Parydise a thousand dollars damiges—or five thousand."

"And suppose I hadn't make her break her oath?"

"Put her on that air witness stand, and put old Parydise in front of her, and I'll bet my bottom dollar he'll worm the oaths all out of her like your picken the seeds out of an Eyetalian orange with a sharp blade."

Not unimpressed by this glowing account of Mr. Paradise's talents, the countess said, after a pause,—

"Well, you'll have her for a witness any how, and she'll speak fair and full what she knows."

"So although your highness has fussilotated things," said Mr. Stump, in all the dignity of a big word, "still the rescue of the blameless ain't no result of your stubborn vengeance and bloodthirsty spirrut."

"For which God be praised," said Martin, devoutly.

CHAPTER VI.

THE TRIAL.

"Heaven is above all yet: There sits a judge
That no king can corrupt!"
KING HENRY VIII.

"I do beseech you,
Make no more offers, use no further means,
But with all brief and plain conveniency,
Let me have judgment."
MERCHANT OF VENICE.

THIS is not a Pickwickian scene. *Intelligence* speaks in almost every face of the assemblage which throngs the entrance and the passage of the court-house; while the confined space of the modest little court-room is crowded almost to suffocation. We are not in London, where a quaint originality must be employed by an author, to cover the absolute stupidity of the mob, to hide the absence of real intelligence by depicting a humorous individuality.

But we are in the State of Massachusetts, and despite the fanaticism which characterizes it as a community, one need only glance at the calm, sharp faces of those twelve jurymen to be satisfied that he would rather submit his case to them than to be judged by twelve peers of England, for here we can recognize acuteness and integrity of mind without *prejudice*.

The judge wears no wig, and sleep is far from his thoughts. He is humble enough to be zealous in his work, he is bold enough to be honest; and yet he is only a simple countryman, with an education barely sufficient, and with only as much dignity as his own merits and his position inspire. What he lacks in idle pomposity he makes up by mother-wit, and his fidelity to the cause of justice, has acquired for him a modest but solid reputation in his limited sphere of action.

Here comes the prisoner, at whose sight there ensues that awful silence in the court-room, which is a dumb plaudit suited to the occasion. Some experience a sensation as if the cravat were too tight, others feel their hearts cease beating, all are impressed by the situation of the man who attracts so much attention, and yet not greeted by one friendly face in all that crowd, who stare upon him as it were with a thousand basilisk eyes.

This is the first act of that drama of real death, at the close of which, instead of dropping an innocent curtain, they often drop the body of the star actor in a manner rather disagreeable to him, though it hands his name down to the admiration of impressible schoolboys and ambitious criminals.

Ernest Montant looked pale, but not agitated. He had been hard at work with his counsel, preparing for the defense, and although he knew his danger, he was more engrossed in his efforts to save himself, than haunted by fears of the result.

When Mr. Paradise entered the court-room, he created a peculiar sensation. "This is the great New York lawyer," was whispered through the audience, and the intelligence of his marked features, and the brightness of his eyes received a dumb tribute from these rustics while pity prevented the derision his deformity might otherwise have excited.

The court being duly opened, and the case called, Mr. Paradise immediately stepped to the judge's bench, and said in a low, clear voice.

"It becomes necessary for me to ask your honor for a postponement of the trial until to-morrow. We are not yet quite ready."

A murmur of disapprobation ran through the audience which so increased as to compel the judge to call them to order, and threaten to have the room cleared if the court was to be interrupted in this manner.

The district attorney, a fine-looking man, with a large head and a deep voice, arose and said,—

"I beg to remind your honor that we have already consented to previous postponements. We can not understand why the defense should thus abuse the leniency of the court."

"Upon what grounds do you request this postponement, Mr. Paradise?" asked the judge. "Haven't you procured all your witnesses yet?"

"Our witnesses are here; but my associates and I have not had the time to consult sufficiently. You know my practice is not a small one—"

"I am afraid Mr. Paradise has not found this defense a very delightful undertaking!" cried the district attorney, with a sneer.

"Am I to be interrupted in this discourteous manner?" asked Mr. Paradise, warming.

"We mean to treat you with all due courtesy," answered the judge, "and we do not forget your extensive practice and pressing occupations; but I must decide that you have had ample time to prepare, and I can not grant the postponement unless you have other reasons for asking it."

For a moment Mr. Paradise seemed to hesitate, and then begged leave to consult with his client and his associates. After a few whispered words, the prisoner shook his head resolutely, and the lawyer said, turning to the judge,—

"We have no other grounds for a delay, and since your honor has overruled them, I suppose we must say that we are ready."

"Go on, then," said the judge.

An irrepressible though faint murmur of applause ran through the room. A celebrated lawyer from New York is always at a disadvantage in country courts, for every one thinks that he is trying to control matters and despises the provincial institutions. It is therefore a satisfaction to the jury and all present, if the judge puts down some celebrity from the metropolis, and Paradise glancing around him, knew full well that the case had opened badly for him so far.

After the clerk had read the indictment, by which the people of the Commonwealth of Massachusetts, on complaint of Bella Van Strom, accused Ernest Montant, of London, England, and late of New York, of the murder of John Jacob Van Strom, and the prisoner had put in a plea of "Not guilty," the district attorney, amidst breathless silence and universal straining of eyes, necks, and ears, opened the case for the prosecution.

This was a peculiar case (as it generally is), and bearing within its issues the bringing to justice of one who had committed the most heinous crime known to social laws or to God's records of human depravity. This peculiarity would be found in the action of the prisoner at the bar, who, when first the foul deed was discovered, when the bleeding body of his wretched victim was brought to light, with barefaced villainy, accused another and an innocent man of the awful deed. That man was then arrested upon the false affidavits of the real culprit, but fortune, who protects the innocent, had directed his footsteps to the residence of one of our most respected citizens where he peacefully remained during the time when the murder must have been committed. That honored citizen, our venerable friend and colleague, Judge Eben Bates, by his testimony, proved so clearly a case of *alibi*, that the wrongly-accused was discharged immediately and stands now in this room, ready to bring forth crushing evidence in just defense of himself and to the certain doom of the prisoner at the bar. Although he (the district attorney) might dwell longer on the forthcoming evidence, he found it so clear, and if he might be allowed to say it, so *easy* a case, that he would yield the floor at once to the witnesses, who would speedily consummate the prisoner's conviction and brand him with the disgraceful mark of perjurer, for having borne false witness against his neighbor to hide his own guilt. His own guilt, gentlemen of the jury, which will shortly be made as clear to the abhorrent sight of man as it is clear at this moment to the frowning eye of God (which was telling).

Mr Paradise now arose to admit, without necessitating superfluous evidence, that the deceased had come to his death by violence, and that the dagger found buried in his breast was the instrument by which death had been caused at the hand of the murderer. After examining witnesses of purely technical importance, the prosecution called Bella Van Strom.

Disdaining to retain her veil, the witness told the court and the jury in a resolute, dispassionate way, that her deceased husband and the prisoner had been great friends at one time, but that serious altercations had taken place between them shortly before the murder. Also, that the deceased had made a will, bequeathing half of his estate to witness, the other half to Josephine Van Strom, his sister-in-law, to whom the prisoner was engaged to be married, appointing the prisoner trustee and executor of the whole estate. That, subsequently, deceased had altered this will, disinheriting Josephine Van Strom, and taking from the prisoner the trusteeship. That, finally, and principally at the instigation of witness, deceased had again changed the will in favor of Josephine and the prisoner, and that this final will was made and filed, to the knowledge of the prisoner, on the very day of the murder.

Here the district attorney put the question·

"Was not, your husband's mind of that wavering, unsettled character, that, in your opinion, the prisoner had reason to fear lest deceased might again revoke the will at some future day?"

Mr. Paradise objected to the question. The court, after some pleading, sustained the question, and Bella answered:—

"Undoubtedly."

Mr. Paradise bit his lips. After fruitless cross-examination, during which Bella remained imperturbable and entirely impassionate, the prosecution called Antonio Stilletto. The Italian's under-lip quivered so violently that he could scarcely articulate his answers to the questions put. It seemed to require an effort whenever he raised his eyes, and when he succeeded there was a malicious and bold impudence in them which resembled the desperate courage of falsehood more than the serenity of truth. Mr. Paradise never took his piercing eyes from him, and the prisoner, who heretofore had kept his glance quietly lowered, looked full into the face of this witness. Although Stilletto occasionally presented a bold face to the district attorney, judge, and jury, he found it inconvenient to stand this double fire of searching glances, the one suspicious and threatening, the other bitterly reproachful and indignant.

Mr. Stilletto repeated boldly what he had already sworn to in his written affidavit, and so terribly telling was his testimony against the prisoner, that the triumphant face of the district attorney, and the loud mutterings around the room compelling the judge to enforce silence, showed Mr. Paradise very clearly that there was no sympathy for his client in that audience. After Mr. Paradise had made the best of a fruitless cross-examination uselessly hurled against the brazen consistency of the witness, a lawyer residing in the village, to whose lodging John had driven on the last day of his life, was placed in the witness-box.

He had drawn up the last will of the deceased, and could testify that the prisoner was cognizant of its provisions, which reinstated him as trustee and again bequeathed half of the estate to prisoner's betrothed wife, Josephine Van Strom. But the most important point to which he deposed, was that he had been present when prisoner and deceased entered the wagon to return to Van Strom's house. Deceased handed prisoner a dagger, with the words—"You had better carry this. It is near dark, and if we are stopped, you are better able to use it than I."

"Can you swear that it was the same dagger which is now in court?" asked Mr. Paradise. The witness could not swear that it was, but thought it was the same.

"Leave your opinions at home," said the hunchback, angrily.

"Not at all," interrupted the district attorney. "Opinions regarding ocular observations are admissible as evidence."

"There is no proof that the daggers are identical," said Mr. Paradise, "and I beg your honor and the gentlemen of the jury, not to forget this flaw in the prosecution."

The district attorney begged the privilege of recalling Bella Van Strom, and she identified the dagger in court as that which her husband had taken with him when he left the house before the murder.

"Now then," said the district attorney, with a bow, "I am only surprised that so eminent a lawyer should advance such trifling quibbles in court. Here we have proof that the dagger which deceased took with him is identical with that which pierced his heart. Here again we have proof that deceased, half an hour before the murder was committed, handed a dagger to the only man known to have been present at the time of the murder. Is this enough?"

"No," said Mr. Paradise; "for the prisoner had another dagger, unspotted by blood, in his possession a few moments after the murder. This was the dagger which deceased handed him at the village, and that which Van Strom originally took with him, and which is now in court, he must have exchanged for the one which he gave to the prisoner. This is the theory which makes proof impossible."

"It is too thin, Mr. P.," said the district attorney, sneeringly. "This theory of yours is indeed too thin."

"We will see how thin it is when we get well into the defense," replied Mr. Paradise; but he knew, as well as every one present, that the prosecution had as strong a case as can well be made of circumstantial evidence; and all hope seemed lost.

Mr. Paradise glanced nervously to the door, and consulted his watch repeatedly before he opened for the defense. He knew what the impatience on all faces around meant. He knew that judge and jury had already condemned his client; but it was now his object to protract the trial, for what purpose we shall soon see, and he made a long and able speech.

In the first place, he said, that he would admit the motive for the murder, just as he or any one else must admit the occurrence of millions of similar temptations in life; but he meant to bring witnesses who would testify so strongly to the prisoner's good character that it would appear self-evident how far even the thought of a dastardly crime must have been from his mind.

Secondly, it was his purpose to show that Stilletto was a liar, a villain, and a perjurer, a vagabond adventurer living on his wits, and a perfectly reckless man; and that this was a conspiracy against the innocent, a vile scheme to exculpate the real murderer. Mr. Paradise had taken a bold stand, and he would have met derision at every turn had not his eloquence, his power of mind and will made a deep impression upon his hearers. The judge grew nervous, the jury opened their eyes wider, and the audience strained every sense to hear and understand.

"Your honor," said the hunchback, "I repeat that I mean to show this Stilletto to be a perjured scoundrel, a vagabond, and a villain well known in New York, and I advise the sheriff to keep his eye on him, for he will be wanted very much, when this trial is closed, and I am sure he will not be here then if he is allowed a chance to escape." Under the spell of the hunchback's eloquence, the sheriff actually sent his deputy to find Stilletto; but he had already vanished.

Mr. Paradise continued:—

"I mean to show that his testimony, which is the main reliance of the learned district attorney, is false—false as malice can dictate, false as cunning can invent, false as brazen deceit can utter, false as the fiend of hell, backed up by all his hellish array, could make it, if he stood in the place of that vile man."

Then followed a sketch of the incidents of that day, with all of which the reader is familiar, and showed from them, and the position of the wagon, horse, and corpse, that a third party *must* have been engaged in the deed, so that the assertion that the prisoner was the only man known to have been present, fails of significance.

"By what witnesses do you mean to assail Stilletto's character so as to cast doubts on his testimony?" asked the district attorney.

"If I can not do it, sir, my case is a weak one," replied Mr. Paradise, confidently.

"I understand that you have subpœnaed Judge Bates," said the district attorney.

"I have."

The first witness called for the defense now made his way to the box. He was an old gentleman, with an air of dignity and refinement that commanded attention and respect.

"What is your name?" asked Mr. Paradise.

"Charles William Going."

"You reside in New York?"

"Yes, sir."

"And what is your business?"

"A merchant, sir."

"Do you know the prisoner at the bar?"

"I know him very well." And then followed a brief account of our hero's parentage, standing and character, which caused all present to feel a new interest in the accused. The impression left by the district attorney, when he pronounced the words, "this is my case," began to change, and the general idea that the prisoner's doom was sealed, gave way to a doubt which increased the excitement and created a feeling of sympathy for our hero. When Mr. Going left the stand, and in an unostentatious but hearty manner, shook hands with Montant, the change in the countenances of the jury did not escape Mr. Paradise, but he knew better than they, that what had been gained was but the result of his own talents and favorable appearances; he knew that in reality his case was as desperate as ever, and that unless he could make good his bold assertions about Stilletto's bad character and perjury—all these outward signs of a favorable turn would melt under the rigor of the law. Again did he consult his watch, and great impatience seemed to possess him. He glanced at his client, and something like sympathy softened his features. He whispered to his associates and his impatience increased to trepidation. At this moment Eben Bates was called, and as he stepped into the box every eye in the room was charmed by his noble and commanding presence; the intelligence in his face, and the dignity, more pompous than

that of Mr. Going, which characterized the man from his venerable locks to his firm planted feet. He was universally known, and everywhere respected. The tongue of suspicion had never dared to assail his good name, and he was credited with every trait of character which belongs to a noble, pious, highly cultivated gentleman. He had sat on the judge's bench many a year, and he fully understood the importance of a case like this. He looked more like the judge than a witness, and at his presence a hush of involuntary homage fell upon the audience, two only excepted. One was Mr. Paradise, whose eyes were now kindled and his nostrils expanded, scenting his prey. He knew that the turning point of the case had arrived. From Ernest Montant he had learned the judge's history, and the prisoner himself now lifted his piercing gaze, full of anger and loathing, to that of the proud witness. The old judge caught his glance only once, and then quailed before him and turned deadly pale.

"Your honor," said Mr. Paradise, "I would respectfully request you to admonish this witness against the crime of perjury. I may as well here intimate that I know all his secrets, and that it would be unpleasant for him should I reveal them."

The district attorney rose angrily, but was involuntarily checked by the change in Eben's face. Already pale, it became livid, the quivering of its muscles changed all its dignity into miserable fear, but he recovered himself so quickly, that probably no one but the two lawyers noticed it.

"Hold," cried the old judge, in a loud, clear voice, waving his hand majestically; "my learned friend, the district attorney, must permit me to speak for myself. I am here as a witness only, but I know the law, and I protest against counsel attempting to intimidate any witness by subtle threats. Another word of that sort to me, Mr. Paradise, and I shall not open my lips again. I defy the court, with all proper respect, to compel me to testify under such circumstances!"

He well knew whom he was addressing. Every eye flashed with indignation against the hunchback; and as he called on the support of the audience, by a look which contained whole volumes, and with a gesture that waved the judge out of existence, Eben read assurance in the thousand recognizing and sympathizing faces which his fiery eye encountered.

"Your honor," he continued, proudly, turning towards the judge, "shall I be respected in this court, or shall I leave the stand?"

"Mr. Paradise," said the judge, frowning, "I can not allow browbeating in this court. If you design to coerce this witness, by threatening the exposure of such matters as belong to a man's sacred privacy, you must be warned to desist from such practice or lose your witness."

Mr. Paradise made a wicked bow, and sneered sardonically. Then he put the question, plumply,—

"Judge Bates, was Stilletto at your house at the time the murder was committed?"

The district attorney objected. He saw no

sense in losing time by compelling witnesses to reiterate what they had previously sworn to in written affidavits, as long as such questions were entirely irrelevant.

"The question is not irrelevant," said Mr. Paradise. "I want to impugn Stilletto's evidence against the prisoner. To that end I must catch him in a previous falsehood."

The district attorney answered the argument, the hunchback replied, and both held their original positions with great tenacity; finally Mr. Paradise, who saw the disadvantageous position he occupied, warmed up into such power and eloquence, that every one listened in wonder.

Suddenly the lawyer ceased in the midst of his powerful address in support of the question to witness, and his face relaxed into a joyous expression of great satisfaction, as his sharp eyes espied two persons who were forcing their way through the packed audience.

During this sudden pause, Judge Bates gathered all his strength. Advancing one foot firmly, he held his head haughtily erect, one hand was uplifted solemnly, his features although bleached by some deadly agitation, were firm set and terribly resolute, his flashing eyes sent fear into the hearts of those that confronted him, and his commanding voice rose high above the tumult occasioned by the persistency of those new comers to reach the front.

"I will cut short this disgraceful quibble and answer the question voluntarily. Antonio Stilletto *was* at my house at the time when the murder must have been committed."

Instantly the prisoner sprang up. His face, hitherto calm and resolute, showed a rage that knew no bounds.

"Eben Bates," he cried, beside himself, and his voice rang in every heart. "Eben Bates. *you lie!* and I call upon God this moment that he may strike to the ground that one of us two which has dared to call on Him to witness a falsehood!"

For a moment the old judge shook with a passion which seemed equal to crushing the world. With clenched fists and quivering lips he was about to hurl defiance at the unexpected voice that had so indecorously interrupted proceedings, when suddenly a change came over him. As if his heart's pulsations had failed him in the moment of need, as if an electric shock had unnerved him, as if a spell of witchery had fettered his utterance and shattered his frame; like a tiger who receives the deadly bullet in the moment of his leap, like a ship which strikes the jagged rock, just as it is rising proudly to master another billow, thus as if God had already heard the voice of the prisoner at the bar, and in answer had sent a thunderbolt to crush the perjurer—he faltered, staggered, and staring as though his eyes would burst from their sockets, was speechless, paralyzed. *His brother Martin stood before him!*

His brother Martin—in whose glowing eyes he read what soon must be heard by the whole world. His brother Martin—in whose face he saw the determination which knew no mercy, and told him too plainly to need words: "Murder

9

breaks all bonds. I am your brother no longer, but your accuser only."

The Italian girl stood beside him. Her face wild with excitement, she commenced to speak. Eben knew every word before she articulated a syllable. With the power that comes to us in such moments, God alone knows whence, he read in the souls of these two new witnesses his inevitable fate. One glance at the faces around him where singular confusion prevailed, a second of time passed (it seemed an age) in which he heard the judge calling order, saw Martin uplifting one lean and withered hand toward him, heard Simonetta's shrieking speech, and he cried in a voice which re-echoed in the breast of every hearer for years afterward,—

"*I confess my perjury! Stilletto was not at my house! He is the murderer!*"

And like an oak struck by the flaming arrow of Heaven, filled by the angel of vengeance sent by God in answer to the prisoner's cry, he sank to the floor a shattered, lifeless wreck.

CHAPTER VII.

BELLA VAN STROM.

"The means that heaven's yield must be embraced
And not neglected."
                                        KING RICHARD II.

"AND now that I have you, again," cried Josephine, "let us sit together on this lounge, by the cozy fire and tell me all about it."

"I declare," said our hero, not yet quite clear from that bewilderment which follows a great and sudden change of circumstances, "I can hardly realize what has occurred."

"Tell me about the horrid trial, Ernest."

"Well, darling, after I had recovered from the shock of being arrested, I looked my danger squarely in the face and made up my mind that I could get out of it, so I put fear behind me and began to think. Especially after Mr. Paradise paid me a visit, I labored unceasingly on my case, not only for my own deliverance, but for Stilletto's conviction."

"Was not I right in securing Paradise?" asked Josephine, proudly.

"I think no one could have defended me better than he."

"He must have been splendid at the trial!" cried Josephine, with enthusiasm.

"He made the best of a bad case, and certainly it was bad enough until Martin Bates and the Italian girl came in."

"I wish I had been there. I think it is a glorious thing to fight the battles of justice, and I adore one who defends a friend!"

"Friendship is not a predominant weakness in lawyers," interposed Montant, with a smile, but he added very gravely: "I confess to a feeling of great gratitude and warmth toward the man when I saw him confront the court in my behalf. Although it might have been a matter of cold business with him to me it bore a nobler aspect, and I shall not forget it."

"Did you not feel terribly ashamed when you entered the court?" asked Josephine.

"No: I felt very serious, as a man upon an errand of life and death would feel. It is the guilt that makes shame. But a shudder came over me at one thought."

"And what was that?"

"As I encountered the curious looks of the audience, the stern face of the judge, and the cold, searching row of countenances in the jury box, a grim fancy presented itself to my imagination. How, if at this moment I stood here *guilty* instead of innocent? I tell you Josephine, the thought alone made me shiver."

"But you were innocent—innocent, as *I* could have told them without that cruel trial, had *I* been the judge!"

"Still," continued Montant, "I knew my danger, knew that Stilletto's testimony had to be disproved, and evidence pointing to him as the murderer had to be procured. And I tell you, Josephine, when Eben Bates broke down at the mere sight of his brother and accused himself as well as Stilletto, I became nearly overpowered. From the gloom and horror of standing as a murderer before the world, from the awful danger of an ignominious death, I found myself in one brief moment saved, and that by an enemy. I was congratulated on all sides; my hands, which just before they had abhorred as blood-stained, were shaken by a hundred sudden friends, and my innocence was acknowledged by acclamation."

"It must have been grand! Had I not promised Bella so faithfully to remain at home, I should have been present in spite of her advice and warning."

"Scarcely had the old man sunk, a senseless heap, on the floor," continued Montant, with animation, "than the Italian woman rushed forward, and, after imprecating a voluntary but truly terrifying oath, declared that she had seen Antonio Stilletto not half a mile away from the place of the murder, about the time that the crime was committed, and that he was running at the top of his speed away from the direction of the bridge. This, with the old judge's self-accusation, made too clear a case for doubt, and the jury returned a verdict of 'not guilty' without leaving their seats. God knows that those two words were music to me. They brought me back to certainty of life and honor unimpaired and my happy mind reverted instantly to you!"

He took her to his heart with emotion, and added, in a low, tender voice,—

"And although I positively *knew* my own innocence, Who was it that stood by me when I was forsaken, and helpless, in prison, and thought well of me while they were preparing to hand my name down to disgraceful oblivion? Who watched for me, while Justice slept, and never doubted, never lost faith in me? *You* did this, Josephine. The woman I love, and who loves me, did it all. God bless her!"

It was a solemn moment. A tribute paid by a strong man to the noble loyalty of a woman. She replied by assurances of unbounded fidelity to his loving words of praise, while both felt more confidence in the other from this incident.

"And is Stilletto in prison?" asked Josephine.

"No; he could not be found. He must have escaped quietly when Martin Bates and the Italian girl first approached the court-room. Paradise had given orders to the officers to keep an eye upon him; but, he succeeded in giving them the slip, though I don't understand how, and he is gone."

"I don't like that," said Josephine, anxiously.

"I don't, either," replied Montant, gloomily.

At this moment the door opened noiselessly and Bella Van Strom entered. Deep mourning did not become her, and there was nothing fascinating in her pale face. Still she bore an air of calm refinement gained since her marriage by contact with the educated world, and not the result of her previous accomplishments. She had not seen our hero since the trial, and Josephine showed her apprehensions of an embarassing scene by turning nervously to the fire, and watching the flames with marked discomfort.

Montant immediately arose, and took the proffered hand of Mrs. John Van Strom quite calmly. Bella was equally undemonstrative, and her speech showed more frankness and honesty than warmth of feeling.

"I need hardly tell you, Mr. Montant, that I congratulate you with sincerity upon the result of the trial."

"Allow me to thank you for your politeness," answered our hero, with dignity. "Of course my delight at the result is limited, because *I* at least could have had no doubt of my ultimate delivery. You also are *now* convinced of my innocence, and I thank you for bestowing upon me the acknowledgment of my unblemished integrity."

Bella looked him straight in the eyes as she rejoined, with imperturbable calmness,—

"The reproach contained in your speech is no less pointed for being couched in delicate language. Yet I can not say that I repent my course of action in unflinchingly, perhaps inconsiderately, assisting justice in its stern pursuits. I stand before my husband's fresh-made grave as his sole representative on earth. and surely it becomes me to cast away false delicacy, and treat the whole world as my enemy until an individual can be found to bear the load of this monstrous guilt. That person probably is now discovered; humanity has again become human in my eyes, and my old-time friends are now friends once more. If you have candor enough to acknowledge that I could not, like this loving heart, divine your innocence and trust to it by inspiration, nor did I accuse you blindly, as I did not blindly acquit you—and if you can pardon me when I make no apology for doing my duty without fear of consequences, then let us shake hands honestly, and believe me that I am happy to welcome you again to this house."

There was more warmth in her last words, and her voice trembled somewhat. Josephine arose, with moist eyes, and held out both her soft hands to her sister-in-law, who took her in her arms and kissed her affectionately. Yet, after good feeling had been restored, it was plain to both of them that the newly-made widow had altered. What mental changes were produced by the terrible shock, what work a review of her past life, accompanied by humiliation and perhaps remorse, had accomplished, besides the ravages of her great grief, let psychologists determine; but no longer was there any of the sprightliness or vivacity, once so noticeable in her manner; with her husband's death the light within her soul had been extinguished, and she sat in the darkness of the tomb, cold and emotionless as a statue.

"I wish to speak to you about a matter which it becomes me to broach," said Bella, after awhile. "I can imagine that both of you intend to postpone your wedding, perhaps for months, on account of me; but I must not allow any such consideration. Life is so closely interwoven with death, that we calculate in vain upon any respite, even in the circle of our nearest friends, from the dreadful monster. Therefore, I consider it man's duty and woman's wisdom to get married while they can, and not wait until another summons may sever you, perhaps, forever."

Josephine glanced timidly at her lover, who said, quietly,—"You are perfectly right."

"Then, when shall it be, since it seems that *I* must arrange for you?" asked Bella.

"We will dutifully consider the question," answered our hero, "and report to-morrow. There is one obstacle, though."

"What?" cried Josephine, with a start.

"Until I have a business, I can not support a wife."

"Such a scruple, it seems to me, is out of place," said Bella. "You are sole executor of our estate, are you not?"

"Yes; since my acquittal, I am restored to that duty; that is, your lamented husband, at my request, appointed Mr. Paradise my colleague, to share the responsibility with me."

"True!" said Bella. I had forgotten that. At all events, our wealth is large; is it not, Mr. Montant?"

"I think," said Montant, with a strange hesitancy, which betrayed his aversion to the subject, "I think that the estate might safely be estimated at a value of two millions of dollars. For generations back, your husband's ancestors habitually invested their surplus income in real estate, in and around New York City. This property has increased in value rapidly, and prices are now advancing fabulously, so I may venture the opinion, that, at no distant day, the sum I have mentioned, as the present cash value, will be largely increased."

"Then, why do you not devote your entire time to the administration of this property?" asked Bella. "I suppose that the law allows a trustee a sufficient percentage to insure you a good living, and, in my ignorance of business, I do not see what more lucrative pursuit a man can follow, than taking care of a very rich wife's property. I do not pretend to give any advice; but since you intend to marry Josephine, you can not well leave her property behind, and I can not see any common sense in refusing to let well-enough alone. Our property requires some one's undivided attention, and, were I in your place, I should be satisfied with filling that post."

"I suppose I will have to come to it!" said Montant, not at all delighted with the prospect.

"Really," cried Bella, "I am beginning to lose all confidence in the wisdom of the stronger sex! They devote all their best energies to the acquisition of money, and here I find you accepting a million of dollars as if it were a bitter pill, as hard to swallow as any sour-faced druggist could make it!"

"You are right, Mrs. Van Strom, but there is one thing you leave out of consideration. It is *manly* pride! It is not so much the possession as the making of wealth which delights us! I came to this country poor enough to accept, with thanks, the lowest situation that would gain me my daily bread, and suddenly, from no merit of mine, from no work, no hard struggle, I find myself with a million of dollars on my hands. This wealth I receive from a woman—a woman I love, it is true, but whose care and support would make me a happy and contented man. I now receive, as a gift, what I intended to work for, and my ambition is gone, my strength wasted, and my pride humbled!"

Josephine felt hurt at this strong language, and it was not immediately that peace reigned among the trio. She could not understand how he could aspire to any thing beyond her love and the means to enjoy it in comfort and luxury. And she had plumed herself not a little on being able to give him all this wealth, and to say that he need not work and plan and contrive and worry about "down town,"—which phrase represented to her mind some wonderful method by which ships, hogsheads, and bales produced endless labor and sour faces at home.

At this pause in the conversation, Bella's thoughts reverted once more to her own affairs, and the hard look settled again around her expressive mouth.

"Mr. Montant, I would thank you to cause a reward to be offered for the arrest of Antonio Stilletto, the murderer of my husband."

"How much shall I make it? I suppose we had better simply give notice to the detective department in New York. Money is the oil to grease that machinery, and a reward is the whetstone which sharpens a detective's wits."

"Very well, how much shall we offer those gentlemen?"

"I would say, five thousand dollars," said he, after reflection. "It is a large amount; but I think you desire me to advise you on the safe side."

"Double it," said Bella, between her teeth.

"I can scarcely sanction that," ventured our hero.

"Ten thousand is the reward," said Bella, savagely.

"Bella!" cried Josephine, approaching her with an imploring gesture, "the wrong you have suffered is great, the crime committed is appalling; but remember that God has branded revenge as a crime, that—"

"I am not seeking revenge," interrupted Bella. "Revenge and justice are as far apart as hatred from well-grounded aversion, stealing from prudence, superstitious bigotry from religion. The one is from heaven, the other from hell. I seek but justice.—Ten thousand is the reward, Mr. Montant!"

"As you wish."

When Bella had left the room, Josephine burst into tears.

"Oh, she is so changed—so changed! Her heart is not broken! It is worse, much worse; it is turned into stone!"

Montant soothed and comforted her, and they finally began discussing a secret and serious affair—the name of Going & Son was mentioned, and a consultation followed about some great things they intended to accomplish.

* * * * * *

On a dismal, rainy, nasty day in March, Ernest Montant arrived, in a very bad humor, at the New Haven railroad depot, in New York City, from Boston. He was tired and hungry, and, to add to his discomfort, he got wet through before he had time to select the least villainous-looking from among the hackdrivers, who surrounded him like fierce hyenas fighting for their prey. He directed the driver to convey him to Delmonico's. At the sight of the luxury, characterizing the place, he realized, for the first time, that he had plenty of money, and ordered a bottle of champagne with his dinner, which extravagance afforded him neither pleasure nor remorse, and he seasoned his sumptuous repast with a train of thought, not calculated to improve the flavor of the fish or the condition of the Stilton.

"I suppose that I am a fool for not feeling as happy as a king," he soliloquized, shoving away an unoffending dish in a manner which impressed the bland waiter with the idea that "Monsieur is either an aristocrat or an upstart."

"As I look around me, I see care and anxiety peeping out on every face, in spite of the assumed cheerfulness, while I, suddenly raised from a suspected murderer to the possessor of a million of dollars, a lovely wife, excellent health, untainted honor, and, on the whole, a tolerably good conscience. What more is there for me to covet?"

Such questions he asked himself, and instead of answering them, he reverted again and again, like a woman, to the words, "And yet I am not happy. What is there left for my ambition? What pleasure can I expect from labor during the smooth and luxurious life I see before me. *I will write*," he muttered fiercely, as he dashed out the last of the champagne into his glass. "I will become an author or something of that sort. I could begin as an editor and work my way up, I know. Something I must have to aspire to beyond mere good luck, for I am now at the top of the wheel without having earned a cent of my wealth, or really deserved a kiss from my Venus."

Mr. Ernest Montant, you, too, have a skeleton in the house. You have a thought, a desire, a secret hope, you would fain hide even from yourself.

The contemplation of his own breast sought utterance in the most distorted philosophy, and rather than dwell upon and acknowledge to himself the truth, he preferred a general grumbling at all destiny had bestowed. He had come to New York, not only on important business relative to the Van Strom estate, not only to confer with Mr. Paradise, his co-executor, but also to pay a visit at a house in Fifth Avenue, whither his heart drew him irresistibly. He had not seen the old gentleman since the day of the trial, after which he had returned home without giving Montant a chance for a conversation. Things were not improving with Going & Son, the firm was faring badly, very badly; the world knew it and Montant knew it, and Mr. Going was too proud to seek the sympathy and consolation of a man who had left him in the hour of need, nor had made any advances since that time.

This very night he had determined to call on his old friends. He lingered a full hour over his coffee, and had a long argument with himself. Perhaps the skeleton stood out in bolder relief, warning him—perhaps his common sense gained the victory—at all events, he determined to wait a few days before gratifying himself with the promised visit, and suddenly called for pen, ink, and paper, and wrote the following letter to Mrs. Bella Van Strom:—

"Although the result of our recent consultation was a determination on my part, to devote my whole time to the. administration of the estate, more mature considerations have determined me to re-enter business. My reasons you will readily discern when you reflect upon what you know of my character.

"I desire to join the firm of my late employers—Messrs. Going & Son—and it is my intention to ask Josephine for a special capital to invest in the house. If they are willing to accept me, I shall examine the present standing of the firm before concluding any arrangement, because I would not willingly risk Josephine's money. In the matter of determining the safety of the investment, I feel perfect confidence in my own ability and honesty of purpose, and I write you on the subject because I desire your sanction of so important a step, and because your approval and encouragement would be a pledge of our future mutual confidence and good understanding."

After finishing this letter, he wrote a long epistle to Josephine, full of love and of his plan to re-enter business as above mentioned.

After a few days he received a reply from Josephine, in which, despite all the affection and devotion therein contained, there was a flavor he did not relish. She wrote that, of course, she had no desire but to carry out her part of his plans, no will but his—no argument other than his reasoning—but that Bella had looked sour over his letter to her, and hinted that it was not gratitude alone which impelled him to come to the relief of Messrs. Going & Son. The letter closed with the assurance that the writer had no fear or doubt of her lover, but it was not quite so strongly worded as he could wish. What did she mean? Was she jealous? Could she doubt him? Did the skeleton rattle its bones?

On the same day he received the following lines from Bella :—

"Sir:—I will reply to your favor in a business tone, for it was a business letter. I take the liberty of saying that I do not sanction your enterprise at all; but, on the contrary, from what I know of the extravagance of a certain family, I have no confidence in the safety of a certain firm. I trust that you will not permit your judgment to be biassed by a gratitude, the causes for which I acknowledge are not quite clear to my inexperienced mind, and I respectfully inform you that, should your resolution remain unchanged, and you form new ties, I would prefer the whole estate to be wound up as soon as possible, the division made, and the control of my portion be left to me alone.

"Before I close, and having said what I had to say, I must assure you of more friendship than these lines may convey at present.

"I remain, truly yours,

"Bella Van Strom."

Montant read it twice, and pondered over it contents for hours in a brown study, biting his lips more than once.

CHAPTER VIII.

SAVED.

"I am not of that feather to shake off
My friend when he most needs me."
Timon of Athens.

His own resolve, alone, and contrary to such advice as he had solicited, made him do it. When matters connected with the estate brought him back to spend a day in Massachusetts, Josephine, in an interview which marked their first difference of opinion, had departed somewhat from the tone of her first letter, and employed all her powers to dissuade him from an alliance which she dreaded—why she knew not, but she had said to him,—

"Take what money you choose, and help them. By so doing, you satisfy all the claims of friendship and gratitude; but do not form a connection which must more or less alienate you from Bella certainly, and perhaps from me."

"They can not take the money, unless I, myself, bring it into the firm," was the answer; and his resolution remained unaltered. On his return to New York, he had consulted Mr. Paradise, who said, with a sneer, that such instances of gratitude were rare in the world, and coolly added, that he would make an ass of himself if he persisted.

So his own resolve alone made him do it.

He approached the house. Uncertainty, fear of a hundred things, had kept him from making a visit sooner. They knew that he was coming. A card, sent up by him during the day, had advised them of his intention; yet now, that it was evening, his mind fluctuated between resolution and hesitancy.

"I know not why a strife seems to be going on in my breast," he murmured, walking faster. "Something tells me that I am about to do the best action of my whole life, and yet I have a foreboding of danger. Well, what generosity dictates, and conscience sanctions, can not be wrong, and nothing but cowardice hinders its fulfillment." Again his thoughts recurred to Josephine's view of the case, and when the well-known house loomed up in his sight, he experienced a sensation which did not altogether contradict the lovely widow's jealous uneasiness. "But what matters it all?" soliloquized our hero, as he rang the bell. "I shall marry Josephine next month, and I do not see what difference it can make if I happen to meet what I might call an old flame! Remote, indeed, from me, is any feeling for Jessie Going, other than friendship!"

In the meanwhile Miss Jessie Going was alone in the parlor, and she listened to every footstep on the sidewalk. Her heart throbbed quicker when some step approached the house, and when it had passed the door, to die away again, relapsed into resigned patience. For many a weary month this had been the first happy day to her. That name on the card had inspired her with a hope, which must be referred to intuition as a cause, that the promised visit might perhaps open the way through a reconciliation between her father and our hero, to the renewed acquisition of his inestimable (so she thought) advice and assistance in her father's business. He was engaged to be married. This she knew; but that made no difference. Had she not told her father that the girlish fancy she once betrayed had been effaced by the serious, all-absorbing struggles which the family had undergone? The feeling which now made her listen to every sound in the street, was nothing akin to love. Oh, no! only friendship, and anxiety for her father. But how could he assist—

Here the bell rang; with a smothered exclamation, she sprang to her feet. The hall door is opened by the servant, while Jessie stands, holding her breath, and clasping her hands, her composure gone, though she knew it not. She hears a familiar voice, and a familiar tread approaches the parlor door. She rushes forward, unconscious of her haste. She beholds him coming rapidly toward her, and a warm blush overspreading her beautiful face, she holds out both hands to him, unable to utter a word.

He has her hands in his; he sees the color rising from her fluttering heart; he looks into her eyes, moist with tears, and unstrung, overpowered by the old influence of her presence, and by her emotion, which strikes home to his heart's core, he presses her hand to his lips, and then turning suddenly away, clenches his fist, and bites his lips savagely. At the movement, her color fled. What her face betrayed while his eyes were averted from her he knew not; but when, after an immense effort, he again turned to her, she was pale, and calm, and stately.

"I am truly glad to see you, Mr. Montant," she said, and invited him to take a chair, by seating herself with the air of a princess. "What an absurdity it is in me," she quietly thought to herself, "to get into such a flutter! Did I not tell papa that he is no more than a friend to me now? And I know I spoke the truth when I said it!" But how now, Jessie Going?

"This is contemptible in me," soliloquized Ernest Montant, at the same time. "An engaged man can greet a sweet friend without acting first like a lover, and then like a fool, I hope! There shall be no repetition of this scene!" Are you certain of that Ernest Montant?

While both were holding these secret conversations, a few every-day commonplaces passed between them to prevent embarrassment, and Miss Going's father entered, and shaking our hero by the hand, said, heartily,—

"So we have you back again at least for one evening, you runaway! Welcome here, my dear friend! Forgotten be the past, and the future untroubled while we make the best of the present."

Montant heard the voice with a pang. It was not so full and ringing as of old. Age and sorrow had weakened its full vibration, while furrowing his venerable brow, and bowing down the proudly erect form of the merchant.

"Mr. Going," said our hero, after the first greetings had been exchanged, "although I am delighted at seeing you all again, after so long a separation, I may as well acknowledge at once that I have not come on an errand of pleasure only. I much desire to have a business talk with you and Walter, if Miss Going will excuse us. I would respectfully suggest that we get over the laborious part of my visit as soon as convenient to you."

The old gentleman's face assumed a more troubled expression, as he at once assented, and led the way down stairs, to the library, where our hero had been on more than one occasion. This was the room where he had taken leave of his employer, and as he entered it again, and considered the difference in his circumstances, between then and now, he felt perhaps for the first time, the proud consciousness of power which is conferred by the possession of wealth.

Jessie remained alone in the parlor. She heard Walter inquiring of the servant where Mr. Montant had gone; she heard him descending the stairs; and through the opening library door the hearty words of welcome reached her ears. She laid her head on her hands, and became lost in thought.

*   *   *   *   *   *

"And now," said Mr. Going, after having related what had occurred in the firm while Montant had been away, "I have voluntarily given you an account of the past, and you can now see what an infamous intrigue it was into which I was coaxed. You see how our Board of Trustees, composed of some of the first merchants of New York, proved to be the very worst selection that could have been made. Respectability is one thing, *work* is

quite another, and no benefit arises from procuring big-sounding names, when their owners have not the time to attend to their business. These high-toned gentlemen left every thing in the hands of Fatman, and Fatman has ruined me. Even without Stilletto, who forsook his post at the factory some months ago; even after the perfect fiasco which that scoundrel made of the manufacturing portion of the business, there was no reason why a sufficient amount should not have been realized out of the company's property to make an honorable settlement with the shareholders, and to leave me enough to discharge my pressing liabilities. As it is, Fatman sold *his* shares secretly, and many of the trustees were enabled by him to do the same, on the strength of a dividend which he caused to be declared, and which created a short-lived demand for the stock. I could not sell any of my interest, because it was all pledged to Mr. Chip, as security for his loan of two hundred thousand dollars, and as soon as the public began to suspect that the dividend was paid with borrowed money, and not from the legitimate earnings, the stock depreciated almost to nothing, and I finally resolved to commence a suit against the company, which suit is now pending, and does not look unfavorable for us. In the meanwhile—"

"In the meanwhile," cried Walter. "In the meanwhile, we must *fail!*"

It was an ugly word, and familiar as was its import to Mr. Going, our hero saw him wince at the sound. He contemplated the old gentleman's countenance, and reflected upon the humiliation it must be to him to acknowledge now, and in this very room, to him, what he as a young clerk had predicted last year. Terribly true was the prophecy the gray-haired merchant had disregarded! At the last speech of Walter's, Montant asked, eagerly,—

"There is an end to delicacy, Mr. Going, and since I know this much. I would thank you to answer me a few questions?"

"Ask away," cried Walter, in despair, walking up and down the room. "If father does not answer you, I will."

"What, then, is the immediate cause of your embarrassment?"

"The notes which you will remember the company gave us for our merchantable property have now been twice renewed, and the last time Fatman promised me faithfully they should be paid."

"But he did not pledge himself personally to their redemption?" interposed Montant.

"Of course not," answered Walter, bitterly. "I'll give that man a thrashing yet, some day!"

"Well, and these notes, Mr. Going?"

"These notes, sir, are due day after to-morrow," answered Mr. Going, despondently, "and this afternoon, in spite of a thousand fair promises which he made to me before I instituted the suit against the company—this *afternoon*, sir, I received word from Fatman that, under the circumstances, meaning the law-suit, the company did not feel inclined to pay the notes, and that even if they had felt so inclined, there was not a cent in the exchequer."

"Then the company will break."

"And we, with it. I have borrowed money upon those notes, and if they are not paid, the lenders will come back on us, and I can not pay. There is no sense in attempting to work through. My shares will be worth absolutely, nothing. Mr. Chip will lose a large sum, and the trustees will have to content themselves with what they have made out of it. So far, I am perfectly certain that Fatman has realized a great deal of money; but why he has assumed such a hostile position toward me—why he appears to have forgotten all his former friendship, and is determined to ruin me, I do not know, I am sure."

"I know," cried Walter. "He was always jealous of us, and I believe Mrs. Fatman has urged him on, because on some occasions I did not feel inclined to be quite as attentive to her as she was graciously inclined to permit."

"He certainly grudged me the Priory," continued his father, without appearing to notice the import of Walter's words, "and besides he has shrewdly stepped into a great portion of my former business connection in the banking and commission line."

"All of which can be recovered from him again," said Montant, quietly.

"A beggar is a child in business, no matter how many years of prosperity and mercantile fame have passed over his head," retorted Mr. Going, sorrowfully.

"Well, then," said Walter throwing himself into an arm-chair, "let us give up the ship gracefully. I have struggled the very life out of me, since you left, Montant, and even if I thought we could stave it off for another six months, I would advise father, in view of the infamous treatment he has received, to declare the truth."

"The public," said the old gentleman, "should know how some of our celebrated merchants do business, and those gentlemen themselves, should be made to understand the duties of a trustee, and that it is not doing what the poor shareholders expect of them—to attend one or two meetings, pocket the price paid for their great names, and then leave all the management to unscrupulous parties, without consulting the public in the matter."

"Mr. Going," said Montant, in the calm, measured voice, he had heard from him once before in this room, "I can not imagine that your firm is insolvent to-day. Am I right in thinking that with the assistance of a large sum in cash, you could, in all likelihood, arrange matters advantageously with the company, and also save much of your property which I know to be scattered far and wide, from sacrifice."

"I think that the company still owns much property of actual mercantile value. This I could undoubtedly recover if I could offer to Chip and others a comparatively small amount in cash. Their eyes are now opened, and I think they would consent to lose a large sum for a small cash percentage. Besides, I have hypothecated a good deal of real estate and other property of my own, which, if I could only redeem at once, could be ultimately, well sold, waiting my time for disposing of it. But this money I can not raise. It is impossible!"

"Father is quite right," growled Walter. "We are not actually insolvent, and yet if we are forced to suspend payment all will go by the board and it will be an ugly failure. Every thing will melt away, for those that own our mortgages will sell for just enough to cover themselves."

"Impossible to help it," said the old gentleman, and when with those words he finished the recital of his trials and present situation, he fell back in his chair the picture of hopeless dejection. Montant felt that it would be inhuman and barbarous cruelty to longer withhold the aid that was at his command.

Yet he reflected one moment. Josephine had given him full power, and he was free to act as his conscience dictated. He reflected whether it was possible that Mr. Going and his son had been over-sanguine in estimating that the firm was not intrinsically insolvent, and he made up his mind that he could take the risk. He arose, stepped up to Mr. Going, and said, in a voice that trembled a little at first:—

"A year ago, I made a promise to your daughter. I have come to-night to redeem it. Both of you, gentlemen, know of my engagement to Josephine Van Strom. After proper consultation with her, I have determined to make you the offer, that, should you accept me as a partner in your house, I will see the firm *through* if it cost a hundred or even two hundred thousand dollars."

He was a boy no longer, and his face showed the change worked by his recent and severe experience. A man who has looked death in the face in as cold-blooded shape as he had encountered it in the form of an indictment for murder is not apt to be timid or to hesitate on assuming a position of power and in calmly asserting it. So he stood before his old principal in a new character as a man to be respected, not alone for the power of the wealth which he wielded, but also for his personal worth.

Mr. Going was too much surprised to immediately recover his equanimity, while Walter sprang to his feet, and seizing our hero by the hand, exclaimed, with impulsive joy,—

"You bring us new life, and we must never be separated any more. You are a noble fellow, Ernest, and we alone can ever appreciate what you have done for us."

"Provided we can accept the offer, interposed Mr. Going, in a low voice, in which hope did not speak.

"Of course we must accept," said Walter, impatiently.

"We will accept if we are solvent, otherwise, not."

"My conviction is, that the capital will be safe," said our hero, quietly. "Of course you would shrink as much from accepting my proposition, as I would be loath to risk another person's capital if there existed any danger for the security of this money. I would suggest that we immediately look into the condition of your affairs provided you have the requisite leisure, and can, from memory, make such extracts from the books as may be required."

In another hour Montant had satisfied himself that, although the great house of Going & Son was nearly ruined, it was not yet beyond redemption. And now the reader might ask the question: How could so wealthy a firm become so quickly impoverished? Montant did not wonder at that startling fact, because, for years Mr. Going had intrusted his business almost entirely to his clerks. While Martin Bates had embezzled money, other employes, representatives, and agents, had squandered it, and Walter had devoted himself to driving four-in-hand and playing cricket. Besides all this, the expenditures of the hospitable, generous, charitable head of the house, were enormous, and when the firm, unknown to the world, had become weakened by these causes, came the Hobgoblin Factory, which swallowed immense sums of ready cash. These large outlays could only be met by incurring large debts, for the discharge of which they had trusted to the realization of large amounts from the sale of Hobgoblin shares. These shares now became worthless, and nothing was left to meet the liabilities that constantly increased by the exorbitant rates of interest demanded on account of the tottering credit of the firm.

But as there is hope while there is life in a body, so there is hope while there is money in a mercantile house, and hope, the great comforter, was strong in the hearts of those three as they discussed their plans for the future.

A silvery voice from up-stairs interrupted them.

"Papa."

Mr. Going went to the door.

"Well, my daughter?"

"Papa, may I come down stairs?" asked Miss Jessie, leaning over the banisters.

"Tell her, yes!" said Walter's stentorian voice. "Come along, Jess!"

Our hero instinctively made a move for his hat; but was checked by the pattering of the young lady's feet on the stairs. He heard the rustling of her dress, and felt a mixed sensation of embarrassment and delight. He saw her enter the room, and became giddy.

There she stood by the door, her hand still on the knob, her delightful figure slightly inclined forward, her lustrous eyes bent upon them in wonder and coquettish query, her rich, raven tresses thrown back, her beautiful face all animation, with her lovely lips half parted—so she appeared for a moment, and again he was spell-bound by her presence, again charmed to the spot, and enthralled by the magic of her loveliness in spite of the world, and in mocking derision of his promises to himself.

"I heard Walter laughing, and papa's voice speaking loudly and cheerfully. Is there any news? Good news?"

Our hero turned away to examine some books on the shelves, while Mr. Going answered his daughter.

"There is news, indeed, my darling. We have made a change in our firm."

"I know what it is!" cried the girl, and stepping up to our hero, who turned around as if by the influence of magnetism, she added, with a heightened color:—

"I always knew it, Mr. Montant! Here is my hand, and take a sister's friendship with it!"

He took the proffered hand, but could not raise his eyes to meet her gaze.

"The old style of Going & Son will be changed," said the old gentleman, cheerfully. "It has been a good name; but I think that Going, Montant & Company will be better still. And now take a seat by me, Jessie, and let us enjoy this bright hour which Providence has prepared for us!"

"And let us pledge the health of the new firm in a glass of champagne," suggested Walter. The proposition seemed in place, and when the wine was passed around, there was a cheerfulness in the room that had long—oh, how long—been absent from that house! Jessie's heart swelled with gratitude. She nestled closely to her father, and her unbounded devotion to him made her forget for the time all that might dampen her happiness. And was there something hidden away in her heart that might have clouded her pleasure? Not so, to judge by her happy face and sparkling eyes, as she listened to a brief account of what had occurred and what our hero had accomplished. Still, she did not favor him with such attention as some might have thought he deserved; and when she finally said, "All will be well now," she addressed the remark to her father, seeming, in the kiss she gave him, to forget all other presence but his own.

All this time Montant sat quietly, with his eyes bent on the floor. Although proud and satisfied, his countenance seemed hardened and stoical, as if the importance of what had been done, and what still remained to be done, repressed all emotion.

"And now let us drink to the health of our new partner," said Mr. Going. "We owe him a debt of gratitude which we can never pay; for by his timely aid, and by his fidelity to me, he has brought peace to my house in my old age."

As Jessie touched her glass to our hero's, he glanced into her eyes and saw them filled with tears. The fervent words of her beloved father overwhelmed her with gratitude toward the man to whom she had just promised a sister's friendship, and he read in their expression more than lips could utter, that he possessed all the admiration and affection she could bestow upon him forever—and no more. Mr. Going continued:—

"Boys, you will have luck in business. I think a good time is in store for this country, and although a war seems at hand, we may be confident that we are on the stronger side. Commerce will not only hold up her head, and assert her power, but will bring us a season of unparalleled prosperity which will create immense wealth in our midst in spite of the war-thunder at our gates. Never forget our late experiences, or that fortune and the advent of a friend in need have saved my name from dishonor, and not the forethought and prudence which should have held the balance in this gray head. I have been like a foolish boy. Henceforth, I will show *you* the wisdom of age, and be certain that to walk the troublesome road of business safely, a man needs only integrity, common sense, and self-respect. No one has any excuse for remaining poor in this country; and, in this advancing age, a merchant is respected as he should be, finding in a successful mercantile career an honor as famous as can be won on the red field of battle. A health then once more to the new house of Going, Montant & Company, and let no one, not here present, ever know how great our need has been."

At this moment our hero looked up. A heightened color overspread his face, and in his eyes there glowed a fire as of a mind made up and resolute, a heart that has dispelled the clouds of doubt, and conquered in a struggle. His eyes no more shunned those of the beautiful girl. He seemed to shake off with an impatient gesture what hesitancy still encumbered the victory he had won, and a warm emotion softened his voice, as he said:—

"And, may I here pledge a health to the woman whose great love for me is the cause of this, to me, unspeakably happy hour. Let me ask you all to join me in remembering Josephine Van Strom, that will be Josephine Montant ere long if God permit. To her I owe life, happiness, wealth. She that never wavered in her faith and trust and love—she, that worked for me day and night, when I was in danger and tribulation—she, that is as noble and true as can be born on earth and inspired by heaven, does not deserve to be forgotten, and let me at this time form in her name a tie of friendship and affection between you and her."

Cheerfully and heartily did he seek Jessie's eyes, as she joined in the sincere response of the others. She saw that all strife (if strife there had been) had ceased in his strong heart, and impelled by curiosity, or solicitude, or egotism, he attempted to read in her face what *she* thought of it.

He could read nothing.

Finally they parted, to meet again to-morrow. A hearty "Good-night," a shaking of hands all around, a half-laughing "Remember our bargain as to sisterly affection, Miss Jessie," and he was gone.

"My dear father," said that young lady, when they were alone again in the parlor, "has he brought a sacrifice to us?"

"No," answered Mr. Going. "The money he will invest is safe in our house. Many wealthy men would have given their sons much greater sums to invest with me on those terms."

"In former times?" suggested Jessie, wisely.

"Yes, but nevertheless he knows full well that his connection with me gives him a standing and position which wealth can rarely buy."

"*Does* he know that?" asked Jessie, doubtfully.

"Most certainly. He has said so, and he is too intelligent not to know it, and too candid not to have meant it."

"I am glad of it. I do not like being under obligations to *any one*," said the young lady, decidedly, but satisfied.

* * * * *

Who is that man walking along the dimly lighted street with a bounding step and a heart as happy as heart can be? Why does he hold his head so high and feel as if he were the inferior of no creature on earth? "*He has done his duty*, and he can look straight and fearlessly into the eyes of all mankind; yes, and lift his eyes to the eternal heavens without a shudder.

Into the eyes of all mankind, and all womankind, too! Into the eyes of Josephine Van Strom he can look and laugh, telling her the while how he stood by her nobly, who nobly stood by him!

He has broken the spell. His strong will has gained the victory over the witchery of Jessie's presence. He has severed the cord that threatened to tear him away from Josephine, regardless of all that she had done for him, forsaking her like a knave, and leaving her to perdition.

No more doubt, no more wavering, no more strife between passion and conscience! He laughed to himself, so light was he at heart, and he wrote a letter to Josephine that night which made her weep with joy.

In fact, our hero was excited and delighted with himself, and felt certain that in all human probability his happiness was assured for a good long comfortable time to come. How, now, Bella Van Strom?

Where are your scruples and warnings and predictions and fancies? You did not know this man when you instilled into Josephine's timid and susceptible soul a fear of that alliance with the Goings. In fact, you have shown yourself to be an unbelieving, suspicious wretch, and were it not that we can excuse you on account of your recent afflictions, the breach in our friendship would become irreparable!

So Josephine told her when she perused Montant's letter, although the lovely widow did not use just those harsh expressions.

Bella read the letter, listened calmly to the enthusiastic eulogies which her sister-in-law pronounced on her lover, and retired unfeelingly to her room without speaking a word in reply.

CHAPTER IX.

MONEY.

"One business does command us all,
For mine is money."
TIMON OF ATHENS.

THAT creature of modern times, the honest, honorable, and honored merchant, dates from England's rise among the nations of the earth as a commercial power. Before that day, trade, money-lending, and negotiations of every kind were confined to Jews and people of the lower classes, and such pursuits were despised and looked down upon by those of gentle breeding, whose ancestry had for generations lived upon the possession of large estates, and gains in foreign wars. But from the time that England began to be counted among the commercial nations, of which she now stands at the head, the merchants became a power in the community, a pillar of the State, the pulse of the nation's life, the extenders of civilization and home respectability. And the American merchant is taking a stand which calls forth the bewildered admiration of old Europe, and in New York the American merchant is to be seen in his greatest power and pride. Among these New York merchants Mr. Going had held his head high, and his position was the reward of his untold labor in the earlier part of his career. And the community knew it, and respected him for it.

But to-day he was expected to fail! Mr. Chip said so as he and the other directors of a certain bank had a friendly confab at their regular weekly meeting, at which meeting the wise gray-haired gentlemen are apt to indulge in scandal and gossip to an extent worthy of equally aged worthies of the other sex.

Mr. Fatman thought so, and the arrangement of "hand-in-hand" with Mr. Going had been out of his recollection for some time previous. He was certain "they could not work through" any longer, and he did not attempt to assume an expression of mourning on his half-jovial, half-vicious countenance.

There were few that did not know it, and the commercial world in general prepared themselves for the ceremony of mourning the event. Many studied pretty speeches, expressive of sympathy, and a great lamentation, suited to the former high standing of the house, was everywhere expected, though the future of the bankrupts was to be forgotten, as speedily as possible, just as if it was a question of the funeral, instead of the failure of Going & Son.

The directors of the bank had all assembled, and Mr. Chip had just concluded a feeling speech about his *old friend Going*, when he exclaimed to the cashier,—

"Here is Mr. Going himself. He seems to be coming in; but I suppose it is time for us to adjourn up stairs, is it not, gentlemen?"

So the gentlemanly directors suddenly discovered that half-past ten, the hour for their official meeting, had arrived twenty minutes ago, and they adjourned to the room above in some haste.

Mr. Going very well understood their spontaneous exit as he approached. Nearly every one of the directors had once been his personal friends, and now they shunned him like an outcast, since he was known to have lost his money!

The old gentleman had to pause a second, so appalled was he by this heartless affront, and the companion who accompanied him, had to whisper in his ear,—

"What they have been to you in the past, they will be again in two short hours. Therefore you have only temporarily lost their contemptible friendship.'

Mr. Going recovered himself. Thank God, it was the last bitterness.

"Mr. Countebank," said Mr. Going to the withered little cashier, "I have come to introduce to you my new partner, Mr. Ernest Montant, who will leave his signature with you, and in future will attend to the finances of my new firm—Going, Montant & Company."

The cashier looked up a moment with that presumption, bordering upon impudence, which our bank officers (in reality our most dependent servants) are allowed to assume, and said, somewhat puzzled,—

"You were a clerk in the house before, I remember you. All right. The paying-teller will show you where to write your signature, and now excuse me, I have to attend the meeting of the directors up-stairs."

Mr. Going left immediately after introducing his new partner. The latter had made no bow, because the cashier had not volunteered a like courtesy, and he now stood before him without removing his hat.

"You will stay a moment, if you please," he said, very quietly, but with evident determination to be obeyed.

Mr. Countebank had his hand on the door-knob; but turned around with the air of a millionaire accosted by a beggar.

"My time, sir,—" he began sharply.

"Of course I know your time is valuable," interrupted our hero, " and the directors have already postponed the meeting twenty minutes; but I request you to give me three minutes more. Mr. Going's firm has deposited in this bank for nearly a century, and I insist upon your attention for the time I stated."

He took out his watch, noted the time, and took a seat near Mr. Countebank's desk. The latter looked bewildered, hesitated a moment, and before our hero had produced some papers from his pocket-book, was again seated at his desk.

"Three minutes," repeated the cashier, gruffly.

"Mr. Countebank," said Montant, without heeding the affront, "our payments are heavy to-day. We have over fifty thousand dollars coming due at your bank alone, and the collaterals which you hold are partly worthless. I refer to the notes of the Hobgoblin Company."

"Well, and what do you propose?"

"I propose," said Montant, slowly, "to continue to keep an account here, *provided*—you continue to treat us with the courtesy which our old name deserves, and will grant us additional accommodations, should we need them."

"But you are *insolvent!*" cried the cashier, hardly knowing what he said from perplexity.

Montant colored with anger at the ugly word, but, controlling himself, answered, with cutting distinctness,—

"These two checks, each for one hundred thousand dollars, will give you the lie more flatly than I can. You will please put them to our credit, and charge what is due to-day to our account. You will also oblige me by kindly contradicting all absurd reports concerning our insolvency, there being no foundation for such scandal, except in the malice of some evil-minded enemies of Mr. Going. Good-morning, sir."

The tactics pursued by Mr. Going and our hero were to prove most telling and successful. He had advised his new partners to keep the change a profound secret. His motives were twofold. In the first place he wanted to see how far the credit of the house could be stretched, and found, that in spite of rumor, and finally, a prevailing certainty of their failure, the personal credit of Mr. Going was not entirely lost. He had sent Walter to borrow small amounts from the brokers, and other small men that were under obligations to the house, and they found that these *small* men responded to the call without hesitation. Unlike the millionaires, such as Chip, to whom Mr. Going had applied for aid, the poorer class came to the rescue, relying on his honor to repay them, even in case of a failure. He was not "a perfect stranger," except to the immensely wealthy.

The other reason for deferring the vindication of the firm was, that Montant thought as much *éclat* as possible was advisable under the circumstances. A gradual improvement in the affairs of the house would have dispelled the floating rumors, and general doubt by degrees; but he knew that a sudden display of power that no one dreamed of, just on the last day, would be noised abroad in the most exaggerated manner, and it needed a trumpet-tone to silence the wide-spread whisperings.

He did not look back when he left Mr. Countebank, to watch the effect he had intended to produce, for he was certain what that effect would be. Mr. Countebank held the checks in his hands, and examined them a moment, not knowing what to think, so well had the busy tongue of Mr. Fatman succeeded in impressing the minds of all he could reach, with regard to the failure of Going & Son. One hundred and fifty thousand dollars in excess of what they had to pay! And notwithstanding a loss of nearly fifty thousand dollars just incurred by the notes of Hobgoblin becoming worthless! But there was no mistake. There were the checks, signed by Mr. Chip, himself, and they were certified by the Bank of Commerce. The astounded cashier called a clerk.

"Change the heading of Going & Son's account, to Going, Montant & Company, and give them credit for two hundred thousand dollars, charging their notes in account!" he almost shrieked, and then fairly flew up the stairs, two steps at a leap, to tell the sage directors the news.

"Let me see the checks," said Mr. Chip. "As I supposed," he added, looking around with genuine satisfaction. "These are my checks, and this is money, belonging to the Van Strom estate; but since Paradise and Montant borrowed it, as executors of the estate, upon collateral security, I am certain that Going did not get them out of charity. Gentlemen, he has had more resources than any of us dreamed of! I am heartily glad of it."

"A clever old gentleman," said one director.

"Can't put him down," said another.

"They were always a strong house," testified a third.

"And will remain so; for, by Jove, any firm that can lose money steadily, as they have done, expend whole fortunes in private extravagances, get taken in by such a business as that Hobgoblin affair, and then come out with a hundred and fifty thousand balance in bank the very day we all expected them to fail—such a house, gentlemen, can be relied on."

"I am very glad of it," repeated Mr. Chip, softly.

"Going is a noble, honorable, charitable man," continued another speaker, in the general eulogy, "and I mean to go and tell him so to-day."

"I always thought he would come out right. He is as smart a man as we have among us."

Oh, the change produced by those two slips of paper! But though the tribute paid by these gray-haired merchants was caused by mammon, and not by true friendship, yet, to be just to human nature, now that all was right again with their former friend, without their aid, probably there was not one in the assembly not honestly glad at heart for what had occurred. *Fatman was not among them!*

Mr. Going sat in his private office that day a proud and happy man. Honor to the weakness that made him derive pleasure from vanity! As to a soldier, so is honor dear to a merchant, and be it sustained as it may, it gladdens the heart and instills new life. And besides, in his happiness, Mr. Going looked back upon the humiliations he had suffered forgivingly. He knew there must be a barrier between the rich and the poor in a country where every man carries his fortune in his own head and hands. He knew that without that barrier, surmountable in this happy land by energy and perseverance, the ambition of the individual would slacken, and the progress of the nation be impeded, and he accepted the good luck that had befallen him with humble thanks, like a Christian gentleman, forgetting the harshness of the world which but a few weeks ago had bowed his head, and almost broken his heart.

Rich men, who saw in him a friend regained, poor men, who saw in him their kind and munificent protector once more, old men, who joyed at a bright spot in human destiny, young men, aspiring to equal such an example of victory in the midst of defeat—all crowded around him, and when Ernest Montant saw the heightened color in his face, and the brilliant light in his eye, he had the blissful satisfaction, so rarely accorded to mortals, of having been the creator of happiness—blissful because Deific.

Then, with a shudder, he thought of what would have occurred had he been unable to help. For a moment his imagination showed him that old man, tottering to his grave with his pride broken and his heart desolate. Perhaps compelled to work for his daily bread, mingling his bitter tears with the sweat of his brow.

And there are such men in the world! They are groping in the night of despair while the sun is shedding golden beams upon the laughing world. And as Ernest Montant finished his reverie, he could have thrown his arms around that old man, *who was saved now* and called him *father*, defying all the smooth-faced tigers of the gay world in his defence.

"*Father!*" he could have spoken the word aloud, but it died on his lips, in his heart before it was uttered. It haunted him, it staid in his mind, rung in his ears all that day, and as he strolled up town he confessed to himself,—

"Yes: hang all doubts and fears—let me tell the truth to myself at least, though never to another. I would rather call that old gentleman by that heavenly name, though he were a beggar, than to be as I am, the praised and honored merchant, the almost idolized friend of those I love, and the possessor of the Venus to whom I owe it all."

He was unhappy. Mark, the man who has an abundance of money, and all that wealth can procure, and who has used his means righteously and nobly—is unhappy still.

*   *   *

A few days after the fame of the old house had taken another flight upward in the manner just narrated, the door of Going, Montant & Co.'s private office was opened softly.

"Good morning, gentlemen," said Mr. Solomons all smiles, "I am happy to inform you that I'm in the stock board again. Debts all paid—old uncle died—rich—miser, you know. Market steady—all stocks in for a rise—bulls victorious. Give me an order—Erie is low, have you any? I'll sell at three a quarter regular—buy three an eighth regular, or I'll give three an eighth sixteenth off *cash*."

"Hurrah!" cried Walter, "*cash* is come to life again, hey, Solomons."

"Cash, sir," answered the Jew, stepping into the room re-adorned with his diamonds, "cash is re-born, and long life to it."

"Amen," added Montant, laughing.

BOOK V.—FATE.

CHAPTER I.

WALTER IS FREED.

"Is this the promised end?"
                                        KING LEAR.

JOSEPHINE VAN STROM was visiting a friend in New York. She that had once been lonely and forsaken, now found no lack of acquaintances, charmed into sudden existence by that sorcerer, *money*. Perhaps, many a gallant, first attracted by the well-founded report of her wealth alone, found more than wealth to fascinate him in the beautiful widow. Our hero called upon her as often as his arduous duties permitted.

"Late, again," she would say, rising with a joyous start to greet him. "Do you know, Ernest, that I can not help wishing you had never entered into that copartnership which keeps you from me so much."

"I think a man can never remain attractive to a woman unless he has a regular occupation. He must be employed during some hours of the day, if it is only to keep him out of the way at home. If he remains with his wife all the time, he becomes the housekeeper's drudge."

"But I am not a housekeeper, you know!"

"But soon shall be," returned Montant, gayly.

"How soon?" she asked, in a whisper.

"Whenever my darling gives the word. Shall it be a month from to-day?"

"Do you think that by that time your business will graciously yield you up to me for a few weeks?"

"Yes. It seems ridiculous to say, one is too busy to get married. Yet such has been my case. There is an amount of enterprise and activity in the commerce of this city, perhaps unparalleled in the history of trade. A man must devote every moment of time and every faculty of his brain to his business, or he can not keep up with the rest."

"But you are independent," she pleaded.

"Not, until that two hundred thousand dollars is returned."

"Oh, you foolish, silly fellow. Isn't it all yours?"

"I might almost call it mine, but as a partner of Going, Montant & Co., I feel the necessity of paying it back to the estate of John Van Strom. I lent the firm that money on my responsibility as trustee, and I must see to its repayment."

"I hate money!" she cried.

"Do not speak so foolishly, Josephine," he replied, gravely. "Money has made us what we are to-day. Money has brought happiness back to Mr. Going's sad and oppressed heart. How can you then speak in derision of this great benefactor?"

"But I want you to leave business, and devote yourself to me."

"There is a time of unexampled prosperity in store for us," continued Montant. "I can name the day when Mr. Going and Walter will be able to discharge all their debts; for the war, which is threatening the life of the country, is rolling wealth into our coffers."

"I thought times were dreadfully hard."

"No; at least not to merchants removed from the immediate scene of war."

"And if you continue to prosper in business will you promise me to retire as soon as Mr. Going has no more need of you?"

"What on earth would I do all day long?"

"*Love me!*" she answered, looking up in his face with the old Madonna expression. He did not answer. After a pause—

"I have a piece of news to tell you, Josephine," he said. "Mr. Going has bought the Priory again."

"How *could* they—"

"Commit such an extravagance? I myself advised the old gentleman to do it. The house in Fifth Avenue will be sold, and their expenses will be comparatively small in the country."

"It seems very strange to me," said Josephine.

"There was a time when we all thought a reconciliation with Mr. Fatman was out of the question, and yet he and Mr. Going have made it all up, and now that we have gained the day, he seems sorry that he ever opposed us. More than that, our old enemy is a *guest* at the Priory. Mr. Going requested immediate possession of the house, and Mr. Fatman consented to the request, on condition that he should be permitted to remain a few weeks as a guest."

"I don't understand it," said Josephine.

"Nor do I; so let us place it among those queer freaks of fortune which we will not attempt to fathom. But there is something more I have to tell you."

"What a day of wonders. Well what is it?"

"It is a case for you to decide alone. I merely want to know whether you do not think, that, since the Goings owe so much to you, it would be but ordinary delicacy to accept the invitation Miss Jessie extends to you, to spend a few days at the Priory?"

Josephine started with dismay; but in his calm, serene, face, she read no justification for the strange doubts and jealous fears that possessed her at his words, and, having reflected, she said, honestly:—

'I do not like to go; but if you think a refusal would look haughty, or, in any way overbearing, I quite agree with you that good taste bids us become their guests if they expect us to come."

"Here is a letter from Miss Going. Walter informed me of its import when he gave it to me."

"So, after some further conversation, the visit was decided on, and the next fine day they rode to Harlem, where Walter, by appointment, awaited them with his little yacht to take advantage of the fine breeze and sail up.

"I think few ladies would venture upon such a trip. Miss Jessie certainly showed that she was cautious," said the handsome widow, who was watching with some anxiety the stiffening breeze, swelling the canvas and forcing the little vessel pretty well over on its side.

"No danger," cried Walter, at the helm. "I have been at this business all my life. Jessie is unwell, or she would have come with me as I told you."

Now, no matter how true this boast might have been, the wind, coming down in puffs and squalls, seemed determined to test his seamanship, and one particular gust (probably made up on purpose in the clouds), struck them very suddenly. The boat careened over, hesitated a moment while the water gushed over the rail, and then capsized in the most deliberate manner. A loud shriek, an oath from Walter, and Mrs. Van Strom, the gentlemen, and the two sailors, found themselves sprawling in the Sound.

Fortunately, none of them became entangled in the rigging, and since there was but one woman in the party they could all combine in their efforts to save her. Clinging to the keel of the vessel, Walter and Ernest held Josephine up between them, but the shock added to the precarious position in which they were placed. The widow was nearly senseless, and Walter and Ernest had a hard struggle until, to their unspeakable joy, a fishing-smack bore down to their relief. With the help of the sturdy fishermen, they were pulled on board in safety, amid odd queries of "Was your sheet jammed?" &c. Though neither the appearance, nor the odor of the boat and its finny freight were enticing it may be questioned if that great sailor Walter was ever so little curious as to what sort of a keel was under him, as he felt that a great responsibility rested on him for the mishap, and, indeed, they were all thoroughly grateful for their deliverance. Finally, a friendly yacht came within speaking-distance, and, by dint of some exertion, they were all transhipped to that more comfortable craft.

"What a superb figure she has," whispered Walter to our hero, when the widow was being wrapped up in an infinity of blankets in the cabin of their friend's yacht.

Little did they dream of the consequences of this accident. Josephine had caught a cold that was to prolong her few days' stay at the Priory, to weeks, and perhaps months. Men's lives have turned on a smaller pivot than this. Who can tell what will be the consequences?

And now we must turn our attention to another scene for a moment, while it is being enacted, and then let it pass away from memory with all its sickening horrors.

A mad-house in New England; a gloomy company of men and women about the grounds, a blank look in every eye, in every face.

As you enter, the air seems uncomfortably still, as if some dread spell was in it. The forms that flit by are like so many pale and restless ghosts — but, instead of the spirit without the body, we have here the body devoid of the mind.

What wonder the young and timid girl, dressed in black and deeply veiled, trembles and shudders at the threshold of this dread abode!

The kind manner of the doctor reassured her; but as he led her along the lane of blubbering, senseless creatures that crowded up to see the new arrival, she realized, with a sickening terror, that these were the best of those confined in the asylum, and her way led to the place where the *worst cases* were imprisoned, and it was there she expected *to see her father.*

Let us not describe the man with the shattered, tottering frame, the wild, blood-shot eye, hands bleeding with the marks of violence, and the teeth set upon the lacerated lips; and this was once Eben Bates.

He had just recovered from an attack of frenzy. His daughter had visited him before his removal to the State Asylum, and the effects had been soothing, even productive of a glimpse of reason. So the doctor caused his fetters to be removed while he led her near him.

The doctor made a mistake.

"Father, do you know me?" Oh, if all was not darkness in that soul, those heart-rending, broken accents would have reawakened him to light.

"Are you the daughter of Judge Bates?" asked a voice unnatural to her ears, and yet it came from her father!

"Father!" she cried aloud, advancing toward him. "Father look at me—oh, it can not, can not be that you don't know me."

"What are you to me?" asked the maniac, with mock grandeur, drawing himself up into a shocking caricature of his former dignity. "Go away! You are the daughter of a criminal! You are dishonored, an outcast, I 'll none of you!"

"Oh, why have I lived to see this," murmured the poor girl, scarcely able to bear up.

"That is the question," he cried, fiercely, having caught her words.

The doctor's practiced ear caught the change in the maniac's voice, and he stepped in sight of the cell. Immediately her father's manner became quiet, and in low, measured tones he said:—

"Why should you live? If you were to die, Eben Bates would have a free conscience and you would be saved from disgrace. I know Eben Bates well—"

Reassured by the change in the patient's demeanor the doctor stepped aside to attend a raving maniac, who seemed determined to win his freedom by battering down his cell door with his thick skull.

"I'll kill you," shouted Bates. A spring, a moan of terror and agony, and the daughter lay on the ground writhing in the iron clutch of her father. He had seized her by the throat and dashed her once-cherished head against the iron-bound walls and flagged pavement, again and again. Before the terrified attendants could interfere, the last prayer of pretty, gentle, loving Bessie Bates had been breathed, and her soul had followed it on to heaven.

They removed the body, a piteous sight, and from the surrounding cells went up such howling, shrieking, curses, and yells as if the demons of hell, rejoicing at the awful tragedy, were incarcerated there instead of human effigies, and the thunder tones of Eben Bates were heard over all as he struggled with the keepers. It seemed impossible to master him. With the strength of a dozen giants, he attempted to free himself, and, whenever he could, he struck his head with unmerciful violence against the bars of his cell.

At last, when exhaustion overpowered him, the reaction came. Unable to stand now, his face became deathly pale, except where the blood flowed freely from the self-inflicted wounds on his forehead. He looked about with strange, wild eyes. His chest heaved unsteadily. Suddenly the life-current gushed from his lips, and he sank to the ground by the side of his daughter, with the light of his immortal soul restored to him, if it so pleased the infinite mercy of God.

CHAPTER II.

ONCE MORE AT THE PRIORY.

"How brooks your grace the air,
    After tossing on the breaking seas?"
"Needs must I like it well."
                                        KING RICHARD II.

THE morning after the funeral of Bessie Bates, Montant was sitting by the window of his room watching the white clouds that chased each other in the distance. Apollo was battling for the mastery of the sky against the hosts of Jupiter Pluvius, and the result seemed doubtful. The broad expanse of the Sound upon which the shadows sailed in ghostly effigies of the clouds above, was hardly disturbed by a ripple. He was contemplating the late events, as detailed in the last chapter, and blessing the kindness of Providence in sparing Josephine. while she who had been laid in the grave but the day before had no happiness in store for her, and could part with life as a loathsome burden.

Bessie's funeral was unostentatious, and no relative of the poor girl appeared to act as chief mourner. Thus alone, though not unpitied, nor friendless, she was carried to a hallowed resting-place, and no remembrance of her father's crimes or uncle's iniquities marked the mound that covered her remains, or embittered her memory, among those who had known and loved her.

It was Sunday morning, and Ernest had before him a day free of business cares, though his mind was full of anxiety. Josephine was sick, very sick, indeed. The shock of Bessie's horrible death, following close upon her own narrow escape, produced a fever so alarming that physicians of the greatest repute were summoned from the city to rub their golden spectacles, and decide that it was best to leave nature to work the cure alone, without being weakened by drugging, and further that they all and severally agreed that the attendant physician was perfectly correct in his mode of treatment.

As our hero arose with a sigh, to join the

family below, Walter stepped in, silent and downcast. He had seen very little of Bessie of late, and though they were engaged, as we know, their affection had never grown into that closer and identifying union of heart and soul which is the result of long intimacy between lovers. Perhaps his late trials had somewhat hardened him against immoderate grief, for we find him mourning his loss with quiet resignation, and looking upon it more as the merciful ending of a terrible existence, than as a cruel bereavement.

After discussing the sad subject, the friends descended to find Mr. Going at the breakfast table, and Miss Jessie presiding over the tea and coffee.

"I have been to Josephine's room," said she, "and am happy to announce that she finds herself much better. Have you seen her, Mr. Montant?"

"Yes," answered our hero, "I think we may consider the danger has passed."

"Do you visit ladies in bed?" asked Walter, with a smile.

"She was up," answered the other, "and lying on a sofa, and she had done this only to enable her to receive my visit. Not altogether according to the directions of the doctor, I am afraid, but I am proud of this mark of her affection, and I am sure it seems to me that she never looked handsomer."

"Will you have tea or coffee this morning, Walter?" asked his sister.

"I think," said Mr. Going, "that the habits of our other guests are intolerable. It is not often that I speak harshly of any one, but this vice of lying in bed till late in the morning is, in my mind, an offense against decency and respectability."

"I do not think that I should submit to it for more than the few days we are compelled to grant them," said the young housekeeper. "I can understand that Mr. Fatman should be fond of sleeping late, and take plenty of time for his toilet, but I am certain his wife only affects the weakness from a desire to ape French manners."

"As for me," rejoined her father, "I can forgive a woman sooner than a business man and head of a family, for if the master of the house does not sit at the head of the breakfast-table, family and house become demoralized."

"Mr. Going," asked Montant, "does it not seem certain that Fatman has lost heavily in his late business transactions?"

"Yes," answered the old gentleman, "and this, added to his much criticised connection with Hobgoblin, seems to be weakening his credit considerably. At least, so I am told in the city."

"How strange that you made friends with him again!" cried Miss Jessie.

Her father shrugged his shoulders.

"This reconciliation," he answered, "brought about, as you all know, by Mr. Paradise, has not been without benefit to us. The suit of my old firm against the trustees has been far more satisfactorily arranged since Mr. Fatman goes "hand-in-hand" with me now, in good earnest."

"And all your old friends have returned to you," cried the young lady. "I understand that Mr. Paradise has promised to spend next Sunday with us."

"Yes, my child. He has never given me cause for complaint, and the services he rendered to Ernest should alone entitle him to a place in our hearts."

"Do these old friends esteem you or your money?" persisted Miss Jessie. "While ruination threatened you, they treated you like a stranger, as you told me yourself."

"There are always two phases of a question," answered the old gentleman, with a smile, "and it is wiser to choose the pleasanter one. I might give it as my opinion that these friends returned to me, not only on account of my regained position, but, also, as a tribute to my supposed sagacity displayed in preserving that position triumphantly in spite of the danger. If they knew how much is due to our good friend here, they might think differently."

The young housekeeper pouted slightly at the mention of Montant's services to the firm, and, rising from the table, busied herself about the room, apparently unconscious of his presence.

Our hero arose from the table and went upstairs to pay another visit to Josephine. As he entered the room, she was seated on her sofa, a little breakfast-table before her, and the words, "Come in," in answer to his knock, were somewhat interfered with by a piece of the cutlet to which she was doing justice. As he approached her, she had just succeeded in swallowing her mouthful, and looked up to him, laughing, and showing an array of beautiful teeth, half-concealed, half-disclosed by her full, rosy lips. Her mouth belonged rather to the ample and luxurious, than to the delicate order, and when a laugh extended over her fair features, she presented such a picture as the god of pleasure would have painted to beguile weary man into forgetfulness of the harsh world.

Montant imprinted a warm kiss upon that upturned laughing mouth, and felt more satisfied than ever with his choice.

"How long do you intend to remain at the Priory?"

"Until my lord and master that is to be bids me leave," she answered, mischievously.

"And how much longer?" he asked, laughing.

"As long as I please."

"But seriously, do you not think we had better leave here as soon as you are able to travel?"

"Are you afraid of falling in love with Jessie? Does your prudence dictate this precaution?"

He drew her toward him, and kissing her again, replied, with singular emphasis, "No."

"Then, why are you so anxious to leave?" she asked. "I like this place. I am very happy with the associations of this dear old Priory."

"Do you remember the masquerade?" he asked, maliciously, "and our walk in the garden, when you proposed to me?"

"I remember that a saucy boy enticed me away from the house, and acted very foolishly, persisting in his nonsense until I engaged myself to him to get rid of him."

"You have not got rid of me yet," he cried.

"No, and I don't wish to!" she answered, with a look that caused him to repeat a certain ceremony previously described. There is no known method of ascertaining the exact number to which these repetitions might have increased, had not the door opened, and a lady stepped in hastily.

"I want to bid you good-bye, Mrs. Van Strom," she said, hurriedly. "I am going to church in the village."

Mrs. Fatman was muffled up in spite of the warm spring weather, and though a veil covered her face, it did not escape Josephine that she was excited.

"Why, what is the matter with you, Mrs. Fatman?" she asked, somewhat perplexed. "Has any thing happened?"

"Oh, no! only I am in a hurry, for it is getting late!"

"Are you going alone?" asked the widow, after the lady had kissed her with a warmth too unlike her usual *nonchalance* not to startle the recipient a little.

"Yes, my husband is just completing his toilet, Jessie pleads a headache, Mr. Going seems fatigued, Walter is still too melancholy to show himself among people, and unless Mr. Montant displays ordinary politeness and offers to escort me, I must go alone."

"With your kind permission, Mr. Montant will stay where he is," said Josephine.

"I must confess, I think this lady more in need of company than you, Mrs. Fatman," said our hero, smiling. "So, since I must choose where my knightly services are most needed, I am compelled to say that my duty keeps me here."

"Oh, irksome duty! How you must suffer under your cruel fetters!" cried Mrs. Fatman, turning to leave the room. Montant assisted her to the carriage, which was waiting at the door, and returned to his lady-love. They were having a glorious good time, when Walter sauntered in.

"Do you know where Jessie is?"

"I have not seen her since breakfast," replied our hero, "nor has Josephine, for I have been bothering her with my company ever since."

"Your calling Mrs. Van Strom by her Christian name reminds me that I have never congratulated you, you vagabond! Here is my hand, old fellow, and allow me to say I consider you about as lucky a dog as I ever knew in my life."

"If you want to tell me sweet things, it is not necessary that you should speak through *him*," said Josephine, blushing a little, but very happy.

"I have only to say to you," he replied, "that, although he hardly deserves his good luck, you have no reason to complain, and I wish you all happiness—more happiness than is in store for me."

After a few minutes of desultory conversation, Walter cried, suddenly:—

"I have something to tell you, Ernest, that I could not recall until just now."

"Well, what is it?"

"I saw a friend of yours at the village yesterday, unless my eyes deceived me most wonderfully."

"And who may that be?"

"Stilletto."

Montant looked at him in amazement. The widow was frightened.

"He was dressed like a farmer," continued Walter, "but his is one of those marked countenances difficult to forget."

"Did you speak to him? If you were certain of the man, why did you allow him to escape?"

"A man in my present state of mind may be excused for slowness of action," replied Walter, gloomily. "He must have recognized me long before I saw through his disguise, for hardly had I noticed his peculiar face, than he quickly turned a corner; and, though I pursued him, seemed to have sunk into the ground, for he was nowhere to be seen."

"You don't know how it frightens me to hear that dreadful man is in the neighborhood," said Josephine, with a dismal face.

"I do not think he will dare do more than sneak around for some object he has in view, and that object, I can't imagine to concern ourselves or this house," said her lover.

"How do you suppose he got away from the court-room in time to avoid a re-arrest after the trial?" asked Walter.

"I think Stump gave him warning that Martin Bates and the Italian girl were coming," answered our hero.

"But Paradise had given this very man, Stump, secret instructions not to lose sight of him, and to prevent his escape at all hazards."

"True. But, for once, Paradise mistook his man," said Montant. "At all events, a mystery still envelops the whole proceeding."

"I hope he will leave us alone for the future," whispered Josephine.

"If he molests us again, I hope I may be awake and present when he appears," cried Walter. "We have all been too good-hearted and too easy of approach by ill-meaning rascals. But, Mrs. Van Strom, let me assure you, that as long as my dogs, my pistols, and myself remain in good condition, Stilletto shall not enter this house without paying for it. Now, don't you think I deserve a kiss for this gallant speech?"

"You do," answered Josephine, laughing, "but as we must all wait for our rewards, I shall postpone yours till our wedding-day."

"When will that be?" asked Walter.

"In a month from now, I hope," answered Montant. "We have postponed it, I might almost say, from week to week; but I do not believe in abusing good fortune, or in trusting too long to the jealous gods."

"Superstitious people say, that a wedding several times postponed is postponed forever," said Walter; and, as his remark was not received with enthusiasm, he chirruped to a dog that had accompanied him on his visit, and left the room.

"Ours won't be postponed forever, will it, darling?" cried Josephine, the tears starting to her eyes.

"No," he answered, firmly. "Not unless Heaven puts in a veto."

"Mrs. Fatman ought to be home by this time," said Mr. Going, in the dining-room, to Walter, who had found his sister communing with herself in solitude, wandering about the grounds, and accompanied her home.

The door opened, and Josephine appeared on the arm of her lover, fresh and blooming as early morning.

"I want to say 'good-morning' to you, sir," she said, stepping up to Mr. Going's arm-chair, and touching his forehead with her lips. Carriage wheels were heard out doors, and the heavy footfalls of Mr. Fatman sounded through the hall, as he came down-stairs to greet his wife. Before any of the gentlemen had determined whether to go to the door and welcome that pious lady on her return from divine service, or to be satisfied with permitting her husband to monopolize her, a confusion of noises reached the dining-room. Soon, Fatman opened the door, violently, and stood before them like one distraught—his eyes starting from their sockets, his features distorted with rage, and a cold perspiration on his fat face.

"She is gone!" he gasped.

"Who is gone?" cried Walter, jumping to his feet.

"My wife!" fairly shrieked Mr. Fatman, every fiber of his fat body quivering with excitement. "My wife! my wife! She has eloped!"

"Who with?"

"I don't know," answered the bereaved husband, breathlessly. "She went to church in the village, and before the service was over, came out and told Patrick to drive home alone, and to tell me that there was a letter for me in the drawer of her writing-desk. Here it is."

Walter glanced at it hurriedly. With a sneer he threw it back to Mr. Fatman, and said, disdainfully: "It does not say who your successor is; but I can tell you."

"Who is it?" roared Mr. Fatman, suddenly reddening till his countenance assumed the hue of a boiled lobster. "What is his name? Speak!"

"Antonio Stilletto."

He seemed to be staggered at the sound of the name; but recovering himself, said, tremulously,—

"Help me, gentlemen, help me to find them. I am like a perfect child."

"I am at your service," said Walter, calmly.

"You are my best friend, Walter."

"Come, let us be off at once."

"At once, at once!"

"Hand-in-hand for good this time," said Walter, maliciously, and they prepared hurriedly for their journey.

"We'll find her, won't we?" cried Fatman, in the heat of preparation.

"Of course we will."

"And bring her back?"

"If she will come," suggested Walter, coolly.

"Sir?"

"I mean what I say."

"You insult me, sir. You wrong—"

"Nonsense!" interrupted the other, who in spite of their recent reconciliation did not care to be very sparing of his late bitter enemy. "You are as silly as most gentlemen of your age; your wife runs away, and you imagine

that if you can only catch her, she will be suddenly infatuated with you again and be willing to return."

"She will, she will!"

"Did she absquatulate, or was she stolen?"

"Well—but—"

"But still you expect her to return, willingly? A queer notion."

"Let me only see her, and all will be right, or I'll get a divorce this very week."

"That would be harrowing to her feelings, to judge by her late action."

"But let me only catch him!" cried Mr. Fatman, indulging in a pugilistic dance around the room.

"Only let us!" Walter joined in, taking a mocking part in the performance.

"Come on!" cried Fatman, puffing and furious.

"Come on is the word," roared Walter, "and damned be he, et cetera."

CHAPTER III.

FRESH COMPLICATIONS.

"Where thou shalt live, till we can find a time
To blaze your marriage, reconcile your friends."
ROMEO AND JULIET.

"Ernest," said Josephine to our hero, "I am well enough to travel, and it would look like abusing the hospitality of our friends to stay longer. I would not for the world impose on their kindness, particularly just now, because they might think, you know—"

"What might they think, baby?"

"They might think that since you and I rendered them a great service in the time of the greatest trouble and danger—"

"Do not distress yourself on that point, Josephine; I have succeeded in making that burden of gratitude as light as possible under the circumstances, and I do not think Mr. Going considers the loan I made him as more than a becoming act of natural gratitude on my part. Besides, fortune has favored all our operations in so great, I may say in an almost wonderful manner, that we can already predict the time when we can repay the money to you. I do not believe the profits of the firm were ever so large as they have been since its credit and standing were suddenly re-established by our timely aid. Their former customers are returning to us, and besides the prosperity of a large legitimate business, every venture that we undertake seems certain to coin gold under our hands."

"All because it is you that manage affairs!" she said, proudly, and with the air of an oracle.

"Since, by rights, a wife should have a good opinion of her husband, I will allow you to think so," he replied, laughing.

They were sitting together on the piazza of the Priory, for a premature summer day made the air soft and warm. A servant approached, and handed Mrs. Van Strom a letter.

"From Bella," she said, breaking the seal.

Montant watched her as she perused it, and marked how the color mounted to her face.

In an excited—almost angry manner, she handed him the note, and he read the following:—

"DEAR JOSEPHINE:—

"It seems that the hand of fate has decided to throw you into the bosom of your present hosts. If you find them desirous of a protracted stay, I would suggest that you had better enjoy yourself at the Priory a little while longer, as I am *house-cleaning*, and can not offer you the comforts or the pleasures you are now enjoying. Perhaps Mr. Montant will agree with me that it is better to defer your return until after the wedding, whenever that may be."

"Your faithful sister,
"BELLA."

Josephine, in turn, observed him closely until he finished the note, and he did not attempt to disguise his disapproval and vexation.

"I declare," said Josephine, "if this was not written in Bella's round handwriting, I would never believe she could have written to me so cold and disagreeable a letter."

"Well, we can't help it now," he replied, in a peculiar tone.

"Can it be that you prefer to remain here? That in spite of all our vows and our approaching marriage, there is something in your heart which ties you to this spot, to this family—*to some one besides myself?*"

She had clasped her hands, and looked up to him imploringly. He replied, almost sternly:—

"There is one duty you seem to have forgotten, and upon it all other duties are based. It is *confidence.* If you wish to preserve my affection and loyalty to you, let me never again hear a question like this, or discover in you a shadow of such feelings as prompted it. I believe that she who doubts loves perfectly no longer."

He arose, angry and perturbed. Miserably frightened, she threw her arms around him, and implored his forgiveness.

"Bella is the cause of it all," he said, not at all modified. "I expected that the simplicity of her mind would keep her from such suspicions and hints as are contained in that letter. As it is, I can not help seeing that she has estranged herself from us in a manner that hardly admits of an effectual reconciliation."

Josephine was unhappy for the rest of the day, and though she did her best to make him forget her ill-timed speech of the morning, while he endeavored to be as affectionate as of old, there was a something between them which was not there before, and they both knew it.

In this unpleasant frame of mind we find him sauntering alone through the park. Though night was fast approaching, he walked to the extreme point of the island; though the dark clouds were hanging low over the blackening waters, he walked along the beach, where jagged rocks were strewn like old weird tombstones.

His soul, agitated with conflicting emotions, took refuge in memory. Looking out over the waves which broke at his feet, the song of the great German poet, Heine, came to his mind, and he quoted to himself:—

"Oh, solve me the riddle of life!
That torturing riddle of old!
Oh! tell me what signifies man?"

　　*　　*　　*　　*　　*　　*　　*

"The billows are breaking high up on the beach,
The winds blow fresh and the waves flow fast,
The stars are shining, unfeeling and cold,
And a fool may await the answer!"

But the powers of the night answered him; in his solitude, the voices of the dark waves spoke to him. He listened, and was answered:—

"Man is the crowning work of the Almighty, and we are created to struggle through life, and conquer the storms and dangers of our existence, just as the tree vegetates into its prime, healing the wound where a limb has been lopped, and resisting the destructive storm. When a tree stands with its leafy head proudly erect, it has fulfilled its mission, and when a human soul conquers the trials of life's rough changes, that soul has done its duty and the Creator is proud of his work. This is the teaching of nature."

"But what sphere is assigned to me? Shall I follow the dictates of my heart, or the cold conclusions of reason. Which points out the path of *duty?* May not human reason be mistaken, and through a mistaken view of duty lead to ultimate mischief? May it not be safer to trust to the heart alone?"

He retraced his steps toward the house, and from afar, the lighted windows guided him through the quickly increasing darkness. Sounds of music greeted him, and as he approached, the front of the grand old mansion, with its columns, broad steps, and substantial balustrades, impressed him with the stateliness of an old château.

He entered. Through the thick walls and closed doors the sounds of music had reached him but indistinctly. He now heard Jessie's sweet, sympathetic voice singing an old ballad —a German ballad. He listened a moment, and then stepped softly into the drawing-room. The young lady, though not alone, seemed to be singing for her own amusement, for her father, interested in his newspaper, at the other end of the room, as well as Josephine, reclining on a sofa, seemed unconscious of the fair performance of the fairer performer.

"If I were a sensual man, when it comes to the question of a love which is to last through life, and as long after life as Heaven permits, I would choose that Venus on the sofa, did the choice lay between these two. But innocence and purity alone can kindle true ethereal love in a man's breast, and though, perhaps, the woman is not born who holds a fairer virtue than Josephine—"

At this moment the widow changed her position, and noticing him, arose with a flushed face and an anxious, tenderly reproachful look in her eye.

"Where have you been, Ernest?" she whispered. "Oh, if you knew what a miserable day I have spent!"

Jessie had finished her song, and when she

left the piano, she cast a casual, indifferent look on the lovers,—then joined her father, and drawing a chair to sit near him, said:—

"I wish Walter would return. I am nervous about him, for who knows what bad men he may meet. Besides, I do not feel safe here without him."

Montant followed her with his eyes, and felt mortified at her last speech. Josephine clung to him, awaiting his answer, and with a great effort to speak kindly, he answered:—

"You must not be too exacting, Josephine! I have been out of sorts to-day, so give me until to-morrow to become myself again. I will be all right to-morrow. And now let me go. I must talk business with Mr. Going."

She looked at him in astonishment; but he had already left her side. He read in her face how deeply his slight and unintentional rebuff had wounded her, so he led her into the hall, and as she passively allowed him to kiss her (she did not seek or return it as usual), he whispered:—

"You are a child. You must not be so sensitive, or how shall we ever get through life, which does not always keep a man loving and smooth-tempered. Excuse me to-day, and to-morrow I will make up for my ill-humor."

"Good-night, then. I am going to my room. I don't feel strong."

He bent over to kiss her "good-night," when her dejected, apathetic manner suddenly changed, and throwing her arms around him, she burst into tears.

"Josephine," he murmured, with surprise and annoyance, "Josephine, do not take my whims to heart. Surely, I have not been guilty of unkindness to you. Not one woman in a thousand would have found cause for sorrow in any thing that I have said to you."

He led her gently up-stairs to the door of her room, and they parted with mutual assurances of love; she to remain sleepless with an aching head and heart for many hours,—he to commune angrily with himself, pacing the hall, while Jessie was talking to her father in the drawing-room.

"'*Nul le rose sans épines*,'" he quoted. "If a man finds a wife who loves him passionately with all her warm and sensitive heart, he must expect to be scolded and accused of heaven knows what nonsense whenever he frowns or speaks an impatient word. 'No rose without a thorn.'"

Then he stepped into the drawing-room to talk about business with Mr. Going.

No sooner had he taken a seat near them, than Miss Jessie arose to leave the room.

"You had better remain, mademoiselle," he said, without looking up from some papers he was examining. "Your father has always confided in you, and I believe has consulted you on some occasions. What we mean to discuss to-night regards some property which your father desires to transfer to your name; so, you see, you are interested."

"My advice, when given, has never been followed," she replied, arresting her steps without condescending to turn back, "and I am tired of exerting my wisdom to no purpose; so, good-night!"

"As you wish, of course!" said Montant.

"The only desire I would express before resigning my position of confidential adviser to the house of Going," she said, languidly, "is that all debts and burdensome obligations be discharged as soon as possible. I think nothing should be given to me until we are relieved from the humiliating debt of gratitude which we now owe to an outside party."

"You owe it to me alone," said Montant, quickly, but repented the words when she replied, quietly,—

"No matter to whom we owe it. I told papa, long ago, that I can't bear to be under obligations to any one, and instead of consenting to have property transferred to me at present, I would far rather be permitted to work with my hands until that disagreeable, odious debt be discharged." With these words, she left the room.

Unobserved by the old gentleman, who seemed vexed and nervous at his daughter's speech, Montant changed color and thought, bitterly,—

"She actually hates me. Calls me an *outside party*, and my loan—*odious!* Her pride inspires her with dislike toward those to whom she owes gratitude. Her injustice is a strange reward for my friendship."

CHAPTER IV.

A VISIT TO THE GREAT PHILOSOPHER.

"Oh, how comes it that thou art thus stranged from
thyself?" COMEDY OF ERRORS.

MONTANT'S conversation concerning matters of business resulted in his leaving the Priory very early next morning to allow himself the requisite time to attend to what they had decided should be done, .so Josephine, who was not dressed in time to see him before he started, spent another miserable day.

He came back from the city quite late, and found that after an absence of three days, Walter and Mr. Fatman had returned from their search after the eloped lady.

"Ernest," said Walter, "we have company in the house, to wit: our two old friends, who have recently received the distinguished title of the Damon and Pythias of New York, because they are inseparable companions. You may guess that we have the honor of entertaining Faro and Wheeler within these justly proud walls. But, eat your dinner, we are through ours long ago, and then join Fatman, father, and me, in the drawing-room, while Jessie and Mrs. Van Strom may amuse the two noble youths in the parlor. We have a great deal to report, and are waiting your presence to begin."

"Have you found her?"

"No; and yes. Go in and eat your dinner!"

And as Josephine was already in the parlor entertaining one of the noble youths, Montant again failed to see her alone. Shortly after his dinner, he was listening to Walter's account in the library, while Fatman sat by, mute and pale—a miserable man.

"That Stilletto is a genius," said Walter. "In spite of our most untiring efforts, we have lost all tracks of the couple. It seems that Madam met him before church was out, and they drove off in a light-wagon together. Where that wagon went to is a mystery. We could not trace it at all, and so went on to New York, quite despondent of success. There we spent a day consulting the police authorities, and this morning, as Fatman was driving me home from town, we passed a cottage situated about twelve miles from here, near the suburbs of the city. Who do you suppose was smoking his pipe in front of the cottage, Ernest?"

"Well, who was it?"

"Muller. The great philosopher. Stilletto's most intimate friend."

Montant listened attentively.

"It occurred to me," continued Walter, that Stilletto, like the majority of rogues, must have a confidant—"

"Pardon me," interrupted our hero, "I am quite certain that Stilletto never had a real confidant in his life. I am convinced that Muller was totally ignorant of the truth about John Van Strom's murder."

"Wait a moment," continued Walter. "We made a halt, and I entered into conversation with him. He said that he had bought the cottage, having saved enough to pay for so modest a home, and that he lived there in peace with his beloved wife and blooming children. When I commenced to question him about Stilletto, he branched off into elaborate nonsense, always avoiding a direct answer to my questions. While indulging in his crazy rhetoric, he watched Mr. Fatman like a cat, and something in his twinkling eye told us that he knew all about the elopement, though we had never mentioned it at all. Suddenly, he said to me, 'Mr. Going, I understand that Mr. Montant is staying at your house. To-morrow is set aside as a day of fasting and prayer, will you tell Mr. Montant to pay me a visit to-morrow, and, Mr. Fatman, will you come also? Come to August Muller, gentlemen, and August Muller will help you.'

"I inquired whether I would be permitted to join you, and having received a gracious affirmative, we promised to come to-morrow; you, Fatman, and I."

After some consultation, they arose and joined the party in the parlor.

"Gentlemen," said Walter, "we three intend to have a ride on horseback to-morrow. Mr. Fatman has not yet removed all his horses from our stables, so we have the necessary outfit to be able to extend an invitation to you, if you would like to be of the party. Only we will be obliged to part company with you for perhaps half-an-hour, or may be an hour, as we have business to attend to at a place about twelve miles down the road. What do you say?"

Messieurs Faro and Wheeler signified their satisfaction, provided the ladies would join them, and Miss Jessie declared, with animation,—

"Oh, yes! I am going. I would love to ride with such a large escort."

"How is it with you, Mrs. Van Strom?"

"I would like to go," she replied, coloring slightly, "but I have not mounted a horse since I was a little girl, and I think I will keep Mr. Going company."

"That's right," said the old gentleman, taking her hand affectionately. "We can take care of ourselves, can't we, Mrs. Van Strom?"

So the party was arranged, and all were busy discussing who should ride this or that horse, while Mr. Faro suggested that one of his pair, now in the stables, should be mustered into service. Josephine only was quiet and depressed. Montant caught an imploring look of her blue eyes, and, understanding it, followed her when she soon after left the room.

"Ernest," she asked, when they met alone in the library, "must you go, too?"

"Yes, darling," he answered, tenderly. His heart smote him when he saw her unhappiness and deep dejection.

"Is it *necessary* that you should? We could have such a happy day to-morrow all alone, and I have so much to tell you," she pleaded.

Since she was one of the few who knew of Mrs. Fatman's flight, she was able to tell her Walter's adventures as he had just heard them, and though to be without him all that holiday to which she had looked forward with delightful anticipation, gave her much pain, she could not help recognizing the necessity.

"Muller would not send for me unless the matter was important. Who knows but what there may be more in store for us to-morrow, than the tracing of that false woman!"

"Who knows?"

*   *   *   *   *   *

Early next morning a scene presented itself calculated to gladden the eye of any jovial gentleman. In front of the house was a gay assemblage of fine horses and bustling grooms, and the equestrians busy with their preparations appeared on the piazza to give the grooms final instructions concerning buckles, bridles, and stirrups. In the center of these stamping, neighing, impatient nags, stood Miss Jessie's horse, awaiting its mistress with dignity, disdaining in calm superiority to join the pranks of the others.

It was a lovely day—the sun bright and warm, the air clear and fresh, the sky unclouded. The evergreen trees looked bright and summer-like, while even the bare branches of the others glittered in the sun and looked less desolate.

Mr. Going came down from his room to see the party set off, and now the knot of gentlemen unties itself to make way respectfully for Miss Jessie, who stepped out on the piazza, looking like the blooming queen of the spring day. Montant, who had already taken leave of Josephine up-stairs, remained in the background when Jessie appeared. Once more did his heart beat violently, when the beautiful girl descended with all her bewitching charms, her graceful blue habit, the color and the bright laugh on her lovely face, and her riding-hat with a gray feather sitting saucily on her rich raven tresses, loosely confined in a long, gracefully-arranged net.

He turned away. She had not noticed him, and he was the last of the gentlemen as they escorted her to her horse in a body. Walter lifted her into the saddle. A few moments of bustle and merry confusion, and away they went, Jessie in front, Faro, Wheeler, and Walter close to her, while Montant, who had been used to the saddle from childhood, curbed his impatient horse to keep pace with Mr. Fatman's heavy cob, imported from England on purpose to carry his bulky weight with ease and safety.

After a sharp ride, they reached a point on the road where Walter commanded a halt, which soon brought the horses' heads together, and a consultation ensued.

"Well," said Mr. Wheeler, "since you three must tear yourselves away, I mean to propose—that is, if Miss Jessie is willing—that we ride on to my father's place, not two miles off. I know my sister Sallie will be—ah—delighted to see you, Miss Going, and if Walter says there is nothing—ah—improper, and as a rest won't hurt the horses—I do, in fact, invite you to come; and the others can call for us when they get through."

All agreed, and a moment later Montant watched them ride off at a hand-gallop, Jessie in the midst, faithfully supported on the right and left by her old admirers.

"Talk about vanity," he muttered. "I do not blame any man for aspiring to the vanity of showing the world such a wife as that! By heaven! she is a perfect queen, and he who possesses her,—the first and only man privileged to kiss those proud lips, and receive the homage that meets her at every turn as half *his own due*,—he will be a lucky man. I wonder whether one of those old beaux will not get her finally, stupid and shallow though they be. I don't think she can love any one, so I suppose she will take it into her head some day to throw herself away, and she will easily succeed."

They reached the cottage described by Walter as the philosopher's home. A neat, well-kept plat of grass covered the slight ascent from the road to Mr. Muller's modest door, and there they beheld the great thinker, basking in the sunlight that shone in under the roof of a neat porch. He had his beer before him on a little round table, and from his pipe ascended the smoke-wreaths of peace, and completed the majestic tranquillity of Mr. August Muller.

"Welcome to my house, welcome to my heart and to my home," he said, rising. "Rarely does August Muller, in the seclusion from the world, which he has of late chosen, enjoy the gratification of receiving so distinguished a trio. Here we have the young merchant, with the good old name (shaking hands with Walter). Here we have the young merchant with an old head (greeting our hero), and here we have the tower of strength and substantiality, bodily, financially, and characteristically, if I may so express myself."

"You may," answered Fatman; "but let us find a place to tie our horses."

"This post is not bulky, but it is true wood," said the philosopher. "Truth is mighty, though it be slim (with a glance at Mr. Fatman's corpulence and at his own meagerness); but to come to business; let me ask you, Mr. Going, and you, Mr. Fatman, to content yourselves with these two chairs, while I take this young gentleman into the house, to speak with him upon matters of some importance."

When they found themselves alone in the parlor, Muller addressed our hero in a whisper :—

"Will you lend me an ear, if I make one preliminary remark before entering upon this sad subject of Mrs. Fatman's strange hallucination, and her unjustifiable elopement with my *late* friend, Stilletto ?"

"So, you know all about it ?" cried Montant. "I do."

"Have they gone very far; and is she determined to stick to her vile paramour ?"

"Let me suggest that the latter of your questions be reversed; and permit me to consider that you have asked me, *Will he stick to her ?*"

Montant looked at the lawyer inquiringly.

"It is even so," said the philosopher. "The question is, will he stick to her who has been another's wife ? It is rare that men fall truly in love with others' wives. Generally, such love is based upon a passion which my good taste forbids me to name. I pretend to be able to prove that even a *widow* can not, and should not, so fascinate—"

"Enough of that," cried Montant, flushed and angry. "Come to business."

"But I must first ask you this question. Are you convinced that August Muller is totally innocent of any knowledge, conniving, or assisting in the murder of John Van Strom ?"

He asked the question in a trembling voice. A feeling nobler than his wretched conceit prompted him, and the "August Muller" came with a sad—almost anguished—tone, from his lips; not at all like his usual sonorous pomposity.

Montant was moved to acknowledge to him his convictions. The fact was apparent, and had been clearly developed in the inquiries made by the authorities, after Stilletto was proved the murderer, that Muller was perfectly innocent of the murder, or of any previous knowledge of it.

"I thank you," said the philosopher, and his face was distorted by a more honest than fascinating twitching around the corners of his homely mouth. "I am truly grateful to you for this satisfaction. It is the only pleasure I have enjoyed for a long while, Mr. Montant. I once hated you; but you see, I am poor now, and poor men seek every one's friendship."

"I thought you owned this house ?"

"I do, sir; but I must sell it again. My creditors have taken a great fancy to cultivate my acquaintance, Mr. Montant, and the enthusiastic manner in which they admire my house when they call to see me, is a subject for any student of human nature."

The philosopher looked very much crestfallen, and as the twitching of his mouth, by some physiognomical mechanism, forced the tears into his little red eyes, Montant felt heartily sorry for him.

"Well, what do you want of me?" he asked, not wishing to yield to his pity for a man he knew to be, if not a criminal, at least a very questionable character.

"I sent for you," replied Mr. Muller, "because you are the most reliable man among those who interest themselves in this elopement. I want to obtain your word that I am to receive a thousand dollars if I bring Mrs. Fatman face to face with the man of her previous choice; in fact, with her husband."

Montant seemed to consider the matter.

"My study of human nature," continued the philosopher, "has always dwelt with peculiar interest upon the subject of *self-preservation*. It is strange how this heaven-born faculty, or instinct, or, if I may so express it, this purely subjective mental moving power is connected with all our nobler attributes. Honesty, piety, virtue, self-control, moderation, abstemiousness, and all their train of dependent virtues. Thus you see that I combine my instinct of self-preservation with the desire to be honest, and help my neighbors. What say you to the thousand dollars?"

"Honesty is its own reward, I have heard say."

"A mere perversion of an old proverb, I assure you. Now—"

"You shall have the money," interrupted our hero, who knew Mr. Fatman's anxiety to behold his wife would not hesitate at such an obstacle. "And, now, *where is she?*"

"I am to receive that sum whether Mr. Fatman induces her to return home, or not?"

"Yes."

"When? Now?" he asked, greedily.

"No. As soon as he has met her; and that must be in a place where he has control over her movements."

The philosopher nodded.

"You see I trust *you*," he said. "I wanted to deal with some one whose word would be reliable. Besides, I feel like a happier, aye, and a *better* man, since you, that have suffered so much from Stilletto, have acknowledged to me that I am innocent."

"Where is she?"

"Here, in this house."

Montant started.

"And Stilletto?" he asked.

"Away; I don't know where," replied the philosopher. "But send Mr. Fatman in, and promise to remain outside, to see that I get my thousand dollars."

"I will give you my check for it if all is as you say."

"I am satisfied."

So our hero went to the front door, and without further explanation, requested Mr. Fatman to step in.

Walter and Montant waited half-an-hour—an hour. The philosopher joined them, reporting that "they are engaged in the deepest kind of soul-engaging discourse"

Finally, Mr. Fatman came out of the house. Muller, with some tact, withdrew. Hot tears rolled down the afflicted husband's round

cheeks, and sobs agitated him, so that it was some time before he could tell them,—

"She loves the scoundrel. She consented to this interview, because she wanted us to understand each other. She has robbed me of thousands, and has turned the money over to Stilletto. She says the rack could not make her disclose his whereabouts; but—hear this, gentlemen! She means to rejoin him unless I prefer to take her, who has robbed and dishonored me, back to my house."

"Cool," cried Walter.

"She says she married me for my money only—I married her from love!"

Mr. Fatman was deeply affected.

"A good riddance, *I* should say," muttered Walter.

"She says that I need not expect her ever to love me, even if I choose to receive her again, and that only her respect for decency induces her to consent to it."

"Do you suppose this cool effrontery is natural to her character, or has her sweet friend probably taught her all this nice lesson?"

"I don't know. I do not understand her. I can not and will not believe that she was always as bad as this at heart."

"Couldn't you have used your riding-whip in there to advantage?" asked Walter, pacing the lawn.

"No. I do not know why I felt nothing like anger—only intolerable grief as she spoke thus to me."

"Now, here we have an instance of the truth that no human being is entirely hard-hearted," soliloquized our hero. "Who would have thought *Fatman* capable of this?"

"Now, gentlemen, what shall I do?" asked the disconsolate man.

"Let her go!" cried Walter.

"I have children by her!"

"Your fatherly duty compels you to keep them away from such a mother."

"My name will be dishonored!"

"Better your name than your home, your house, your bed, and good conscience!" cried Walter.

"Well, I will—but, though a higher power will punish *her*, if I catch Stilletto—"

"Don't kill him," interrupted Walter. "If Madame has only tenacity enough to stick to him well, she will be quite sufficient punishment. As far as the money is concerned—is it cash, or checks, or bonds, or what?"

"Mostly railroad bonds, I only happened to carry in my pocket-book over Sunday. I had not thought of them since."

"Then it is possible to recover a portion. The detectives are on his track any way to earn the ten thousand dollars reward offered for his apprehension as the murderer of John Van Strom. If you advertise the numbers of the bonds—"

"She took the leaf out of my book where I had a list of the numbers, so that is impossible. That devil's whelp told her how to make all safe."

"A wonderful fellow is this Stilletto," exclaimed Walter.

And so Mr. Fatman got rid of his wife.

After another conversation with Mrs. Fatman, her husband turned his cob's head homeward, alone and in deep melancholy, while the others rode on to find the rest of the party at Mr. Wheeler's house. This family belonged to the old settlers, very nice people, who abound in Westchester County, and they knew how to entertain their guests so well that it was late before the latter found themselves on their homeward road.

Miss Jessie, surrounded by her four cavaliers, directed the order of the march.

"We have only a few minutes of good daylight left," she said, to Mr. Faro, "so let us have some excitement before darkness sets in. I propose that Mr. Wheeler and Mr. Montant have a race from here to where yonder tree marks the foot of the hill. On, gentlemen!" she cried with animation. "The winner shall kiss my hand."

"Well, I suppose that Mademoiselle must be humored," said Montant, who was riding behind her.

"Mademoiselle is accustomed to being humored," she replied, turning toward him, and laughing merrily. "Now, then! Walter and I will be judges."

Off they started. Montant had so far had trouble in restraining his horse, which now darted off with frantic delight.

"How well Ernest rides," exclaimed Walter, in honest admiration.

"Splendidly," corroborated his sister, with sparkling eyes. "Let's after them."

They galloped on, and were near enough to the tree to distinguish Montant as the winner.

"You may touch your lips to my hand, you most fortunate of knights," said Miss Jessie, blushing considerably through her hilarity, and proceeded to extract said hand from her riding gauntlet. He rode up close to her, and bending low, that no one else could understand his words, he said,—

"*You* do not like to be under obligations. *I* do not like to receive rewards."

He dropped her little hand, and resumed his old place by Walter, just behind her.

Miss Jessie flushed with vexation.

For awhile they rode at a rapid pace, which the lady selected, and in consequence but few words were exchanged. The sun was down, and the new moon stood bright in the sky. Half the homeward road had yet to be passed, when Miss Jessie checked her horse, and said:—

"Gentlemen, I think I have done my duty to you as your hostess, and have entertained you splendidly all day. You must now excuse me. I want to speak to our dumb friend, whom Walter seems quite incapable of cheering into a sign of life."

So saying, she deliberately reined in her horse to Montant's side, and Walter, accustomed from boyhood to humor his sister, rode on with the disconsolate Wheeler and the invective Faro.

"Mr. Montant," said Jessie, "I have been, and am still, a wayward, spoiled child. The hard lessons of life found me unprepared to meet them as I should, and they have perverted many of my better impulses. Especially in speaking and acting when with my friends, on trivial occasions, have I been more than

silly—often very, very wrong. Will you forgive me?"

This was one of her moods—the only mood worthy of her real character. Her noble heart, her good sense, and generous disposition, spoke when she accosted him in this strain, and the maidenly modesty, the holy purity of the girl, lent her a fascination he knew of old, and no vow, no duty, no strength of will could enable him to shake it off now.

He answered her with a fervor to which she listened with downcast eyes and half-averted face.

They spoke of the days that were gone. Of the Priory as it was when old Mr. Van Strom held his crazy revelries—of the jolly times they had enjoyed in the Fifth Avenue house, and the merry dances they had danced together. The moon, which stood high and shone into their hearts, had before this been the only witness of many an earnest, many an enthusiastic exchange of thoughts between them. Their conversation turned upon the deeper and holier subjects of life, and Montant, inspired by the genius of the hour, spoke with an eloquence he rarely felt disposed to develop. And she replied with all the warmth of her young heart, filled with a sense of the intelligence, the worth, and the power of the man at her side. Completely lost in each other, they rode on, while their horses seemed to understand that the riders were in no hurry, and crept on slowly as docile lambs. Her rich and manifold character, her loyal and devout soul, and her warm, generous heart, disclosed themselves to him, while she realized his whole excellence. Once she had loved him, but never had she understood him as to-day. It was an hour in which they forgot the whole world; it was an hour to remain in their memories for ever!

"I wish," he said, as they approached the Priory bridge, "I wish I had always known you as I know you now. My confidence in human nature would have suffered less."

"'Tis woman's part to increase that confidence, by showing that human nature is worthy of trust and belief."

"If I had always known you as well as this," he began. "If I had read you better—" He ceased.

"What, then?" she asked, in a whisper, trembling violently. "Would you have left us in the hour of need? Would you have remained, out of friendship for me?"

"Yes, I would," he answered. He felt a strange dizziness, and had to gather all his strength to retain his self-possession. A few moments passed in silence, when the horses, with a sudden affection for the stable, gave a jump, and dashed over the Priory bridge.

They rode through the woods.

"Why, the others have been out of sight a long while," said Miss Jessie, anxiously.

"Yes, too long," he said, quite as anxiously; and added, in a tone she could not or would not understand, "*Josephine will be worried.*"

"Walter always plays me such tricks," she exclaimed, with a feeling akin to alarm, and giving her horse the lash.

When they rode up to the house, they found

that the three gentlemen, who, instigated by Walter, had spurred on, were, indeed, in the parlor, having sent their horses to the stable some time before. Walter came out to meet them. Montant called out for him to help his sister from her horse, saying that he could not hold his own nag and attend her also. He forgot that the groom was in waiting.

They stepped into the hall. Without turning to the right or left, Jessie ran up-stairs. Later she sent an apology that a headache would not permit her to descend.

As Montant entered, he saw Josephine. As he approached, he noticed that she was pale, and trembling, and now, in the glaring light, she could see his flushed face and unsteady, feverish eye. She watched him in spell-bound misery for a moment, and then, rising with an effort, greeted him as usual, though not quite so enthusiastically. She did not say a word about his late return and in *whose* company; and he, grateful for her forbearance, devoted himself to her all the evening, and they tried to be once more the lovers of old!

CHAPTER V.

SIMONETTA'S INHERITANCE.

"Nature her custom holds,
Let shame say what it will."
HAMLET.

THE flimsy ornaments adorning the ceiling of the Italian dance-hall do not bear a deathlier yellow hue, than the face of the countess, as she lies on a faded lounge where they have carried her, in a sudden attack of illness. Her wicked heart is fighting its last struggle, her wrinkled, sallow face, shows the contortions which forebode the end.

In one convulsive hand, she holds the manuscript of the "Maniac's Story;" in the other, she clutches the newspaper report of the "Horrible tragedy in a New-England mad-house," where the end of her lover, Judge Bates, is recorded with all the sensational extravagance of a reporter, and yet only a faithful record of the terrible event.

She was comparing the two, and laughing at the analogy. It had been her last laugh, for, in the very midst of the exultation which filled her Satanic soul, the avenging angel had sent a thunderbolt and felled her to the earth.

The dancing-girls stand around. They are not attired in their glittering, evening costumes, for the sun has not set, and the afternoon hangs dull and leaden over the scene, showing, in its blank light, the creatures of sin and the abode of vice in all their repulsiveness, in their natural decay. The wanton faces have lost their leer; appalled and frightened, they stand about their dying mistress; not a tear softens their hollow eyes, only fear—terror, and the knowledge that *they*, also, must come to this. And, besides these women, other persons are in the room and surround the countess. They are police officers—they have come to close up the den. They have come, to find that, in an-

other hour, it will be closed without their aid; for, as soon as the countess has breathed her last foul breath unto the world, her companions and followers will scatter to the winds. Poor winds!

But, there is one face in the crowd which tells a different story. By the side of the ragged couch, a woman kneels, weeping. The officers ask her how it is, that she seems to bewail the loss of one so depraved, and what their relationship has been.

"She has been kind to me!" answers Simonetta Marini, and truly, in this place and associations, there is enough relationship expressed in those words. Yes, the withered hag had been kind to her, and now her glazing eye rests with fond sorrow upon the still attractive face of the girl. Here is the "tender spot" of which the countess told Martin Bates. And if a prayer can rise in that heart, it is in thanking God, whose awful presence is before her now, for the mercy of bringing to her death-bed the one creature upon whom had centered all that was left in her of love and tenderness.

The countess, speechless and almost paralyzed, made a desperate effort for some purpose which seemed to weigh heavily in her fast-departing soul. With great difficulty she made Simonetta understand, and the girl opened the dying woman's dress, and procured two documents, sealed, and addressed to "Simonetta Marini," which the hag had secreted near her bosom. This accomplished, the countess, with a gasp and a grimace, gave up the ghost.

The police officers surrounded the corpse, while the dancing-girls stole a last and awe-stricken view of their late mistress. Only Simonetta bewailed the hag's death, and her hand closed the stiffening eyelids. Then the girl realized with a pang and a shudder, that she was lonely and deserted in such a crowd as this, and she tried to make her way to the door. Half-bewildered and truly affected, she seemed scarcely conscious of her movements, when a friendly hand touched her shoulder. She looked up, and saw Martin Bates. The old man's face almost expressed the resignation of despair, but a pitying, friendly light shone in his eye as he said, simply, "Come with me!"

She hesitated a moment, and then followed him, willingly. They reached the street, and forced their way through the multitude of queer people fast assembling to gaze upon the remains of the countess—the news having spread in an instant over the Fourth Ward.

Martin (walking hurriedly). "Let us get to some quiet place as soon as possible; I have much to say to you."

The girl. "It seems wonderful to me that you should seek me out, after what has happened between us."

Martin. "All is forgotten,—all forgiven. I am now alone in the world, alone with the burden of my memory, which is haunted by hideous shapes of sin and misery and horror."

Simonetta (bitterly). "And you have come back to me because no one else would keep you company!"

Martin. "Not so. I have come to you because you are the one living being that is not associated with my shame and crimes, the one being whom I can look in the eyes and say, honestly: 'Old Martin Bates has been a friend and a comforter to you.'"

Simonetta. "It is true. No one can deny it; and as I also am without a kindly being to help me, except yourself, I will once more confide in you, and consult you about what is to become of me."

They reached a place where abrupt stairs led down from the street, into one of those dens known as "music halls," and by mutual consent they descended. The rooms were nearly deserted at this hour, and they easily found a corner where they could converse without fear of eavesdropping.

"Let us examine these papers which the countess gave me before her soul fled to the clouds," said the girl, producing one envelope, upon which was marked, "Simonetta's inheritance, number 1," and a second bearing the title, "Simonetta's inheritance, number 2."

Martin (having opened the first, greedily). "This is her last will. She leaves all to you, her house, her money in bank, her bonds, stocks, and all other property. I knew she must have saved something, but I did not think it would be as much. Simonetta, you are almost rich."

The girl (disdainfully). "Open the second envelope."

Martin. "Here is a letter addressed to Antonio Stilletto, and you are directed to read it before delivering it. Listen: 'Son and villain, if ever you dare to touch a hair of Simonetta's, after I am dead, my ghost will haunt the life out of your black heart. Mark this: a curse be upon all you undertake, withered and blighted will be all your future life, and eternal damnation shall receive you, unless you leave her unmolested, unscathed by your foul revenge or pestilent approaches of any sort. But before you die, you'll suffer tenfold the tortures of hell, for my spirit will be like the furies of old, and you'll not have an hour's rest unless you obey my last command. You knew me in life. You know that I was not to be turned from any purpose. Know, then, that after death I will keep my resolves with tenfold vigor, so heed what I say, because dead or alive, I am determined to save that girl from you. Fear me, obey me, or go hang—'"

Martin ceased.

Simonetta (after a pause). "The second inheritance is more a kindness to me than the first!"

Martin. "Oh, no! Nothing like money! nothing like money!"

Simonetta. "What is the blessing of money to me if *he* kills me."

Martin. "Do you fear that?"

Simonetta. "I did fear it until I read this admonishing message."

Martin. "So you think that he will be frightened."

Simonetta. "Most miserably frightened. The countess knew him, knew the weakness of his superstition, and she has drawn a circle of witchcraft around me which will protect me. May the Virgin reward her for it."

Martin. "Still I would not suppose that one so hardened in sin should be so much the slave of the most miserable of human weaknesses."

Simonetta. "What bad man is not?"

Martin (with a sigh). "I am bad enough, but—"

"You are not bad," cried the girl, suddenly, and stretching both her hands out toward him. "Let the world and the law say what they will, *I* say you are a good, kind, generous man. Take this money. You are poor and old. I do not want it as much as you."

He looked at her intently for a moment. His hard, square, cadaverous face softened with emotion, and a ray of hope. With tears streaming faster and faster down his bony cheeks, he said,—

"Simonetta, I found you a poor organ-grinder girl. I attempted to draw you away from the brink of the abyss whose hungry jaws were ravenous for another victim. You despised, betrayed me."

"But I was not ungrateful!" cried the girl.

"Betrayed me," repeated Martin, "but you can make it all up if you will go with me, away from this land of iniquity, away to the far hills of Scotland—"

"As your wife?" asked the girl, bewildered.

"As my wife, until a few short years shall free you."

"And do you know what I am?" cried Simonetta. "Do you forget that Stilletto—"

"I forget every thing—I forgive every thing. You have sinned—so have I. Neither can take the responsibility of forming any ties with pure and blameless people, without heaping another and far greater sin upon our heads. But let me tell you, Simonetta, that since we both know every crime which rests upon our consciences, we can best regain peace by uniting in the task of repentance and reform. Then do not hesitate. Let people talk as they will, let them sneer in derision, let the world continue to snarl at us like the wild beast—we will go among new people, seek a new world."

"When shall we go?" cried Simonetta, jumping to her feet.

"At once, at once! Oh, that old Martin should be happy once more."

"As soon as we can turn into hard money the inheritance of my benefactress?"

"Yes, yes. I also have realized a little fortune out of poor Eben's estate, so we are comfortable, all comfortable, my dear girl. I feel that my crimes, committed from brotherly love, which had grown into the infatuation of a madman, are all forgiven, and you also will leave behind you the dirt and dishonor which this vile town and that murderous Stilletto have cast upon you. Will you not, carissima?"

"If the Virgin lends a gracious ear to my prayers, she can cleanse the worst of us," replied Simonetta, devoutly.

CHAPTER VI.

A VOICE FROM HEINE.

"Shall I hear more, or shall I speak at this?"
ROMEO AND JULIET.

FOR several days Jessie kept her room, descending only for a short time in the middle of the day; though remaining longer when her father's business permitted him to spend the day with her. She was invisible when the gentlemen left the house in the morning, and when they returned from the city, she had already retired, pleading a continuation of headaches.

Montant was very busy for the week following the holiday described in a previous chapter, and his relations with Josephine remained the same as on that evening. They conversed constantly, but he was so much engrossed by business that he was more desirous of rest and entertainment than of the passionate love previously characterizing their private moments. Josephine was kinder and more studiously affectionate than ever, but through it all there appeared a languishing weariness in her look and manner. It was an important week for Going, Montant & Co., and at its close they repaid to the estate of John Van Strom, or rather to Josephine, the two hundred thousand dollars Montant had borrowed. He seemed relieved of a burden after the transaction had been completed, and Josephine was delighted with his animated spirits. For the first time since a cloud overshadowed the serenity of their affection, the subject of their marriage was discussed.

"No more postponement of that day," said Montant, more firmly than enthusiastically. "In ten days all will be fixed."

"Shall we stay here till then?" she asked, somewhat startled by his tone.

"As you desire, my darling!" he cried, more heartily than before. "I am yours already, and will follow your wishes in all such trivial matters."

"Well, then, let us have the wedding here, according to Mr. Going's pressing invitation. It will be a very quiet one. No show, or white dresses for me!"

Montant's face fell, but she failed to notice it, and they agreed that the wedding should be in ten days, at the Priory, and only a few of their most intimate friends were to be invited.

"Will Bella come?" asked Montant.

"I think so."

"It does not seem likely, from the tone of her letters."

"That tone will change when she sees —"

"What?"

"That we are really to be married, dear."

Sunday came, and Mr. Paradise, who had promised and postponed his visit, finally arrived. He brought Mr. Going a letter from a gentleman in New York, which he read carefully and with a thoughtful brow. The subject treated in the letter seemed very important and worthy of deep consideration, for his looks rested pensively upon his daughter, whose improved health permitted her to join the family again,

and then wandered with the same thoughtfulness to Montant and Josephine. Something occupied his mind which probably caused him many a doubt and struggle, and he was absentminded even during dinner, the time of all others when he was wont to be scrupulously attentive in his manners.

It was a Sunday dinner, so like the olden times, with the sunbeams dancing on the richly-papered walls, and the old air of refinement, elegance, and stateliness marking all that was done or spoken, always excepting Mr. Paradise, who sneered as usual at every one, though in truth his sarcasm was not so biting nor his sardonic taunts so bitter as of old.

"Walter seems to enjoy this new state of affairs," he said.

"Yes," replied that gentleman. "Fatman has now left us; but the port wine crust remains on the doors and the honeysuckle is on the walls. I will live and die in this place."

"A palatial residence, Mr. Going," said the hunchback, imitating Fatman. "But, speaking seriously, I would as soon have expected to see the dog kiss the cat, or a Prussian embrace a Frenchman, as to find you two reconciled. I thought the feud between you and my fat friend was too deep to be easily bridged over."

"When kind fortune smiles on a man already prepared for an old age embittered by poverty, perhaps disgrace, he is readily disposed to forgiveness," replied the old gentleman. "Although friends spring up to greet the fortunate as quickly as they forsake the unlucky, yet they are always welcome. To-day I feel as if I never had cause to complain."

Paradise was silent. When her father had concluded, Jessie raised her eyes to Montant, to send him a look of gratitude; but finding his gaze riveted upon her face with an expression of which perhaps he himself was not conscious, her eyes were hastily cast down and she colored crimson. Josephine noticed and read him; but she concealed her impressions under the guise of unusual good humor, and became quite hilarious.

Neither the shadow of pecuniary cares, nor the business anxiety which had dampened many a family party in the old house, now rested upon them, but a more threatening burden was on their hearts, though they attempted to laugh it off, succeeding remarkably well, if the general merriment could be considered a criterion.

"By Jove, she is a lovely—a *superb* woman," said Walter to himself, referring to his fair neighbor, Josephine Van Strom, who showed to advantage in her ripe, glowing beauty, when intentionally sprightly, entertaining, and fascinating.

When the ladies retired, it happened that Mr. Going was talking to Montant, and both removed themselves and their cigars to the bow-window, leaving Walter and the hunchback alone at the table.

"Walter!"

"Well, your honor?"

"Why the devil don't you marry that widow?"

Walter stared.

"That's pretty good," he cried.

"Have you never thought of it?"

It was impossible to say whether he had or not, since he did not answer the question.

"She has a million of dollars. She is young. She is not only passionate, but as *true* a woman as ever lived; to which I can testify. She is as handsome as I am homely (which is saying a good deal); you are young—"

"But what are you talking about?" said Walter, lowering his voice that the others might not hear. "You know she is engaged to Montant. What would *he* do?"

"Humph!" growled the hunchback, and quickly changed the subject.

They soon rejoined the ladies, and a walk was proposed.

"I do not feel well, Ernest," said Josephine. "I am afraid I left my room too soon after my sickness. I feel oppressed, as if another illness were in store for me, so I think I will remain at home. Will you keep me company?"

"Of course."

"Montant!" called Mr. Paradise.

"Well!"

"Walk with me, I have something to tell you."

"I am going to remain at the house with Mrs. Van Strom."

"Can't let you off. I am compelled to ask you to break the Sabbath with me and talk business, offending this glorious sunny afternoon by speaking of dusty agreements, moldy records, and other nasty law documents. As it is all for the benefit of our fair client there, I call upon you, by your duty as trustee, to obey, for I will not soon have another opportunity."

"What a burden too much wealth is," sighed Josephine. "But go, Ernest, since Mr. Paradise will have it so."

Why was it that the business talk did not last long—how came it that Montant and Jessie walked together along the little beach, while Mr. Going, Walter, and the lawyer strayed far behind?

In the course of the conversation—that free *causerie* characterizing the idle moments of old friends—they spoke of German philosophy.

"I believe it is all nonsense—that is—I think there is some sense at the bottom of it; but carried to a point above the sphere of ordinary life where alone it can be made useful," said Miss Jessie, wisely.

"You commenced a very intelligent speech by a very hasty sentence," he replied, smiling. "Nonsense it certainly is not, and though you are correct in praising the philosophy of life, the most abstract teachings of the German school (not so the French) can be applied to the most obscure lesson of life, because *logic* is the life of German intelligence, and logic can not lose itself in vague speculation."

"Why do they indulge in all those dreadful half Latin appellatives, though, making their books horribly unintelligible, to me at least?"

"It is a fact," he answered, "that when Emanuel Kant speaks of his *Kategorische Imperat vus* he might possibly have couched the same idea in terms comprehensible to all!"

"He was a great man, I understand."

"Yes, and do you know why?"

"No. If you want to tell me, let's rest awhile. Here is a seat between two trees, where we can see the Sound as well as by wading in the sand."

"I will tell you in a very few words."

"That's right. Philosophy should be laconic," said the young lady, decidedly.

"He was great," he continued, when they were comfortably seated, with only a small space of the rustic bench separating them. "He was great because he established a *reason for virtue.* He selected *human conscience* for his subject, and made of that mysterious intuitive monitor a definite, tangible *principle,* based on irresistible logic, *proving* its cause and strengthening its existence by the pillars of *reason,* absolute argument, and clearly defined and logically derived truths."

"But does not religion serve the same purpose?" she asked.

"Reason and religion serve in reality one and the same purpose. They both come from God, and to-day Emanuel Kant stands as the savior of many who are convinced by reason; but would not be converted by religion. Happy are those who can combine the two!"

"Can you?"

He looked into her eyes, which spoke more than interest,—more than attention to what he had just said, or what his answer might be. Even her beauty, calculated to thrill the breast of any man, was not so fascinating as the bright intelligence and depth of mind that shone in her when the mood permitted, and he was delighted above measure.

"I can try," he said, with a smile.

"You laugh at my earnestness!" she cried, disappointed. "Talk to me more about your German philosophy."

"I must make it short, then," he answered, "for there is no telling how long you will be pleased with the subject. In a minute you will be wanting to see which of us can throw a white pebble to the greater distance over the water."

"How does Kant establish the logic of our conscience?" she asked, persistently.

"I am not sufficiently learned in his doctrines to answer that question satisfactorily, but I know that he entirely separates the inner man from the outer world. All objects he treats as *impressions* only, and even demonstrates our inability to *prove* their existence. We *think* that is the Sound before us, but we can not *prove* that it is. This is one of his fundamental theories which aids him in showing us our individual self in contrast to all the rest of creation."

"Or what we consider creation."

"Thank you," he replied, with a quiet smile. "From this isolation of Self, he shows the grandeur, the majesty of the self-sufficient soul, and consequently the dependent and inferior importance of the outer world. He teaches us to judge the objects around us, not by their own, but by *our own* light, and, in belittling their importance, elevates our individual soul to the place where it belongs."

"Then, in subjecting the outer world to the individual and self-existent soul, he must also think less of the *mind,* which judges from outside objects entirely, than of the *heart*, whose mysterious intuition is the life of the soul. It is a doctrine which centers upon the heart, Mr. Montant!" she cried, with enthusiasm.

"But the mind brings the heart (as *you* call his *Imperativus*) to a disciplined knowledge of its true worth."

"Does not this theory affect the abstract outer world as well as the material? Can we *prove* that a recognized law, a signed pledge, a given vow, is our duty any more than that a horse is absolutely, and beyond doubt, a horse? Does he not subject the tangible duties of life to his *Imperativus* as well? He must!"

"Yes," answered Montant, "if you put it in that light, I can not but admit that if *I* understand him correctly, a law, a pledge, or a vow, should be sanctioned by the *Kategorische Imperativus*, else it is not right to keep it—for the *Imperativus* is the highest, holiest judge!"

"The heart, you mean," she said, slowly, as if to take in the whole meaning of the sentence as she amended it. "The *heart* must approve, or the law, the pledge, the vow, is unholy!"

He looked at her as though he had received a shock! Did she think,—could she know what she was saying? Did she purposely throw the firebrand into his inflammable soul, to kindle there an unquenchable flame?

She saw his agitation, which was indeed incapable of control or suppression, and suddenly burst upon her the *meaning* which might be put upon her words. Coloring deeply with confusion and alarm, she abruptly rose, and it was some moments before she could call a woman's weapon to her aid. Changing her manner, she cried, coquettishly,—

"I am tired of philosophy. Let me fulfill your prophecy. I dare you to throw white pebbles into the dear blue water against me."

When the rest of the party joined them in that innocent amusement, Montant stepped aside and watched her, fascinated more than ever, as he saw her laughing and dancing around with all the gayety of a perfect child. Her hair had escaped from its confinement, and the merry wind played in the waving tresses—a fresh bloom was on her face, and the sprightliness of youth sparkled in her bright eyes.

"Who would think that this girl could talk as she has just talked to me?" he said to himself, and a rebellious evil voice in his heart whispered, "Josephine, with all her charms, can neither talk philosophy nor run along the beach like this girl;" but he silenced the voice, and, with a conscience that would *not* be silenced, walked to the house to hear, with a sharp pang of distress and self-denunciation, that Josephine was quite ill again with a relapse of fever.

After whispering a few loyal and loving words through the half-opened door, he wandered around the house, lonely and disconsolate, until tea was served, upon the return of the strollers. The rays of the sinking sun gilded the dining-room and shed a beauteous light over that face, from which he could not always avert his looks. Miss Jessie had entirely recovered her self-possession, and the delicate tint upon her cheeks was the hue of health only. After tea, as they were sitting a quiet family party in the drawing-room,—

"I do not think it would disturb Mrs. Van Strom if you were to sing, Jessie," said her father.

"I have studied those songs you brought me, Mr. Montant," said the young lady.

"I am glad of it. In my humble opinion, they were composed by the greatest master that ever wrote a note."

"Schuman?" she said, reading the name on the title-page.

"Yes."

"I wish Germans would adopt *musical names*, also," said Miss Jessie.

She arranged the notes before her by his assistance, and, while she was singing, he remained in such a position as to command a partial view of her face.

Indeed, she had studied the songs! Although her voice was not remarkably powerful, it was very sympathetic, and as she sang the magnificent melodies correctly, the feeling with which she was inspired was sufficient to interpret correctly the great composer's immortal thoughts.

He had selected the celebrated series of Schuman's songs, with words by Heine. They are short, but precious *bijoux*, and as she sang one after the other, she entered more and more into the spirit of love, longing, and complaint, her eyes grew moist and were cast down when he stepped up to lay another of the songs before her. Unfortunately, she was obliged to sing the English translation, but borne up by the sublime strain of the melody, the plaintive, passionate words spoke to every heart among her few listeners.

"What is this?" she asked Montant, in an uncertain voice, as he laid the last of the songs before her. He read the first line:—

"*Warum sind den die rosen so blass.*"

She began the song. As the music and words wailed forth the lament of a blighted love, her emotion became more and more apparent. The last words:—

> "Why am I sick and sad at heart,
> Oh, darling, answer me!
> Oh, tell me, my sweet love, wherefore
> *Hast thou forsaken me!*"

fell from her lips in trembling, thrilling accents. She ceased. Not a sound broke the silence. She lifted her brimming eyes and met the gaze of Montant bent upon her with the full agony of love that knew no more reason or control. For a moment she returned the gaze, though it burned her eyes like fire; for a moment she trembled like a leaf, and her bosom heaved convulsively, then she arose and glided hastily from the room.

What she said to herself and to her God, as she stood on the dark piazza, leaning her aching head against a massive pillar—what her thoughts were and what a struggle she had to undergo, none knew, and no one offered to intrude upon her moment of weakness.

After a few minutes, during which those that remained in the drawing-room kept an awkward silence (even Paradise was speechless), she returned, calm and collected, and said, in a firm, clear voice:—

"Papa, I want to speak to you in the library."

Montant had left the room, unwilling and unable to encounter the wondering glances of the others, and paced the hall like one steeling his iron will in the white heat of the furnace of tribulation. Jessie entered the drawing-room by a door which opened directly upon the piazza, so he had not seen her re-enter. But he was very much astonished to see Josephine descend the stairs soon after the music had ceased, and approached her to expostulate. She looked flushed with fever, and excused herself in advance.

"I could not bear that dreary room any longer, and I have been separated from you so long already, dear, so I made an effort, wrapped myself up well, and came to look for you."

Although he was not satisfied that it was not imprudence, he was glad to have her near him, and he consented that she should stay long enough for a good walk in the hall.

"I want a glass of water," said Josephine, finally, so they stepped into the dining-room and procured the refreshment. The sound of voices from the library reached them through the door which separated the two rooms, and as he had not heard Miss Jessie asking for a private interview with her father, it did not suggest itself to him that they might be involuntary eavesdroppers.

"Then I will answer Mr. Van Hagen's letter to-morrow," said the voice of old Mr. Going. "Although his age is an objection, his high respectability, his excellent name and family, together with all that accomplishments, education, and wealth can do to make a gentleman a desirable connection, prevent me from gainsaying your decision."

"It is not a decision yet," answered Jessie, in a distinct, composed voice, "but you may tell him, that, in your opinion, I will accept him."

Montant staggered to the wall. A suffocating pain almost mastered his senses, and faltering the broken words, "O, my God!" he pressed his hands to his temples, trying in vain to recover himself. When he succeeded (in a moment, which seemed to him ages), Josephine stood before him without a sign of the feverish flush upon her face. Her eyes met his, and he saw her anguish, her deathly suffering. With her hands clasped against her heart, she stood motionless, petrified, and her face, from which no suffering could banish the Madonna expression, resembled that of the Virgin when she looked upon the Cross where all her hopes were crucified.

"Josephine," he said, huskily, in his agony, and sinking upon his knees, a thoroughly wretched man, "Josephine, can you forgive me?"

"Forgive you," she muttered, and it seemed to him that he heard a stranger's voice. "Forgive you? Yes, yes, all is forgiven." And now the fever sent the blood boiling to her temples, and with a low moan, she sank to the

floor. She was carried up-stairs to her room, and laid upon her bed, from which she did not rise for weeks.

<hr>

CHAPTER VII.

THE BALL.

"Was't you that did so oft contrive to kill him?"
As You Like It.

DREARY days passed at the Priory while Josephine was ill—too ill to be visible to any one but those two grim guardians of the sick, the doctor and the nurse.

The scene at the library door so vitally affected Josephine, as to cause a relapse of brain-fever. Montant refused to explain, and answered all queries of "How did it happen?" by a shrug of the shoulder and a frown, which ill became his open and habitually serene countenance.

From that hour he avoided Jessie, who returned the compliment with a frigidity her experience in society had taught her to sustain to perfection. Thus separated from Josephine, and further than ever removed from Jessie, Montant began to find his stay at the Priory intolerable; so he concluded to remain in town, devoting himself exclusively to business, until Josephine should be sufficiently recovered to receive him. Miss Jessie seemed to suspect that both her father and brother believed her to be very unhappy, and to evade their sympathy, she intrenched herself behind a wall of imperturbable indifference, or a cold serenity that must have appeared strange in one so young; but the gentlemen recognized her quiet determination to settle matters by herself alone, and left her undisturbed. Under these circumstances, neither Walter nor his father enjoyed the best of spirits, and when at home, eschewed conversation and society.

"I have not yet written to Mr. Van Hagen," said her father, one morning, as he was breakfasting with his daughter alone.

"Why not? I thought that point was settled," replied the young lady, carelessly.

"Well, but we were interrupted that evening, you know!" said he, looking out of the window, and feeling uncomfortably embarrassed.

Miss Jessie shrugged her shoulders, and replied: "Do as you wish, papa. I have told you that I am willing to encourage him, so the matter rests entirely in your hands."

"I think that since we owe so much to Mrs. Van Strom, and considering that she is to be connected with us by every tie except blood-relation, we owe it to ordinary delicacy to postpone a step like this until she is well, or at least out of danger."

"I am satisfied, if you are," said Miss Jessie, and the subject was dismissed.

Not many days after Josephine had been rudely hurled back into the horrors of a sickness from whose perils she had just emerged, a carriage drove up to the house from the railroad-station, containing a lady in deep mourning, who alighted, and was greeted with some surprise on the part of Mr. Going and his daughter. When she threw back her veil, her face, pale and stoical, with her monotonous tone and impassive manners, were those of a person having lost all interest in life. It was Bella Van Strom, whom Mr. Going had informed of Josephine's illness, and who had come to nurse her. After several days of calm consideration, Bella had deliberately arrived at her conclusion, but when she entered the sick-room of the fair patient whose beauty no fever could distort, her heart melted, and she was happier than before.

During the whole of that anxious time which preceded her convalescence, Montant remained away, and Bella stayed with her charge day and night, her only relaxation being an occasional walk when she visited her parents. Smith, the tailor, was still residing with his worthy spouse, in the same house where the mare had paused to meditate, though he had abandoned his trade, living in the ease and comfort provided by Bella.

Josephine's convalescence, depending fully as much upon regaining her peace of mind as upon her physical recuperative powers, was, perhaps, due in the greatest obligation to Bella. We will not inquire by what means or by what arguments the tailor's daughter succeeded in bringing peace to that storm-tossed soul; but with the regained bloom of health, serene tranquillity began to subdue the strife which had heightened the ravages of the fever, and toward the end of May, she was in full possession of health and beauty, her figure a little less luxurious, her face a shade paler than of old, but altogether—charming. Thus Montant found her when he returned from the city, with stronger resolutions than ever, and consequently far happier than while his doubts and struggles threatened to master him.

His first conversation with Josephine took place in Bella's presence, and she noticed that they talked more like friends than lovers. Montant offered to kiss her—she refused, half laughing, half seriously.

"Not before a certain day!" she cried.

"Then let us fix the day for good this time," he said, with slight impatience.

So they fixed the day which they had so often appointed before. Was this arrangement to fare better than the last?

It soon became known to the small company that Jessie desired to give a ball, and although Bella's presence, and recent widowhood, made the originators of the idea hesitate about carrying it out, Bella spoke to Jessie as soon as she heard of it.

"Nothing would trouble me more than to have you postpone your party on my account. If I thought I could not prevail on you to ignore me, I would at once take my leave. I would much prefer to remain a few days longer, and if you desire my acceptance of your hospitality, give your party by all means. I will simply remain up-stairs for that evening. And so the fête was decided upon.

What a difference there was between the Priory of to-day and when old John Jacob Van Strom gave his masquerade ball, where caricature seemed the order of the day, or rather, of

the night, and the house haunted by a ghost. The dismal lamp which then scarce disturbed the darkness around the gallery of Van Strom portraits was replaced by a gas chandelier (for the gas-mains had reached even the Priory), and the walls—once so dark—were frescoed in the day when Fatman was lord of the manor, so that now it resembled a grand salon more than a tomb-like vault.

And the company attending Miss Going's ball were very unlike the fantastic mixture of unadorned old-fogyism, and grotesque fancy, that then thronged the hall. A good band played for the dance, instead of the four negro fiddlers who then stamped the floor, and shrieked out the figures of the quadrille, and tortured their poor fiddles until they squeaked like so many demons, regardless of the dreadful scene of lunacy and death there enacted before them.

The company now present was elegant, and the arrangements for the ball corresponded. True, those tasty ball costumes, those excruciating toilets, those ladies and gentlemen, attired in their best, moving among their friends, and conversing so delightfully, were only component parts of Vanity Fair; but many a real intellect was there, and many a stout heart beat within a lace-covered bosom. Not all vanity in Vanity Fair.

"What a delightful house for a ball!" Such was the universal verdict, as the spacious apartments received the brilliant concourse of guests; and few of those who had come from the city on purpose to attend, regretted the exertion.

Soon the ball opened, and the dancers began to flit through the hall, and around the parlors, while the graver portion of the company—the solid men and heavy fathers—congregated in the library and dining-room, where supper was to be laid later in the evening.

Mr. Paradise was there, of course. Strange as it may seem, Mr. Going liked the hunchback beyond merely paying the ordinary tribute to his talents and powerful intellect. But to-night the lawyer seemed to have something to do, besides conversing with his host and the elderly gentlemen who crowded around him,—gentlemen of wealth and influence, and among them Mr. Chip, who looked quite refined, in his dress suit; but his white cravat was too tight, giving him a flushed face, that reminded one of the symptoms that accompany human choking.

Mr. Paradise was preoccupied. The reader must have noticed, in the course of his experience, that during a ball at a country house, there is always a multitude, composed of the servants and their friends, who throng the piazzas, and peep in at every window, to catch a glimpse of the gay world within. Now, Mr. Paradise thought it fit to mingle with these outsiders, and, in fact, appeared to pay more attention to them, or rather to one person among them, than to the brilliant company who were dancing and laughing, unconscious of the person who had captivated the great lawyer. This one person amused himself by sneaking around the house, and fixing a pair of lynx-eyes upon every individual within and without the illumined mansion. He was a little man, with a conspicuous black beard, having the air and dress of a foreigner. Finally, Mr. Paradise requested the foreign-looking gentleman to step into the drawing-room, and there introduced him as,—

"My friend, Baron de Stombe. Mr. Going. I have taken the liberty of bringing the baron along with me, because I wanted him to see something of American society."

Mr. Going, considerably astonished at this late introduction (for the lawyer had not mentioned his friend before), made a bow, without exactly knowing what to say.

"Your most obedient, sir," said the baron, displaying more vulgarity than foreign accent, and making an awkward, low bow.

"Have you arrived in this country lately, sir?" said Mr. Going; and arming himself with studious politeness, he added, "I am most happy to receive you, or any other friends of Mr. Paradise, at my house."

"Sir," answered the baron, with another bow, "my cratitude is only excelled by my—"

"Beauty," suggested Mr. Paradise, who stood near him, biting his lips.

Whereupon the foreigner grew very red, and Mr. Going, quite perplexed; but the lawyer came to the rescue, and took his friend away.

"Well, Stump," he asked, laughing, "how do you like fashionable society?"

"It is beautiful," replied the detective, whom it was next to impossible to recognize, so carefully had he disguised himself. "Beautiful," he repeated, looking around him. "Sich lovely gals, and sich music. It's bully, sir!"

"Do you see the man you want?"

"No, sir; but I think I will 'fore mornin'."

"You are sure he's here?"

"Miller swears that our mutual friend, Staletoe, has confided in him in privit. He has got Mrs. Fatman and lots o' chink, all stowed away safe in Canady, waitin' for him to go to Europe, but he wants to be r'venged on Mountain 'fore he goes to rest in the buzzum of Venus, and take the donations of Mercoory. R'vengo is strong, Mr. Paradise, and when Miller told him of this 'ere party here to-night, Staletoe straightways axed him sich questions, and in sich a way, that I'm sure he's here, or means to be."

"No letting him off this time!" said Mr. Paradise, in a threatening tone.

"Oh, no! no, no!"

"I am certain that it was you who got him out of that court-room before the judge had time to issue a bench-warrant for his arrest!"

"Oh, no! no, no!"

"But mind you, if you don't arrest him to-night, and that before he does any mischief, d'ye hear? If you don't, you'll have a fight with me, and you know I don't joke when I say fight!"

"Rely on me, guv'ner."

"Can't you imagine in what disguise he means to appear?"

"No. You see, all I know is what I've told yer. Miller was scared out of his wits, and the strangest thing is that I found it out at all. The way of it was this yer: I had to see Miller on a matter of business, which was Hob-goblin. I wanted to see if my shares was any good, so up I goes to Miller, and on my way, thinks I, there is a reward of ten thousand set on John Van Strom's murderer. Now, what a nice thing that 'ere ten thousand 'ud be for my family in my old age. I have three, and the old woman, Mr. Paradise. So knowin' Miller was more like to be awears of Staletoe nor any one else, I cross-questions him a bit, and got out of him what I told yer. He said, too, that since Mr. Mountain had been very kind to him, he'd like to keep danger away from that gentleman's head; so he told me all that Staletoe had told him, which I have told you, and I made up my mind that our Eyetalian friend will be here to-night."

"No letting off, now!"

"Rely on me," said Mr. Stump, honestly. "He was an old friend of mine, but now there's an end to all that. Ten thousand in money and a bully newspaper notice is worth more than friendship with a mankiller."

In the ball-room, Miss Jessie queened it without a rival. Never was her beauty more radiant, never did her spirits flow merrier, never had she been so sprightly, lovely, fascinating. Mr. Faro and Mr. Wheeler were but diminutive objects in the host of adorers gathered around the young lady; and among the gossip enlivening the party, the report (true for once) was prominent, that she probably was as great an heiress this night as before the time when the world considered Going & Son doomed to poverty.

Miss Jessie had granted to every one of her friends a lively turn around the room,—every one except Montant, who had not asked the honor, so, at last, she became quite exhausted, and requested Walter to take her to the dining-room for a glass of lemonade. The elderly gentlemen, who had first taken refuge here, had just been requested to leave, that the waiters might prepare supper, so the room was deserted.

"I don't like negroes around the house, Walter, and you know it," said Miss Jessie. "Why did you order black waiters?"

"Because I thought it better tact to order most of the supper from the village than to have the whole brought out from Delmonico's at an absurd expense. Of course, I was obliged to take what waiters these people could give me, and they are lamentably, though unmistakably, black."

"Get me the lemonade, like a good fellow," said his sister.

"*Why don't you dance with your lover? it will be his last chance,*" suddenly whispered a voice behind her, with marvelous rapidity, yet perfect distinctness.

She turned around, with a start, so frightened that her heart stood still; but no one was near except a black waiter, busy at the sideboard, which stood not far from her chair. She scanned him closely. He was apparently an old darky, with gray wool, and stooping considerably. He quietly followed his occupation, without noticing her motions.

"Did you dare to speak to me?" inquired the young lady, sternly.

"What did you command, Miss?" inquired

the negro, running up with great servility.
"Did you speak to me?"

"I want to know whether *you* spoke to
me?"

"Oh, no, ma'am," answered he, with humble surprise.

"All right, then," said Miss Jessie; but
when Walter returned with the lemonade, she
related the queer circumstance to him.

The consequence was, that Walter took occasion to watch the old negro whenever he
could do so unobserved by the latter. Then
he drew the attention of Mr. Paradise to something indefinitely strange in the man's appearance, when closely watched, and finally, the
Baron de Stombe was advised by Mr. Paradise to favor the same individual with his
regards.

"Can it be he?" inquired the hunchback.

"'Pon my word," replied Mr. Stump, "with
all due respect to my friend Staletoe, I don't
believe he is cunning and bold enough to
come *in here*, and in *that* rig. No, no, it ain't
him."

CHAPTER VIII.

A BROKEN HEART.

" Like the lily,
That once was mistress of the field and flourish'd,
I'll hang my head and perish."
                              KING HENRY VIII.

THE small conservatory which, as in most
American country mansions, adjoined the
dining-room, was illumined by Chinese lan-
terns, whose colored lights gave the room and
the flowers around a fantastic appearance.
Here, a few couples sought refuge, when the
dining-room was thronged with guests, and
among them were Miss Jessie Going and her
cavalier, the fortunate and envied Mr. Wheeler.
Miss Jessie, who had not deigned to invite our
hero's attention to her any more than he had
volunteered to approach her, seemed, nevertheless, to keep him slightly in sight, and
when she noticed him in company with Mr.
Paradise, walking through the conservatory in
whispered but earnest conversation, she concluded to seat herself there among the
flowers.

"You may bring me an ice into the conservatory," she said, to her escort.

She could not see Montant and Paradise,
though she knew they were on the other side
of the stand on which the flower-pots were
placed; but being seated near the door, could
see who entered or left the room.

Presently Mr. Paradise stepped out. Then
she knew that Montant was there alone, and
surmising that he might soon follow, and on
his way out, find her alone, she arose to meet
the gallant Mr. Wheeler half-way, when the
old negro waiter, who she was certain had
made that queer speech to her, in the early
part of the evening, appeared at the door of
the conservatory. In his hand was a bottle
of champagne, and he seemed to be looking
for some one he could help to wine.

"Waiter," called Montant, from the other

end of the conservatory behind the fragrant
partition, "I wish you would bring me a glass
of champagne."

His tone was weary, as if he had seated
himself to rest, and was loath to go after the
desired refreshment in person.

"Yes, sir," replied the waiter, with great
alacrity, and turned to the table to get a
clean glass. Miss Jessie watched him from
simple desire to keep out of his way, while
the darky was too much occupied with something that seemed greatly to excite him to
notice her in the nook where she had again
retired immediately upon noticing his hateful
face. He was doing something to that bottle!
In another moment he hastened away to bring
Montant his glass of wine, and as he passed
her a small crumpled piece of white paper
came out of his pocket as he withdrew his
hand therefrom. Intuition suggested drug—
Montant—and danger. At this moment Mr.
Wheeler brought her the ice, and was horrified at the treatment he received. She
pushed him violently aside, and hastily turning
the corner, saw Montant at the other end of
the room, alone with the waiter, who was
just filling his glass. Our hero held it in his
hand, and in another moment would have
swallowed the contents, when the glass was
snatched from him, and while it fell to the
floor in fragments, a voice he knew well,
gasped:—

"It is poisoned! I saw him pour it in!"
And there stood Jessie, white, and shaking
with emotion. Montant sprang to his feet; he
seized the negro by the throat, and cried,—

"Confess, or I'll throttle you!"

In an instant the conservatory was filled
with people from the dining-room. Montant,
fast losing control of himself, perhaps would
have made his threat good, but the darky,
with great dexterity, drew a dagger. A shriek
from the ladies, a stampede among the gentlemen who stood around, as usual, with open
mouths—yet Montant was saved from the
murderous weapon, for a little man with a
black beard and foreign appearance intercepted
the threatened stroke, disarmed the assassin,
and handcuffed him in a instant. Then the
guests saw with astonishment that the skillful
foreigner was Mr. Paradise's friend, the Baron
de Stombe. The baron clutched his long
beard, it came away, disclosing the bland and
smiling face of Mr. Stump, and pointing to the
handcuffed prisoner, with all the delight of a
showman exhibiting a gorilla, he exclaimed,—

"You knows me, Mr. Mountain; but do you
know your sweet black friend?"

Our hero suddenly guessed the truth.

"If I could only get a leetle soap and water,"
continued Mr. Stump, amiably, "I would show
the ladies and gentlemen here assembled the
white face of Mr. Antony Staletoe, the most
no-to-ryus falsefire, stubborn thief, and mankiller in all this enlightened kentry!"

"Take me away!" snarled Stilletto, the expression of whose face was happily obscured
by his disguise. So Mr. Stump obligingly
escorted his capture out of the room, followed
by every one except our hero and Miss Jessie,
who stood by him, not knowing what to do—

bewildered, confused by a thousand emotions.

"You have saved my life!" he whispered, in that soft, caressing tone that no woman mistakes.

"Thanks to the mercy of Heaven," she replied, trembling violently.

"Do you mean what you say?" he continued, quickly. "Do you mean that you are not indifferent to my existence?"

"Indifferent?" she cried, convulsively, clasping her hands, and striving in vain for composure.

"Oh, do not turn away from me! Look up—look in my face and see a man who is about to make a strange confession."

Completely at the mercy of the moment, she looked at him. In her tearful eyes he read what she could no longer disguise.

"Jessie," he whispered, taking both her hands, "I owe you my life. I belong to you. I can not continue the struggle. My strength is gone. It must find utterance. Now, at this moment when Providence has thrown us together, I must confess it, though it cost the life you have just preserved."

She could not find it in her soul to resist him. Like a charmed bird she awaited what she knew must come. Trembling, and beside herself with agitation, she felt her heart leap with delight—and a thrill of ecstacy run through every fiber of her pure body as he put his arms around her, and whispered,—

"Jessie, I love you!"

"Since when?" she murmured.

"From the moment I first saw you."

"And you never told me till now!" she moaned, stepping back and burying her face in her hands. With shivering terror she realized the misery, the deceit, the *sin* of his confession.

Not so he. With a ruthless, almost fierce, determination, he cast aside all consideration, and all the duties he owed to Josephine, for he felt that this moment separated him from both forever, and he was resolved to taste the sweet cup before accepting the endless bitterness he knew was in store for him. His arm tightened around her.

"Answer me," he whispered, intoxicated by the bliss of holding her trembling form, her throbbing bosom close to his heart. "Answer me. Tell me once, at least, what I see, what I feel, what I *know* already. Do not withhold from me the height of blessedness, but tell me that you love me."

"I do," she sighed, in a heart-broken, yet fond tone, and hiding her face in his bosom. "May be it is wrong and sinful; but I can't help loving you."

And their love, gathering strength, quickened his boldness and conquered her timidity. Their lips met, and for a moment they forgot that they were standing on the brink of destruction, and that this foretaste of heaven must be their farewell to all happiness on earth.

Although nearly unconscious of all surroundings, and of the danger lest an eavesdropper watch them, he had instinctively drawn her into the farthest corner of the room, where the tall plants almost concealed them.

11

But their voices might have been overheard in the deserted apartment, and when, from the intoxication of love, she returned to reason, and strove to free herself from his embraces, she suddenly whispered,—

"I hear footsteps on the other side of the room. Could some one have heard us? For the peace of all of us, I hope not!"

Yes, there had been steps, though they quickly glided from the room. Josephine's misgiving heart led her to discover the absence of those two from the company. She had stolen into the conservatory, and from behind the wall of flowers heard all. She was gone now, and the two looked with guilty uncertainty at each other's doubtful faces.

"Guilty? No," he said to her, warmly. "What the heart dictates can not be wrong. I will save Josephine from a life of misery by disguising no longer what had better be known now, than after marriage."

"But, merciful heavens! how will this all end?" she cried, wringing her hands.

"Jessie," called her father's voice, and the old gentleman appeared at the door. The young lady hastened to his side, heedless of her disordered hair and the treacherous blush scarce yet departed from her forehead and beautiful neck.

"Our friends talk of going home," said her father, not noticing her rather strange appearance and manner.

"At this hour?" she cried. "Why, the dancing has hardly commenced yet. Walter, order a galop, and we will lead it off." Walter obeyed, and they so inspired the rest that in spite of the cloud cast upon the party by Stilletto's murderous attempt and subsequent arrest, dancing really commenced with renewed vigor. Jessie seemed indefatigable. Not a friend among all the gentlemen failed to obtain her hand for a turn; but her father saw what escaped most people, that the tears stood in her eyes, and she had to bite her lips before she could laugh or make a merry remark. And thus she danced on and laughed away, weeping incessantly. She would have given any thing for "a good cry," and at last, unable to stand it any longer, she ran up-stairs with a laugh and a jest, to throw herself sobbing on her bed.

Her father softly followed her, and, as his anxious ears caught the sounds of her distress, he turned away with a heavy sigh, leaving her to conquer herself alone.

Montant paced the library a long while, wondering what to do. Finally he re-entered the parlor where Josephine was conversing with Walter, who soon yielded her to our hero, to attend to his duties as host.

"Josephine," he said, in a low voice, bending over her chair, "I have a confession to make to you."

"Not to-night," she replied, hastily. "Wait till to-morrow."

"Why to-morrow? It is a serious matter, and weighs on my heart heavily."

"Wait till to-morrow," repeated the widow, rather decidedly; and without paying any more attention to him, she left the room.

Did she already know what he had to confess to her? Had she listened in the conservatory? As he tortured himself with these doubts, Jessie entered the room, and Montant saw that she had been weeping. He watched her, the queen of the dance, glancing quietly around the host of admirers that flew to her side, and longed to be near her to shield her from the gay throng that little suspected the cause of her agitation.

"Dance with me, or it will look strange," he said, below his breath. "Walter has asked me twice why I have neglected you in this conspicuous manner." With a strange smile she accepted the offer, and they danced until both were tired out, when she took her brother's arm and walked away, without having looked at him or moved her lips.

Josephine came to the door and saw them dancing, and then retired to Bella's room. She entered softly, leaving the door ajar, and sitting down by her sister, she took her hand. Bella looked quietly up from the book she was reading, to see what was wanted.

"Do you hear that beautiful waltz?" said Josephine, gently, as the strains of music reached their ears like fairy melodies from dreamland. "Those notes remind me of the merry days of my girlhood. Once I could dance and laugh with any. I am too old for them now."

In mute sympathy Bella pressed her sister's hand tighter, gazing earnestly and inquiringly into her face, and so the two women sat in silence for some time, in the dimly-lighted room, while below the dancing was at its height.

"Bella," said Josephine, "I shall never marry."

Still Bella did not speak; but a grave, sad expression settled on her face.

"That waltz is divine," continued Josephine, in an unnatural voice. "He is dancing with her now. I saw them dancing together."

And Bella leaned over to her sister, and tried to lay Josephine's head upon her breast.

"What has happened," she asked, fearfully.

"He has betrayed me! He has kissed her! He has confessed that he loves her!"

"And you heard him; saw him?" asked Bella, more excited than her sister.

"Heard them only. It was enough. I do not know what makes me so quiet. I have talked and acted like a rational being ever since. Isn't it strange?"

"Strange, indeed!"

"Well, Josie," said Bella, after a pause. "Was I not right, when I suspected that this would come to pass? Has he said any thing to you about it?"

"No. He told me that he had a confession to make, but I put him off till to-morrow."

"How calmly you speak of it," said Bella, alarmed. "To hear you, one would think you never loved him!"

Josephine shrugged her shoulders.

"What do you intend to do?" asked Bella.

"Go home with you by an early train to-morrow—provided you will take me with you."

Bella pressed her tightly to her heart, and no further answer was needed. Then the tailor's daughter spoke long and soothingly to her, and before the music had ceased Josephine was weeping, but not altogether miserable, in the embrace of her faithful sister.

That same night, Mr. Going promised that he would not divulge their intended departure, and before any one in the house was astir, except one servant, Bella and Josephine had left the Priory, and were on their homeward way. Montant found a note left for him by Josephine, and his misery was not lightened when he read the following:—

"I overheard every thing in the conservatory. I thought I had a right to listen to all that *you* would say. I was wrong, and ask your pardon. I am certain you intended to tell me *all*; but I would save us both from that humiliation. I begin to feel that our engagement was a very foolish affair. I am too old for you—you want a young girl for your wife, and since you have found her, be happy with her. You are hereby released from all that you have ever promised me; but I beg you to believe that I bear no malice, nor do I blame you for, at last, succumbing to a passion born in your heart before you ever knew me. I am happy in the remembrance of the good that has come to you and your friends through poor me, and it will be a comfort to me in my future loneliness.

"Good-bye, Ernest; good-bye!

"As I respect and honor man, so I respect and honor you, and I thank God that a hasty marriage has been prevented from condemning you to an everlasting struggle between your duty to me and the dictates of your own heart.

"Ever yours, affectionately,
"JOSEPHINE."

Two hours after the receipt of this letter he left the Priory to take up his residence in New York. He wrote to Josephine that he had not even attempted to see Jessie again, and he begged her to forget and to forgive, insisting so far as he could upon marriage on the appointed day.

He received an answer in Bella's hand. It was a courteous, even friendly letter, but it told him only too plainly that even if Josephine were disposed to relent, Bella would never allow it, and he knew that the weaker woman would abide by the better judgment of her stronger sister. Then he wrote to Josephine once more:—

"My pride is so humbled by Mrs. Van Strom's very kind letter, that I do not care if the ship sinks, that is to take me to Europe to-morrow. I will try if my home in England and life with my parents will afford me that peace of mind I can never again enjoy in the society of my friends here. I am now a singular spectacle! A man who has had the greatest successes in mercantile life, and who has been blessed by the love of two noble, beautiful, and true women, yet finding himself so miserable and sick of life that it is a question whether it is possible to bear all and live.

"I will not ask you again to marry me. I have too much respect for your pride and your womanhood to do so; but I can not either marry the girl, for whom I confess I have a maddening passion, I am also certain that under the circumstances Miss Going would never consent. And so—farewell—for ever!

"ERNEST MONTANT."

He sailed for Europe, where he arrived just in time to see his father breathe his last. He had not dissolved partnership with Mr. Going; but on the contrary, his visit to England was employed to extend the British connections of the house. In consequence of the continued good fortune which crowned the operations of the firm, and his mother's excellent standing in English society, he came in contact with many of the first families, and as his calm dignity, solid sense, and high principles suited the tastes of the English aristocracy of birth and commerce, he made many warm friends, and had capital opportunities of marriage.

But he discarded all such ideas. He was well aware that the love born in his heart when he was hardly a man, had grown with his growth, sending its root and tendrils through and around his heart until separation had become impossible.

And then every letter which reached him from across the ocean bore that name so dear to him. Not only *that* name, but his own linked with it. In his replies, he never mentioned her own name, which intoxicated him with a thousand sweet remembrances, for he dared not. How beautiful Walter's clumsy penmanship became when he wrote those six letters! Every letter seemed to tell its own tale, and call him back across the water where he had left his heart, his hope, his happiness!

* * * * * *

It is not to be supposed that Josephine left the Priory in a happy mood. The peace Bella's faithful friendship promised her was too widely different from the happy prospect that had beguiled her dreams. Weeping in silence, she implicitly followed Bella's counsel, and though her gentle soul could not harbor bitterness against Ernest Montant, her distress was overwhelming.

On their way from the Priory, Bella called religion, that great refuge of woman, to her aid, and painted to Josephine's loving heart a world of goodness, and charity, which they would erect in the midst of this cold, harsh world of enmity and unkindness. The immense wealth they had inherited would enable them to carry out any project for the relief of misery, and active benevolence would keep her mind too thoroughly occupied to brood over her sorrows. And though these two women despised pomp and pride, their consciousness of the power of goodness they wielded in their large fortune, caused them to exult in its possession, and in making their plans for the future, they forgot for a time the present distress.

And so, planning, they came to the old house where poor John had breathed his last. The day was lovely, and the genial breath of spring was in the air. The carriage rolled up to the door, where the servants awaited them. Home again, but *how?*

Josephine Van Strom was not a woman to surrender all the blessings of love without a sharp struggle. All is glorious and beautiful without—the bursting buds and blooming flowers; the waters murmuring a melodious accompaniment to the songs of the birds newly-awakened to their music; and the soft winds, breathing a thousand perfumes, rustling softly in the new foliage overshadowing the lonely path of that poor traveler, homeward bound to a desolate peace. All nature is attired in a triumphal garb, and all things earthy seem to rejoice—but there is a broken heart in the midst of all these splendors. Although this heart be but an atom in the earth, though this whole earth be but a speck in the universe—yet this poor broken heart, infinite in its sorrows, cries to the Lord of worlds, and is heeded by the Omnipotent. Another appeal for mercy!

And can this poor broken heart be mended?

CHAPTER IX.

HOW IT WAS MENDED.

"Fate, show thy force: ourselves we do not owe."
TWELFTH NIGHT.

FALL was approaching; the wind blowing around the old Priory brought an autumnal chill, and Mr. Walter Going kindled a wood fire in the old-fashioned fireplace of his chamber with his own aristocratic hands. Mr. Walter Going gazed into the merry flames, which, to the music of the dismal moaning wind, danced a cheerful defiance to the howling lamentations sweeping through the parks and around the walls of the old mansion.

It was a splendid room in which we have seen the fire built. Implements of gunning and fishing, cricket bats, raquets, all sorts of weapons, portraits of noted horses and dogs, reminiscences of sporting life, such as Derby paintings and hunting scenes;—here and there some lovely woman's picture looking dismayed in such masculine company, a book-case, a gun-rack,—in fine, a crowd of objects to cheer the cheerless life of a bachelor.

Mr. Walter Going sat before the glowing logs, and being in want of something to do, recalled to his mind "Reveries of a Bachelor," and philosophized. And to that grand conclusion did he arrive, not for the first time either :—

"I want a wife!"

Mr. Walter Going took a fresh cigar from a box just opened, displaying an aristocratic array of weeds from the "Vuelta Abajo." The fresh cigar soothed his nerves, but the old conclusion came back :—

"I want a wife!"

The fresh cigar was emitting fantastic wreaths of smoke, and Mr. Walter Going, stretching himself on two chairs, watched the ascending rings. Either they inspired him, or his own vague fancies assumed shape, for he suddenly pushed away the second chair, moved closer to the fire, and, as addressing the coquettish flames, said, audibly :—

"I have an idea!"

The sound of his own voice seemed to arouse him; he laid away his cigar immediately, and descended to his sister's room. He knocked, and upon being admitted, found his father there, writing a letter on Miss Jessie's pet *escritoire*.

Walter kissed his sister affectionately. He noticed (not for the first time) that she was looking pale, and her beautiful face was more apathetic than usual. "Are you writing to Mr. Van Hagen, father?" he inquired.

"Yes," replied his father.

"Do you mean to accept him, Jessie?" asked Walter, lazily throwing himself on the sofa.

"I do," replied his sister, indifferently. "He is a *gentleman*, and that should be enough, nowadays!"

"You intended to accept him some months ago?"

"Yes; but circumstances prevented."

"Will you do me a favor, Jessie?"

"Any thing reasonable; but pray don't ask any thing difficult to perform?"

"Postpone this engagement for two months."

"Why?" exclaimed Mr. Going, looking up quickly.

"Because I, as an always dutiful son and ever attentive brother, ask this as a special kindness and favor to me."

The engagement was postponed.

That same night Walter wrote a long letter to Ernest Montant. It ended with this sentence,—

"I know what I am talking about. Trust to me, as far as the girl is concerned. At the same time, I ask you not to show your face here until after Jessie's wedding, unless you know what you are talking about. Write to me, and I will answer immediately."

With this mysterious paragraph the letter closed.

A few days later, Mr. Walter Going made a trip to an Eastern watering-place, where he found, as he expected, two widows. They were both immensely wealthy, and while the elder and plainer-looking of the two had received some offers of marriage, the younger, a very beautiful woman—quite as rich as the other, and of an excellent family, being the daughter of the late General McLane—was besieged by a host of suitors coveting her money, and perfectly willing to take her into the bargain.

At first, Walter was almost afraid to attempt to approach the fairer of the two, so difficult was it to fight a passage through the phalanx of admirers that surrounded her; but he found that Josephine Van Strom loved to talk to him. With easy freedom she conversed about the old times, and inquired about Ernest Montant in a manner that made him hope she had learned to regard her love for him as a past dream.

For a week or more he courted her, and one evening, when the moon was shining brightly, he asked her to walk with him out over the white sea-beach. There lay the ocean, hushed in sleep and coated in silver. Only in faint murmurs did the drowsy breakers roll up, while high above, in the starry sky, rode the brilliant sovereign of the night, shedding her luster of love over the endless, mighty sea, and expanding all human souls far beyond their own littleness amidst the solemn, glorious majesty of nature.

"Mrs. Van Strom," said Walter, "I want to talk to you about a friend of ours in England."

"Is he well? Heaven knows I wish him all good."

"Do you care for him?" he asked, with some agitation.

"Yes; he was my lover once, as you know very well, and now, although we are separated for ever, I have nothing but prayers for his welfare and earnest hopes for his happiness. What do you hear of him? What is he doing?"

"He is miserable!"

"I know why," said the widow, drearily.

"Now," Mrs. Van Strom, began Walter, summoning all his energy, "it is very well to be kindly disposed toward a friend, but it is altogether a different thing to *do* something for that friend. I want to ask you whether, for his sake, you are willing to make a sacrifice—one that may be great, yet may result in great happiness for you."

"I don't know what you mean."

"Let me explain myself. We are alone, with the ocean, the moon, and our thoughts. At such a time I think two human beings may so far throw off the shackles of society as to be frank with each other, and discuss freely the subjects nearest their hearts."

The widow signified her acquiescence, and slackened her steps, perfectly willing to listen.

"Ernest Montant loves my sister. He always did, and always will."

"And she loves him."

"Then," said Walter, "why don't they marry?"

Josephine was silent.

"Because their pride keeps them from it," he continued. "He feels as if he had committed a great wrong, and is stubbornly resolved to make himself and my poor sister miserable. All from honorable motives!"

Still, the widow did not speak.

"There is a remedy," said Walter, hurriedly. "And two weeks ago, when I found that my father had determined to marry Jessie off to an old man, who would make a respectable husband for her, and a wretched thing of her. I wrote a letter to Montant, telling him that I knew my sister too well not to be aware of the state of affairs, and asking him to write to me immediately whether he was still in love with Jessie, and if he would come home at once, providing I could succeed in removing the obstacles his pride and conscience have created."

"What obstacles? How can you remove them?" said Josephine, with emotion.

"I can't remove them; but *you* can. You must marry!"

Josephine was silent. She could not see her way clear through the thousand conflicting emotions that disturbed her.

"If you will marry—*marry me*, you will free Ernest from his imaginary obligation and make my poor sister happy for ever. But you will do more. You are certain to marry again some day; but you will never find a man more devoted to you or more jubilant over the hope of taking you to his arms as a loving wife. Do not hesitate; let your generous heart speak, and give me just a little of your great love, which little I hope will grow in time, if you will only accept me."

"Give me till to-morrow to decide," said Josephine, not knowing what to do.

"Do you want to inflict a sleepless night upon me?" cried Walter, much agitated. "Can you be cruel enough to make me linger in suspense, like a desperate beggar at the door of opulence? Come Josephine! I love you with all the fervor of my heart, and if you want an honest, affectionate fellow for your husband, take me now."

She reflected a moment, and following the impulse of her heart, which told her that she was doing right, said softly,—

"Well, I am satisfied."

With a cry of exultation, Walter caught her in his arms, and as he pressed her close to his heart, he said,—

"I don't understand why all men don't fall in love with you, Josephine!"

* * * * * * * *

A month later, Walter stepped into the library, at the Priory, where his father and sister were sitting. "In this practical age," he said, "there is nothing like announcing news laconically. So oblige me by reading this letter, Jessie."

Jessie read—"I am engaged to be married to Josephine." It was dated from New York a month before, and addressed to Montant, in London. She started from her chair, and, coloring crimson, threw herself on her brother's breast.

"Read the answer, Jessie."

She took the paper from his hand, and read—"I start for New York a week from to-day."

In vain did she attempt to hide her emotion. In vain did she strive to be calm, or to conceal that she understood the whole situation perfectly. Unwilling to betray too much, she left the room; while Walter said to his astonished father,—

"It's all right now! I hope, sir, you approve your children's choice. This is the day set to answer Mr. Van Hagen."

* * * * * * * *

Walter drove down from the Priory on the day that Ernest Montant was expected to arrive, and met him on the pier where the steamship made fast.

"All well?" was Montant's first question, as they warmly shook hands.

"All well," replied Walter.

"How is business?"

"As fine as can be, my boy; we have marvelous luck."

"If we are only sharp enough to reap our harvest in time, and not wait till the storms come, which must break in upon us soon!"

"I'll leave that to you now. You are smarter than I."

"And what general news is there of our friends?"

"Of our enemies I have to report that Stilletto has escaped from the punishment which, as the newspapers say, he so richly merited."

"What! has he broken out of State prison?"

"He never got there."

"Why, how is that possible?"

"Ask of the winds," quoted Walter, tragically. "Or, rather, ask the police justices, ask Mr. Stump, ask the district attorney, ask the judge of the sessions,—but please don't ask me."

"Is it possible that justice in this city is so loosely administered that a murderer can slip through and gain his liberty in the very face of the most positive evidence of his guilt?"

"Not only possible, but true," replied Walter. "By a complication of somehows he is enjoying the society of the delightful Mrs. Fatman in some part of Europe, and I only hope that she has kept control of the money she stole from her husband, or she will find herself deserted pretty soon, I fancy."

"And what has become of Fatman?"

"He seems to have loved his wife, and is leading a life of miserable loneliness. We do not see much of him; but I understand that he has lost a great deal of money, besides losing the darling of his heart."

"What have you heard of Martin Bates?" inquired Montant, with some hesitancy at pronouncing the name.

"I understand that he really took that girl Simonetta Marini to Scotland and married her."

"They are a couple well met!"

"He was a good fellow," said Walter, softly.

"My dear fellow," replied our hero, "in this age of crime and dishonesty, we can not afford to excuse a felon's villainy by praising his good-heartedness. Martin Bates was guilty of many offenses, and, as a good citizen, I must set my face against the placing of a martyr-glory around such heads as his."

"Yet it was a noble act to take that poor polluted girl and save her from all the horrors of her fate, by marrying her."

Ernest shrugged his shoulders, and then said,—

"Let us forget the strange people who haunted our lives, and came near dragging us down to destruction with them."

"And let us now have a good dinner at Delmonico's, and then we will drive to the Priory. I brought down a pair of horses for you."

"A pair of horses, Walter? You extravagant dog, there is no help for you."

CHAPTER X.

HOW IT ALL ENDED.

"What is decreed must be, and be this so."
TWELFTH NIGHT.

GLORY to the September breezes blowing freshly across the country, as Walter and Ernest Montant drove along on the road from New York to the Priory. If ever the sky was blue, it was on this splendid day, and the trees already showed, in the gilded edges of their leaves, indications of the coming splendor of color that would soon turn the woods into a magnificent display of golden and fiery tints, laid on by the master-hand of Nature. And with this external glory of beauty, when Nature puts on her most gaudy robes, the hearts of the two young men expanded with a foretaste of the joys that were now insured for the future. Still, they did not discuss the objects of their love—the good dinner at Delmonico's, followed by a cigar and a delightful drive to the Priory, were inspiring, but it was not until the swift horses began to smell the approach of the stable that Montant ventured to say:—

"Has Miss Jessie finally refused that old fogy, Van Hagen?"

"There she is to answer the question herself," answered Walter, laughing, as he pointed into the distance, where a lady on horseback, attended by a single groom, became visible.

Montant tried in vain to conceal his agitation. "What shall I do?" he asked.

"Tell the servant to give you his horse, and let him jump in with me," was the answer.

When they approached near enough to recognize each other, Miss Jessie halted, and a deep color heightened the blush of exercise that already rested on her cheeks. She then rode up and said, with a pleasure she did not care to conceal,—

"Welcome home! This is, indeed, a delightful surprise."

Without a word of reply, he jumped from the wagon, and to the utter bewilderment of the groom, grasped the reins of his horse, and asked him to dismount immediately.

As the servant knew him, he touched his hat respectfully, glanced at Mr. Going to receive his approval, and then did as he was bid, and held the stirrup for our hero to mount.

Walter waited for the attendant to take the vacant seat in the wagon, and touching up his horses, drove off with a merry ringing laugh.

How lovely she looked in her closely-fitting riding-habit, her black hair waving beneath her hat and feather, and her eyes bright with happiness.

"Welcome home once more!" she said, when Montant was fixed in his saddle; "and we'll have a gallop to see if you have forgotten how to ride."

As England is not the place where gentlemen are apt to grow rusty in horsemanship, she had reason to be satisfied when she cast a sidelong glance at him as they rode abreast. He had grown a little stouter, and a full beard gave him a manlier look than before. When they checked their panting horses, after the gallop, she said:—

"You have not spoken to me yet!"

"Wait till we reach the spring in the woods, hard by the road," he replied, with a smile and sparkling eyes. "Will you please follow? I am very thirsty, and really require a drink of water."

So saying, he wheeled abruptly from the road, and she turned with him under the

trees to a spot in the center of a small clearing, where they knew of a romantic, bubbling spring. He swung himself from his horse, and tied him to a tree, without saying a word, and came to her side to lift her from the saddle. His eyes spoke volumes; and though suddenly seized with trembling confusion, she allowed herself to be assisted to the green turf by his strong arm.

In an instant he had fastened her horse's reins to a branch, and they stood opposite each other, alone in the sanctuary of Nature, alone with themselves and the love that needed no more restraint.

"Jessie," he cried, opening his arms.

And there she was in another moment, nestling her beautiful head on his breast; and as they exchanged the holy vows of love, and sealed the eternal bargain with their lips, such a happiness was theirs as reconciles one to all past sufferings.

"Say, 'Ernest, I love you!'" he dictated, pressing her close to him.

"Ernest, I love you!"

"Tell me you have loved me for years, through all the changes and sorrows we have experienced together."

"Yes, yes. I have loved you ever since I first saw you."

"But there were times," he said, "when you thought you did not love me, or why did you slight me so often, and give me cold looks and cold words? If you only knew what I have suffered for you!"

"Have we not suffered together?" she whispered. "It is true, that when I saw my father sinking under the weight of his trials, I forgot all but my anxiety for him; and were you not engaged to another? That night, when your precious life was saved through my poor instrumentality, when you took me to your heart in my distraction and grief, I felt that I had no strength to oppose you. Oh, what changes have we lived through!"

"But no more sorrows now," he said, joyously.

Her eyes corroborated the statement.

"You will never forsake me? Oh, do not deceive me now! Do not whisper one word but what you mean to keep through all time."

She looked up into his eyes, the celestial light of unbounded love beaming through her tears.

"Forsake you! Deceive you!"

Did he not hold her in his arms, her trembling form throbbing in his embrace, her lips sealed to his? What further assurance was necessary. And then they rode home together—home through the luscious sun-set—exhilarated by the freshening breezes from the Sound, reveling in the words and looks whereby their exultant hearts sought utterance.

"Home again!" he cried, as he lifted her from her horse, stealing a kiss while he held her in his arms in the darkling twilight. "Home again, for good and forever!"

*   *   *   *   *

What a grand double wedding it was at the old Priory! How beautiful Walter's bride looked. "Body of Venus and face of Raphael's Madonna," said Mr. Paradise. But who could find a simile for Montant's young and blooming wife!

When the words, "love, honor and obey," came from her trembling lips, and she bound herself to be his wife until death should part them, his heart swelled with a happiness, greater than he had believed possible, and, although he was sufficiently a man of the world to acceptably entertain the merry company, he felt an insufferable longing to be alone with her, to tell her again and again how he loved her, and how he was rewarded for all his troubles by the one blissful privilege of calling her his wife.

When all was ready for their departure on their wedding trip, a parting glass of champagne was proposed, and the intimate friends and as many more as could crowd in, gathered in a circle around the two couples, Mr. Going and Mr. Paradise, who gave the toast in the following words:—

"Let us drink to the health of these two men and their wives. By the solemn vows of matrimony they have this day pledged themselves to a life of honor, and the discharge of the noblest duties on earth, the duties of husband and wife—father and mother. May their homes be blessed and may we see many a happy day in this magnificent house, which the spirit of hospitality has chosen for his favorite abode. And, further, and I am certain my old and beloved friend (taking Mr. Going's hand and speaking with true emotion) will join me in the sentiment; further, I say, let us drink success to the new era, whose happy inaugurators have joined hands this day, and whom we congratulate with our whole hearts. May the old spirit, which has for so many years troubled this house, depart to oblivion. Gentlemen and ladies, a bumper!"

"And let Hobgoblin rest among the dead," added the lawyer, in an undertone to Mr. Going. "A plague upon all such."

"Amen," replied the old gentleman, deeply moved. "Two children at once," he whispered. "It is not an easy day for one so old as I."

When they approached the carriages to take their departure, a man stepped forth from the crowd of spectators congregated in front of the house, and made his way to Montant.

"August Muller is desirous of shaking hands with you, sir," said the philosopher, heartily, "and let me tell you, sir, that he does not often descend from his high sphere to congratulate mortal man, even were he the Czar of all the Russias."

Montant, delighted with all the world, willingly gave him his hand, saying: "We have traveled rather closely together through life, Mr. Muller. Let us forget what little differences of opinion we have had, and let me thank you warmly for the kindly feeling which of late you have displayed toward me. Goodbye!"

Amid a general hurrah the carriages drove off, watched to the last curve in the road by the excited spectators.

"My friend," inquired Mr. Muller of the next bystander, "do you know what has made this so happy a day for my worthy friends in yonder carriages?"

"Love, I suppose," said the young man addressed, the rustic poet of the village.

"You judge matters by secondary or tributary causes, my friend," replied Mr. Muller, with the old sickly smile, and metaphysically raising his eyebrows. "But what fundamental, creative principle caused this love, to-day culminating in matrimony?"

"I don't know," answered the village poet, suspecting that the other intended to laugh at him.

"*Money*," replied the great philosopher, and walked off with dignity.

THE END.